Ethics for International Business

Business takes place in an increasingly global environment, crossing political and cultural boundaries, and consequently ethical dilemmas arise. The central focus of this successful and innovative text lies in how to make and explain "best choice" judgments in international business situations.

The newly-updated version of this groundbreaking textbook continues to provide a topical and relevant analysis of the ethical dimensions of conducting business in a global political economy. From a starting point of applied ethics, the book introduces a common set of normative terms and analytical tools for examining and discussing real case scenarios.

Extensive real-world examples, presented in the form of exhibits, cover issues including:
- foreign production, including sweatshops
- export of hazardous products
- testing and pricing of HIV/AIDS drugs
- advertising tobacco, alcoholic beverages and infant formula
- deceptive marketing techniques and bribery
- religious and social discrimination
- cultural impacts from "music, movies and malls"
- environmental issues, including oil spills, rain forest preservation, global warming and genetically modified foods
- Internet censorship and privacy issues in China
- fair trade certification and consumer boycotts
- oil companies in the Sudan
- foreign investors in Burma

To keep pace with the changing landscape of global business, this new edition features:

- Updated exhibits that introduce new issues and are sourced from more international publications
- Increased coverage of issues arising in emerging markets
- Updated descriptions and assessments of relevant international agreements
- Seventeen new photographs that were chosen to accompany cases designed for classroom discussion
- Three new figures that help depict the ethical analysis process

The continued globalization of business increases the relevance of this textbook and its unique focus on specifically international ethical challenges faced by business, where governments and civil society groups play an active role. While most business ethics texts continue to focus heavily on ethical theory, this textbook condenses ethical theory into applied decision-making concepts, emphasizing practical applications to real world dilemmas.

Anyone with an interest in the ethical implications of international business, or the business implications of corporate responsibility in the global market, will find this book a thought-provoking yet balanced analysis. Clearly written, this has become the textbook of choice in this increasingly important field.

John M. Kline is a Professor of International Business Diplomacy in the Walsh School of Foreign Service, Georgetown University. He is a past Director of the Master of Science in Foreign Service Program and the Karl F. Landegger Program in International Business Diplomacy. His teaching focuses on international business-government relations, international investment strategies and negotiations, and international business ethics.

Ethics for International Business

Decision Making in a Global Political Economy

Second Edition

John M. Kline

Routledge
Taylor & Francis Group

NEW YORK AND LONDON

First edition published 2005
by Routledge
270 Madison Avenue, New York, NY 10016

This edition published 2010
by Routledge
270 Madison Avenue, New York, NY 10016

Simultaneously published in the UK
by Routledge
2 Park Square, Milton Park, Abingdon, Oxon OX14 4RN

Routledge is an imprint of the Taylor & Francis Group, an informa business

© 2010 John Kline

Typeset in Minion by
RefineCatch Limited, Bungay, Suffolk
Printed and bound in Great Britain by
TJ International Ltd, Padstow, Cornwall

Library of Congress Cataloging-in-Publication Data
Kline, John M.
   Ethics for international business : decision-making in a global political economy / John M. Kline.—2nd ed.
      p. cm.
   1. Business ethics.   2. International business enterprises—Moral and ethical aspects.   3. Globalization—Moral and ethical aspects.   I. Title.
   HF5387.K578 2010
   174'4—dc22   2009043143

ISBN13: 978-0-415-99942-7 (hbk)
ISBN13: 978-0-415-99943-4 (pbk)
ISBN13: 978-0-203-88059-3 (ebk)

Dedication
For my family and my students

CONTENTS

LIST OF FIGURES

PREFACE

The first edition of this book focused on ethical dilemmas confronting international business, using news article exhibits to illustrate issues and stimulate discussion regarding the responsibilities of corporations, governments and civil society. Given a favorable reception, these elements are retained in this second edition that features numerous new issues, over a dozen more recent article exhibits, and updated information on international standards and agreements. Responding to suggestions, several pedagogical elements are added, including photographs, more figures, and suggested "framing questions" to guide discussions in Chapters 4–9. The main objective remains the same. The textbook seeks to encourage the development of a personal value framework that can help guide decisions on international business issues while simultaneously exploring the evolution of global agreement on core value principles.

Scandals periodically erupt in the media that focus renewed attention on business ethics. However, these incidents seldom reflect difficult ethical dilemmas. Whatever the technical arguments about legal culpability, most reported business scandals represent actions the perpetrators surely knew were improper but decided to take anyway, either rationalizing their decisions or simply expecting not to get caught. Preventing or punishing such misdeeds falls to corporate governance and management, or civil and criminal law. The real task for business ethics is to assist individuals with more common but also more difficult "best choice" judgments, where good moral arguments can be marshaled to support alternative courses of action. These types of ethical dilemmas are especially frequent for international companies doing business in complex cross-cultural environments.

Ethics involves a reasoned search for the value framework that should be used to judge and guide action. Formal theory provides valuable intellectual insights that enrich and elucidate this task. However, the opaqueness of theoretical formulas can also lead people to associate ethics with abstractions too idealistic to apply in every-day life. This gap in perception must be bridged through an approach to applied ethics that can encourage and facilitate consciously normative decision making. The expanding scope and influence of international business underline the practical importance of developing skills in applied ethical analysis among current and future business leaders.

When facing ethical dilemmas, executives often make decisions under time constraints with too little (or sometimes too much) information. Pressures become magnified in a global political economy where companies must respond simultaneously to multiple governments and diverse societal groups. "Best choice" outcomes require clarity on value priorities, a tested decision-making process, and frank assessments of both the motivations and the expected impacts of proposed actions. Individual participants in collective deliberations must also display personal courage to assure that explicitly normative concerns receive full and direct consideration. Although sometimes uncomfortable to use in standard business settings, the language and techniques of ethical analysis can help promote more open and candid evaluation of available decision options.

This textbook emerges from many years of teaching and consulting in the field of international business and public policy. The book owes much to numerous students whose valuable contributions in class discussions over the years helped shape the book's suggested approach to ethical reasoning as well as the use of applied case scenarios to illustrate international business dilemmas. In sharing their post-graduation experiences, these students also encourage the author's hope that time spent on studied reflection in an academic setting can make a difference in real-world judgments and actions.

Writing a textbook on ethics invariably incorporates personal value bias, both conscious and unconscious, in developing the approach, coverage and examples for discussion. In this instance, conscious goals include favoring simplified ethical analysis to promote a broader use of normative decision making and focusing particular attention on ethical choice issues where business operations span wide international political and socioeconomic divides. Manifestations of unconscious value bias undoubtedly exist and likely reflect the lessons and limits of the author's own experience. Some readers may perceive instances of apparent bias, especially on issues whose content involves sensitive personal or cultural value differences. Potentially controversial topics cannot be avoided in a textbook purporting to examine international ethical dilemmas, but no offense is intended in the selection or discussion of specific issues or case illustrations. The author acknowledges a debt of gratitude to the many students, colleagues, friends and family who have so positively contributed to the development of this book. Shortcomings in the text, however, are the responsibility of the author alone.

1

THE VALUE FOUNDATION FOR A GLOBAL SOCIETY

INTRODUCTION

Global economic interdependence surged over the past quarter-century, significantly reshaping business strategies while exerting a powerful influence on international politics. The impact on business and politics is now widely recognized and generally assumed to be irreversible. Corporations adapt research, production, marketing and service strategies in an effort to "think global, act local."[1] National governments grudgingly accept growing constraints on their sovereign scope for unilateral action even as they maneuver for competitive gains from global commerce. These changes supply both the building blocks and much of the driving force behind the emergence of "globalization" as a contemporary phenomenon. Less well recognized among the effects of global interdependence is the way traditional boundaries between business and politics can become blurred, particularly where the growing impact of "foreign" ideas and products raises normative issues in diverse societies around the world.

Does the advent of globalization portend the formation of a global society? Societies develop on a foundation of shared values that shape the structure and supply the bonds necessary for collective human interaction. The nation-state system imposes political boundaries on populations around the globe, dictating with varying degrees of success the rules that organize behavior within national borders. Societies may be coterminous with these national boundaries, but they can also be subnational or supranational in scope.

Accelerating the pace of global change, modern international business techniques are quickly outdistancing the ability of traditional political mechanisms to control external impacts on national populations. Economic, social and cultural patterns are being altered by global commerce, often without the considered assent or even the conscious recognition of the people most affected. Who is deciding the direction of these changes and what values are guiding the objectives?

This book uses applied ethical reasoning to explore many of the normative issues posed by the contemporary interplay of international business and political activities. The central focus is on business operations but recognizing that international enterprises operate within a distinctly global political economy. The normative dimension of globalization often appears in the form of protests against the power and impact of international business, generally represented by multinational enterprises (MNEs). Frequently the standards used to reject or affirm MNE actions lack clarity in terms of their origin, rationale and breadth of support. Identifying and evaluating the normative debate over globalization and MNE impacts can help gauge whether a sufficient consensus is developing on core values to support the emergence of a truly global society with commonly accepted rules and objectives to guide international business.

WHY ETHICS MATTERS

As pursued in this book, ethics deals with the identification, assessment and selection of values to be used as standards for judgment and guidelines for action. Values lie at the heart of all decisions, providing the normative basis for choosing among alternative conclusions and courses of action. As a term, "ethics" is commonly misused to signify some ideal but unrealistic standard that bears little relationship to practical daily decisions. In reality, ethical analysis offers a way to examine the values that do guide daily decisions in all aspects of human life. Decisions involve choice, and choice is guided by values. Ethics matters because its methodologies offer a way to identify, understand and consciously choose among the values embodied in different judgments and actions. The fundamental importance of ethics stems from the belief that intentional, informed choice produces the best decisions and outcomes.

Explicit considerations of ethical choice often appear absent from many discussions of politics, economics and business. Yet decisions made in these fields inherently involve choices among competing and sometimes conflicting values. When the political system exacts retribution for actions adjudged wrong, some value standard determines what punishment a person justly deserves, and why. When economics traces the flow of scarce resources, some value standard determines the allocation of those resources among individuals based on distributive justice choices such as equality, contribution, effort or need. When business seeks to obtain or retain a public charter to operate within a host country, some value standard determines whether those operations offer sufficient public good to merit approval by the sanctioning authorities.

The important role of ethical choice often escapes notice because the common use of instrumental terms can obscure the value standards that actually guide political, economic and business decisions. For example, nation-state actions typically find justification in the pursuit or preservation of the "national interest," but the exact nature of that interest, or what values are sacrificed on its behalf, are seldom specifically identified and evaluated in public debate. Economics may focus on the pursuit of efficiency, assuming the term functions in a value-neutral fashion while demurring on the choice of which ends are served by enhancing efficiency. Business operations can define goals in terms of maximizing profits, ignoring broader impacts and disregarding the instrumental nature of profits as a means to some end that is decided by whoever receives the distributed profits. Ethical analysis helps strip away the instrumental terms that obstruct a clear view of the underlying values, baring them for a conscious assessment and informed, intentional choice.

Globalization fosters an array of complex ethical dilemmas where clear assessments and informed choice become difficult. Yet choices are being made, by default if not intention. The motivation for studying the possible value foundation for a global society springs from the fact that economic and political interdependence, facilitated by MNE business activities, forge patterns of global interaction that reflect embedded values. Globalization as a process is happening anyway. Whether or not that process leads toward a global society bound together by shared fundamental values is still an open question. The decisions and actions taken by business, government and civil society leaders will help determine the outcome of this process. Explicit attention to ethical analysis and decision making can increase the potential for "best choice" results for a global community.

STUDYING ETHICS FOR INTERNATIONAL BUSINESS

This book differs in several respects from standard business ethics texts. First, only an introductory summary is offered to some basic philosophical concepts that provide both the foundation and the tools for ethical reasoning. Excellent books on philosophical ethics are available from many authors, including some with an orientation toward business applications.[2] The assumption here is that readers are either already generally familiar with this material or else can gain easy access to it if more in-depth explanations are needed. This restriction permits broader coverage of more business issues while still retaining the framework of ethical reasoning necessary for the examination of applied cases.

A second difference stems from the specific concentration on *international* business ethics. Since the mid 1970s, business schools (especially in the United States) have introduced or expanded offerings on business ethics, usually as separate classes on corporate social responsibility or, less frequently, as integrated components in traditional courses in accounting, finance, marketing or management. However, just as most US schools were tardy in adapting courses to reflect the increased importance of international business operations, so too have approaches to teaching business ethics been slow to address the complex and demanding task of applying ethical business principles in diverse countries and cultures around the globe.

This book provides extensive and varied coverage of ethical issues raised by international business operations. The purpose is to complement, rather than substitute for, offerings already available, with an emphasis on examining the particularities of international business situations. This textbook is also intended for use outside business schools, especially as an encouragement for schools of international affairs and departments with political economy majors to integrate the study of international business ethics into their curriculum. Global corporations are recognized by political scientists as important international actors, but few programs incorporate the study of how businesses should respond to differing international, intercultural situations, or how political and business actors might best interact on such issues.

Explicit attention to the political economy context for international business ethics constitutes the third major distinction of this book's approach. In the academic community, politics, economics and business exist as largely separate fields, even though an increasing number of interdisciplinary bridges are being constructed. In the "real world," academic field distinctions hold little meaning, particularly for businesspeople who must operate in a global economy that is continually influenced by political authorities. In applying ethical analysis to international business situations, it is both reasonable and realistic to pose questions that explicitly examine the comparative role responsibilities of both business and political actors. An important objective of the case analyses presented in this book is to consider the factors or circumstances that might lead to assigning greater levels of ethical responsibility to various societal actors (political, business or others). This approach may also prove useful in Business and Society courses.

Finally, the book uses a case analysis methodology based on real-life scenarios, often utilizing actual news stories. The incorporation of news articles replicates the type of information initially available in many new situations and is designed to practice techniques for applied ethical reasoning rather than to argue for particular conclusions in any individual case. Readers are encouraged to distinguish the factors in each case that: (1) establish the normative importance of the issue; (2) determine the comparative degree of responsibility for relevant actors; (3) identify appropriate actions; and (4) suggest possible guidelines for managing future situations with similar conditions. Although most case scenarios are recent, some older articles are used where ethical dilemmas are especially well illustrated and the scenarios still reflect contemporary value choices.

The case scenarios depict factual circumstances at a particular point in time and challenge the reader to consider "best choice" decisions for relevant actors, specifying the normative rationale and criteria used for the selected choice. In most case scenarios subsequent developments are not discussed in the text, to avoid prejudicing discussion about what "should" happen with the knowledge of what "did" happen. Although this approach may frustrate some readers, the technique keeps a focus on ethical analysis and prescriptive decision making rather than on factual knowledge of descriptive events. Independent research can satisfy the desire for follow-up information on any particular case.

ORGANIZATION OF THE BOOK

Drawing on framework concepts from ethical theory, Chapter 2 provides normative language and analytical tools to help examine, understand and evaluate situations that raise important but difficult value choices. The selective summary offers useful terminology and possible criteria for assessing the factors presented in ethical dilemmas. Setting out the context of a global political economy, the discussion differentiates legal and social norms while comparing the roles and functions of governments, businesses and other non-governmental actors. The chapter concludes with an illustration of the case scenario methodology, employing the suggested tools of ethical analysis to examine a controversy over a proposed MNE mining investment in Peru.

Chapter 3 considers the concept of human rights as a recognized expression of international principles that might provide a value foundation for a global society. After examining the content and interpretation of the United Nations Universal Declaration of Human Rights, the narrative offers case scenarios that test how such principles might apply to international trade rules and economic transactions. The specific relationship of international corporations to human rights principles also receives attention, considering how responsibilities to respect and promote such values might influence MNE actions, including issues surrounding expanded internet access in China.

The next six chapters survey a broad range of ethical issues raised by the operations of contemporary international enterprises. Each chapter examines a related set of issues, with a central "framing question" offered in the Introduction to provide a general context and guide subsequent analysis of the issues and case examples. The discussion uses normative terminology and analytical tools to explore the nature of relevant ethical questions, the relative role responsibilities of governments, MNEs and other non-governmental actors, and alternative "best choice" decisions for responsible actions. Discussion incorporates various normative criteria that might be employed in ethical analysis as well as identifying the status of international agreements or other emerging global standards relevant to those issues.

These chapters focus on ethical dilemmas, i.e. situations marked by several contrasting but ethically reasonable arguments supporting different courses of action. By omission, little attention is paid to studying clearly wrong actions by international business. Although such examples certainly exist, this text eschews the goal of convincing readers not to do something they likely already know would be unethical. Instead, the objective seeks to enhance analytical skills that can help identify the best available decision when confronting difficult ethical choices.

The penultimate chapter reviews various mechanisms used to control or guide international business activities. In addition to governmental mandates, an array of market-based instruments can influence corporate actions, as illustrated by increasingly organized and active civil society groups that seek to alter the nature, scope or impact of international business operations. These instruments can be employed to move business actions in the direction of "best choice" normative outcomes.

The concluding chapter presents a broad appraisal of contemporary trends shaping the global community, summarizing areas of both consensus and disagreement on important value principles. After surveying the types of ethical issues analyzed in the previous chapters, the narrative considers the extent to which common morality standards are emerging that could support a global society. The assessment considers the practical challenges MNEs confront when business operations must span the current diverse array of political, economic and sociocultural environments. MNE activities, and the value decisions that guide those actions, will play an important role in determining global relationships and their ultimate impact on people's daily lives.

PERSONAL AND ORGANIZATIONAL DECISION MAKING

Globalization evokes a sense of scope and scale beyond the reach of individual influence. Yet it is precisely at the individual level that crucial value judgments must be made and follow-up actions taken if conscious, rational decisions are to guide societal decision making. Individuals hold simultaneous memberships in multiple groups, ranging from family and friends to job and profession to community and nation. Societal bonds that organize human interaction develop from interrelated decisions taken within diverse organizations, reflecting value choices that can be consistent or chaotic, conscious or unthinking. Value selection begins with individual judgment and choice that shape the decisions taken by broader private and public institutions.

This book challenges readers to identify and refine their own value principles while engaging others in the development of guidelines for managing difficult international issues. A minimum objective aims to help legitimize the use of ethical reasoning and normative language in pragmatic discussions of complex business decisions. Corporate meetings often follow a routine shaped by comfortable and customary business jargon that can cloud rather than clarify real value choices.[3] Individual courage is sometimes required to disrupt prevailing patterns to introduce normative considerations of what *should* be done because it is the *right* decision to take. Effective identification of value choices and constructive communication of decision rationales form the essential basis for such a reasoned dialogue. The following chapters offer some decision-making tools to assist this process while testing their application on issues that affect the prospects for a truly global society.

NOTES

1. This term's origin is usually credited to Percy Barnevik, former head of the global enterprise ABB, and is generally associated with an interview contained in W. Taylor, "The Logic of Global Business: An Interview with ABB's Percy Barnevik," *Harvard Business Review*, March–April 1991, pp. 91–103.
2. For example, see T. Beauchamp, N. Bowie and D. Arnold (eds), *Ethical Theory and Business*, 8th edn, Upper Saddle River, NJ: Pearson Prentice Hall, 2009; R. De George, *Business Ethics*, 6th edn, Upper Saddle River, NJ: Pearson Prentice Hall, 2006; T. Donaldson and T. Dunfee (eds), *Ethics in Business and Economics*, Brookfield, VT: Ashgate Dartmouth, 1997; T. Donaldson, et al., *Ethical Issues in Business*, 8th edn, Upper Saddle River, NJ: Pearson Prentice Hall, 2008; W. Shaw, *Business Ethics*, 6th edn, Belmont, CA: Wadsworth, 2008; R. Buchholz and S. Rosenthal, *Business Ethics*, Upper Saddle River, NJ: Prentice Hall, 1998.
3. Some reasons for executive reluctance to use normative language in business discussions are cited in F. Bird and J. Waters, "The Moral Muteness of Managers," *California Management Review*, vol. 32, no. 1, pp. 73–88.

2

ETHICS AND INTERNATIONAL BUSINESS

INTRODUCTION

International business operates in an interdependent global economy where market functions are influenced by national political and cultural diversity. The scope and influence of international enterprises grew enormously during the latter part of the past century, spurring debate over what normative standards should guide business decisions. The study of ethics and international business is an exploration of the analytical techniques available to help answer this question.

ETHICAL ANALYSIS

Ethics focuses attention on the choice of values. One useful definition of ethics is "the systematic use of reason to interpret experience to determine values worthwhile in life and rules to govern conduct."[1] This conception of ethics sets the parameters used in this book. Past experience is examined, principally in the form of applied case studies, to assist the identification of values and conduct standards to guide international business activity. A related term is morality, which defines what persons should do in order to conform to a society's norms of behavior.[2] Ethical analysis can help determine moral norms. In common discussion, including in some cases contained in this book, references to ethical and moral actions are sometimes used interchangeably.

Moral values and standards deriving from a process of ethical analysis should be distinguished from religious-oriented morality that is based ultimately on revelation rather than experiential examination. This distinction does not deny the importance of religion as a source of personal values that can guide conduct in society. However, absent broad-scale conversions, religious prescriptions do not provide as useful an approach to developing internationally agreed principles compared to rationality-based debates that examine past experience. People who have not shared the same revelation or profess the same faith will not be convinced simply by the assertions of committed believers. Ethical analysis offers a more promising avenue for identifying and developing shared value principles in a global society that encompasses multiple faith-based belief systems.

Ethics concerns the nature and the justification of right actions. Prospectively, ethical norms are prescriptive, identifying values to guide actions now or in the future. Ethical norms may also provide standards for judgment of current or past actions. These uses apply to the fields of politics, economics and business. For example, normative standards can determine how economic benefits and burdens are distributed within a society while providing a basis for political or legal decisions regarding retribution (punishment). Sometimes economics is viewed as non-normative—simply the description of how economic forces work, or the determination of the most "efficient" system of resource utilization. This portrayal, of course, begs the normative question regarding which economic system is "best" or the purpose and consequences of "efficiency." Similarly, a cynical public too often reacts to business ethics as a joke, calling the term an oxymoron. At best, corporations are considered to be amoral mechanisms that simply produce goods and services for society.[3] This perspective vastly understates both the role of business within society and the essential relationship of ethical values to business operations.

Legitimate businesses, including international enterprises, need a societal foundation of ethical values in order to operate efficiently and effectively. At a minimum, enterprises must be able to assume that contracts will generally be honored and employees will not continually steal from the firm. Legal restrictions can support such standards by acting against periodic deviations, but there must be an assumption of general adherence to values such as promise keeping and honesty in order to permit rational business operations. Confirmation of this claim can be found in societies where extortion, bribery and other forms of corruption are endemic. When there is no basis for believing that an enterprise offering the best product or service at the best price can make the sale, legitimate business transactions will cease. One might argue that business transactions will still occur (as in a sense they do when commerce is dominated by criminal elements or corrupt public officials), but while this point is theoretically debatable, few if any businesspeople or public officials would defend such a conception of business or argue that it provides a sustainable basis for global commerce.

Another common objection to applying ethical analysis to business is a view that ethics relates to value choices made by individuals and does not apply to organizational entities such as corporations.[4] This view perceives business enterprises as no more than a collection of individuals whose own personal values determine their actions. Although personal value is fundamental to any discussion of ethics, exclusive attention to the individual ignores the reality of societal interactions and the effects of organizational mechanisms designed to influence behavior.

Corporations can be seen as a collective entity, with a discernible identity, decision-making power, and action capability.[5] Societies accept this notion when they permit the chartering of corporations as legal persons, distinct from the individuals who comprise the collective. Peter French[6] identified the essence of a corporate personality with the notion of a "corporate internal decision" structure. Under this concept, actions can be considered organizational, or corporate, actions if they are approved by a chain-of-command structure and are consistent with established corporate policy. Corporations establish this decision process to assure that individuals do not pursue personal goals to the detriment of the corporation's long-term interests. Thus, actions taken outside of approved channels or in violation of corporate policy should be seen as individual rather than corporate behavior, because the individual has forfeited his or her authority to act on behalf of the corporate organization. This notion assumes practical importance in assigning responsibility (credit or blame). It is also essential to the discussion of business ethics as distinct from personal or individual ethics.

ETHICAL CONCEPTS AND PRINCIPLES

Philosophical debate over the centuries has produced a wealth of material on ethical concepts and principles, including their more recent application to business issues. This book does not attempt to replicate, or even to summarize, the excellent treatment offered in these texts. Most readers will already be familiar with the principal lines of debate in philosophical ethics or else have ready access to reference materials if elaboration is desired or needed beyond the limited analytical tools suggested here.

In order to concentrate on the examination of contemporary international business applications, only a few major ethical concepts and principles are reviewed to establish some common terminology for later case analyses. The richness of theoretical distinctions is admittedly sacrificed to make the process of ethical analysis more accessible and understandable to more people, including current and future business and public policy practitioners. Too often students of business or politics discard ethics as irrelevant because its philosophical formulations appear too complex, demanding or disconnected with "real-world" situations. The following brief discussion of contrasting ethical approaches is meant to encourage individuals to undertake basic ethical analysis that may help identify some value factors or belief systems which already shape their reactions and response to different situations. By reviewing simple ethical terminology, or "tag terms," that can be attached to often unconscious value systems, this process may bring normative standards more clearly into focus, permitting more conscious choices and perhaps an improvement in decision outcomes.

The major debate in traditional ethical theory contrasts teleological and deontological points of view. *Teleological theory* is best represented by the *utilitarian* writings of John Stuart Mill.[7] This theory focuses on consequences, seeking the greatest good for the greatest number. The related decision rule argues that an action is "right" if and only if it produces as great a value/disvalue function as any available alternative action. Adam Smith's notion of an "invisible hand"[8] provides one business-related application of a utilitarian concept, i.e. each person seeking his or her individual interests in a competitive system is thought to produce the best possible outcome for the society. The main problems with the teleological or utilitarian theory stem from the difficulty in defining, quantifying and comparing units of "goodness";

determining the appropriate point in time (how far into the future?) to measure outcomes; and the fear that "unjust" consequences may result, especially in terms of individual rights.[9]

Concern that utilitarian outcomes could prove unfair to individuals and minorities spurred interest in *deontological theory*, drawing heavily on the writings of Immanuel Kant, who focused on what a person "deserves" and an action's motivation rather than its outcome.[10] Under this philosophical concept, a decision rule was considered ethical if all rational beings, thinking rationally, would accept the rule whether they were the giver or receiver of the action. John Rawls adapted this concept to a theory of justice in his famous "veil of ignorance" test, asking what principles we would call fair if we did not know our place in a society (and therefore could not anticipate how the principles might impact us).[11] Individual conscience may provide a popular embodiment of this notion, but most deontologists would favor strengthening this internal mechanism with a set of external rules that define a person's duty. The concept and enumeration of fundamental human rights are basically deontological in origin, as are ideas that certain positions carry distinctive role obligations (such as chief executives, auditors, etc.). Business relies on deontological views when it supports rules or boundaries on certain activities, even when those rules may impair maximum profit in individual cases. For example, most enterprises attach value to a contractual agreement (promise keeping) that transcends and generally supersedes the value of any particular transaction's outcome.

The deontological approach lends itself to the creation of standards or rules to cover various situations, depending on the circumstances and motivations of the persons involved. Problems with deontological theory include the difficulty of separating psychological motivation from justification, deciding how far back in time or how deep in detail to search to determine what a person "deserves," and choosing between ethically based standards when they clash and create a moral dilemma.[12] Teleologists postulate one decision formula (value/disvalue) to apply in each and every situation while deontologists develop rules (with varying levels of generality) to cover differing circumstances. In their simplest form, the former concentrates on outcomes, or "ends," while the latter focuses on the process, or "means."

Philosophical ethics offers a number of variations as well as alternative theories to this basic debate.[13] For example, *rule utilitarianism* bridges the teleological and deontological theories. It maintains the emphasis on consequences but acknowledges the difficulty of knowing the outcome of each individual action. Therefore, rules are accepted as appropriate for certain types of actions in the expectation that abiding by the rules will yield the greatest good for the greatest number in the long run.[14] Most business support for sanctity of contracts may fit this description as much or more than a purely deontological concern with the justice of the process.

A similar attempt to bridge the main debate is suggested by *common morality theory*, which establishes a deontologically oriented list of *prima facie* obligations but permits these priorities to be overridden in special individual circumstances.[15] This approach best reflects contemporary efforts to determine normative international business principles in a global political economy. International agreements are inherently deontological in their attempt to set forth general rules to govern conduct among nations, creating the initial outlines of a more closely integrated global society. Without the recognition of commonly agreed norms, interaction among separate societies would remain severely constricted. Teleological reliance on case-by-case determination of the best outcome in each unique circumstance provides little support for building shared goals among nations while posing a threat that case outcomes may be determined more by national power quotients than by an appeal to common values.

In a global political economy, the incipient stage of common morality principles suggests that these precepts should constitute a presumptive standard for judgment and guidance that still permits opposing arguments, where the burden of proof is borne by advocates of an alternative course of action. While perhaps falling short of the rigors imposed on ethical theory in philosophical debates, this approach offers practical promise in applying ethics to the realm of contemporary international business. The ethical theory continuum in Figure 2.1 portrays a deontological focus on justice principles and rules versus a teleological calculation of the best cost/benefit outcome as extreme opposing poles for approaches to ethical decision making. The mixed variations of common morality and rule utilitarianism are arrayed along the continuum according to whether the approach's basic belief rests more on deontological principles of justice or on teleological outcome projections.

Readers are encouraged not to choose a single philosophical theory at the beginning of this textbook. If an individual begins analysis with a predetermined ethical theory, the tendency is to apply that view to each case in a deductive, top-down fashion, trying to make case facts fit the philosophical theory (see Figure 2.2). Instead, the textbook's methodology follows an inductive approach to reasoning. This bottom-up approach examines which specific case factors provide a reasoned basis for the "best choice" decision in each ethical dilemma. Then, by assessing the cumulative decisions from multiple cases in each chapter, decision guidelines can develop for that chapter's set of issues. Comparing the various chapters, more general decision principles may emerge that illuminate broader ethical concepts. Perhaps (but not necessarily), the concepts may connect to an established ethical theory that can be located along the continuum.

The important objective in an applied ethics approach is to assist individuals to build and test a personal, practical process for making "best choice" decisions. Opting for a theoretically consistent philosophical approach to decision making may be more intellectually satisfying, but conceptually tight theories are not always compelling when confronted with real-world ethical dilemmas. As this section's previous discussion suggests, the best ethical theories still have problems in their specific application. Ideally, an action that is guided by deontological principles of justice can lead to the best teleological outcome, but such philosophical coherence is not always

Deontological Principles and Rules	Common Morality	Rule Utilitarianism	Teleological Cost/Benefit

Figure 2.1 Ethical Theory Continuum.

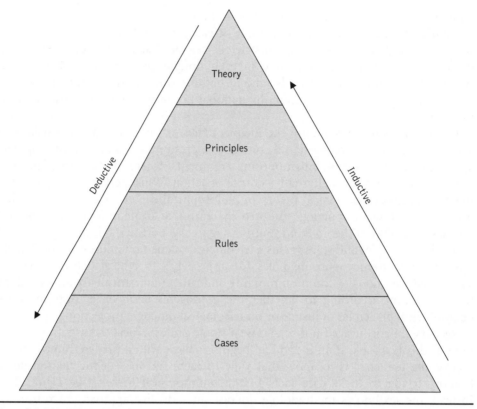

Figure 2.2 Ethical Theory Pyramid.

possible. Ethical dilemmas occur when two or more ethically reasoned arguments favor mutually exclusive courses of action. In these circumstances, "best choice" decisions are necessary, but not fully satisfying.

LEGAL AND SOCIAL CONTRACTS

As a legal creation, a business enterprise does not possess an inherent right to exist. Corporations are granted their existence by the human societies within which they are chartered. The corporation's charter and the laws governing its operations form the legal contract between the society's real people and the created business person. The corollary of this power of legal creation is a society's ability to revoke a corporation's charter or, effectively, to "kill" the enterprise. The justification for such an action springs from the rationale for the corporation's initial creation. Fundamentally, a society sanctions a corporation's existence if the enterprise (1) will create something useful for the society and (2) will not harm the society or, if harm is done, the useful good outweighs the harm. Rationally, what society should grant, or sustain, the operational life of a corporation that creates no good or, even worse, actively harms more than helps that society?

Written legal requirements constitute an explicit "floor" for corporate behavior.

Indeed, national laws could be taken as the embodiment of a society's standard for ethical corporate conduct. This position, however, encounters two challenges. First, as discussed in some later case studies, a nation's constituted laws could require unethical actions. Just as individual persons may act unethically, national governments may adopt laws based on unethical principles. In such cases, should a corporation knowingly violate an unethical law? What ethical standards should be used to judge whether a national law demands unethical action? This issue arises more frequently for international enterprises than for corporations doing business in only one country. Often national laws not only differ but may, in fact, directly conflict, forcing enterprises to choose to follow one legal standard while violating the other. A corporation's choice of action should obviously be based on some moral norm other than the law when two or more mutually exclusive legal standards conflict. Later case analyses will seek to elucidate how such a corporate decision might be made.

The second challenge to the position that national law fully embodies the ethical standards for corporate conduct derives from the concept of a social contract. A society's set of expectations regarding desirable corporate behavior can be considered a social contract between the enterprise and its chartering society. The social contract will presumably include legal requirements but may go much further as well. In addition, a social contract evolves as societal expectations and mores change. Within any given society, expectations regarding corporate behavior and responsibilities undergo progressive change over the years. Business responsiveness (or unresponsiveness) to these changing expectations will help define the society's legal contract with its corporations. Law is fundamentally reactive. Most laws are adopted to regulate behavior that has offended changing societal expectations to such an extent that political forces mobilize to enact new legally binding standards. Hence, as long as corporations act within the evolving boundaries of the social contract, restrictive new legal standards are less likely to be adopted.

This dynamic between social and legal contracts presents corporations with a dilemma. On the one hand, most businesspeople like the certainty provided by clear and enforced rules of the game. If fair and transparent legal requirements are equitably applied, a "level playing field" exists for free market competition. Under these conditions, corporations following standards higher than those imposed by legal norms could risk additional associated costs that might place the firm at a competitive disadvantage. On the other hand, executives also desire flexibility to adapt their business operations to differing societal conditions, especially with the diversity presented in global commerce. This disposition leads business generally to oppose more legal requirements (particularly when they fear regulations designed by politicians without business experience may prove unnecessarily constraining and inefficient). The desire to avoid additionally burdensome law thereby provides a possible incentive for business to abide by a social as well as a legal contract. By conforming sufficiently to evolving societal expectations, business may avoid the reactive adoption of more binding national regulations, including the potential for greater conflict between the legal formulations adopted by different nations.

CONTRACTS WITH A GLOBAL SOCIETY

International enterprises operate in an increasingly global economy that is still essentially governed by national laws. Modern statecraft busily pursues negotiations on standards to facilitate international commerce but, absent an effective world political authority, the domain for international law is limited and generally applies to corporate entities only through the intermediary of national legal authorities in the enterprises' country of incorporation. The stubborn fact of contemporary global life is that insufficient consensus exists among national governments regarding fundamental societal objectives to support agreements on business conduct standards that could be negotiated in sufficient detail to be adjudicated in court as international law. In fact the inability of governments over the last quarter-century to agree on binding "hard law" standards led to the creation of numerous "soft law" alternatives.

International "soft law" standards for business essentially date from the mid 1970s when international enterprises were under broad attack in the world community, exemplified by acrimonious debate in the United Nations.[16] The Guidelines for Multinational Enterprises adopted in 1976 by the Organization for Economic Cooperation and Development (OECD) marked an important stage in the relationship between national governments and international enterprises. Unable to develop enough common consensus to support legally binding standards even among relatively like-minded industrialized country members, the OECD governments enunciated voluntary business conduct guidelines that each government would recommend as standards for good corporate citizenship wherever international enterprises operate. Unenforceable as legal requirements, the OECD guidelines were "soft law" standards backed by the moral sanction of public pressure. Such formulations of multilateral or international "soft law" standards[17] constitute one element of the evolving social contract between international enterprises and the globalizing society within which these firms operate.

The inability of nation states to agree on enforceable international legal standards raises questions about whether truly global norms exist regarding ethical business conduct. In philosophical terms, the issue is often argued in terms of ethical relativism. In this debate, the possible existence of universal (or, more modestly, global) norms is challenged by the view that ethical standards are relative, varying according to the culture or belief systems prevailing in different societies. The admonition "When in Rome, do as the Romans do" reflects such a relativist perspective. This dictum may have provided practical guidance when companies operated in reasonably autonomous national economies. However, greater global interdependence brought growing public criticism when companies appeared to use ethical relativism to escape responsibility for difficult choices where national norms conflicted.

Globalization has increased public awareness and concern regarding conditions and events in other countries, resulting in greater scrutiny of associated business activities. A global social contract appears to be emerging wherein international enterprises are held increasingly responsible for upholding ethical standards that go beyond, and may even conflict with, prevailing norms in a particular nation. Although the emerging consensus on global norms may not yet support international legal agreements, business faces the practical reality that appealing to ethical relativism no longer offers corporate action in one nation effective protection against the consequences of adverse public judgments in other nations. Subsequent chapters will examine case studies illustrating many such contemporary situations.

The emerging and evolving nature of global norms poses a difficult challenge for international corporations. In many situations, there will be no clear choice between a "right" and "wrong" action. Rather, ethical dilemmas will occur where legitimate arguments can be made for several competing alternatives. The challenge thereby becomes how to decide on the "best" action rather than simply deciding to do what is "right." Making the "best" choice when confronted by an ethical dilemma also raises issues regarding *who* should decide. In many cases, international corporations may not be the most appropriately responsible actor. Business ethics in a global political economy also involves determining how to allocate responsibilities among relevant international actors.

DELIMITING CORPORATE SOCIAL RESPONSIBILITY

Debates over corporate social responsibility often begin with two contrasting views regarding the scope of business obligations. One perspective, typically associated with Milton Friedman,[18] claims near-exclusive primacy for the fiduciary obligations owed to a firm's owners (shareholders for publicly traded companies). A differing viewpoint, offered by writers such as Edward Freeman,[19] asserts broader corporate responsibilities to stakeholders (incorporating groups such as employees, consumers, suppliers and local communities, along with shareholders).The *shareholder* perspective focuses on a firm's founding financial contract and expected return on investment, while the *stakeholder* approach uses social contract notions to extend responsibilities to groups that significantly affect, or are affected by, the corporation's activities.

Other factors are used to evaluate the nature of a firm's responsibilities and the types of obligation falling on other relevant actors. Issues pertaining to business ethics in a global political economy generally encompass multiple public and private sector actors with varying levels of responsibility. Hence, conceptual tools are needed to determine when and why business enterprises bear an ethical responsibility in a given case circumstance as well as their degree or level of responsibility compared to other potential actors.[20]

One common distinction in assigning variable responsibility relates to *causation*. Corporations whose actions cause harm are more responsible (to stop such actions and rectify the harm caused) than firms not causally connected to the harm. Causation is sometimes further differentiated depending on whether the results stem from corporate action (an act of *commission*) or inaction (an act of *omission*). An important related factor is *capability*. Ethical responsibility can be placed on only those corporations or other potential actors that possess a capability to act. Greater responsibility may be associated with greater capability (reflected in the adage that with greater power goes greater responsibility).

Awareness and *knowledge* are two other factors used to determine degrees of ethical responsibility. Similar to capability, a corporation can be held ethically responsible to act only in cases where the firm is aware of the need for action. Awareness can generally be assessed in a bipolar "yes" or "no" fashion; however, actors are not allowed ethically to close their eyes in order to remain unaware or uninformed about ethical needs. Good-faith efforts must be made to stay alert to situations requiring ethical action. Knowledge functions as a more variable concept. The more a corporation possesses relevant knowledge in a case, the more that corporation is expected to act ethically.

Proximity may be associated with awareness and knowledge in the belief that actors closest to a case situation are likely to be more cognizant of it than groups operating at a greater distance. This concept lies at the heart of the *subsidiarity principle* that assumes the actors closest to a situation are going to be the best placed to respond to its circumstances,[21] thereby giving them principal ethical responsibility. The subsidiarity principle also establishes a type of responsibility chain. If the most proximate actor fails to act, then responsibility shifts to the next most proximate actor(s), continuing along an outward chain until ethically required action is taken. Hence, an imperative for ethical action can be passed along the *subsidiarity chain*, as ethical failures by the most proximate actors make others, in effect, parties of *last resort*.

While the notion of a subsidiarity chain of responsibility expands the reach of ethical requirements, other concepts introduce possible limits to such mandates. For example, an appeal for action down the subsidiarity chain to a party of last resort may be confined to cases of *critical need*. Even in these important cases, limits can exist on the type of ethical response that is required. While some degree of self-sacrifice may be called for, ethical obligations do not generally extend to the point where a person would be called upon to give up his or her own life. (This limitation on natural persons, however, may not apply to the same extent for legal creations such as a corporate person.) In this context, ethical obligations identify *minimal* required actions that constitute a normative duty. More extensive *maximal* responses may be taken, but such actions would be voluntary and go beyond the concept of the duties required by ethical standards.[22]

Levels of ethical responsibility may also be assessed according to the type of action required. The most basic notion is the general ethical mandate to *do no harm*, which constitutes a type of negative injunction. More positive ethical obligations require affirmative actions, such as to *help protect* others from harm or to *provide assistance* to improve their conditions.[23] A negative injunction that simply limits one's own action is generally associated with minimal ethical obligations, while affirmative duties may either require a greater degree of ethical responsibility, or be considered discretionary maximal actions.

Of course, these various concepts and factors often interrelate and may be used in various combinations to help delimit corporate social responsibility. For example, in the controversy over "sweatshop" labor conditions in foreign apparel factories,[24] social activists called for ethical action by US retail firms that had a capability to act through contracting and monitoring arrangements, even though the retailers did not own the foreign "sweatshop" factories and were not proximate to their operations. Other actors, including the factory owners and local governments, were more causally connected, as well as more proximate and knowledgeable, but either chose not to act ethically or lacked the capacity to do so. In evaluating the ethical issues presented in subsequent chapters, the reader will be encouraged to draw upon these various ethical concepts, assessing the relevant factors involved, in order to develop a framework or process to guide ethical decision making.

USING ETHICAL ANALYSIS IN A GLOBAL POLITICAL ECONOMY

International corporations emerged in the past half-century as important private actors on a world stage long dominated by sovereign nation states and their associated international organizations. In a global political economy, governmental institutions and other non-governmental organizations (NGOs) share with business enterprises a responsibility for ethical conduct. The concepts and factors used to delimit corporate social responsibility, as discussed above, simultaneously serve to evaluate the relative social responsibility of these non-business actors as well.

Governments, in particular, carry a heavy presumption of social responsibility. The fundamental purpose of governments is to protect and enhance social welfare; they also possess significant resource capabilities as well as the power of mandatory sanctions. By contrast, corporations are chartered by governments fundamentally to serve an economic purpose, within societal expectations. When considered in a global context, however, the resources and reach of many modern international corporations may, in certain respects, exceed the capabilities of some governments, even though sovereign governments still possess ultimate legal authority within their political jurisdictions.[25]

The palpable dichotomy between powerful international corporations and relatively less capable governments arises most often in cases involving developing countries and, more recently, economies in transition from communist or other centrally planned structures to a free market system integrating with the global economy. These conditions can place relatively more social responsibility on corporations. One formulation, offered by Lee Tavis as a *productivity/social separation principle*,[26] suggests that corporations have little responsibility beyond increasing productive outputs when operating in societies governed by both efficient market forces and effective democratic governments which operate in the best interests of their people. These dual conditions essentially mirror Milton Friedman's assumptions regarding a business environment that would constrain business responsibility to shareholder interests.[27] Conversely, in societies where one or both conditions are absent or impaired, Tavis argues that corporations should accept correspondingly greater social responsibility, essentially adopting the broader notion of stakeholder interests.

In many cases where local government and/or market regulation are insufficient to assure public welfare, other governments or intergovernmental organizations may constitute the next most proximate and capable actor in an international subsidiarity chain of social responsibility. However, the machinations of global politics often impede government measures needed to address ethical concerns in other sovereign countries, shifting an increased burden on to other actors. Developments over the past quarter-century showed that international corporations possess a capacity for action in addressing ethical issues existing in various countries. As demonstrated in cases discussed in later chapters, social activist pressures that failed to produce government action have sometimes found international corporations more responsive, whether to ethical appeals to good corporate citizenship, market sanctions, or both.

DEVELOPING AN ETHICAL FRAMEWORK

Ethical analysis can serve to answer four "W" questions about applying norms of social responsibility in a global political economy, including its relevance to international business: *Who* should do *What, When* and *Where*? The practical persuasiveness of these answers, however, depends on determining and explaining the crucial fifth "W"—*Why*? The fifth "W" is critical because it sets forth the rationale for distinguishing between the factually descriptive "is" and the normatively prescriptive "ought." Ethics deals with the "ought" of society, the value definition and direction to the way things should be. Applied ethical analysis seeks to operationalize these value choices in a practical manner.

Ethical analysis offers a way to use rational reasoning to clarify differing views and potentially bridge or minimize disagreements among individuals and groups. Although such a task could be undertaken case by case, the presumptive guidelines proposed by common morality theory offer a more efficient approach that complements the international system's search for common standards to facilitate closer integration in the global community. Through an experiential evaluation of past cases, as illustrated in upcoming chapters, ethical guidelines can be formulated to answer questions of Who, What, When, Where and, especially, Why, providing an ethical framework for exercising corporate social responsibility in a global political economy.

CASE SCENARIO METHODOLOGY

Brief case scenarios are used throughout the book to facilitate discussion of ethical dilemmas that confront corporations and other actors in a global political economy. Often the scenarios will encompass several different but related issues where value choices have interactive and sometimes conflicting effects. This complexity reflects contemporary reality. Many of the scenarios are reprints of actual news stories that retain the journalist's technique and story line. While offering a refreshing change in writing style, this methodology also challenges the reader both to analyze critically the facts presented and to identify which additional missing information may be considered necessary for drawing an ethical conclusion. The process will help highlight the factors considered most important for making ethical decisions and the value standards that best reflect such judgments.

This section offers readers an early sample of the case scenario methodology. One article is presented without the surrounding context of a chapter's discussion on a particular set of issues. Although this sample corresponds most closely to issues examined in Chapter 8, "Culture and the Human Environment," the main objective in presenting the example now is to demonstrate how case scenarios may be used. The following discussion illustrates how issues can be identified in such case scenarios and which types of ethical concepts or factors might be employed in their analysis.

The article "A Life Worth More Than Gold" appeared on the front page of *The Washington Post* on 9 June 2002. The story portrays a contemporary clash of views and values where a poor rural community's way of life in Peru is challenged by a foreign corporation's plans for an open-pit gold mine. The case encompasses issues of cost/benefit measures and distribution questions, representative governance concerns, private property and contract rights, and the role of foreign organizations in national decision making.

To begin the analysis, the article illustrates some difficulties with teleological decision making that relies on comparing the good and bad impacts of alternative actions to seek the best outcome. This approach is especially tempting for many international business issues that appear susceptible to economic cost/benefit assessments. The main questions revolve around identifying comparable units of value, measurable at specified times, with parallel questions concerning the relative distribution of benefits and burdens.

Certain case facts are clearly stated in monetary terms (the company's $350million investment in an estimated $1billion project; the valley's annual $100million agricultural production). Some items appear susceptible to monetary calculation (300 mining and 1,500 spin-off jobs; potential tax revenue and export earnings). With other factors, assigning a monetary value becomes problematic. How is a "way of life" quantified financially? Project advocates suggest that development will improve living standards through such measurable steps as better housing and paved roads. However, Tambogrande already has electricity and running water, and residents such as Alejandro Silupu Riofrio believe their current mud houses are just fine. Is more always better, and who should decide the specific goals of further "development," as well as whether such improvements offset associated "costs?" For example, if a mine transforms the village's evangelistic Christian social life into "honky-tonk" entertainment replete with discos and prostitutes, is this effect on Tambogrande's "way of life" a cost or a benefit, and what quantifiable value should be attached to such a lifestyle change?

Equally problematic is choosing a point in time to calculate cost/benefit outcomes. Should outcomes be measured after two years; ten years; the time when the mine's gold deposit becomes exhausted; or the village's condition some years after the mining company has departed? Each point in time might yield a different outcome conclusion. With what degree of certainty can outcomes be predicted? Farmers fear the mine will devour farmland and water while contaminating their crops, forcing them into another occupation. And should the outcome calculation consider only this one Manhattan Minerals project, or also the other nine mining companies that hold similar concessions nearby?

Distribution consequences raise related ethical issues. Should cost/benefit outcomes be evaluated only in macro terms, or should the distribution among individuals and groups be considered, including whether those bearing the greatest adjustment costs should obtain the greatest benefits or at least an outcome that leaves them no worse off than before the project was initiated?[28] The article suggests most profits from the

Exhibit 2.1   A Mine for Tambogrande, Peru

A Life Worth More Than Gold

Peruvian Town Tries to Turn Away Mining Company

By SCOTT WILSON

Washington Post Foreign Service

Tambogrande, Peru. Just below the lime, mango and avocado orchards that have sustained life in Tambogrande for generations lies a thick deposit of valuable metal. Gold and silver sit on top, copper and zinc underneath. The deposit could be worth $1 billion to the Canadian mining company that has the rights to tap it.

Doing so, however, would require demolition of a crescent of homes bending down from the highest hilltop of Tambogrande, which is crowned with a peach-colored statue of Jesus. The open-pit mine would open up just blocks from the central square, replacing about a third of this comfortable town beside a slow river in Peru's arid north.

Although this is a place where most streets and houses are made of dirt, the 20,000 residents of Tambogrande have decided that they prefer their homes, their hillside and their fruit orchards to gold. In an unofficial referendum held here last Sunday, nine in ten voters made known that the mining company, Manhattan Minerals, was not welcome.

Despite that message, the company intends to proceed. In doing so, it has embarked on a confrontation that involves such enduring national themes as gold and greed, murder and foreign interests—and even ceviche, the seafood delicacy that is Peru's most celebrated contribution to Latin American cuisine.

The confrontation has brought the debate over global capitalism to this dusty corner of Peru. A flock of international nonprofit organizations have arrived to advise townspeople in their fight, precipitating a war between a foreign mining company and a foreign anti-globalization movement, with Tambogrande in between.

Towns like this one have rarely been allowed to harness their own wealth. The eventual result here in the fertile San Lorenzo Valley may be a mine that sends most of its profits abroad and the remainder to the government in Lima, 540 miles to the south. But the residents of Tambogrande have resolved to prevent that. They are counting on a tentative democratic revival underway in Peru after a decade of quasi-dictatorship, hoping that a clear expression of their will can counter the promise of contracts and cash.

"If they don't respect these results, we will have to rely on the power that comes from the whole world knowing that these are our wishes," said Hugo Abramonte Ato, a retired schoolteacher born fifty-five years ago to landless peasants. "We don't want to change our life in exchange for this supposed bonanza."

The referendum was the first of its kind in a country that has known only fifteen consecutive years of democracy in the past century. It followed months of debate characterized at times by the type of violence traditionally used to solve problems in this part of the world.

A leader of the anti-mine movement, Godofredo Garcia, was killed in his lime grove last year by two hooded men, a month after a mob torched the first section of "model homes" that Manhattan Minerals planned to give to 1,600 families displaced by the first phase of its project. The Vancouver-based company, with its sole interests in Peru, saw $16 million in property burn.

Underlying the debate is Peru's dark, unfinished legacy of struggle over property rights for the rural poor. Many of these farmers are first-generation landowners, the sons and daughters of parents who worked as indentured servants on the valley's vast haciendas. They became the first beneficiaries of Peru's grand experiment in land reform three decades ago. Now that the haciendas are gone, many of these peasants' children view the foreign mining company as a new enemy in the same struggle.

Manhattan cannot proceed without buying the houses at the site of the proposed mine. It will likely sweeten its offer to the town to persuade the owners to sell.

The negotiations are also a test for President Alejandro Toledo, who took office less than a year ago after pledging to turn the page on corruption and energize Peru's underdeveloped agricultural sector.

His predecessor, Alberto Fujimori, fled to Japan and faces charges in Peru ranging from corruption to murder. If Toledo backs Tambogrande, it would mean nullifying a Fujimori-era contract and risk spooking foreign investors at a time when exploiting gold deposits has become a linchpin of national economic development policy.

Peru is the world's eighth-largest gold producer—the largest in Latin America—while a decade ago it did not appear on the list at all. Gold accounts for a third of Peru's export revenue, and only 10 percent of the country has been explored.

"This is part of an anti-development campaign that is going to be unfolding across Latin America, and I think it needs to be understood in that way," said Lawrence M. Glaser, chairman and chief executive of Manhattan Minerals, who called the referendum a ploy by anti-globalization activists to undermine the project.

The company has had the concession here for five years. Along with guaranteeing new homes for displaced families, the company has promised that 300 mining jobs will be filled by town residents and predicts that another 1,500 spinoff jobs will be generated by the project. The company plans to invest $350million in the operation, and estimates a billion-dollar profit over the life of the project.

In a phone interview, Glaser said the fact that the referendum was held three weeks before the scheduled release of a company-funded environmental study "should be seen for what it is, a public relations campaign." Before it was held, the vote was deemed illegal by Peru's minister of energy and mines, Jaime Quijandria, one of the government officials who have refused to comment on the project until the environmental study is released.

"There has been almost no investment in the agricultural sector in this area since land reform, and we don't see the foreign [nongovernmental organizations] that are opposing this project offering any development alternatives," Glaser said.

Almost a century and a half ago, German scientist Ernest Wilhem Middendorff got off the boat in the nearby port town of Paita, made his way to Tambogrande, and discovered gold. In those days, mining gold from the Piura River was a low-tech, low-bother operation. Most residents saw a greater potential for riches in the fruit trees that sprouted from the dry soil.

A century later, starting in the late 1940s, an irrigation system financed largely by the World Bank turned 150,000 desert acres of the San Lorenzo Valley into some of Peru's richest farmland. The large hacienda owners reaped the early benefits, their cotton plantations flourishing under the care of peasants. That system persisted until the early 1970s when land reform turned peasants into landowners for the first time. Today, the valley's hundreds of small and medium-size plots account for $100million a year in agricultural production

The region produces 25,000 tons of mangoes each year, many bound for the United States, and almost half of the limes that Peruvians use to make ceviche, a savory, spicy cocktail of raw seafood seared by lime juice. That fact has been exploited by shrewd anti-mining activists, who have popped up on Lima's busiest streets wearing fluorescent lime costumes and chanting the slogan: "Without lime, there is no ceviche."

What farmers fear most is that a mining operation would consume farmland, contaminate their fruit and siphon off too much water, forcing them into mining jobs they know nothing about. Manhattan is one of ten mining companies with concessions in and around Tambogrande, and residents fear it is the Trojan horse for an industry with designs on the whole valley.

In the past year, two chapters of Oxfam International have joined the town's cause. Oxfam America has spent an estimated $20,000 on the community, including commissioning a study last year that predicted dire environmental consequences if the mine opens. The Environmental Mining Council of British Columbia and the Washington-based Mineral Policy Center, two groups opposed to mining, helped underwrite the study.

In addition, Oxfam America has contributed $4,000 to the Defense Front of Tambogrande, a local group formed to fight the mine, to help defray legal costs for several people facing charges for destroying Manhattan's property last year. Cathy Ross, a program officer for Oxfam America in Lima, said the group has not taken sides in the debate but is only helping Tambogrande determine its own future.

"There are few cases as clear-cut as this one," Ross said. "There's a lot at stake for the company, a lot at stake for the government. And from their perspective, those look a lot more important than what's at stake for the local community."

It is perhaps Manhattan's bad luck that, on the surface at least, Tambogrande doesn't want for much. All 8,000 people living in the urban center have running water and electricity. While not generating the opportunities it might with more technology, agriculture has meant that the town is fully employed.

"Why would I want a new house?" asked Alejandro Silupu Riofrio, thirty-five, a shop owner whose home has crumbling mud walls. "We're fine with this one."

Those resources make Tambogrande different from Peru's other mining zones, usually distant, desolate mountain regions where towns, if they exist at all, have nothing. But several reports, including a second study financed by Oxfam America, suggest that surrounding communities hardly benefit from mines.

While local jobs are created, they do not last forever and most of the revenue is sent elsewhere, the reports have found. Last year, for example, the Denver-based Newmont Mining Corp. paid $50 million in taxes to the government from its gold mine near Cajamarca, 450 miles north of Lima, the most profitable gold mine in the world. The city received $800,000 of that and is resisting the mine's expansion plans.

In the past year, scores of Tambogrande residents have heard this message in workshops organized by Oxfam Great Britain. Many now worry that the mine would transform a place where the Saturday evening gathering of Christian evangelists has been the most popular form of mass entertainment into a honky-tonk town with a disco on every street corner.

"In mining zones, poverty is the highest and prostitution the greatest," said Eligio Villegas Salvador, an evangelical Christian, recounting what he has picked up in the workshops. "So we say no thank you."

---

mine will be sent abroad for the corporation and its shareholders, while Peru's national government claims the remainder, returning little to benefit Tambogrande. The village site of another Peruvian gold mine received less than 2 percent of the $50million in taxes collected by the national government.

Governance structures raise ethical issues of who decides outcome and distribution questions because political systems differ in how authority is allocated among national, regional and local institutions. The article cites corruption problems in Peru's previous national governments, with the representative effectiveness of the new democratic regime still unproven. Do national government decisions always provide the "right" answers? Should current political decisions give weight to past injustices, such as the indentured servitude suffered by the parents of many present Tambogrande residents? A local referendum showed 90 percent of the voters opposing the mining project, but the vote was considered illegal by the national government (and the article does not report what percentage of the population voted). Should the local majority of voters rule but only if the national government sanctions the referendum?

Tambogrande residents line up outside an elementary school to vote in a referendum on Manhattan Minerals' proposed gold mine. Ninety percent of voters opposed the mining project in the non-binding referendum, deemed illegal by Peru's minister of energy and mines. Photo by Scott Wilson/*The Washington Post*/Getty Images.

A somewhat different view of local choice would give preferential decision powers to a certain class of people who hold property rights to the land needed by the mining company. Do property owners have a right to sell their land whenever the company's proposed compensation package offers a sufficiently attractive personal gain or is this right limited by potential difficult-to-quantify effects on nearby residents? On a related legal consideration, should sanctity of contract be upheld for the mining concessions granted corporations by the previous national government, or should those contracts be invalidated if the government was corrupt or otherwise politically illegitimate?

Several other elements in the article may also raise ethical concerns. Environmental impact studies are mentioned, but insufficient information is presented to offer a basis for substantial analysis, making it difficult to weigh the relative importance of this concern. The justification for methods of opposition and resistance could be evaluated, with the story containing examples of voting, public relations campaigns, destruction of property and even murder. A special consideration is whether the "foreignness" of certain actors makes a difference. Would ethical considerations be different if the mining company were owned by Peruvians, or by neighboring Chileans, rather than a Canadian enterprise? Foreign NGOs are supporting local opposition to the mine with money, advice and the prospect of mobilizing international public opinion against the mining company. Could this foreign involvement constitute improper foreign interference in Peru's internal affairs, particularly if it contravenes the national government's development policy priorities on increasing export revenues? Should foreign NGOs bear a counterpart, long-term obligation to contribute toward alternative development strategies for Peru?

A discussion based on ethical analysis techniques would explore these and other facets of the article, seeking to employ terminology and concepts that can help clarify the five "W" questions. In the process, priority would be assigned to the factors or concepts that most persuasively inform decisions about Who should do What, When, Where and Why. The resulting conclusions would provide one piece of a framework for ethical decision making based on experiential analysis.

The relative difficulty a reader encounters in responding clearly to the "W" questions posed in this case scenario may reflect the current clarity of the person's recognized ethical framework for making decisions. Most importantly, the specificity of the Why answers given to other "W" questions can indicate which value standards are being used to guide decision making. For example, some readers may focus on process standards for choice, determining Who should decide What happens by favoring either individual rights or majority rule (democratic voting) procedures (either at the local or at the national government level). For other readers, calculated outcomes and their distribution effects may be more important, seeking to determine What cost/benefit ratio is likely to result from the proposed mining project. The distribution of resulting benefits could take into account such criteria as the greatest number of (Peruvian) people, ownership of physical or financial property, the development needs of proximate local villagers, or the harm caused certain persons by the project's costs.

As noted in Chapter 1, the actual outcome of this case scenario is not presented to avoid possibly prejudicing a reader's analysis of the "best choice" by interpreting what eventually occurred. The object in each of these cases is to develop and practice an approach to ethical decision making rather than ascertain the outcome of a particular event.[29] Subsequent chapters will use this same methodology to examine various sets of ethical issues that arise as international business operates in a global political economy. The reader is encouraged to build his or her own ethical decision-making framework through this process. The result should yield a more identifiable, consciously adopted standard for making ethical judgments and guiding ethical actions.

NOTES

1. This particular formulation is adapted from a definition used by R. De George in *Business Ethics*, New York: Macmillan, 1982, p. 12.
2. T. Beauchamp and N. Bowie (eds), *Ethical Theory and Business*, 6th edn, Upper Saddle River, NJ: Prentice Hall, 2001, p. 1.
3. P. Samuelson and W. Nordhaus, *Economics*, 15th edn, New York: McGraw-Hill, 1995, p. 6.
4. J. Kline, *International Codes and Multinational Business*, Westport, CT: Quorum Books, 1985, p. 120.
5. R. De George, *Business Ethics*, 2nd edn, New York: Macmillan, 1986, pp. 92–9.

6. P. French, "The Corporation as a Moral Person," *American Philosophical Quarterly*, vol. 16, no. 3, July 1979, pp. 207–15.

7. For example, see J. Mill and J. Bentham, *Utilitarianism and Other Essays*, Alan Ryan (ed.), New York: Penguin Books, 1987.

8. A. Smith, *The Wealth of Nations*, New York: Modern Library, 1937, p. 423.

9. For more discussion on these points, see W. Shaw, *Contemporary Ethics*, Malden, MA: Blackwell, 1999; and J. Smith and E. Sosa (eds), *Mill's Utilitarianism*, Belmont, CA: Wadsworth, 1969.

10. I. Kant, *The Critique of Judgment*, trans. J. Meredith, Oxford: Clarendon Press, 1952, pp. 359–61.

11. J. Rawls, *A Theory of Justice*, Cambridge, MA: Harvard University Press, 1971, pp. 136–42.

12. For more discussion on the particular strengths of deontological and teleological approaches, see W. Shaw, *Business Ethics*, 3rd edn, New York: Wadsworth, 1999, pp. 43–68; R. Buchholz and S. Rosenthal, *Business Ethics*, Upper Saddle River, NJ: Prentice Hall, 1998, pp. 24–9; J. Boatright, *Ethics and the Conduct of Business*, 2nd edn, Upper Saddle River, NJ: Prentice Hall, 1997, pp. 32–65; De George, *Business Ethics*, 2nd edn, 1986, pp. 44–80; and Beauchamp and Bowie, *Ethical Theory and Business*, 2nd edn, Englewood Cliffs, NJ: Prentice-Hall, 1983, pp. 21–40.

13. Other variations include: (1) rights theories, which emphasize individual or human rights. For example, see P. Davies (ed.), *Human Rights*, New York: Routledge, 1988; and T. Regan and P. Singer (eds), *Animal Rights and Human Obligations*, 2nd edn, Englewood Cliffs, NJ: Prentice Hall, 1989; (2) virtue ethics, which adopts the goal of cultivating virtuous traits such as truthfulness and compassion. For example, see A. MacIntyre, *After Virtue*, Notre Dame, IN: University of Notre Dame Press, 1984; (3) psychological egoism, which maintains that everyone is motivated to act in their own self-interest, however defined. For example, see M. Slote, "An Empirical Basis for Psychological Egoism," in R. Milo (ed.), *Egoism and Altruism*, Belmont, CA: Wadsworth, 1973, chapter 8; and F. Snare, *The Nature of Moral Thinking*, New York: Routledge, 1992, chapter 4; and (4) ethical egoism, which argues for the desirability of self-interested actions but denies they are psychologically necessary. For example, see D. Gauthier (ed.), *Morality and Rational Self-interest*, Englewood Cliffs, NJ: Prentice Hall, 1970; and J. Osterberg, *Self and Others*, Boston, MA: Kluwer, 1988.

14. J. Urmson, "The Interpretation of the Moral Philosophy of J. S. Mill," *Philosophical Quarterly*, vol. 3, no. 10, 1953, pp. 35–7.

15. A. Donagan, *The Theory of Morality*, Chicago: University of Chicago Press, 1977.

16. A. Fatouros, "The UN Code of Conduct of Transnational Corporations: Problems of Interpretation and Implementation," in S. Rubin and G. Hufbauer (eds), *Emerging Standards of International Trade and Investment: Multinational Codes of Conduct*, Totowa, NJ: Rowman & Allanheld, 1984, pp. 101–18.

17. Other examples of early soft law standards can be found in Kline, *International Codes*.

18. M. Friedman, "The Social Responsibility of Business Is to Increase Profits," *New York Times Magazine*, 13 September 1970, pp. 32–3, 122–6.

19. R. Freeman, *Strategic Management*, Boston, MA: Pitman, 1984.

20. Many of the factors suggested below are adapted and expanded from the formulations suggested in J. Simon, C. Powers and J. Gunnemann, "The Responsibilities of Corporations and Their Owners," reprinted in Beauchamp and Bowie, *Ethical Theory and Business*, 5th edn, Upper Saddle River, NJ: Prentice Hall, 1997, pp. 61–6.

21. "Corporate Social Responsibility and Transnational Corporations," in *World Investment Report 1994*, New York: United Nations, 1994, p. 315.

22. This application of corporate minimal and maximal duties is drawn from T. Donaldson, *The Ethics of International Business*, New York: Oxford University Press, 1989, pp. 62–4.

23. These terms are adapted from T. Donaldson's application of H. Shue's duty categories. See Donaldson, *The Ethics*, p. 83; and H. Shue, *Basic Rights: Subsistence, Affluence, and US Foreign Policy*, Princeton, NJ: Princeton University Press, 1980, p. 57.

24. This issue is discussed in Chapter 5.

25. In the most common, simplistic portrayal of business power, critics compare corporate sales figures to the gross national product of countries. Assuming the statistics are comparable, corporations would outnumber countries among the top 100 economies in the world. Other commentators challenge both the validity of this statistical comparison and resulting assertions that corporations are therefore more powerful than many countries. For a brief discussion of these views, see M. Wolf, "Countries still rule the world," *Financial Times*, 6 February 2002, p. 17. This debate over macroeconomic numbers unfortunately often distracts from a more general assessment of ability to act, where international

enterprises may, indeed, have greater situation-specific practical capability for action, especially when large corporate investments are disproportionately important in small developing country economies. These types of situation-specific assessments will be tested in many of the case scenarios presented in subsequent chapters.

26. L. Tavis, "The Multinational Corporate Responsibility for Third World Development," *Review of Social Economy*, vol. 40, no. 3, December 1982, pp. 427–37.

27. M. Friedman, *Capitalism and Freedom*, 3rd edn, Chicago: University of Chicago Press, 1963, pp. 119–36.

28. This calculation of distributional outcomes reflects concern similar to the application of the "Pareto principle" in welfare economics. For a brief description, see E. Kapstein, "Does Globalization Have an Ethical Problem?" in J.-M. Coicaud and D. Warner (eds), *Ethics and International Affairs*, New York: United Nations University Press, 2001, p. 250.

29. The Tambogrande case is far from unique. Other local protests erupted several years later over the initiation or expansion of other mines in Peru, including Newmont's Yanacocha gold mine and BHP Billiton's Tintaya copper mine (a project that initially boasted good community relations). There, multiple incidents reinforced the need for a general policy, based on "best choice" value priorities. Readers might discuss and decide how to formulate such a public policy position. See H. Weitzman, "Mining Groups Struggle to Find 'Social Licence' to Operate in Peru," *Financial Times*, 4–5 June 2005, p. 4; and Weitzman, "Peru's Mining Areas Haunted by the Spectre of Violence," 12 August 2005, p. 7.

3

HUMAN RIGHTS CONCEPTS AND PRINCIPLES

INTRODUCTION

A discussion of human rights provides both historical and contemporary contexts for examining ethical decision making on the international business issues presented in subsequent chapters. The concept of human rights attempts to set out global deontological standards that place priority value on the individual rather than on groups or institutions. In theory, these basic individual rights cannot be ethically overridden by teleological claims that outcomes in particular cases would yield better results, even for a majority of people. In practice, the specific enumeration of human rights principles, including potential conflicts between different rights, presents implementation difficulties for use as consensus guidelines. Despite this practical challenge, international policy debates increasingly appeal to human rights concepts and principles as the basis for nascent global conduct standards.

INDIVIDUAL RIGHTS, STATE AUTHORITY AND HUMAN RIGHTS

The deontological notion of rights can encompass a broad scope of standards with a wide range of derivative authorities. History records recurring competition between different standards of rights promoted as the moral foundation for a given society. Religious authorities have pronounced specific standards for guiding behavior and administering justice according to principles revealed through divine inspiration. Royalty has claimed for itself a "divine right" of kings to decree standards of justice applicable throughout their realm. The rise of nation states essentially conferred authority on the national government to set a society's civil standards. However, after the French and American revolutions, state power was often based on a constitution that, in theory if not always in practice, derived its authority from the consent of the governed and recognized certain individual rights that should not be infringed by state actions.

Considerable variation obviously existed among these diverse sets of rights. Indeed, even rights derived from the same general authority evolved over time as the understanding or interpretation of religious revelations changed, succession altered royal decrees, or particular national governments succumbed to the ballot or the bullet. More generally, the specific substance of recognized rights developed progressively under the cumulative impact of knowledge and insights gained from societal experiences. The idea of an evolving social contract, incorporating a set of recognized rights, helped structure relationships among participants in a given society.

The specific application of rights to the concept recognized today as human rights arguably can be traced back at least to the Code of Hammurabi in 1750 BC. Related principles appear in authoritative statements from the Roman Republic to Great Britain's Magna Carta before resonating in the US Declaration of Independence and, more elaborately, the US constitution (including the Bill of Rights). Often formulated in universal language, most documents actually applied these rights only to defined groups of citizens. Therefore, the practical application of rights principles depended on a government's slowly evolving definition of citizenship while the political focus of rights claims depended on a nation state's jurisdiction. Although some international agreements articulated human rights ideas, the concept's application was essentially confined to domestic polities until after World War II.[1]

The Universal Declaration of Human Rights, adopted by the UN General Assembly on 10 December 1948, stands as the most broadly accepted international statement of normative values that constitute a "common standard of achievement for all people and all nations."[2] Nearly two decades later, the UN General Assembly attempted to give these principles more precise legal formulation, approving two separate covenants in 1966 that addressed civil and political rights in one document and economic, social and cultural rights in another document. By 1976, enough countries had ratified the covenants to bring them into force, but only countries ratifying the agreements were bound by their provisions and enforcement depended on a weak UN Human Rights Commission whose mandate covered only the Covenant on Civil and Political Rights.[3]

These UN actions nevertheless set the parameters for contemporary debate over using human rights principles to evaluate actions and guide the conduct of international actors, including business enterprises, in a global political economy. Without an appeal to some overriding normative principles, such as human rights, governance of corporate behavior would be reliant on the legal standards set by sovereign national political authorities. However, the Declaration provides a higher (and potentially conflicting) "standard of achievement" that can be used to evaluate and guide corporate actions. Human rights also can serve to justify the use of coercion or intervention to breach the protective barrier of national sovereignty when state authorities egregiously violate the rights of their own citizens.[4]

An appeal to individual human rights standards that may supersede even the key interstate tenet of national sovereignty suggests the potential for a principled social contract for a global society. In fact, the central role accorded human rights issues in contemporary debates about globalization echoes the opening lines of the UN Declaration's preamble that states: "recognition of the inherent dignity and of the equal and inalienable rights of all members of the human family is the foundation of freedom, justice and peace in the world."[5]

Of course, common public understanding usually associates the Declaration and its obligations only with governmental actors, leaving in question how business enterprises might relate to such a document. In actuality, the Declaration's preambular recognition of a global "human family" places obligations on non-governmental organizations as well. Indeed, the Declaration proclaims that "*every individual and every organ of society*" (emphasis added) shall promote respect and secure the effective observance of the enumerated human rights.[6] Thus, when globalization advocates urging international corporations to respect and promote human rights, their calls echo the Declaration's concept of shared ethical responsibility in a global society.

CIVIL AND POLITICAL RIGHTS AND/OR ECONOMIC, SOCIAL AND CULTURAL RIGHTS

In addition to positing human rights as a fundamental premise for a global society, the United Nations shaped much follow-up debate on the Declaration of Human Rights by approving the two separate covenants that distinguished between civil and political (CP) rights and economic, social and cultural (ESC) rights. This distinction reflected disagreement over whether one group of human rights was more important and obligatory than the other set of rights. Embedded in resulting discussions were elements of ethical analysis relating to prioritization, relativism, causality and the extent of duties or obligations incurred by a respect for human rights.

Much of the disagreement during the latter half of the twentieth century over categorizing human rights mirrored geopolitical differences between largely Western developed nations, and Eastern and Southern developing nations. Although generalizations did not always hold, developed nations tended to view CP rights as fundamental human rights while viewing ESC rights as desirable goals. Developing nations often favored the opposite prioritization, arguing that the achievement of ESC rights was often a precondition for the realization of CP rights. Much debate centered on sequential assumptions as to whether recognition of CP rights in a society would lead to improvements on ESC rights, or whether progress on ESC rights would create the conditions necessary for the attainment of CP rights.

The disagreement on human rights categories also played out within the US government as different administrations addressed the UN Declaration, with resultant implications for US foreign policy and programs. Exhibit 3.1 contains the opening summary from a State Department document on traditional US policy toward human rights through the Cold War era. The document describes human rights as rooted in America's self-identity and lying at the core of US foreign policy. However, the US policy definition of human rights clearly recognizes only those principles associated with civil and political liberties. Economic, social and cultural rights are termed an "additional concept" that may constitute "desirable ends" but apparently lack the weighty mandate accorded to CP rights. What are (or should be) the core values that define America's self-identity and guide its policy decisions? Is "life, liberty

Exhibit 3.1   US Human Rights Policy

Background. Human rights are central to America's concept of itself and are at the core of US foreign policy. In 1776, our government became the first specifically created to preserve human rights; our Declaration of Independence even speaks of "certain unalienable rights" with which all people are "endowed by their Creator." Such rights cannot be granted by any government; rather they are "unalienable" because, based on "the laws of nature," they belong to everyone. Because human rights have always been inseparable from American identity, it follows that a human rights policy is more than just an appendage to our foreign policy. Our humane traditions separate us from those who deny human rights and embody America's attraction to people all over the world. Unfortunately, this intention to secure rights everywhere does not translate itself easily into an effective human rights policy. Devising a policy that works well is a complex matter.

Definition of human rights. The US Government recognizes two categories of human rights. First, all individuals should be free from violations of the "integrity of the person," such as political killings, torture, cruel treatment or punishment, arbitrary arrest or imprisonment, denial of fair public trial, or arbitrary interference in personal life. Second, the government recognizes a group of political and civil rights, encompassing freedom of religion, speech, and press; freedom of association, including the right to form free trade unions; freedom of movement both within and outside national borders; freedom from discrimination on grounds of race and sex; and the right of citizens to change their government.

The additional concept of "economic, social, and cultural rights," as it has evolved over the last twenty-five years, includes such desirable ends as the "right to economic development," the "right to employment," and "the right to health care." Considerable American foreign aid efforts have been activated by the moral imperative to eliminate starvation, poverty, and disease from the world. The idea of "economic and social rights" is easily abused, however, by repressive governments claiming that in order to promote these "rights" they may deny their citizens the right to integrity of the person as well as political and civil rights. We believe that no excuse justifies the denial of basic human rights . . .

Source: "Human Rights," *Gist,* "a quick reference aid on US foreign relations. Not a comprehensive policy statement," Bureau of Public Affairs, Department of State, September 1984.

and the pursuit of happiness" confined to CP rights, or must ESC rights exist as well to give those terms full meaning and practical effect? Do such rights inhere only to US citizens, or are all men created equals, with the same human rights? And what duties or obligations should be imposed on US foreign policy and programs by the recognition of human rights, civil/political, economic/ social/cultural, or both?

In a dramatic departure from traditional US foreign policy, the Clinton Administration, following the 1992 election, dropped its previous insistence on distinguishing between CP human rights and lesser goals dealing with ESC values. In addition to supporting issues such as development rights and women's rights at international meetings, then Secretary of State Warren Christopher announced that the United States would finally ratify the Covenant on Economic, Social and Cultural Rights. However, the Clinton Administration could not overcome substantial domestic concern that ratifying the treaty would commit the United States to subsidizing repressive governments which claimed to promote ESC rights. Furthermore, in 1996 the US government rejected a "right to food," reportedly fearing lawsuits from poor countries claiming a right to assistance. The US position declared that "any 'right to adequate food' or 'fundamental right to be free from hunger' is a goal or aspiration to be realized progressively that does not give rise to any international obligations."[7]

How should rights be defined or prioritized? Can there be a "right to life" without a concomitant "right to adequate food," at least enough food to sustain life? If the US government feared that recognizing a right to food might provide a basis for lawsuits from poor nations seeking aid, why was there no similar fear of lawsuits from oppressed foreign citizens seeking assistance to attain long-recognized CP rights to free speech, freedom of religion, and the right of citizens to change their government? What is the nature of the relationship between rights (of others) and duties (on us) to respect (or actively support the attainment of) those rights?

The "right to food" concept is usually discussed in terms of whether developed nations have a moral obligation to actively assist hungry (often starving) populations in developing nations. If no "right to food" or more general "right to development" exists that obligates developed countries to assist impoverished people in developing countries, then development aid contributed by the richer countries may be viewed as a non-obligatory "maximal" action. If a priority "right" to food or development exists, then relatively small foreign aid totals fall far below both the critical need in developing nations and the ability of developed nations to assist. Indeed, most developed nations consistently fail to reach their self-accepted goal of devoting 0.7 percent of gross national income to development aid. Only a few smaller, northern European nations usually meet this target, while the average assistance from industrialized nations in the Organization for Economic Cooperation and Development (OECD) lingers at a paltry 0.22 percent of gross national income (down from 0.33 percent in the early 1990s).[8]

On the other hand, ethical analysis could judge developed nations more harshly, perhaps even falling below a "minimal" obligation not to harm impoverished people, if those country's policies can be causally linked to continuing poverty in developing countries. Just such a charge arises in international trade debates over the agricultural policies of developed nations, particularly in Europe and the United States. To take one example, EU sugar policies blocked imports of cheaper sugar from developing nations, denying those countries income from sugar sales in the European Union. To compound the damage, dumping surplus EU sugar on world markets effectively undercut the developing countries' export prices in sales to other countries. The EU sugar policy could reduce a South African farmer's income by as much as one-third while guaranteeing sales for a French farmer at well above the world market price.[9] Protectionist policies extend into many agricultural areas. A report issued by the Catholic Agency for Overseas Development (Cafod) calculated that EU support for dairy farmers amounted to an average of $2 per day for each cow in the European Union, which exceeds the daily income of nearly one-half of the world's human population.[10]

The EU altered its sugar regime in 2006, largely responding to a World Trade Organization (WTO) decision that subsidies were illegal under existing international trade rules. Price supports were to be reduced 36 percent over four years (still leaving the EU price at double world market prices), while compensating EU farmers and encouraging their transition to other production.[11] However, the EU also took advantage of the time between the WTO's ruling of illegality and its enforcement to dump nearly 2 million tons of surplus sugar on the world markets, nearly 10 times the 2003 EU export level. An EU spokesperson acknowledged that the WTO had "condemned our regime" but stated that "we are fully within our rights" until an official compliance date is set.[12] Although legal, is it ethical to exploit this type of gap between the letter and the spirit of international trade rules? Negotiations in the WTO's Doha round of global trade talks floundered when countries failed to reach agreement on further agricultural policy reforms. Future multilateral trade accords will need to find broader common ground on "fair" rules for trade in agriculture to overcome this obstacle to expanded global commerce.

ETHICAL MINIMUM CONDITIONS AND COROLLARY OBLIGATIONS

Reaching consensus on a specific enumeration of human rights presents difficulties, whether the task is approached through contrasting categories or a single list. The UN Declaration clearly stands as the central document in this field, drawing primarily on its established status as the broadest official agreement. The text itself derives from a post-war era when US power dominated UN organs and the majority of current UN members did not even exist as independent nations. A contemporary political attempt in the United Nations to draft a new consensus list of human rights would likely fail. While this political reality should not denigrate the existing Declaration's standing or practical function, it does indicate the challenge for ethical analysis to clearly identify and communicate normative values that underlie human rights principles in a global society.

In the contemporary human rights debate, ethical analysis faces two main challenges. The first challenge is to identify and, when necessary, prioritize specific rights that should be respected for all individuals. The second challenge is to evaluate which individuals or institutions bear an obligation to act as a corollary duty to respecting human rights, as well as determining the type of actions that would fulfill this ethical obligation. In the illustration of US human rights policy reflected in Exhibit 3.1, the first step would be to determine whether food or other specific items constitute fundamental rights that must be respected. The second step then queries which individuals or institutions have a duty to act and what specific actions (for example, the provision of food aid) would fulfill their obligation to respect the human rights of others.

Ethical analysis might respond to the first challenge by attempting to identify a set of fundamental human rights that constitute basic minimum conditions for any individual member of a global society. The UN Declaration of Human Rights offers one possible formulation of such an answer. Ethicists have suggested more abbreviated versions of the Declaration's list, attempting to identify a fundamental core of normative values.[13] To begin, such a core list might start with an individual's basic right to life, moving quickly to associated (perhaps derivative) rights such as security of person (freedom from killing or torture) and the minimal food, shelter or health care necessary for survival.

Formulating a list of rights beginning from a blank slate does not ask whether valued rights are civil/political or economic/social/cultural in nature. Instead, the approach is somewhat similar to Rawls's "veil of ignorance" test to determine which principles would be termed "just" or "fair" by individuals who did not know their place in the world. Which rights would individuals consider basic or fundamental, a type of ethical minimum condition inherent as a right for every human person, if such rights were chosen without knowing in advance where in the world each individual would reside, and under what conditions?

Exhibit 3.2 offers a seemingly extreme yet instructive case scenario involving international trade in human organs. Driven by the extreme poverty in Moldova, Nicolae Bardan sold a kidney (albeit illegally) for $3,000. This sum far exceeded his local $6.50 monthly pay as a welder (especially since his salary had not been paid in three years) and provided essential financial support for himself and his family. The fact that the transaction was illegal suggests a certain societal level of moral indignation regarding the act of selling an individual's organs to improve his or her economic circumstances. Yet such real-life scenarios are more common than is generally recognized and pose significant normative issues regarding individual human rights, corresponding duties, free choice conditions and market-driven economic processes.

For example, should a list of fundamental human rights include the right for each individual to retain his or her own body organs, or is such a right contingent on the person's economic circumstances? If Nicolae cannot obtain basic essentials such as food and shelter without selling a kidney, should he have a (legal) right to do so? If not, do other societal actors (who?), in Moldova or in other nations (where?), have a moral obligation (when?) to do something (what?) to assist Nicolae? Why?

If a priority value is placed on free choice, Nicolae should be free to choose to sell his own kidney. However, is such a choice really "free" when his life circumstances are so desperate that he appears to have no other viable alternative (and thus no real "choice")? If Nicolae must provide for himself and has the ability to do so by selling his kidney, does the market process serve as an efficient (and ethical) intermediary? The European soccer player who received Nicolae's kidney may have paid as much as $100,000 for the operation, while Nicolae received $3,000 in addition to some days of rest and good food in Turkey. If such transactions were confined within each nation state's borders, it is doubtful Nicolae could have found a financially capable buyer in poverty-stricken Moldova. Therefore, this international business transaction (albeit illegal) probably provided Nicolae with an otherwise unavailable option (however distasteful). Should this case scenario constitute evidence for, or against, international trade? What normative criteria should determine when such trade should be permitted or regulated?

As extreme as this case scenario may appear, the issue of trade in human organs is real and actively debated. An article published in the 2 October 2002 issue of the *Journal of the American Medical Association*[14] cited evidence of kidney sales occurring as commercial transactions in South America, the Middle East, South Africa, China and Pakistan. This article reported on a study of over 300 individuals in Chennai, India, who had sold a kidney at least six years earlier. The study investigated whether

Exhibit 3.2   Selling Kidneys in Moldova

Selling of Kidneys Becomes Moldovan Cottage Industry

Desperate Villagers Recruited by Illegal Organ Network

By DMITRY CHUBASHENKO *Reuters*

Minjir, Moldova. Nicolae Bardan took his five-year-old son off his bicycle, entered his modest limestone house, threw some wood into the stove and put a large loaf of homemade bread on the table.

All this—bicycle, house, firewood and bread—Nicolae bought with the money for his kidney, which he sold illegally to an Istanbul clinic eighteen months ago. For the kidney, Nicolae, a twenty-six-year-old welder in a tractor brigade, pocketed a modest $3,000.

But in his native village, which lies forty-four miles west of Chisinau, the capital of this former Soviet republic, the sum appears huge. Nicolae would have had to work thirty years to earn that much.

"The one who got my kidney is a good bloke; I talked to him," Nicolae said. "He said he had played soccer in Europe; his kidney was injured in one of the matches."

Nicolae's story is typical of those of many of his countrymen seeking to keep body and soul together. Nicolae, whose monthly salary of about $6.50 has not been paid in three years, said his woes started in the mid-1990s when he was left out of Moldova's nationwide land privatization campaign. Because he did not belong to a Soviet-era collective farm, he was not entitled to an allotment of land.

Tiny Moldova, wedged between Romania and Ukraine and once known as "the blossoming orchard of the Soviet Union," is now Europe's poorest country. Most of its population of about 4 million survives on small private farm plots.

After the birth of his son, Nicolae and his family were forced to move from one place to another for four years, living for a while with relatives and friends, but moving on sooner or later because there was never any money to pay their hosts.

Driven by despair, he went to work in Russia but soon returned. "I spent a few months in Moscow, but there was no normal life there. The police would chase you everywhere."

Hope gleamed unexpectedly in his native village. A woman from Minjir, who is now being interrogated by Moldovan police, told Nicolae he might earn easy money in Turkey if he sold one of his kidneys there. A police spokesman said that another woman, allegedly the head of an illegal transplant network in Chisinau, is being sought by Interpol.

But months before police cracked down on the transplant syndicate, Nicolae was given a foreign passport and sent to Turkey by bus to sell his kidney. "I spent three weeks in Turkey, including the first week in a hotel on the Mediterranean coast," he said. "I just had a rest and ate as much as I could. I had not eaten that much for ages."

The second week he spent in Istanbul, where several Moldovans were undergoing a series of medical checks in preparation for kidney transplant operations. Finally, the man who was to receive Nicolae's kidney arrived. The operation, with the use of modern equipment unavailable in Moldova, was performed without complications. A week later, Nicolae was on a bus heading back to Moldova.

Nicolae said recipients of kidneys had to pay up to $100,000 for such operations, which he said are performed in private Istanbul clinics. Moldovan donors are entitled to 3 percent of this sum. "They say Romanian donors also came to Istanbul but were paid $10,000," he said.

"In Turkey this is very well organized; some donors were brought to Europe by planes for operations," Nicolae said.

On his return to Minjir, Nicolae paid off his debts, bought an unfinished house for $950, a ton of wheat for $100 and a truckload of firewood for another $100. He built a summer kitchen and dug out a cellar.

Thanks to precise laser surgery, the operation scar running across Nicolae's waist and back is almost invisible, and he boasts how he and three of his neighbors recently handled a truckload of several tons of grapes.

Village doctor Simion Mitu disapproves. "All of them are crippled people," he said. "In five or seven years they will really suffer from lacking one kidney, but Moldovan hospitals will not be able to help them."

Official police data show that thirty-six Moldovan citizens have donated organs illegally abroad. Medical experts say the actual figure is much higher. Mitu said he knew of at least seventeen villagers in Minjir, which has about 7,000 inhabitants, who had sold kidneys abroad.

Maria Golban, twenty-seven, who lives in the nearby village of Brateanovca, said the same woman who advised Nicolae to sell his kidney advised her to sell one of her kidneys in Turkey.

"The operation went all right. A forty-year-old Turkish woman got my kidney. I saw her but never spoke to her," she said. "This was my own decision, no one forced me. I did not want my husband to sell his kidney; he needs to work," she said.

Maria's husband is paid about $50 a year for tending village cattle, and the couple and their two children, age five and eight, survive largely on the cottage cheese they make.

Maria's daughter remembers the day her mother brought her nice dresses and candy from Turkey, and it is an open secret how these treasures were acquired. "When I grow up, I will also sell my kidney if I need money," the little girl said.

Maria said many villagers had asked her for help in selling their kidneys in Turkey. "I would not wish my greatest enemy to follow the same path as I did," she said. "I know, God also does not like the way I acted, but I hope he will forgive me."

The local Orthodox priest, known as Father Antoniu, is dismayed by the organ sales.

"This is like suicide, when a human being gives away what he was given by God," he said. "But [the villagers] are pushed to that by despair . . . and sacrifice themselves to their children."

---

an improvement in economic circumstances might justify such sales for the donor while, more obviously, benefiting the recipient when an insufficient supply of donated kidneys exists for needed transplants. The findings demonstrated that most donors had become worse off in both their financial circumstances and their health.

This study, however, can also illustrate the nature of ethical criteria for public policy choices. If the study had shown that donors had improved their financial position, should commercial kidney transplants then be made legal? Is the relative health of the donor also a necessary part of the calculation, or is that factor up to the donor as a potential trade-off choice? Or do commercial kidney sales fail an ethical "free choice" test? If so, who bears what responsibility, where and when, to assist someone in Nicolae's position so that other alternatives become available? These questions are pressing and their answers are important to many individuals, including the young daughter of another kidney donor, Maria Golban. As noted in the Exhibit 3.2 article, this young girl already seems to know that any rights to her own body may have practical limits when the need for money is paramount.

The WHO proposed a worldwide ban on trade in organs, reportedly because the "legal sale of organs is likely to exploit the poorest and weakest groups in society, to undermine altruistic giving and may also lead to human trafficking."[15] The global shortage of kidneys and other organs for transplants, however, generates some contrasting movement to permit fixed monetary compensation for organ donations in order to increase the supply, a position adopted in Israel. Iran has paid donors for kidneys since 1988 and boasts the highest unrelated living donor rate in the world, although foreigners are legally excluded from becoming buyers or sellers. In practice, the system reportedly can function like a market, with sellers and recipients agreeing on prices that exceed the officially sanctioned amount. Countries such as China and Pakistan have strengthened laws and enforcement efforts directed against practices that provided a commercial "tourist" market for transplants. The Philippines, where foreigners accounted for almost half of the kidney transplants in 2007, banned transplants for non-Filipinos the following year.[16] Clearly, societies are struggling to manage the gap between supply and demand for organ transplants without permitting rich recipients to exploit poor potential donors, especially in a global marketplace with huge disparities in personal income.

One way to define human rights is to formulate a list of ethical minimum conditions deserved by any individual. Many potential rights (ESC and/or CP) will involve relatively objective factors such as rights to your own body, adequate food or owned property. Other factors may involve more subjective concepts such as the right to a fair trial, to participate in government, or respect for an individual's "human dignity." Some items may test the limits of a "minimum" conditions criterion, such as the UN Declaration's endorsement of a right to free elementary education and periodic holidays with pay.[17] As the development of such lists would suggest, identifying certain items as fundamental human rights necessarily involves issues of prioritization.

Prioritization is inherent in decisions regarding which (priority) values to include and which (less essential) values to exclude. Prioritization issues also arise when valued rights clash, as when one individual's right to adequate food seemingly conflicts with another individual's right to private property. The further one progresses from the central core right(s), the more potential also exists for interactions among various rights, raising analytical questions regarding sequential cause-and-effect conditions. In such circumstances, priority may be assigned to one right that is causally necessary to attain another right of equal or even higher inherent value. This calculation often occurs in debates over whether CP rights lead to the achievement of ESC rights, or whether the latter rights are preconditions for enjoyment of the former. Even if rights in both categories were considered equal in inherent value, practical priority would be assigned to the rights believed to be necessary causal agents for attainment of the other valued rights.

[As an exercise, readers might develop a list of fundamental human rights, either beginning with a blank slate or by reviewing and possibly revising (additions and/or deletions) the UN Declaration's list. The exercise could rank-order priority items and indicate likely areas of potential interaction among listed rights.]

Despite the challenges of defining an agreed list of human rights, some specification of rights appears essential to provide practical standards for judgments and a guide for future actions in a global society. Beyond meeting this first challenge, however, ethical analysis must also provide a way to respond to the second challenge as well. If defined individual human rights are agreed upon, what corollary duties are thereby imposed on other individuals or institutions, and what types of actions should be taken to fulfill these obligations?

This second challenge can be tackled by employing the concept of levels of ethical responsibility. A minimal duty is to respect the human rights of individuals by not violating their rights (i.e. do no harm). In many cases, this minimal obligation is termed negative or passive because one's duty is fulfilled by inaction (refraining from actions that would violate an individual's rights). This viewpoint is often associated with basic CP human rights reflecting freedom or liberty argued to inhere naturally to the individual unless violated by others. Of course, a condition of natural freedom would hold only so long as all individuals respect such a right for all other individuals. The negative/passive approach thus begs the question regarding whether a violation of someone's CP human rights would impose any duty on third parties to help protect or actively assist the harmed individual. By recognizing specific CP human rights, does the US government incur an ethical obligation to help protect those rights for individuals in other countries?

Discussions of ESC human rights generally incorporate a more active or positive sense of ethical duty. Many human rights classified in this category appear to require some minimum allocation of resources to permit their attainment. In a global society characterized by resource scarcity or significantly unequal resource distribution that leaves some individuals below the minimum required to realize their human rights, ethical duty may entail some resource transfer. The US government's rejection of a human right to adequate food appeared motivated by a desire to avoid any such ethical obligation to provide active assistance to hungry individuals in other countries.

If human rights do impose corollary ethical duties or obligations on others, are there varying degrees of responsibility on different actors or limits to the type of action required? Under what circumstances, and to what extent, should an ethical US foreign policy allocate resources to aid foreign populations, whether to avoid starvation or to escape from political repression? Ethical analysis provides tools to examine this question by employing concepts such as causality, capability, knowledge, proximity, critical need and last resort. These factors, identified in Chapter 2's discussion of delimiting corporate social responsibility, can be used to evaluate, and compare, relative levels of ethical responsibility among various international actors.

Thomas Donaldson presents an example of applying guidance from ethical analysis to international financial policy in an article on "The ethics of conditionality in international debt."[18] The International Monetary Fund (IMF) can offer loans to nations that confront serious balance of payments problems. Many heavily indebted developing nations have used IMF facilities to avoid default on large foreign debts. The loan agreement generally requires recipient governments to change certain policies in ways designed to stabilize and improve the nation's economy, but often with short-term financial hardship on local populations, especially among the poorest segments, with no guarantee that financial conditions will actually improve in the future.

The general ethical justification for such IMF policy requirements is that current economic hardships may be necessary to achieve longer-term economic improvements. However, this teleological approach is traditionally based on macroeconomic projections that sometimes prove inaccurate and do not generally address how the policies will distribute costs and benefits on individuals or segments of the developing countries' populations. The uncertainty of the projected outcomes, combined with the apparent heavy cost paid by already poor segments of the public, leads ethicists such as Donaldson to favor the incorporation of more deontologically oriented policy rules based on distributive justice concerns. Donaldson argued that the condition of the poorest segment of a developing nation's population should not be made worse by an IMF loan's requirements, even in the short to medium term.

One way such a value choice might affect policies in organizations such as the IMF and the World Bank would be in how a policy's success is measured. Traditional approaches focused on macroeconomic measurements of poverty reduction such as a nation's per capita income growth. However, per capita income measures do not reflect the distribution of income within a population, so impacts on impoverished segments of the population would remain unknown. Even if the policy changes benefited the majority of the population (similar to a utilitarian's "greatest good for the greatest number" standard or a democratic majority), Donaldson's criteria would adjudge such a policy action ethically unacceptable due to its disproportionately negative impact on individuals already occupying the society's least advantaged position.

The IMF policy example illustrates a traditional tendency on economic or business issues to employ teleological reasoning that draws on the type of cost/benefit outcome calculations familiar to professionals working in these fields. These outcome projections can be used prescriptively to guide operational programs. Conversely, viewed from a consequentialist perspective, possible ethical duties to act may also be diminished if projected outcomes will not attain the desired objective. Theoretical human rights obligations to aid oppressed or starving individuals in other countries may thus be offset by judgments on the likely feasibility of attaining the goal. Even though such issues of practicability raise legitimate considerations in ethical reasoning, a teleologist should guard against making rationalizations into justifications. For example, the reliability of outcome projections depends on probability assessments at a selected future time, subject to potential influences from numerous unforeseen variables. An equally appropriate test for practicability might be the less demanding standard of progress rather than achievement. Ethical decisions might require only action that advances conditions to make a desired goal more attainable at some time in the future rather than a goal's assured achievement at a time certain.[19]

INTERNATIONAL BUSINESS, HUMAN RIGHTS AND GOOD CORPORATE CITIZENSHIP

Discussion in this chapter thus far has illustrated primarily issues relating to national government responsibilities on human rights concerns. In line with the UN Declaration's call for "every organ of society" to respect and secure these rights, how should international business define and respond to human rights obligations? Perhaps surprisingly, corporations increasingly acknowledge a relationship to human rights issues. The most obvious connections arise from direct economic activities, although resultant impacts occur, both directly and indirectly, on other types of human rights as well.[20]

Historically, international corporations rejected responsibility for CP human rights, usually asserting a stance of political neutrality in the domestic affairs of host nations. As discussed in the next chapter, this posture initially accorded with the preferences of national governments that demanded foreign corporations not interfere in a nation's internal political affairs. By contrast, business could hardly deny a relationship to economic goals and, consequently, some role in influencing the potential attainment of ESC rights. The central assertion of capitalist market philosophy holds that private corporations, pursuing their self-interest, will (through the guidance of Adam Smith's invisible hand) achieve the greatest economic good for the greatest number of people. Of course, this utilitarian belief does not address distributional consequences for minorities, or in general whose individual rights may be serviced for the benefit of the majority. Still, corporations could claim that their activities generate a larger economic pie and that governments bear any responsibility to redistribute resources to benefit disadvantaged individuals.

In the early 1990s, business made broader assertions, declaring that the economic growth stimulated by international commerce will produce progress on the realization of CP human rights as well. For example, a 1994 *Business Week* editorial argued that expanding foreign trade and investment promotes middle-class growth that, in turn, will lead to greater respect for individual human rights, even under oppressive political regimes.

> The idealists are right to pursue their agenda of supporting individual human rights around the world. But linking that agenda to US trade policy can and has hurt the American economy. Just as surely, rapid economic growth in the Third World is a solvent of the bonds of oppression. Building a strong middle class overseas through foreign investment and trade has led to greater individual rights in South Korea, Taiwan, and elsewhere, even in the face of authoritarian governments ruling in the name of communitarian values. The truth is that delinking trade from human rights policy is the pragmatic way to promote human rights overseas.[21]

This rationale offers a teleological argument that should be testable at some point in time. However, when should projected results be expected, and should the policy be abandoned if anticipated outcomes are not achieved? Such a policy test arose in 2000[22] when the United States established normal trade relations with China, cutting the link between periodic congressional renewal of bilateral trade policy and evaluations of human rights conditions in China. However, subsequent reviews of China's progress, including in the US State Department's annual human rights reports, often found that China's record improved little and sometimes actually worsened even as US–China trade and foreign investment ties increased dramatically.

Does such a record call into question the projected sequential impact of economic growth on respect for human rights? Should international business be held responsible for making a positive impact on respect for CP human rights, or is business responsibility met simply by avoiding any direct involvement in contributing to the violations of such rights? Some international companies specifically endorse human rights principles, such as the UN Declaration, employing various formulations to express the nature of their perceived responsibilities to respect, support and/or promote such standards.[23]

The phenomenal growth of internet usage in China brought new "best choice" dilemmas for international companies regarding how to respect and promote core human rights values. As a transformational technology, the internet has unparalleled ability to collect and distribute information as well as connect users across the world. Based on principles of freedom and openness, the internet can serve as an instrument of reform and promotion of human rights, even assisting democratic activists to popularize their struggles and recruit supporters. However, national governments are developing sophisticated control mechanisms for restricting internet access to sensitive information and penalizing violators. China is notorious for stringent censorship practices, but other countries such as India, Vietnam, and the United States all impose limitations on the privacy and expression of internet users.

The task facing MNEs in the internet and communication technology (ICT) industry is how to expand business and respect local legal requirements that may entail restrictive censorship, while still honoring obligations to internet users to support freedom of information, expression and the protection of personal privacy. Governments can establish censorship regulations that restrict access to information, whether the subject is pornography or political opinion. National standards vary widely depending on both sociocultural norms and a country's degree of political freedom. Privacy values are at stake when government officials ask ICT enterprises to turn over identifying information on customers. The officials may allege potential legal violations without divulging what offense or law is involved.

These issues gained prominence in 2004 when Shi Tao, a Chinese news reporter, used his private Yahoo! e-mail account to distribute a purportedly secret document urging media to refrain from reporting on an anniversary of the Tiananmen Square massacre. Yahoo! was among the first internet MNEs to establish offices in China in line with improved US–China trade relations. The company followed China's internet regulation policies without fully anticipating the challenges that emerged. In this instance, Chinese police demanded that Yahoo! release private information on a particular e-mail user, alleging he had violated Chinese law. Lacking formal guidelines for disclosing such information, Yahoo! complied with the request. The police used information provided by Yahoo! to trace the e-mail user and arrest Shi Tao, who was eventually convicted and sentenced to 10 years in prison.[24]

The incident sparked international controversy. In 2006 congressional hearings, Yahoo!'s chief executive maintained that the company was obligated to follow the laws of countries in which it operates and under Chinese law was bound to comply with the police request.[25] US lawmakers and human rights organizations asserted that Yahoo! had pursued a politically expedient option, abdicating its responsibility to protect the welfare of its users and protest an unjust Chinese policy. Yahoo! later reached out-of-court settlements in US lawsuits filed on behalf of Shi Tao and another activist.[26] Yahoo! also sold its Chinese operations to Alibaba, a local firm that follows Chinese policies, but Yahoo! retained a minority investment in the operation. Should Yahoo! have refused the police demand for information or taken other actions to resist? Does Yahoo! still carry an ethical responsibility for Alibaba's censorship policy and privacy actions, or does the transfer of management control remove Yahoo! from a subsidiarity chain of responsibility?

On censorship, the Chinese government did not provide internet firms operating from China with "black lists" of impermissible words. Instead, the Chinese government required firms to withhold search results or eliminate blog posts that discuss content that " 'damages the honor or interests of the state' or 'disturbs the public order or destroys public stability' or even 'infringes upon national customs and habits.' "[27] Firms must largely interpret these vague prohibitions for themselves. Fearing severe and arbitrary penalties for lax censorship, many firms vigorously censor content while others claim to provide greater openness. Does self-regulation as opposed to adhering to specific restrictions dictated by a government alter the nature of a firm's ethical obligations?

Yahoo! was not the only foreign-owned MNE that encountered difficulty in China. Operating from its California headquarters, Google had captured about one-quarter of Chinese internet search traffic. Since Google staffed no offices in China, the government could not legally require that Google voluntarily censor its search content. However, the Chinese government used the so-called Great Firewall to block many topics for searches from people inside China using google.com, and even temporarily shut down all access to the Google site in September, 2002. The Great Firewall was not wholly effective in blocking sensitive content, but the filtering action significantly slowed search traffic and when Chinese users searched impermissible content, the Firewall could prevent reloading the search engine, creating an impression the Google site had shut down. The slowdowns and shutdowns drove consumers to local competitor Baidu, which efficiently processes content inside China, producing (self-censored) search results more quickly and reliably.[28]

Google's eroding Chinese market share posed a difficult ethical dilemma. The company could continue to operate outside of China, safe from Chinese government demands for self-censorship and user information, but face the prospect of losing more users to Baidu (in which Google also had an investment stake it later sold). Conversely, Google could place its servers within Chinese territory and again yield hits in milliseconds, but confront political and legal pressures to comply with Chinese censorship and information demands. Exhibit 3.3 discusses Google's response—an announcement in 2006 that it would offer a limited version of its popular search engine to Chinese users.

To avoid being forced to release private information, the dilemma encountered by Yahoo! a few years earlier, Google decided not to offer popular e-mail and blogging services. Blogging attracts 70 million users in China, representing a higher proportion of internet users than in the United States.[29] By forgoing such services, Google offers a less competitive product that reduces its profits. In terms of its search engine, Google announced it would comply with China's self-censorship laws but would seek minimal limitations. Has Google struck an ethical "balance" in terms of its ethical obligations?

Exhibit 3.3   Google and Internet Rights in China

Version of Google in China Won't Offer E-mail or Blogs

By DAVID BARBOZA

SHANGHAI, Jan. 24—Google is bringing a special version of its powerful search engine to China, leaving behind two of its most popular features in the United States.

In an effort to cope with China's increasingly pervasive Internet controls, Google said on Tuesday that it would introduce a search engine here this week that excludes e-mail messaging and the ability to create blogs.

Google officials said the new search engine, Google.cn, was created partly as a way to avoid potential legal conflicts with the Chinese government, which has become much more sophisticated at policing and monitoring material appearing on the Internet.

Web sites have exploded in popularity in a country eager for freer flow of information. But Web portals and search engines trying to win Chinese users face a significant balancing act: they do not want to flout government rules and guidelines that restrict the spread of sensitive content, but they want to attract users with interesting content.

One result has been that search engines and Web portals have censored their sites and cooperated with Chinese authorities. Indeed, the move to create a new site comes after Google itself, as well as Yahoo and Microsoft, have come under scrutiny over the last few years for cooperating with the Chinese government to censor or block online content.

Currently, people in China use Google by accessing its global engine, Google.com. But industry experts say that the site is often not accessible from inside China, possibly because it is blocked by Chinese authorities culling what is deemed to be sensitive or illegal information.

Google's new Chinese platform, which will not allow users to create personal links with Google e-mail or blog sites, will comply with Chinese law and censor information deemed inappropriate or illegal by the Chinese authorities. This approach might help the company navigate the legal thickets that competitors have encountered in China.

Foreign companies say they must abide by Chinese laws and pass personal information about users on to the Chinese government. In one case two years ago, Yahoo provided information that helped the government convict a Chinese journalist, who was sentenced to 10 years in prison, on charges of leaking state secrets to a foreign Web site.

Another challenge, though, is trying to attract Chinese users to a censored engine. Google officials conceded that the company was struggling to balance the need to bolster its presence in the China market with the increasingly stringent regulations that govern Internet use here.

"Google is mindful that governments around the world impose restriction on access to information," a senior executive wrote, responding to questions. "In order to operate from China, we have removed some content from the search results available on Google.cn, in response to local law, regulation or policy. While removing search results is inconsistent with Google's mission, providing no information (or a heavily degraded user experience that amounts to no information) is more inconsistent with our mission."

The Chinese government has been particularly strict in recent years about filtering antigovernment news and opinion pieces from the Web and blocking Web sites or blogs that question governmental authority.

The government also has employed a variety of techniques to control what appears on the Web—temporarily blocking sites, redirecting viewers to government-controlled sites and even shutting sites altogether. Government officials have even been able to block references to specific words, like Tibet, Falun Gong and Tiananmen Square.

A year ago, when Google first started a Chinese-language version of its global service, the company filtered out and omitted some news sources that were already being blocked in China. The company said at the time: "There is nothing Google can do about it."

Now, Google officials say they hope they have struck the right compromise. The new site will improve access and speed up regular search engine service in a country where Internet traffic is skyrocketing, even if that service is limited in scope, the company said.

China has more than 100 million Internet users, making it second only to the United States in Web surfers; and blogging, podcasting, playing online games and surfing the Web are wildly popular.

Google says it plans to disclose when information has been blocked or censored from its new site, just as it does in the United States, Germany and other countries.

The regular Google.com site, based outside China, will continue to be available for access from China.

Difficulties using the site have put Google at a disadvantage in China, where the Google.com site had lost ground to a Chinese rival, Baidu.com, which went public last year.

Baidu is called the Chinese Google, and Google even has a stake in the company. But officials at Google say that recently they have been losing share in China, partly because of difficulty people had using Google.com.

The Paris-based group Reporters Without Borders, which tracks the activities of Western technology companies seeking to do business with repressive regimes, condemned the Google-China deal as "hypocrisy" and called it "a black day for freedom of expression in China" in a statement published on its Web site.

"The firm defends the rights of U.S. Internet users" the statement added, "but fails to defend its Chinese users against theirs."

When criticized for the decision to launch Google.cn, Google's chief executive responded: "I think it's arrogant for us to walk into a country where we are just beginning operations and tell that country how to run itself."[30] Are appeals to political or cultural relativism valid? Or is such a position "hypocrisy" as Reporters Without Borders might charge? From a deontological perspective, should a company, at a minimum, publically protest Chinese actions as a violation of international human rights, or even refuse to operate under conditions that do not protect freedom of information and personal privacy? From a teleological viewpoint, could foreign company compliance with Chinese restrictions be justified by claims that, over time, increased internet usage will result in changes that improve human rights in China? How should such progress be measured, and when?[31]

In 2009 the Chinese government presented ICT MNEs with another challenge, announcing that by 1 July, all personal computers sold in China must be shipped with a local company's software called Green Dam-Youth Escort. Reportedly aimed mainly at blocking access to pornography, the software would link each computer to a central list of blocked sites, allowing periodic updates. Critics pointed out that the list could be used to block any type of content, might permit the collection of personal data, and could expose the computer to cyber attacks or interfere with other software programs. This time, computer hardware manufacturers such as Hewlett-Packard and Dell were caught between defying a Chinese government order or facing charges of aiding information censorship and jeopardizing privacy.[32]

Although Acer, Sony and Chinese-owned Lenovo reportedly agreed to comply, other individual companies commented cautiously on the difficulties of meeting the new requirement, particularly so quickly without thorough tests of the software. Industry and broader business organizations opposed the Chinese order more vocally, calling for its suspension or repeal. Government officials in the United States, the European Union and other countries also protested the Chinese order. One day before the 1 July deadline, China's Ministry of Industry and Information Technology suspended the new requirement, purportedly to provide more time for consultations to perfect the plan.[33]

The earlier ethical dilemmas encountered by ICT MNEs, coupled with public and government scrutiny of their actions, encouraged the development of a voluntary

Two people use a laptop computer at a wireless café in Beijing on 1 July 2009, the initial government deadline for all new computers to be sold with Chinese-made Internet filtering software. Implementation was postponed hours before the deadline, but some companies had already complied and general government censorship continued. Photo by Frederic J. Brown/AFP/Getty Images.

industry code to protect the freedom of expression and privacy of ICT users. Yahoo!, Google and Microsoft, in consultation with groups such as Human Rights First and the Committee to Protect Journalists, engaged in a nearly two-year effort to draft a set of guidelines that could be applied in all countries. When announced in October 2008, the Global Network Initiative laid out "a common set of principles for how to do business in nations that restrict free speech and expression." The document acknowledges that companies must obey local laws but pledges to protect personal user information and "narrowly interpret and implement government demands that compromise privacy" while evaluating a country's record on freedom of expression and privacy before launching new business operations.[34]

Proponents endorsed the initiative as meaningful progress in the development of global standards on ethical ICT business practices. Some critics found the Initiative's principles too general and faulted its implementation procedures. Early corporate support for the Initiative was limited, principally to the companies whose dealings with China have been most sharply criticized.[35] As the industry matures and companies look for a decision-making framework to address new ethical challenges, such voluntary codes may gain greater support.

Arguments for business responsibilities on human rights issues can draw on citizenship notions, particularly for those firms that participate and benefit extensively from the global political economy. When a private business enterprise is granted rights as a legal "person," that corporation owes citizenship duties to the nation within which it operates. However, most MNEs hold simultaneous citizenship in literally scores of nations, creating the potential for a clash of loyalties should the interests of its various host nations conflict. Although the concept of global citizenship does not yet correspond to a sanctioned political authority, a growing number of corporations promote increased international integration among national economic and political systems, and pursue global business strategies that supersede the interests of individual nation states. As principal beneficiaries of globalization, these enterprises owe some type of corporate citizenship responsibilities to the global society they serve, even if that society still lacks a correspondingly organized polity.

Human rights concepts and principles can provide emergent guidelines for international corporate citizenship where diverse and sometimes conflicting national legal standards offer insufficient direction for ethical decision making in a global political economy. Nation states are struggling to negotiate a legal framework to manage the impacts of globalization, clearly recognizing the need for agreed standards to govern the rapidly growing range of political, economic and social interactions.[36] While the drive to devise an international legal framework merits attention and effort, legal standards must be based upon a sufficient societal consensus on underlying values and norms. Comparatively less attention has been paid to the type of ethical analysis that can help identify, clarify and communicate these norms for an emergent global society. The deontological standards suggested by human rights principles may provide a starting point for this analysis as well as a background context for the following chapters that examine topical sets of global ethical dilemmas in an attempt to determine Who should do What, When, Where and, especially, Why?

NOTES

1. T. Gladwin and I. Walter, *Multinationals Under Fire*, New York: Wiley, 1980, p. 132.
2. "UN Universal Declaration of Human Rights," online, available at <http://www.un.org/en/documents/udhr/index.shtml> (accessed 2 June 2009).
3. The United States has ratified the Covenant on civil and political rights but is only a signatory to the Covenant on economic, social and cultural rights. The UN High Commissioner for Human Rights maintains an up-to-date list of countries' adherence to human rights treaties, accessible through a UN website at http://www.un.org/en/rights/index.shtml (accessed 2 June 2009).
4. For example, an appeal to human rights helped justify outside military intervention against Serbia's actions in its province of Bosnia in 2000. Chapter 4 discusses several similar appeals to human rights standards by groups urging private international corporations to take actions directed against the apartheid regime in South Africa and a military junta in Burma.
5. UN Universal Declaration.
6. Ibid.
7. P. Holmes, "At Forum, US Rejects Foods 'Rights'," *The Washington Post*, 18 November 1996, p. A18.
8. S. Daneshkhu, "Richest Nations' Aid Falls to $51 Billion," *Financial Times*, 14 May 2002, p. 14.
9. R. Thurow and G. Winestock, "How an Addiction to Sugar Subsidies Hurts Development," *The Wall Street Journal*, 16 September 2002, p. 1. For other articles on the effects of US and EU agricultural subsidies, see J. Madeley, "Agricultural Subsidies Hit Poor Farmers," *Financial Times*, 24 September 2002, p. 22; and K. Hassett and R. Shapiro, "How Europe Sows Misery in Africa," *The Washington Post*, 22 June 2003, p. B3.
10. J. Filochowski, "EU Cows Richer than Half World's Population," letter to the editor, *Financial Times*, 25 September 2002, p. 14.

11. J. von Repert-Bismark and S. Miller, "EU to Cut Support for Sugar Prices by 36%," *The Washington Post*, 25 November 2005, p. D4.

12. R. Minder, "Fury at EU Plan to Offload Surplus Sugar," *Financial Times*, 23 September 2005, p. 9.

13. For example, see T. Donaldson, *The Ethics of International Business*, New York: Oxford University Press, 1989, p. 81. Another approach is the formulation of "hypernorms," drawn from values of most major religions and acceptable to all cultures and organizations; see T. Donaldson and T. Dunfee, *Ties that Bind: A Social Contracts Approach to Business Ethics*, Boston, MA: Harvard Business School Press, 1999.

14. M. Goyal, R. Mehta, L. Schneiderman and A. Sehgal, "Economic and Health Consequences of Selling a Kidney in India," *Journal of the American Medical Association*, vol. 288, no. 13, 2 October 2002, pp. 1589–93.

15. Anonymous, "International: The Gap Between Supply and Demand: Organ Transplants," *The Economist*, 11 October 2008, vol. 389, iss. 8601, pp. 79–81.

16. Ibid.

17. UN Universal Declaration, Articles 26 and 24, respectively.

18. T. Donaldson, "The Ethics of Conditionality in International Debt," *Millennium: Journal of International Studies*, vol. 20, no. 2, 1991, pp. 155–68.

19. J. Langan, "Defining Human Rights: A Revision of the Liberal Tradition," in A. Hennelly and J. Langan, *Human Rights in the Americas*, Washington, DC: Georgetown University Press, 1982, p. 86.

20. See the graphic representation of how international corporations impact human rights contained in exhibit 5.2 in Gladwin and Walter, *Multinationals Under Fire*, pp. 144–5.

21. "To Spur Human Rights, Spur Trade," *Business Week*, editorial, 7 March 1994, p. 138.

22. M. Vita, "China Trade Bill Clears Hurdle in Senate," *The Washington Post*, 14 September 2000, p. A2.

23. J. Kline, "Political Activities by Transnational Corporations: Bright Lines Versus Gray Boundaries," *Transnational Corporations*, vol. 12, no. 1, April 2003, pp. 1–25.

24. P. Goodman, "Yahoo Says it Gave China Internet Data," *The Washington Post*, 11 September 2005, p. A30; P. Pan, "U.S. Firms Balance Morality, Commerce," *The Washington Post*, 19 February 2006, p. A17.

25. D. Milbank, "Searching for an Explanation: No Results Found," *The Washington Post*, 7 November 2007, p. A2.

26. C. Rampell, "Yahoo Settles with Chinese Families," *The Wall Street Journal*, 14 November 2007, p. D4.

27. C. Thompson, "Google's China Problem (and China's Google Problem)," *New York Times Magazine*, 23 April 2006, p. 64.

28. Ibid.

29. A. Jacobs, "Chinese Learn Limits of Online Freedom as the Filter Tightens," *The New York Times International*, 5 February 2009, p. A8.

30. J. Yardley, "Google Chief Rejects Putting Pressure on China," *The New York Times*, 13 April 2006, p. 7

31. In January, 2010 Google announced its intention to stop censoring its Chinese search engine, even if it meant leaving China. Although the company had clashed periodically with the government over censorship issues, the immediate impetus for this decision was a cyber attack Google discovered, alleged to originate in China, against several U.S. sites, including attempts to hack into the e-mail accounts of Chinese human rights activists. The controversy will likely spark a new round of developments on this issue. See J. Vascellaro, J. Dean and S. Gorman, "Google Warns of China Exit Over Hacking," *The Wall Street Journal*, 13 January 2010, p. 1.

32. L. Chao, "China Squeezes PC Makers," *The Wall Street Journal*, 8 June 2009, p. A1.

33. E. Wong and A. Vance, "China Intent on Requiring Internet Censor Software," *The New York Times*, 19 June 2009, p. A8; L. Chao and J. Dean, "Chinese Delay Plan for Censor Software," *The Wall Street Journal*, 1 July 2009, p. 1; M. Wines, "After Outcry, China Delays Requirement for Web-Filtering Software," *The New York Times*, 1 July 2009, p. A6.

34. J. Vascellaro, "Google, Yahoo, Microsoft Set Common Voice Abroad," *The Wall Street Journal*, 28 October 2008, p. B7. For more information on the Global Network Initiative, see the website at http://www.globalnetworkinitiative.org.

35. M. Helft and J. Markoff. "Big Tech Companies Back Global Plan to Shield Online Speech," *The New York Times*, 28 October 2008, p. B8.

36. For an analysis of the legal context for this debate, including the "Draft Norms on the Responsibilities of Transnational Corporations and Other Business Enterprises with Regard to Human Rights" discussed within the UN Commission on Human Rights, see P. Muchlinski, "The Development of Human Rights Responsibilities for Multinational Enterprises," in R. Sullivan (ed.), *Business and Human Rights*, Sheffield: Greenleaf, 2003, pp. 33–51.

4

POLITICAL INVOLVEMENTS BY BUSINESS

INTRODUCTION

Globalization challenges national political sovereignty as growing economic inter-dependence ties national political fortunes to developments and decisions taken outside a nation's territory. When trade comprised most of world commerce, governments viewed foreign business as an external influence subject to customs controls at the border. The rise of multinational enterprises (MNEs) in the post-World War II era introduced a new actor on the international political stage. Utilizing foreign direct investment (FDI), MNEs established locally incorporated but foreign-controlled entities inside numerous economies, simultaneously taking on multiple national citizenships. These foreign subsidiaries penetrated more deeply and exerted greater influence on national economic processes than traditional export/import transactions. Controversy ensued over how MNEs should interact with national political authorities and their resulting impact on local societies.

Value standards related to political involvements by MNEs evolved from simple admonitions on non-interference or neutrality to more complicated and sometimes conflicting calls for companies to exercise political influence. A broadly accepted standard proscribes MNE activities that corrupt governmental processes or subvert national interests to advance corporate profits. More controversial are cases involving countries whose governments are ineffective, unrepresentative or repressive to their own people, typically involving systematic violations of civil and political (CP) human rights. In these circumstances, MNEs may be viewed as complicit in govern-mental violations and/or capable of influencing political change. When and where should MNEs become involved in political activities? What should they do? Who should decide? And why? That is, which reasoned value principles should guide these determinations?

This chapter explores a series of prominent cases where international corporations became involved in national political activities. The most distinctive illustrations arise when large natural resource MNEs exert disproportionate influence in small economies governed by ineffectual or abusive national regimes. In most cases, business involvement stems either from a causal connection to human rights violations or potential business capability, in the absence of action by more responsible political parties, to bring about positive change. Core issues involve whether companies should always obey national laws and how to respond when laws of different countries conflict.

The central framing question of this chapter is: Should corporations invest in, or do business with, any country where it is legally permissible (or should corporations follow voluntary ethical standards with minimum conditions that must be met above and beyond legal requirements)?

CONTRASTING STANDARDS OF CORPORATE RESPONSIBILITY

Two cases in the early 1970s seemed to set polar opposite guidelines for business involvement in political activities. A standard for non-interference in a nation's internal affairs emerged from widespread allegations that ITT Corporation conspired to overthrow a democratic government in Chile. The election of socialist Salvador Allende engendered fears that Cuban-style communism would spread in Latin America, leading to US support for efforts to debilitate or topple the regime. Investigations revealed that ITT Corporation encouraged CIA assistance to Chilean opposition groups seeking to destabilize the economy, worsen social unrest and prompt military intervention.

The Chilean case embodied the worst fears regarding MNE involvement in political activities. A foreign corporation, invested in a developing country, appeared to collude with its home government to subvert Chile's political sovereignty and democratic processes in order to advance both US foreign policy goals and ITT's business interests. This case helped inspire a non-interference principle set forth in UN and other intergovernmental documents that admonishes MNEs against involvement in a nation's political activities.[1] The standard reinforces national political sovereignty, shielding national regimes from outside interference in their internal affairs. Many corporations adopted a parallel principle, eschewing any role in political processes and professing neutrality in all political matters.

The second case, contemporaneous with the ITT affair, dealt with foreign corporations doing business in or with an apartheid-ruled South Africa. In this case, apartheid denied non-whites basic CP rights based solely on racial discrimination while concomitantly condemning the majority black population to inferior socioeconomic conditions. As the international community began to press for changes in South Africa, MNEs became sandwiched between the apartheid rules of South Africa's political system and increasing calls in the United Nations and among civil society groups for business to adhere to international human rights standards.

The dilemma confronting MNEs invested in South Africa was complex. Following international human rights standards in their employment practices meant violating, at least, some petty apartheid laws mandating racial segregation in lunch rooms and rest rooms, and prohibiting non-white supervision of white employees. Going further by pressing for political reform of the apartheid system required direct involvement in domestic political processes. At the extreme, MNEs could withdraw from the country in an effort to weaken the economy and loosen the government's hold on power. However, such motivated action would essentially constitute an effort to overthrow an existing national government. In fact, even political actions by business to abolish apartheid laws could be viewed as an attempt to promote regime change, because the minority white government could not remain in power if the apartheid system was dismantled.

The argument for MNE political involvement in South Africa was generally presented as an exception rather than an abandonment of the general non-interference or political neutrality principle. The rationale for this case exception—the Why of the ethical determination—rested on a judgment that the egregious circumstances in South Africa presented a case of critical need, requiring a response from any capable actor along the subsidiarity chain, if other more responsible (political) actors failed to take action. Although many governments historically practiced racial and other forms of discrimination, few regimes so blatantly enshrined the rules in law and systematically enforced them against the majority through police-state repression. And while the United Nations and some governments rhetorically censured South Africa, the limited economic sanctions imposed on the regime seemed unlikely to end the apartheid system.

These two cases, which reflect disparate norms for MNE political involvements, pull corporations in different directions. Business identifies most easily with the non-interference standard, asserting a posture of political neutrality when caught between the conflicting policies of different national governments. The clear trend since the 1970s moved in the opposite direction, however. Governments seldom encourage MNEs to undertake political activities in other countries, but civil society groups increasingly urge corporations to act against governments that violate the human rights of their citizens. The rationale for intervention holds that international human rights values take priority over the principle of national political sovereignty, especially when a national government forfeits its legitimacy by systematically violating its citizens' rights. Although other international political authorities should act in such situations, their failure to do so can shift greater responsibilities on to MNEs as the next most capable actor in the subsidiarity chain. The challenge for business is determining who decides when and where corporations should become politically involved, and what specific actions they should undertake.

LESSONS FROM THE SOUTH AFRICAN EXPERIENCE

Business responses to apartheid in South Africa offer a wealth of case experience that significantly shaped subsequent views on international corporate social responsibility. Despite widespread abhorrence of apartheid, corporations faced difficult ethical choices regarding who should guide their determinations of when and where to do what. An examination of decisions taken by MNEs in South Africa illustrates how ethical concepts can be employed to help guide these value choices.[2]

In deciding who should guide them, many MNEs initially turned to their own governments for a determination of whether to conduct business in South Africa. Governments can (and do) prohibit or restrict their corporations from doing business with certain countries as a foreign policy tool. However, most governments in Western industrialized countries, home to nearly all MNEs, placed only limited restrictions on trade with South Africa, primarily affecting arms exports. Without support from these governments, UN economic sanctions went no farther. The United States was especially reluctant to impose heavy sanctions against an allied regime in the Cold War fight against communism, particularly given South Africa's important geographic location for ocean commerce and its endowment of scarce strategic natural resources, including manganese, vanadium, chrome, platinum, gold, corundum and rhodium. Without governmental restrictions, legal guidelines left MNEs free to conduct business in the South African economy.

The failure by governments to exert more pressure on South Africa's apartheid regime came despite growing political activity in many countries aimed at forcing stronger legal measures. Groups agitating for tougher action in the United States included civil rights organizations, religious institutions, university students and other coalitions that supported a more activist US policy in favor of human rights standards. These groups forged cooperative ties to coordinate their activities in ways replicated in later years in other human rights issues. Failing to achieve satisfactory policy change in the political arena, the groups next directed their efforts at corporations with substantial business investments in South Africa, calling upon MNEs to use their economic position to oppose the apartheid regime.

Should business take guidance from civil society groups on political involvement issues when those groups have been unsuccessful in achieving government action through established political channels? The activist groups advanced an affirmative economic argument by using shareholder resolutions, stock divestments, demonstrations and boycotts to bring marketplace pressures on corporations doing business in South Africa. However, an ethical argument also suggests that MNEs should choose the best normative action, even on political involvement issues, whether or not they are forced to do so by legal mandates or marketplace threats. In particular, the case for contravening the non-intervention or neutrality principle in South Africa rested on a determination that the prevailing government was illegitimate. Despite retaining the diplomatic recognition of numerous governments, the regime's power rested on an apartheid structure that violated basic human rights and denied representation to a majority of its population.

Besides home governments and civil society groups, MNEs could also seek guidance from the host society, especially from the people most affected by their actions or inaction—in this case, the non-white population of South Africa. Although it seemed evident that victims of apartheid would favor its abolition, their ability to provide practical guidance for MNE action was less clear. The consensus leader of black South Africans, Nelson Mandela, was imprisoned. Alternative representatives, such as African National Congress leader Oliver Tambo, Anglican Archbishop Desmond Tutu, Zulu Chief Gatsha Buthelezi, and spokesmen for various labor federations, sometimes offered conflicting views and advice. Attempts at public polling proved suspect or indeterminate. Many corporations turned to their own employees for guidance, placing prime importance on the individuals most closely connected with the company and, hence, arguably most directly affected by its decisions.

Business also faced When and Where questions about actions in South Africa. The When question arose as the issue of apartheid gained international salience. Apartheid as a systematized form of enforced legal discrimination dates from the Afrikaner Nationalist Party's assumption of power in 1948, ironically the same year the UN Universal Declaration of Human Rights was adopted. World attention did not initially focus on apartheid, however, until the 1960 Sharpeville massacre of 69 blacks, and not until Soweto street demonstrations resulted in 700 deaths in 1976 did public revulsion galvanize opposition to the government's brutal enforcement of apartheid policies.

Corporations establishing operations in South Africa prior to these landmark dates may have lacked sufficient awareness of apartheid's repugnance and therefore may have had less responsibility for their choice of actions. Certainly corporate responsibility increases as decisions to invest in South Africa occur closer to the 1970s. As a general principle, corporate responsibility may be greatest when a decision is pending to initiate business in a new country because, at that point, the corporation retains the greatest degree of control over its actions. Just as MNEs regularly conduct political risk assessments prior to investing in a country,

South African police beat black women with clubs in 1959 after they set a Durban beer hall on fire in protest against apartheid. The more deadly Sharpeville massacre the following year captured the outside world's attention, raising awareness about white minority oppression of the black majority and generating initial support for the anti-apartheid movement. Photo by Hulton Archive/Getty Images.

corporations could and should undertake "ethical risk assessments" to identify and evaluate the nature of ethical issues such an investment may confront. Once a business relationship is established, the MNE incurs complicating responsibilities to other stakeholders in its new project and may be less capable of taking unilateral action (as will be illustrated below in examining what actions MNEs took in South Africa).

The Where question primarily concerned whether a corporation had to be present in South Africa (through FDI) or if a trading relationship (exporting or importing) also established corporate responsibility for political action against apartheid. An invested enterprise acquired local citizenship, employees, customers, suppliers and other stakeholder responsibilities inside the country. These linkages created direct, proximate and sometimes causal connections between invested MNEs and the surrounding apartheid-based society. By contrast, a company engaged only in international trade transactions, selling to or buying from a South African firm, remained external, lacking a physical or legal presence in the country.

Case experience with imports from South Africa provides few lessons regarding corporate responsibility determinations. The most notable example involved the sale of Krugerrand gold coins. Opponents of these purchases objected to the benefit provided to South Africa's export earnings as well as the symbolic importance of a product closely associated with both the South African government and the exploitation of black labor in the country's gold mines. Retailers of Krugerrands faced sporadic public demonstrations protesting their sale, but import trade generally appeared too limited and indirectly connected to apartheid to spark the level of opposition generated against export sales to South Africa.

A prominent early case involving exports arose when allegations surfaced in 1970 that the South African government employed Polaroid cameras for photographs in identification passbooks used to restrict the movement of blacks inside the country. Polaroid had no investments or employees in South Africa and its exports went through an independent distributor. Still, Polaroid decided that "We have a responsibility for the ultimate use of our product. . . . We as a corporation will not sell our product in instances where its use constitutes a potential abridgement of human freedom."[3] After failing to prevent the distributor from making clandestine sales to South African government agencies, Polaroid terminated its exports to the country.

Polaroid's acceptance of end-use responsibility for its products represents a far-reaching standard that will be addressed more fully in a later chapter on marketing issues. In terms of political involvement, this step constituted an attempt to cut all connections between the company and the South African government's violation of the black population's right to freedom of movement. From a deontological perspective, even this rather indirect connection to the violator had to be terminated.[4] From another viewpoint, a teleologist would question how Polaroid's action affected the outcome. Even though the company prohibited direct sales to the government and then stopped all exports to the country, Polaroid cameras could still be purchased in third countries and resold into South Africa, albeit probably at a somewhat higher cost. Thus, the cameras might still be used in the passbook system. Of course, in measuring the full consequences of an action, teleologists might also evaluate whether Polaroid's high-profile public decision increased pressure for action by other MNEs that possessed greater political ability to oppose apartheid policies.

Perhaps the most important trade relationship involved financial services, most specifically international bank loans to the South African government. Although MNE banks sometimes established branches in the country, the clear importance of a loan relationship involved a transfer of funds from external private lenders to the South African government for its disbursement in support of public policies, potentially including apartheid enforcement. Particularly as the South African economy weakened, these loans became more important to the government's viability, giving private banks increased potential capability to influence outcomes, including public policy choices involving apartheid. Banks with significant South African loan operations received considerable attention from civil society activists pressing for business action against the apartheid structure.

Financial services face heavy regulation in most countries, drawing foreign banks into a close relationship with government agencies. For banks dealing directly with the government as a customer, the connection is closer still. The "product" in these cases constitutes the loan funds transferred to the government for its disposition. Although loans must be repaid, with interest, the government benefits from the immediate increase in available monies and the banks thereby provide support for the government and its activities. Where loans go only to private sector borrowers, an argument can still be made that MNE banks indirectly support the prevailing government by injecting external financial resources into the South African economy.

Among the banks that accepted social responsibility for their business with South Africa, some institutions employed a teleological process by adopting policies permitting loans to South African government agencies only for programs with projected good consequences for the black population, such as improvements in their housing or education. This conditional loan method attempts to control product end use, similar to Polaroid. The use at issue with bank loans is clearly government policies and conditioning loan use represents involvement in the political process by denying funding options for any program that supports the apartheid system. Alternatively, banks could choose a more deontological approach, deciding that the ultimate use of loan funds is indeterminate because money is fungible within a government's budget. Under this principle, the ultimate outcome of the loan cannot be accurately projected, so no commercial relationship should be maintained with the apartheid government, or perhaps even with the South African economy.

One event stands out as an illustration of how bank actions can impact an economy and affect a government's political fortunes. Under anti-apartheid economic pressures, South Africa faced increasing difficulties obtaining foreign loans to fortify its economy. In 1985 over two-thirds of South Africa's foreign debt of $16.5billion comprised short-term high-interest loans from private banks, enabling the government to sustain its financial activities. These loans could be called in for repayment at any time. Although apparently motivated by financial risk concerns rather than anti-apartheid objectives, Chase Manhattan Bank called in its loans in August 1985, sparking similar action by other banks. South Africa confronted loan repayment demands totaling $13billion over four months. The government was forced to freeze the debt, impose foreign exchange controls and reschedule repayments, severely damaging the country's currency and sending living standards into a tailspin that seriously weakened the government's position, even among the white population.[5]

This discussion of bank capabilities clearly moves into the realm of decisions regarding what actions MNEs should take, once a social responsibility link is determined. Four principal options emerged in the South African experience that also frame later choices in other human rights cases. (1) Where MNEs deny responsibility, the firm may continue to conduct its normal business and refrain from deliberate attempts at political involvement. (As noted earlier, the company's business may nevertheless have unintended political impacts.) (2) The MNE can remain engaged in South Africa but implement reforms within its operations to eliminate direct participation in apartheid practices and present an alternative "model" for responsible business behavior. This approach avoids direct political activities but actively opposes apartheid practices within the boundaries of corporate operations while passively suggesting other companies do likewise. (3) Overt political activity can be added to the second option, including public statements against apartheid, financial support for opposition groups or lobbying activities to change apartheid laws. (4) Corporate withdrawal constitutes the fourth choice, with the MNE disinvesting from subsidiary operations and perhaps terminating any business dealings with South Africa. Firms choosing disengagement may or may not intend the potential political consequences of their action, including weakening the South African economy and thereby perhaps hastening a collapse of the apartheid regime.

An ethical assessment of these choices can be illustrated through the story of the Sullivan Principles for MNEs doing business in South Africa. The Reverend Leon Sullivan, a black Baptist minister from Philadelphia, had joined General Motors' (GM) board of directors in 1971. Immediately discarding the first option that GM lacked social responsibility for its South African operations, Leon Sullivan initially urged the company to withdraw. However, during a trip in 1975, he heard pleas from blacks in South Africa that MNEs use their resources to bring change from within the country rather than withdrawing. In response, he helped develop a set of business conduct principles that bore his name, asserting that the only ethical justification for MNEs to remain in South Africa stemmed from their ability to create positive change for the black population. Hence, the original Sullivan Principles outlined six workplace reform standards covering issues such as equal pay for equal work, training and promotion for non-white employees, and desegregation in corporate facilities. The sixth principle reached outside the workplace, seeking community improvements such as housing, education and health facilities.

Essentially the original Sullivan Principles represented option 2, promoting reform from within the South African economy but without overt political activity. Implicitly, however, the standard overlapped into political involvement. Although desegregation actions were confined to the workplace, the area where corporate responsibility and control are arguably greatest, certain steps could violate so-called "petty apartheid" regulations on racial segregation. Adopting this position suggests that business can ethically violate certain laws, rather than viewing legal standards as an absolute mandate for business behavior. (In practice, the South African government failed to challenge the MNEs on these regulations, which were ultimately abandoned.) Formally, the Sullivan Principles only obliquely hinted at this type of political effect by vaguely referring to seeking "modification" of existing working conditions through "appropriate channels." Leon Sullivan was clearer in his interpretation, saying "implementation of the Principles placed companies in confrontation with the law, but the changing practices of those companies brought modifications of the law and its enforcement."[6]

By 1980 nearly one-half of US companies invested in South Africa had signed the Sullivan Principles. Several times the principles were elaborated in greater detail and expanded to include items such as support for the right of black workers to form unions. An auditing process monitored and then publicly rated each signatory firm's progress in implementing the principles. This evaluation process is consistent with the teleological nature of the principles, which were based on projections of achieving measurable progress in improving conditions for non-whites in South Africa. Nevertheless, Rev. Sullivan deemed progress limited, primarily because business actions directly impacted only those non-whites with employment ties to the companies, which probably constituted no more than 1 percent of the country's workforce. Possible multiplier effects from other firms adopting this "model" behavior appeared slow and uncertain at best. He favored adding overt political activity to the principles, effectively moving to option 3.

The so-called Fourth Amplification of the Sullivan Principles shifted formally into the sphere of political involvement, specifying corporate commitment to work for the elimination of apartheid laws and customs. Disparate reactions arose among MNEs regarding the appropriateness of such overt political activity. Some companies balked at undertaking a political role in a country where the MNE operated as a "guest"; other firms felt obliged at least to speak out to support rights for their black workers. Leon Sullivan clearly expected the companies to "do more than make public statements . . . They must do their utmost to change the laws and the system."[7]

The intended outcome aimed at helping millions of non-whites, as quickly as possible. Such an impact necessitated reaching far beyond the factory walls and engaging in the society's political processes.[8] Sensitive to the severity of the critical need that existed in South Africa, Leon Sullivan next established a timetable to achieve system-wide outcomes. Excerpts from a speech presenting his ethical reasoning calling for action are presented in Exhibit 4.1. Declaring that "The evils of apartheid must come to an end," he announced in mid 1985 a two-year deadline to abolish apartheid in South Africa. When this outcome failed to materialize, Leon Sullivan withdrew his support for the principles bearing his name and moved to option 4, calling on companies to withdraw from South Africa and for the US government to institute an economic embargo.[9]

The story of the Sullivan Principles in South Africa thereby illustrates a range of corporate responses to calls for business action against apartheid. This experience established some parameters for business choice options when faced with pressure for political involvement in opposing regimes that systematically violate the human rights of their citizens. The action choices can be roughly categorized as (1) business as usual, (2) stay and reform your operations, (3) stay, reform, and become politically

Exhibit 4.1   The Choice to Reform or Withdraw

The Role of Multinational Corporations in Helping to Bring About Change in South Africa

LEON H. SULLIVAN

... We are all aware that the most racially segregated nation in the world today is the Republic of South Africa. The inhumanities practiced there against blacks and other non-whites are well known around the world. Apartheid and its policies of separate development, and all of the laws and regulations that follow from these policies, are a blight on civilization. The roots of 300 years of racial discrimination in South Africa go down so deep that one wonders if the only realistic answer might have to be a violent one involving massive human and property destruction. I hope not. . . .

It was for this reason, looking for a peaceful solution, that my efforts with the multinational businesses were begun and the so-called Sullivan Principles were created. The Sullivan Principles must be viewed as a moral, humanistic, and economic effort to persuade companies of America, Europe, and other parts of the world with interest in South Africa to use their great resources, power, and influence for meaningful change in South Africa, and to help build a bridge of understanding, cooperation, and reconciliation between the races before it is too late.

I fully realize, and it must be made very clear, that the companies alone cannot solve the problem of apartheid. . . . But the companies can and should play the major role in helping to bring an end to the racial injustices, because more than any others, the companies have been the main beneficiaries of the cheap labor and the inhumane practices. Billions and billions of dollars of profits have been made on the agonies, torn families, and broken bodies of blacks and other non-white South Africans. Therefore, starting in the workplace and extending to the communities, the businesses must do all they can to help change the inequalities of and injustices against black people.

And the businesses must work to influence the government to rescind its unjust racial laws. Otherwise, the multinational companies have no moral justification for remaining in South Africa and should be compelled to leave the country. . . .

Among other things, the Principles call for an end to all vestiges of discrimination in the work place for all companies operating in South Africa; equal pay for equal work; massive programs of education and skilled training; Blacks being uprated in all companies to management and supervisory jobs at all levels, including management of white workers; the recognition of representative black trade unions; support of black businesses in large numbers so Blacks will one day own shops, stores, factories, and mines; development of extensive housing schemes and health programs; and the lobbying of the South African government for an end to all apartheid laws, including influx control and separate development.

. . . But the efforts of the companies must go beyond fair employment and jobs. The urgent need in South Arica is not fair employment and jobs at this time, but freedom: freedom for the black masses that they might have equal status throughout South African society.

Therefore, in a recent amplification, an addition was made to the Principles that calls for American companies to actively work for an end to all apartheid laws. . . . In a word, the latest amplification to the Principles requires that the companies challenge the South African Government to abolish apartheid and requires the companies to become part and parcel of the liberation movement for social, economic, and political justice. . . .

American companies must stand up and be counted. Now is the time. And they must be measured and judged by the extent to which they take a stand against that unjust system. But time is running out. People are being killed daily in South Africa, and South Africa does not have ten years, or six years, or four years to bring an end to its unjust system of government. Therefore, a deadline is necessary for decisive action to be taken. In this regard, as of May 7, 1985, I announced a

24-month deadline for United States companies in South Africa, taking the position that if in 24 months apartheid is not actually and in fact abolished in South Africa as a system, all American companies should withdraw from South Africa, and there should be a total United States embargo against South Africa, including all exports and imports. And it is my hope that other companies and other nations will do the same. The gauntlet

must be laid. The evils of apartheid must come to an end. . . .

Source: Leon H. Sullivan, speech to the Sixth National Conference on Business Ethics, published in W. Michael Hoffman, Ann E. Lange and David Fedo, *Ethics and the Multinational Enterprise*, Lanham, MD: University Press of America, 1986, pp. 379–86. Reprinted with permission.

---

active, and (4) leave. Historically, MNEs arrayed themselves along the full range of responses. The majority of US firms supported the Sullivan Principles, many even after Leon Sullivan abandoned this approach. By early 1991 all but some 100 US MNEs had withdrawn from South Africa, although many enterprises maintained trade or technology relationships with the new owners of their former firms.

The method or completeness of corporate withdrawals generated controversy regarding business intentions. Retaining some non-investment business ties could be viewed as a cynical way to relieve public pressure on the MNE without sacrificing all profits. On the other hand, corporations generally justified such actions as a balancing of responsibilities to many stakeholders, including black employees who could lose jobs and customers who could lose access to important products or services if the MNE terminated all business relationships. How should a corporation calculate the trade-off between the immediate harmful impacts of job loss on its black employees, whose conditions had improved through the Sullivan Principles, measured against the possible effect the MNEs' withdrawal might exert on eventually weakening the apartheid system? This weighing of direct and indirect, micro and macro impacts reflects the integrated network of stakeholders an MNE develops after deciding to invest in a country. As discussed earlier regarding ethical risk assessments, these ties complicate later determinations of how a business withdrawal will impact various parties. Of course, retaining some business connections and customer loyalty also makes reentry to the South African market easier under a post-apartheid regime.

Even retrospectively, calculating the impact of business actions on the demise of apartheid proves exceedingly difficult. A myriad of international, national and local political and socioeconomic factors influenced developments in South Africa in complex and interactive ways. Certainly MNE actions increased pressure on the South African government to contemplate reforms while business retrenchment and withdrawals contributed to the country's declining economic health. Because a full accounting would gauge cumulative effects over time, attempting an outcomes-based decision regarding any one particular business decision becomes problematic. Yet the cumulative impact is built on such individual decisions, which can dynamically influence each other as they are taken. A teleological method of projecting outcomes requires this type of case-specific calculation. A deontological, rights-based emphasis on rules and relationships brings its own challenges, especially determining which values standards take priority and whose rights and welfare lay the strongest claim on a corporation's social responsibility.

HISTORICAL CHOICES IN ANGOLA AND UGANDA

Two other early cases join with South Africa's apartheid experience to illustrate some of the fundamental ethical dilemmas of political involvement by business. Historical circumstances in Angola sequentially posed two political involvement issues for MNEs, particularly for the dominant foreign investor, Gulf Oil. Gulf began exploring for oil in Angola's Cabinda province in 1954 and three years later received a drilling concession from the Portuguese colonial government.[10] Hence, the first issue relates to Gulf's involvement with colonialism. Striking oil in 1966, the company invested over $150million to achieve production of 150,000 barrels a day by 1971, with substantial long-term prospects. This success drew the attention of civil society groups opposing colonialism, who demonstrated against the company, charging that Gulf's strategic oil investment and growing tax and royalty payments supported Portugal's exploitation of a disenfranchised Angolan population.

Similar to apartheid, corporations could point out that colonialism had not always evoked strong opposition, at least in their home countries, whose governments permitted business relations with most colonial territories. Still, the post-World War II movement to grant independence to former colonies should have raised some ethical concerns. As early as 1961, armed insurgents against Portuguese control had temporarily captured most of Cabinda province, forcing Gulf to suspend its exploration activities, and undeniably creating an awareness of this issue. When confronted by critics of colonialism, Gulf claimed political neutrality but asserted its contribution to Angola's economic development.

The controversy over Gulf's involvement with a colonial regime in Angola was overtaken by events in Portugal, where a military coup occurred in April 1974. The new government sought to reduce the high costs of fighting Angolan independence groups and offered a referendum on self-determination. Independence and the withdrawal of Portuguese troops were planned for 11 November 1975. Unfortunately, well before that date, competing factions within Angola caused serious instability in a provisional government, leading to armed conflict among three major groups. Portugal aided the evacuation of its citizens and other refugees but then left the country to the developing civil war. During the conflict, foreign governments, including the Soviet Union, Cuba, the United States, China and South Africa, provided significant support, including weapons and financial assistance, to competing groups.

The Popular Movement for the Liberation of Angola (MPLA), the group backed by the Soviet Union and Cuba, quickly seized control of Cabinda province, the capital city of Luanda and roughly one-quarter of the country. Gulf maintained its stated position of political neutrality but faced a dilemma putting this stance into practice. The issue concerned tax and royalty payments due the government of Angola for Gulf's oil operations. In late 1975 Gulf paid over $100million to the government's account in Banco Angola, located in the MPLA-controlled capital city. Another $95million was due at the end of the year, followed two weeks later by an additional $30million. All three armed groups in the civil war now demanded receipt of the monies. To put this revenue in perspective, US CIA financial assistance provided to groups opposing the MPLA totaled $30million. Should Gulf continue to transfer payments to the Soviet-backed MPLA, whose military (including Cuban soldiers) provided security around Gulf's facilities in Cabinda, or should it recognize the claim of anti-communist opposition groups, as urged by the US government? Certainly Gulf's payments represented a significant capability to affect political outcomes and its decision would constitute political involvement.

In the end, Gulf chose a path that seemed to maintain its neutral posture. The company suspended operations but made its contractual payments as required, depositing the funds in an escrow account to be held for an Angolan government recognized by the world community. Of course, perspectives differed on whether this action constituted political neutrality in the conflict. Gulf could claim it was deciding not to act by refusing to choose which faction should receive the payments. However, the MPLA could view such purported inaction as, instead, a deliberate act to deny it access to the funds, because establishing the escrow account was an action that changed the existing practice of making payments to MPLA-controlled government accounts. In this case, taking no political decision as to which group should receive the funds still constituted political involvement by altering the *status quo ante* regarding the civil war factions' comparative financial resources.

The MPLA accused Gulf of acting in response to US political pressure and threatened to find other oil companies to operate the Cabinda facilities. While discussions ensued, however, the MPLA made rapid gains on the battlefield and by early 1976 controlled enough of the country to achieve formal diplomatic recognition by the Organization of African Unity and many Western European nations. Although the continued role of Cuban troops in Angola delayed US government recognition, Secretary of State Henry Kissinger reportedly approved Gulf's release of escrow funds to the MPLA and subsequent resumption of its Cabinda operations—an involvement that challenges the political neutrality claim Gulf had advanced.

The Angolan case experience illustrates both the wisdom of carefully assessing possible ethical risks prior to undertaking a business initiative and the difficulty of anticipating all potential developments, especially over the longer-term life of a major project. Growing opposition to colonialism should have alerted Gulf to ethical questions regarding involvement in Portuguese-controlled Angola; however, once invested, Gulf was drawn into an unanticipated civil war featuring Cold War intervention by foreign powers. Turning the rhetoric of corporate political neutrality into the reality of actions proved difficult if not impossible.

Even after the MPLA became the acknowledged government of Angola, Gulf still faced ethical choices relating to political involvement. Armed anti-communist forces continued to oppose the MPLA government and US conservative groups, backed by some members of Congress, harshly criticized Gulf for its support of a Marxist government.[11] Chevron later acquired Gulf, including its operations in Angola. As the company transferred into new ownership, what ethical norms should guide Chevron's decisions relating to political involvements? Discuss how Chevron should evaluate its Angolan situation and decide whether the change in ownership should also occasion an adjustment in corporate policy. Why, or why not?

In the Uganda case, trade rather than FDI formed the primary business connection between foreign corporations and the estimated murder of 100,000–300,000 Ugandans in the 1970s during the brutal seven-year rule of Idi Amin.[12] Most killing occurred along ethnic and tribal lines, serving to demonstrate and maintain Amin's power while eliminating potential opposition. Actions by other governments seldom exceeded diplomatic protests, with neighboring African regimes especially reluctant to support outside intervention. Pressure therefore built on coffee importers, who bought as much as $750million of Ugandan coffee beans, representing over 90 percent of the country's foreign exchange earnings. The revenue went direct to a state marketing board and funded Amin's purchases of weapons and luxury goods for his military and police.

The coffee connection indirectly linked importing firms to the Amin regime, but more dramatically demonstrated a potential ability to influence the regime's actions. The coffee industry's oligopolistic structure concentrated purchasing decisions in the hands of relatively few firms. Because Ugandan coffee beans could be substituted quite easily from other sources, coffee companies risked little financial penalty and few alternative replacement buyers were available. Even the potential for adverse impacts on peasant coffee growers in Uganda appeared minimal because they already received little or nothing for their crops, which could be sold only to the centralized state marketing board.

In late 1977 the president of the US National Coffee Association wrote to the US Secretary of State and to a congressional sponsor of legislative trade sanctions on Uganda. The letter acknowledged that "the violations of human rights occurring under the government of President Idi Amin are abhorrent and morally repugnant," causing pressure on coffee firms to end purchases of Ugandan coffee beans.[13] However, rather than individual firms acting alone or risking potential antitrust problems for collusive market actions, the coffee companies favored the adoption of a uniform government policy and action to ban such imports. Opponents in the administration and Congress, worried about such a step's effectiveness and precedent, delayed legislative approval of trade sanctions. By mid 1978, faced with continued government inaction, several large coffee companies individually ended purchases from Uganda. Shortly thereafter, Congress adopted a trade embargo. The sanctions weakened Amin's hold on power and encouraged opposition rebels. The following year, after border conflicts with neighboring Tanzania, an invasion force drove Amin into exile in Saudi Arabia. Milton Obote, the President before Amin, returned to power.

This case history illustrates the application of several tools of ethical analysis. The subsidiarity chain of ethical responsibility shifted pressure on to coffee companies when governments, as the more appropriate and responsible political actors, failed to act in a case of clear critical need. The potential ability of coffee companies to affect the Amin government's resources through trade sanctions appeared to give those companies greater responsibility to act than other firms more proximate and, at times, with a more direct causal link to the human rights violations. For example, reports indicated that Bell Helicopter trained Ugandan police, Page Airways sold Uganda jet aircraft, several charter airlines helped service Ugandan planes and Harris Corporation provided a satellite communications system. Although these individual commercial deals may have drawn protests, the principal pressures aimed at stopping coffee bean purchases because the coffee companies possessed the greatest ability to influence outcomes, even though the outcome sought was political change in another country.

A deontological rules-based approach would support trade sanctions that ended all these business ties. The Ugandan case experience showed more of a teleological orientation in targeting coffee firms in the expectation that stopping their revenue flow to the Amin regime would weaken its hold on power and lead to a new government. Indeed, the trade sanctions most likely speeded Amin's departure. However, teleologists derive mixed satisfaction from the Ugandan case and its projected outcome. Judged from the event in 1979, Amin's overthrow appeared to vindicate preferred outcome projections. Following the slightly shorter but just as bloody rule of Milton Obote, the results did not appear so good. Although Obote's violence fell mainly among different ethnic and tribal groups, the total number of murders committed by the undisciplined military during his regime likely equaled if not exceeded Amin's slaughter. At what point in time should outcome projections be made; with what degree of certainty can outcomes be known?

Yoweri Museveni, the guerilla leader who assumed power following Obote's ouster in 1985, brought greater stability, security and economic prosperity to Uganda. Complaints against his administration focused on the suppression of political opposition through the creation of a "non-party democracy" that limited the exercise of political participation and freedoms. The murder sprees carried out under Amin and Obote clearly argued for an ethical judgment of critical need. Should the less violent suppression of political freedoms under Museveni also reach that threshold and motivate action? Should it matter that the achievement of substantial economic progress under Museveni is argued to depend on the stability achieved by denying certain political and civil liberties?

SUDAN'S INTERNAL CONFLICTS

Oil also features prominently in the long-running but escalated civil conflicts in Sudan that encompass a variety of human rights issues, including racial, ethnic and religious discrimination, forced displacements, slavery, violence against civilian populations, and genocide. Root causes lie in both historical circumstances and the lack of representative governance, along with an unjust distribution of economic resources. At the center of Sudan's civil war, both geographically and financially, sit foreign MNEs that exploit oilfields located largely in the center of the country, dividing the dominant Arab and Muslim North from rebel regions in the black, animist and Christian South as well as the neighboring Darfur region. MNE investors face charges that their involvement fuels the political and military conflict, and exacerbates human rights violations, directly and indirectly, intentionally or unintentionally.

Colonial decisions laid the groundwork for contemporary civil strife. Britain had administered the two dissimilar regions separately, but map boundaries and the grant of independence in 1956 described Sudan as one nation. The South quickly rebelled, initiating a conflict lasting until 1972 when the Northern-based government promised the South greater autonomy and funding. Two years later, Standard Oil of California (Socal), now Chevron, began oil exploration and found significant reserves in 1978. The oil discovery helped rekindle tensions over power and resource-sharing arrangements, leading to renewed violence. When several Chevron employees died in a rebel attack in 1984 the company suspended operations and sold its rights nearly a decade later. The purchaser, a Sudanese government-sponsored consortium, added MNE partners from China, Malaysia and Canada, with the Canadian firm (originally Arakis, later acquired by Talisman) supplying key technical expertise and industry credibility. Another lull in the conflict permitted renewed oilfield operations around 1997.[14] By mid 2001, civil society groups organized a campaign similar to the anti-apartheid struggle to pressure Talisman to withdraw from Sudan.

The enormous revenue stream from new oil production to Sudan's government coffers presents the most obvious connection linking Talisman at least indirectly to increased civil war violence, especially with the close correlation between increased oil revenue and growing military expenditures. The desire to develop new oilfields in a secure setting also appears to motivate the forced displacement of local villagers, with military forces or armed militia groups using tactics ranging from bombing and burning to rape and slavery. No direct evidence suggests the MNEs order, require or even encourage these tactics, any of which would establish ethical intent and causally link the MNE to the harm, even if the company did not itself carry out the brutalities. However, if a company is aware of such violence and benefits from its results, the company may be viewed as complicit in the actions.

Talisman's home government of Canada faced the most direct pressure to implement MNE investment sanctions. Following an investigation in early 2000, the Canadian Foreign Minister rejected forcing Talisman to withdraw and instead concluded that "engagement and dialogue" constituted the most appropriate tools, with monitoring by NGOs of company and Sudanese government activities. The US government criticized Canada's inaction against Talisman and expressed concern about companies providing "a new source of hard currency to a regime that has been responsible for massive human rights abuses in Sudan and sponsoring terror outside of Sudan."[15]

Although Socal/Chevron initiated oil exploration in Sudan, US-based oil companies were absent from subsequent controversy because the US government imposed restrictions on US business activity in Sudan. The primary US motivation stemmed not from the civil war but from a determination that Sudan had assisted international terrorism. In fact, following terrorist bombings of two US embassies in East Africa during August 1998, cruise missiles were launched against a Sudanese factory alleged to be involved with terrorism. Should the Sudanese government's involvement in human rights violations constitute an equally compelling case for US government sanctions against the regime?

Despite broad condemnation of Sudan's regime and widespread calls for corporate withdrawals, some uncertainty was expressed about the ultimate impact of disinvestments by firms such as Talisman. An article appearing in *The Washington Post* in 2001 reported in its headline that "Activists in Sudan Fear Loss of Western Oil Firms' Influence."[16] Some commentators credited Talisman with at least quietly trying to

Exhibit 4.2   China Invests in Sudan's Oil Fields

China Invests Heavily In Sudan's Oil Industry

Beijing Supplies Arms Used on Villagers

By PETER S. GOODMAN
Washington Post Foreign Service

LEAL, Sudan—On this parched and dusty African plain, China's largest energy company is pumping crude oil, sending it 1,000 miles upcountry through a Chinese-made pipeline to the Red Sea, where tankers wait to ferry it to China's industrial cities. Chinese laborers based in a camp of prefabricated sheds work the wells and lay highways across the flats to make way for heavy machinery.

Only seven miles south, the rebel army that controls much of southern Sudan marches troops through this sun-baked town of mud huts. For years, the rebels have attacked oil installations, seeking to deprive the Sudan government of the wherewithal to pursue a civil war that has killed more than 2 million people and displaced 4 million from their homes over the past two decades. But the Chinese laborers are protected: They work under the vigilant gaze of Sudanese government troops armed largely with Chinese-made weapons—a partnership of the world's fastest-growing oil consumer with a pariah state accused of fostering genocide in its western Darfur region. . . .

In the case of Sudan, Africa's largest country, China is in a lucrative partnership that delivers billions of dollars in investment, oil revenue and weapons—as well as diplomatic protection—to a government accused by the United States of genocide in Darfur and cited by human rights groups for systematically massacring civilians and chasing them off ancestral lands to clear oil-producing areas. The country once gave safe haven to Osama bin Laden and is listed by Washington as a state supporter of terrorism. U.S. companies are prohibited from investing there. . . .

China National Petroleum Corp. owns 40 percent—the largest single share—of the Greater Nile

Petroleum Operating Co., a consortium that dominates Sudan's oil fields in partnership with the national energy company and firms from Malaysia and India.

From its seat on the United Nations Security Council, China has been Sudan's chief diplomatic ally. In recent months, the council has neared votes on a series of resolutions aimed at pressuring Sudan's predominantly Arab government to protect the African tribes under attack in Darfur and stop support for militias by threatening to sanction its oil sales. China has threatened to veto such actions while watering down the threat of oil sanctions.

"China has a long tradition of friendly relations with Sudan," Wang Guangya, China's ambassador to the U.N., said in a recent interview in New York. He confirmed China's veto threats, though he dismissed as "categorically wrong" suggestions that oil interests were a factor, asserting that the resolutions would have eliminated the Sudan government's incentive to cooperate. China—itself often criticized on human rights issues—has a philosophical predisposition against outside pressure. . . .

One of the poorest countries in the world, Sudan has long aimed to extract oil riches but lacked the necessary capital. It needed the help of deep-pocketed outsiders. In the 1960s and 1970s, Chevron Corp. took the lead. But as the civil war flared in the south in the 1980s, Chevron abandoned its concessions. During the early 1990s, the Canadian firm Arakis Energy Corp. took up the task, later selling out to a larger Canadian company, Talisman Energy Inc.

China National Petroleum Corp., still owned by the Communist Party government, bought into the Sudan consortium in 1996. It joined with Sudan's Energy Ministry to build the country's largest refinery, then last year invested in a $300 million expansion that nearly doubled production, according to a report in the Shenzhen Business Post.

The consortium's Heglig and Unity oil fields now produce 350,000 barrels per day, according to the U.S. Energy Department. Separately, CNPC owns most of a field in southern Darfur, which began trial production this year, and 41 percent of a field in the Melut Basin, which is expected to produce as much as 300,000 barrels per day by the end of 2006. Another Chinese firm, Sinopec Corp., is erecting a pipeline from that complex to Port Sudan on the Red Sea, where China's Petroleum Engineering Construction Group is building a tanker terminal.

Sudan's bloody north-south conflict began long before China arrived, but oil has dramatically increased the stakes as well as the government's ability to pursue the battle. The war is a struggle over the resources of the south, pitting the mostly Muslim, Arab elite that runs the government in Khartoum against the largely Christian and animist African tribes who live in the lower half of the country.

For years, the government lacked the arms to vanquish the Sudan People's Liberation Army, the rebel group that controls much of the south. With the dawn of oil production in 1999, Sudan's government began collecting $500 million a year in revenue. About 80 percent went to buy weapons, said Lam Akol, who was Sudan's transportation minister from 1998 to 2002 and is now a rebel commander. Over the same period, Sudan's military budget has doubled, according to the International Monetary Fund. A study by PFC Strategic Studies concluded that the Sudan government could collect as much as $30 billion in total oil revenue by 2012, with the potential for much more if exploration succeeds.

As the oil began to flow, Sudan relied on Chinese assistance to set up three weapons factories near Khartoum, Ryle said. Human rights groups say oil receipts have helped pay for a government-led scorched-earth campaign to remove mostly ethnic Nuer and Dinka tribes from around the oil installations. The goal is to deprive the rebels of a base of support in their bid to attack the industry and undermine the government's oil revenue.

A report by the U.S.-funded Civilian Protection Monitoring Team, which investigates attacks in southern Sudan, asserted that government troops have "sought to clear the way for oil exploration and to create a *cordon sanitaire* around the oil fields." . . .

[F]ield reports produced by human rights groups describe a connection between the people extracting the oil and those waging the war. Some of the helicopter gunships used in the attacks on civilians are Chinese-made, according to Akol, the former Khartoum transportation minister. The helicopters, he said, have frequently been based at airstrips maintained by the oil companies—a statement consistent with the findings of Canada-based World Vision when it interviewed survivors of attacks and defecting government soldiers in 2001. . . .

The exit of Canada's Talisman company from Sudan was largely a reaction to public pressure. China National Petroleum has felt similar pressures. In April 1999, the company announced plans to sell shares on the New York Stock Exchange—the first Chinese state-owned firm to land on the Big Board. It was to be the largest initial public offering in the exchange's history, valued at $10 billion. But human rights groups said the deal would be the effective use of U.S. financing to aid the killing of innocents in Sudan. Eventually, CNPC restructured the transaction. It sold $2.9 billion in a newly created subsidiary, PetroChina, asserting that none of the money would be used in Sudan.

Ultimately, it may be peace that presents the Chinese firm with its greatest challenge. Under the terms of an agreement still being negotiated, oil contracts are supposed to remain secure. But three commanders of the southern Sudan rebel group said in interviews that the SPLA will seek to punish China once the rebels gain a formal decision-making role in the government.

The stakes could be considerable: Peace would allow the world's major energy companies to enter Sudan's oil patch. Moreover, roughly two-fifths of all known reserves—oil worth more than $16 billion—are now in rebel-controlled territory, according to the study by PFC, the strategic analysis group.

"The suffering of the people is on the hands of the Chinese," said commander Deng Awou. "The agreements for the Chinese company may be terminated."

influence the government on human rights issues and speculated that the Canadian firm would be replaced by increased investment from Chinese or Malaysian firms less likely to respond to human rights concerns. In fact, Talisman sold its share of the Sudan project in late 2002.[17] How should the potential for an unknown replacement buyer be calculated in making ethical decisions regarding possible withdrawal?

Exhibit 4.2 describes the increased role played by China National Petroleum Corporation (CNPC), which became the largest investor in Sudan's dominant oil field consortium. Should CNPC's corporate responsibility for the violence in Sudan be assessed any differently than the earlier involvements by Chevron and Talisman? The Chinese firm appears less vulnerable to pressures from civil society groups based largely in Western markets, but increased global financial and commercial linkages may expand levers for future action.[18] Subsequent to Exhibit 4.2's publication, China openly urged Sudan to change its politics. Chinese President Hu Jintao reportedly urged Sudan in February 2007 to accept a larger UN role to achieve peace in Darfur.[19] At what point in time should CNPC's impact be judged?

This Sudan case scenario captures only a snapshot portrayal of an ongoing saga, but real decisions must be taken at definitive points in time, benefiting from some retrospective knowledge and perhaps calculated projections on possible alternative futures. MNE control and options are greatest upon entry to a country, where ethical risk assessments might carefully evaluate the compatibility of business and government partners in a project. Prospective development of deontological rules may also provide a starting point for negotiations and decision making; for example, agreements on how security forces should be deployed or used to protect an investment and how local communities would be impacted by the project's development. As discussed later in the chapter, the Sudanese experience, and others like it, stimulated progress on guidelines such as the Voluntary Principles on Security and Human Rights. This type of exercise may help sort out relative role responsibilities among government, business and NGO actors when human rights issues require major political involvements.

MILITARY REPRESSION IN BURMA

Serious and systematic human rights abuses mark military rule in Burma,[20] ensnaring business investors and importers in protests aimed at the regime's ouster. Compared to other cases, clearer answers emerge with Burma regarding who should guide decisions, when and where. Somewhat less agreement exists on what business actions should be taken, but even these options and arguments have narrowed, along with the rationales for alternative choices. Over time support has broadened in both the public and private sectors for the termination of business relations with Burma, driven partly by a deontological rejection of ties to a notoriously abusive regime as well as the absence of convincing projections that continued engagement will bring substantial and sustained improvements.

Burma gained independence from Britain in 1948, launching a fledgling democracy that lasted until a military coup in 1962 replaced it with a single-party constitutional dictatorship that enabled the military to maintain control. Failed policies and ineffective administration led to economic failures that sparked social unrest in 1988, with protests and demonstrations calling for democratic change. The military dissolved the government and assumed direct control, killing and imprisoning thousands of protesters in the ensuing crackdown. In 1990 the junta permitted relatively free parliamentary elections in which an anti-government party, the National League for Democracy (NLD), won 60 percent of the votes and 80 percent of the legislative seats. The military then nullified the electoral results and imposed further restrictions on political activities. NLD leader Aung San Suu Kyi, who won the Nobel Peace Prize in 1991 for her vigorous but peaceful pursuit of democracy, has spent most subsequent years under house arrest, while many of her supporters were imprisoned.[21]

The military regime's well-documented human rights violations include extra-judicial killings; torture; rape; restrictions on speech, the press, association and religion; village displacements; forced labor; and military conscription of children. Few regimes have faced such widespread international condemnation of its practices. Although some governments matched their rhetorical criticism with progressive economic sanctions, insufficient consensus existed for broad embargoes, particularly because neighboring Asian countries favored engagement over isolation. In 1997 the US government prohibited any new investment in Burma but did not force existing investors to withdraw or restrict key imports from Burma, particularly textiles. Civil society groups increased pressures on MNEs to withdraw and most US and many European manufacturing and retail firms left the country, including enterprises such as Hewlett-Packard, Motorola, Pepsico, Heineken and Philips.

The British government took an unusual step in April 2000 when the Foreign Office publicly called on Premier Oil to withdraw from Burma but did not seek legal authority to force disinvestment. Business organizations castigated the move and Premier rejected the advice, endorsing "constructive engagement" as a better approach. Groups such as Amnesty International supported the government's position but urged similar action toward alleged human rights violations in China and Saudi Arabia. Eventually Premier sold its Burmese interests as part of a restructuring deal in 2003. Later that year the BAT tobacco group became the last large British MNC to leave Burma. Although BAT also had resisted earlier pressure to withdraw, the company reconsidered, saying, "The overriding factor is that if you are a UK multinational then it is hard to ignore the political will of your government."[22] Should a home government apply public pressure but not legally require MNEs to take actions designed to weaken or remove a foreign government?

The largest and most important remaining foreign investors in Burma are oil companies engaged in an offshore natural gas production and pipeline project. This enterprise was led by Total of France in partnership with Unocal (US) and a Burmese state enterprise. Costing over $1 billion, the Yadana natural gas project primarily aims to export gas overland to Thailand, yielding export earnings for Burma and profits for the corporate partners. Most controversy about the project centered on its construction phase that ended in 2000 when commercial production began. Opponents focused on several issues tying the project to human rights violations, including financial benefits the military regime gained from investment funds and projected export sales; displacement of villages along the pipeline route; forced labor to build roads and support military units providing security for the pipeline; and the implicit credibility provided the military regime by its involvement with major Western MNEs.

Total and Unocal (later acquired by Chevron) denied involvement in the abuses, claiming that any forced labor or village displacements occurred without their knowledge or support. Critics argued MNE complicity in the military's abuses, even if indirect, because the firms were joint-venture partners with a state enterprise, benefited from the roads and security provided by the military's use of forced labor, and supplied key expertise for a project that helped sustain the junta's rule. While the critics pressed for withdrawal, the two companies argued that other firms would replace them and the project would go forward anyway. Additionally, probable replacement firms were less likely to press the government for reforms or provide philanthropic support to improve local community education and health programs.[23]

Many of these arguments were raised in lawsuits brought by Burmese citizens against Unocal and Total in the firms' home countries. Without admitting any wrongdoing, both companies agreed to out-of-court settlements reportedly worth around $30 million and $6.1 million, respectively.[24] Controversy continued to follow the firms, however, stoked by periodic flare-ups in Burma including the violent suppression of protests led by Buddhist monks in 2007, the government's inadequate

Two Burmese refugees chain themselves to a Unocal tanker in Los Angeles, California on 12 December 1996. They were arrested along with other demonstrators protesting human rights abuses and environmental destruction linked to the company's construction of a pipeline in Burma. Photo by Eric Slomanson/AFP/Getty Images.

response to a devastating cyclone in 2008, and the repeated extensions of Aung San Suu Kyi's house arrest.[25]

One question for ethical analysis concerns how such contending claims should be evaluated. Should a judgment be formed based on cost/benefit projections, selecting quantifiable factors to measure at a given point in time, or should decisions follow priority rules of conduct based on concepts of justice and human rights, as asserted by selected organizations or spokespeople for the Burmese people? Would it make a significant difference to know that Aung San Suu Kyi has spoken out against foreign investment while Burma is controlled by the military regime[26] and is quoted as saying: "Total has become the main support for the military government in Burma."[27] Should fears that less responsible investors might replace Total, especially now that the pipeline is completed, diminish pressures for withdrawal? Which reasons offered for withdrawal or for continued engagement are most ethically convincing? Why?

A related element in this case pertains to trade rather than FDI connections. Governmental action lagged the development of unusually broad private sector support for tougher trade sanctions against Burma. The International Labor Organization (ILO), a tripartite institution representing government, business and labor participants, took the unprecedented step (in its 81-year history) of recommending to member governments that sanctions be imposed on Burma for its violations of prohibitions against forced labor. No new national government measures immediately resulted from this call, but an increasing number of US retailers took unilateral steps to end their purchase of Burmese products. On 15 April 2003 the American Apparel and Footwear Association asked the US government to impose a ban on all imports from Burma because of continued human rights abuses.[28]

The US Congress contemplated imposing an import ban, but some officials initially suggested such a governmental restriction would violate World Trade Organization rules. The US government finally did impose trade sanctions on Burma in late 2003 after the military government again used severe travel and speech restrictions to essentially confine and isolate Aung San Suu Kyi in her house. Should international trade rules permit trade sanctions against governments that systematically violate their citizens' human rights, or should trade sanction decisions be left to private sector business initiatives?

GOVERNANCE AND RESOURCE ALLOCATION IN NIGERIA

Nigeria gained independence from Britain in 1960, another troubled product of colonial construction. Patterned on British territorial demarcations, Nigeria's borders drew together over 300 different ethnicities into Africa's most populous state. Although a federal structure recognized some of the internal diversity, in practice the central government consolidated control over most resources, not least because strong military governments exercised power for nearly three-quarters of Nigeria's first 40 years. Oil resources, discovered in 1956, represent the country's principal source of national income, providing roughly 80 percent of government revenue and 90 percent of foreign exchange over the 1980s and 1990s. Not surprisingly, invested oil MNEs play the central business role in Nigeria, led by Shell as the dominant producer.[29]

Several issues and events figure prominently in ethical debates over Shell's involvement in Nigeria, including allegations regarding collusion with oppressive military regimes, complicity in violence against local populations protesting Shell's activities, and environmental damage to land and water resources. Exhibit 4.3 reports on many of these issues but requires careful analysis to untangle the interrelated strands of charges and counter-charges. One central ethical issue appears to underlie, if not instigate, most of the controversial actions. The core issue relates to Nigeria's system of governance and the resultant resource allocation decisions emanating from that system. From the standpoint of corporate social responsibility, the key judgment is whether MNEs should attempt to influence internal resource allocation policies of the national government, disinvest from the country, or proclaim political neutrality and non-involvement in Nigeria's internal affairs.

Protests against Shell originate principally among two ethnic groups in the main oil-producing regions of the Niger River Delta. The Ogoni people numbered only about 1 million, while the Ijaw represented Nigeria's fourth largest ethnic group at nearly 4 million. Nevertheless, neither group counted among the top three ethnic factions (Hausa-Fulani, Yoruba and Igbo) who primarily competed for power. Hence, both the Ogoni and the Ijaw derived little economic benefit from the oil resources extracted from their land but suffered most of the detrimental effects, particularly environmental pollution. In fact, Nigeria as a whole benefited little from its vast oil wealth, as widespread governmental corruption siphoned off most monies, creating a wealthy elite centered around military leaders while leaving the general population among the world's poorest.

This cost/benefit disparity among the Nigerian people raised issues of economic distributive injustice that drove most of the protests against Shell and other foreign oil firms. MNEs require central government permission to invest and usually operate as minority partners in joint ventures controlled by the Nigerian state oil company as the majority shareholder. This legal relationship connects MNEs directly to the government while leaving questions regarding their control and influence capabilities. Indirect ties to the government also arise from MNE technology inputs and revenue outputs from the oilfield ventures. Another form of linkage derives from association with military and police violence against populations located near oil facilities threatened by protest actions. Real threats to MNE operations (facilities and employees) existed, but requests for government protection often resulted in disproportionately brutal actions that left civilians dead, villages razed and local populations displaced.

Protest actions also appear responsible for some, although certainly not all, environmental damage from oil spills. Sabotage of oil pipelines may be attempts to reduce corporate profits, gain monetary compensation for local leaders, or simply represent efforts by poor people or criminal gangs to acquire crude oil for sale. Shell also contends that some spills resulted from inadequate investment in the maintenance and upgrading of pipeline equipment but blames the government's refusal, as the controlling joint-venture partner, to spend necessary funds for improvements during an oil price downturn in the mid 1980s.[30]

Exhibit 4.3   Defining Shell's Role in Nigeria

Nigeria's Oil Exploitation Leaves Delta Poisoned, Poor

By DOUGLAS FARAH
Washington Post Foreign Service

Eriemu, Nigeria. The swamp and palm trees surrounding Well 19 are still black, seven months after thousands of barrels of crude oil spilled into the jungle and caught fire, fouling the water and scorching the tropical forest. Nearby, a stream of natural gas hisses from a pipe that has recently been sabotaged.

Not far away is an immense natural gas flare that shoots a flame 300 feet into the sky, noticeably raising the temperature at the nearby village of Oshie by several degrees.

The scenes are repeated all around the Niger River Delta, a fragile wetland of about 42,000 square miles that produces 2 million barrels of crude oil a day and that is worked by five multinational firms. It is home to about 7 million Nigerians. Abandoned by the government, hostile to the oil companies and ecologically ravaged, the delta is in a dismal state that sometimes seems impossible to remedy, one perpetuated by a seemingly endless cycle of distrust and violence.

By any measure, the delta is an environmental basket case.

Whether caused by carelessness, human error or sabotage, oil spills have dumped at least 2.5 million barrels of oil—equal to 10 Exxon Valdez disasters—into the delta from 1986 to 1996, according to a recent unclassified study commissioned by the CIA. Oil companies acknowledge that at least 100,000 barrels were spilled in 1997 and 1998.

And every day, 8 million cubic feet of natural gas are burned off in flares that light the skies across the delta, not only driving off game, hurting the fishing and poisoning the agriculture, but contributing to global warming.

The CIA study found that while oil extraction has "generated immense profits, the delta's inhabitants have suffered increasing poverty and a general decline in the quality of their lives due, in part, to the environmental impact of oil extraction. Corruption and bureaucratic incompetence have led to an almost total absence of schools, good drinking water, electricity or medical care."

Around Eriemu, ethnic Ijaw communities blame the oil companies for the August spill and months-long delay in cleaning up. The villagers, who said cleanup efforts did not begin until last month, want economic compensation for the ruined lands and water, as well as more oil-company investment in health, education and water systems.

"We will not be able to use this land for the next twenty-five or thirty years at best," said Peter Akpagra, at Eriemu village. "There is no way all that oil can be cleaned up—Shell can't do it—so our farming has stopped."

Such disputes have often spilled over into violence, with young people in the communities taking oil workers hostage, occupying pumping stations or sabotaging pipelines, and oil companies relying on the often brutal and corrupt Nigerian military and police to maintain order, sometimes even paying military and police salaries in the region.

Ijaw leaders have taken strong public stands against such violence. But they said the jarring sight of foreign oil camps with running water, electricity and health care beside the villages with none of those amenities has led to more and more radical actions by disaffected youths.

"The oil companies must and should be subordinate to the people," said Oranto Douglas, deputy director of Environmental Rights Action, a Nigerian advocacy group. "Right now they are lords and masters."

The Shell Petroleum Development Corp., Shell's Nigerian branch that runs the site and is by far the largest oil producer in the delta, says the problem at this wellhead is not so simple.

Executives said there can be no compensation because the well was sabotaged and the cap ripped off, something community leaders reluctantly acknowledged. Compensation, they said, would lead to more sabotage.

And, said Shell executives, the community blocked cleanup efforts in an effort to force the company to pay, leaving the oil to soak into the water and land.

Shell also argues that, while it funds some regional development, it is up to the government, not the company, to provide basic services.

Hubert Nwokolo, Shell's general manager of development, said that the company has radically altered its approach and raised its community development spending from about $10million in 1996 to $55million last year in 150 communities.

But Shell officials argue that, while they have an obligation to the communities, so does the government, which is largely absent. They said they were trying to get the government to use its own oil revenue to establish services in this region.

"If it did, the pressure would be much less on the oil companies," Nwokolo said. "We build schools, put in water systems and electricity. But we also pay our taxes. It is really the state's job to take care of its people."

Douglas and other activists say that while there is some truth to that argument, the oil companies have often functioned as virtual arms of the government. In doing so, they have developed close relations with the brutal and corrupt military regimes that ruled Nigeria until twenty-two months ago.

Shell has been forced to shut down its oil production in the eastern Ogoni region since 1995, for example, when ethnic Ogoni leaders and youths carried out a campaign of violence against the company after the execution of Ogoni leader and environmentalist Ken Saro-Wiwa. The executions were carried out by the military government under dictator Sani Abacha, and the Ogonis alleged that Shell did not use its influence with the government to try to free Saro-Wiwa.

"The Niger Delta is not a law-and-order question," Douglas said. "It is primarily and almost purely political and a question of survival. The communities want to protect their air, water and forest."

There are some small signs that the situation could be improving. Violent incidents such as kidnapping and sabotage dropped sharply last year. Activists such as Douglas and Moffia Akobo, a former oil minister who now heads the Southern Minority Movement here, who were driven underground during the years of military rule, now operate openly.

The democratic government of President Olusegun Obasanjo, who took office in May 1999, has slowly begun fulfilling its constitutional obligation to give 13 percent of the country's oil revenue back to the six Niger Delta states to use for development. Under the military, 1 percent was allocated, but even that didn't make it.

The first oil money was disbursed to the states in January, and government officials, activists and oil company executives say it has given the local and state governments an incentive to keep the oil flowing.

In addition, the government has formed the Niger Delta Development Corp., which is supposed to use a new 3 percent tax on oil companies to fund regional development. Since its establishment four months ago in Port Harcourt, the largest city in the delta, the corporation still has no working telephones and very limited office space. But as Akobo and other community leaders are quick to point out, almost every Nigerian government has set up some version of a development corporation here and most of the money has simply disappeared into the pockets of officials.

Source: From *The Washington Post*, 18 March 2001, p. A22 © 2001 *The Washington Post*. All rights reserved. Used by permission and protected by the Copyright Laws of the United States. The printing, copying, redistribution, or retransmission of the Material without express written permission is prohibited.

The most infamous event involving Shell was the arrest, summary trial and hanging execution in 1995 of the well-known Nigerian writer Ken Saro-Wiwa, along with eight other activists. Saro-Wiwa had led protests against Shell's operations in the Ogoni region. Much early criticism of Shell focused on the company's inaction. Critics held Shell responsible in the case because the government sought to protect the company's oil facilities whose operations had sparked the protests and Shell was assumed capable of intervening with the government to prevent the hangings. Shell's chief executive reportedly did fax Nigeria's military ruler to urge a pardon for Saro-Wiwa, but the executions were carried out.

Other critics assert that Shell was more directly, causally related to the arrest and execution. Saro-Wiwa's son was among the plaintiffs in a case that reportedly claimed Shell engaged in "a systematic campaign of human rights violations" to stop the protest and provided both transportation and pay for Nigerian soldiers who committed human rights abuses. These charges formed the central elements in a case brought to trial in the United States under the Alien Tort Claims Action of 1789 (discussed in more detail in Chapter 10). Shell strongly denied the allegations, labeling them "false and without merit."[31] While maintaining its denial, the company settled the case out of court a few days before the trial was to begin, agreeing to pay $15.5 million to compensate the plaintiffs and support a trust fund for the Ogoni people.[32]

Fundamentally, all these issues spring from Nigeria's unrepresentative governance, particularly the refusal of corrupt regimes to allocate revenue from the country's oil riches to improve their people's welfare, especially in the Ogoni and Ijaw oil-producing regions. With oil revenues going to the central government, these regions initially received less than 1 percent of the reallocation, later raised to 3 percent in 1992 after early protest actions. Following the return of civilian rule in 1999, a new formula allocated 13 percent of the revenue to the main oil-producing states. The movement toward more democratic political processes and increased revenue commitments for decentralized development projects reduced somewhat the extent and level of violence against oil facilities. However, protests continued in some areas and not all revenue commitments were fulfilled.

In recent years, militant groups stepped up attacks against pipelines and other oil facilities, kidnapping some workers and demanding a greater share of the revenue in return for peaceful production. Foreign MNEs such as Shell and Chevron increased spending on community projects and reportedly hired some individuals connected with militant groups in efforts to quell the violence. The central government vacillated between negotiations with militant leaders and military incursions into the Delta region where creeks and swamps make pursuit of local groups difficult.[33]

MNEs confront two key ethical questions regarding their role when invested in a country such as Nigeria. Should the firms stay in the country and, if so, exactly what steps would constitute socially responsible action? Most specifically relevant to the nature of this case, should an MNE become publicly involved with how the government handles protest actions? Should MNEs also attempt to influence the highly political nature of governmental policies and decisions that allocate national revenue to various regions and purposes within the country?

Reflecting on its historical experience in Nigeria, Shell appears to have developed several policy positions that respond to these questions. Previously, the company argued that it had no authority to "interfere with the government of Nigeria" on issues such as Saro-Wiwa's trial. Shell contended that it had "a legal obligation to notify authorities" of perceived threats to oil operations and, therefore, was "compelled" to seek security assistance on occasion.[34] Later, Shell's General Business Principles committed the company "to express support for fundamental human rights in line with the legitimate role of business." Shell cited its efforts in the Niger River Delta, including lobbying the government in 1998 to withdraw Mobile Police from Ogoni land and urging support for the highest human rights standards after the arrest of an Ogoni activist, Barom Mittee. The police force withdrew and the activist was later released. Although not claiming credit for these outcomes, a Shell spokesperson states: "It does, however, illustrate that local managers feel empowered and are committed to taking a public position on these issues." Shell also adopted a policy against involving Mobile Police security, even where demonstrations disrupted production, choosing to evacuate personnel rather than risk potential human rights abuses by security forces.[35] This position is reinforced by Shell's endorsement of the Voluntary Principles on Security and Human Rights, as described in a following section of this chapter.

Beyond actions related to governmental human rights abuses, Shell also expanded its community involvements through both increased financial contributions to development projects and improved communication with local leaders and NGO representatives. As reflected in Exhibit 4.3, however, Shell still confronts an ethical dilemma in defining an appropriate corporate role in providing needed social services to underserved populations. How far should MNE investors go in funding schools, hospitals, or water and electricity systems for local communities? Are such steps included in a list of moral minimum obligations for a socially responsible company to remain invested in a region, or are such actions laudable but fully discretionary decisions of corporate philanthropy? How does a foreign company assure funds truly benefit local communities in areas effectively under the influence of militant groups?

More broadly, should a company lobby the government to redistribute its tax revenue or oil income differently among diverse local populations; if so, according to what allocation formula? For example, to meet distributive justice goals, how should the following three factors be rank-ordered in determining the distribution of oil revenue: regional *per capita* population; the relative welfare needs of regional populations; whether the oil came from a particular region? MNE involvement in these types of questions will inevitably overlap domestic political processes, leading to participation and impact on a nation's internal affairs.

"FOREIGNERS" ALLOCATE CHAD'S OIL REVENUE

Decades of varied experiences with oil extraction in Africa set the stage for a novel approach to developing oil resources in Chad, a desperately poor nation landlocked in the heart of Africa.[36] Knowledge of oil deposits existed for decades, but potential private investors hesitated to commit the enormous sums required to exploit the reserves and Chad lacked the ability to develop the oil on its own. A consortium led by ExxonMobil finally pursued a project costing over $3.5billion but faced strong opposition from environmental and human rights NGOs when news of the prospective investment became public in 1996. International NGOs, reflecting on problems with oil investments elsewhere in Africa, favored leaving the oil in the ground, at least until Chad evolved a more democratic, less corrupt government and strict environmental guidelines could be enforced. However, locally based NGOs and community leaders saw the project as a unique opportunity to exploit Chad's only known resource to generate revenue that could lift the country's impoverished population—if public monies were actually spend on improving people's lives. Thus began an unusual cooperative experiment between oil MNEs, the government of Chad, international and local NGOs, and the World Bank.

Certainly many trademark concerns present in other African oil conflicts also existed in Chad: a dictatorial, politically repressive regime; murder, torture and other human rights abuses against civilians; corruption in government administration;

Villagers walk by an ExxonMobil rig at Kome, Chad. A $3.5billion, 660 mile pipeline was needed to exploit land-locked Chad's reserves, transporting the oil through Cameroon's jungles to export at the Gulf of Guinea. Despite unprecedented commitments on using oil revenue for social development, Chad's population has enjoyed few sustainable benefits from the project. Photo by Tom Stoddart/Getty Images.

ethnic and religious divisions; potential environmental damage and social disruption from a massive oil project. Protracted negotiations among the parties proved difficult, with some 250 NGOs involved in 145 meetings with ExxonMobil over 1993–9. The final agreement appeared to strike a balance between economic, social and environmental interests, promising sufficient MNE profits to justify the investment while allocating most resultant public revenues under an established formula to address major educational, health and development needs of the population. As reported in one news account:

> For the first time, a nation has agreed to surrender part of its sovereignty over how to spend the money earned by unlocking its oil wealth. Proceeds from Chad's sale of oil from the first three fields—expected to exceed $100million a year, nearly doubling the nation's fiscal revenue—will travel a financial pipeline designed, and insisted upon, by the World Bank and other outsiders and monitored by a Chadian committee that includes Muslim and Christian religious figures and other community leaders. Their job is to ensure the money is spent on development projects such as schools, clinics and rural roads, and isn't siphoned into secret overseas bank accounts, as happened in neighboring Nigeria, or funneled into civil wars, as in Angola and Sudan.[37]

Despite the superficial attractiveness of this new approach, especially compared to the adverse experiences in some other cases, several aspects merit further ethical inquiry. The central consideration in this case concerns the choice of who decides, which entails probable trade-offs among competing values. On a macro political level, the issue posed involves national sovereignty. Foreign private and public organizations were imposing on Chad's government a formula determining how it could spend public revenue inside its own country. Technically, the government voluntarily agreed to this arrangement, but in reality it had little actual choice because the only alternative was to forgo any development of its oil resources. Who determines which governments lack the political legitimacy to exercise spending authority over their country's revenue? In practice, will the international community impose such arrangements only on small, poor and relatively powerless nations?

The contrast between value choices of international NGOs and local citizens illustrates how this same question of who decides applies at the micro level, especially when differing time horizons are employed. International NGOs initially favored killing any oil project but relented after appeals from local leaders to allow them this opportunity for development. The NGOs' time horizon foresaw a possible future with a representative government in Chad when development decisions could be taken more responsibly for the general population's benefit. Current citizens of Chad, however, confronted a life expectancy of 47 years on an annual income of $230. Their value scale tipped more heavily toward seeking immediate improvements in living conditions over the possibility of greater or more secure development opportunities at some point (how far?) in the future.

Unfortunately, this new model failed in its attempt to assure a resource allocation that would reduce poverty. Periodic disagreements arose between Chad and the World Bank as the project neared completion and Chad's government sought a larger share of the growing oil revenue. Chad pointed to increased military needs to counter a rebel movement and other costs resulting from refugees fleeing the Darfur region in neighboring Sudan. Although the World Bank agreed to some loosening of spending controls, it concluded in September, 2008 that "Chad failed to comply with key requirements of this agreement" and "did not allocate adequate resources critical for poverty reduction."[38] The experiment ended with Chad repaying the remaining $65.7 million owed on the initial World Bank loan, using revenue from income taxes on the oil companies and the prospect that other companies will invest in developing new oil fields (neither of which was restricted in the initial agreement).

Assessments of the project's impact painted a dim picture. Child mortality actually rose from 1990 to 2006, while 37 percent of children were underweight and three-quarters of adults remained illiterate. A 2005 report by the independent board that was to oversee poverty-reduction spending found "much of the money was being wasted on abuses like shoddy school desks made of buckled wood, computers and printers purchased at inflated prices, and wells, schools and hospitals not completed."[39] Documented problems and board recommendations for change were often ignored while corrupt officials and firms were not investigated by the government.[40]

While this novel experiment failed, the central issues still remain and the ethical questions for corporate responsibility loom large. Should ExxonMobil continue in the project even though the agreement for revenue allocation and use collapsed? Should other companies enter Chad to exploit potential new resource areas, especially with the attraction of much higher world oil prices? Should civil society groups now pressure companies to withdraw or not invest in Chad, leaving the country's potential wealth in the ground? Who should decide What happens?

ETHICAL ISSUES AND CASE EXPERIENCE ON BUSINESS POLITICAL INVOLVEMENTS

Cases reviewed in this chapter cover the second half of the twentieth century, with most playing out over the last couple decades. This time period mirrors the global expansion of MNE operations and increased civil society activism on human rights issues. MNEs faced growing pressures for greater corporate social responsibility in host countries, even when such actions involved them in the nation's internal political affairs. The campaign against apartheid in South Africa still stands as the definitive example, encompassing a broad array of companies responding in diverse fashion to orchestrated marketplace and political pressures. Actions in other cases often draw from the South African experience but generally represent less extensive or well-organized efforts.

The most striking similarities among the reviewed cases are their overwhelming concentration in Africa, with Burma's Asian locale as the only geographic outlier, and the central role played by natural resource companies, principally oil firms. The significance of these observations lies in their representation of contrasting capabilities. With the exception of South Africa, the nations involved fall along the lower end of the spectrum for both economic and political efficacy. By contrast, the MNEs involved, particularly oil industry firms, constitute some of the largest, richest and most effectively organized global enterprises, and their business operations represent a significant share of each host country's economic activity. This contrast suggests that relative capability constitutes the most significant case experience factor on these political involvement issues, helping to determine who may be held responsible, where and when, to do what. Similar case experience has not occurred where individual small companies are called upon to oppose the actions of powerful governments in large nations.

Two other factors in ethical analysis—causality and critical need—often link with capability to answer the question why the capable party should act. In some cases, arguments alleged an MNE causal connection to human rights violations, either directly (asking security forces to suppress protests or move villages; providing support for military actions; selling equipment to the government) or indirectly (business partnerships with government enterprises; paying royalties or tax revenue; providing foreign exchange by purchasing exported goods).

The Voluntary Principles on Security and Human Rights, mentioned earlier, address one of the most direct causality risks between MNEs and security forces in host countries. Signed on 20 December 2000, the principles establish guidelines for corporations in selecting and monitoring security personnel, including government-related forces, and reporting cases of human rights abuses. Negotiated under the sponsorship of the US and UK governments, the principles have been endorsed by major oil and other natural resources companies as well as several NGOs, including Amnesty International and Human Rights Watch.[41]

The strength of causality arguments is being tested in US courts, where cases have sought to use the Alien Tort Claims Act of 1789 to seek judicial penalties against MNEs for alleged involvement in human rights abuses in other countries. In 2004, the US Supreme Court upheld this statute's use in limited cases where corporations or other actors (but not sovereign states) can be sued in US courts for such actions as crimes against humanity or torture. The same year, Unocal settled a case out of court involving accusations of slave labor during construction of the gas pipeline in Burma. The Nigerian case involving Shell was cited earlier and others are discussed in Chapter 10. Whatever the outcome of specific legal decisions, these cases illustrate the type of causality connections that should be explored in ethical evaluations of MNC involvements with abusive regimes.

The concept of a connection continuum[42] may help evaluate the nature and strength of causality factors when examining MNE links to harmful actions and how such factors could determine relative degrees of corporate responsibility. Figure 4.1 illustrates a range of connections that could link a business actor to a human rights violation, with correspondingly diminished responsibility moving from left to right on the continuum. On the extreme left, an MNE's actions bear a direct, causal link to the harm (for example, if the allegations against Shell in the Saro-Wiwa case were valid). In the center, the notion of complicity rests between contributory and coincidental links and can be differentiated into direct, beneficial, and silent variations. Direct complicity might involve selling arms or providing significant financial support that permits a repressive regime to carry out human rights abuses. Although perhaps not intentionally causal, an MNE aware of the impact of its involvement is directly complicit in the human rights violations. Beneficial complicity suggests the MNE benefits from the results of the human rights violations even if its involvement is indirect and unintentional (for example, construction of the gas pipeline in Burma benefited from the forced labor used by the Burmese military). Silent complicity, which is more ambiguous and primarily coincidental, occurs when an MNE is aware of human rights violations but remains passively silent because the company has no substantial ties to the actions or their results. In such cases, a minimum ethical responsibility still might be to inform other relevant actors and encourage an appropriate response. At the extreme right on the continuum, an MNE could be unaware of human rights violations occurring in an area outside of its commercial sphere and

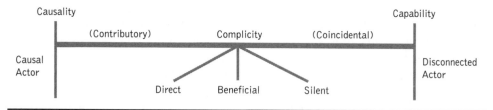

Figure 4.1 Connection Continuum.

therefore cannot be held ethically responsible (as long as it is unintentionally unaware of the violations).

The connection continuum concept highlights an important shift in assigning ethical responsibility to MNEs across an increasing range of international issues. Traditionally, causality was the dominant determinant of responsibility; that is, the actor directly causing harm was held responsible for stopping the harm and providing compensation or restitution. In the political arena, national governments are responsible for protecting their citizens from human rights violations. When a government is the violator, other national governments are looked to as next in line to bring pressure on an offending government to stop the violations. However, national sovereignty inhibits effective international action and significant harms often continue unabated. Beginning most significantly with apartheid in South Africa, attention turned toward other actors connected to the harm through a subsidiarity chain of ethical responsibility. MNEs appeared next in line, with varying degrees of complicity in apartheid harms and some capability to affect change.

Capability thereby became an increasingly important factor in assigning ethical responsibility to MNE action (or inaction). Linking critical need to corporate capability throws a broader net of ethical responsibility over more potential actors than looking only for causality connections. From the cases in this chapter, capability evaluations led most easily to responsibility judgments where a single corporate actor (Gulf/Chevron, Shell), or a small number of companies (coffee buyers) could exercise dominant business influence. Even then, however, if causality connections were unclear or absent, sufficient critical need was necessary, along with the failure of more responsible governments or other political parties to act, before MNEs became ethically bound to do something.

The relationship between capability and critical need therefore relates to an MNE's relative position on the subsidiarity chain of ethical responsibility. The company's relative responsibility largely follows its assigned role in a society. On most political involvement issues, absent causality connections, MNEs should come after governments or international organizations with defined political role responsibilities. Only when such political actors lack the ability to act, or fail to exercise the political will to take sufficient action, should MNEs consider involvement in political affairs—if the critical need criterion is met.

Cases reviewed in this chapter showed governments slow to act against political authorities in other nations, even where evidence pointed to clear, serious and systematic human rights abuses. Political processes in democratic nations can be notoriously slow to build a broad enough consensus to support foreign involvements that do not directly threaten the homeland. Many competing, and sometimes conflicting, issues crowd foreign policy agendas. And without the support of major national governments, most international organizations are powerless to act. Hence, following the South Africa experience, MNEs drew greater attention. Many MNEs are more vulnerable to direct and effective pressures than national political institutions, can respond in a more timely fashion, and often possess significant capability for action, sometimes with the beneficial side effect of increasing subsequent pressures on governments to intervene.

Case experience can also be used to test critical need determinations, including possible rank-ordering among multiple human rights issues. In most cases reviewed, violations were blatant, multiple and egregious. Undemocratic governments suppressed political and civil liberties; carried out murder, torture and rape against civilian populations; oppressed ethnic and religious minorities; and allocated economic resources corruptly or unfairly. In such instances, critical need judgments appear relatively easy. However, consider how hypothetical variations on these cases might influence ethical determinations regarding when and where MNEs should become involved in political activities.

For example, is the critical need threshold met when an undemocratic regime denies elections and freedom of speech but does not commit mass murder? How much difference would it make if the regime imprisoned opponents and perhaps engaged in some torture? Several civil society groups might describe China in this manner. Or should MNEs become politically involved in countries governed by democratically elected majorities, but where majority rule results in discriminatory action against ethnic, racial or religious minorities? How much difference would it make if the discriminatory action involved physical violence, or an unfair allocation of economic resources, or perhaps only social bigotry? Would India's policies or practices that result in discrimination against Muslims and lower-caste individuals qualify as a critical need situation? (Of course, both China and India also fall toward the higher end of the economic and political efficacy spectrum, where individual companies or MNE coalitions may possess relatively less capability to exert political influence.)

If capability and critical need judgments point to MNEs as the "who" to act in a case situation also designating "when" and "where," then "what" types of political involvements should the MNEs undertake? For instance, should foreign companies openly oppose a host government or actively assist efforts to overthrow a ruling regime? Could such extreme actions (perhaps on an exceptional basis) be justified in cases where an illegitimate regime rules the country? But then who determines the political legitimacy of a nation's government? Was the apartheid government in South Africa illegitimate when so designated in UN General Assembly resolutions but not by UN Security Council action or the withdrawal of diplomatic recognition by the home countries of most MNEs? What particular actions could MNEs ethically take in opposing a government: public statements; urging home government sanctions; breaking host country laws; withdrawing investments or boycotting exports; providing money or goods to rebel groups? Should deontological rules restrict certain types of MNE actions, or should judgments depend on teleological case-by-case evaluations?

Case experience suggests that answers to "what" questions regarding MNE actions may also cover political involvements where companies influence public policy changes or sometimes provide a supplement or substitute for host government programs. In cases dealing with a government's allocation of national revenue, what steps should MNEs take if political corruption or discriminatory policies result in a maldistribution of economic benefits? Who should decide which distributive justice criteria to apply in judging whether a specific allocation policy is unfair (according to equal share, need, contribution, property rights, historical or social status, etc.)? In instances where benefits from corporate activity are distributed unjustly within a host country, what steps would fulfill an MNE's social responsibility? The Chad case represents an extreme example of foreign interest groups, including but not limited to MNEs, imposing a specific revenue allocation formula on a host government. Another approach advocated by some civil society groups calls on MNEs to publicly release contractual terms that reveal how much money is paid to government entities, relying on transparency and public pressures to force appropriate allocation policies and avoid corruption.[43]

MNE capabilities also generate calls for more direct action to assist local communities where government services are insufficient, either as a result of the government's allocation decisions or because the government lacks the financial or administrative capability to provide needed social services. In some reviewed cases, natural resource MNEs pursued investment projects in poor rural areas where minimal government presence existed. In such instances, should the companies assume quasi-governmental roles in providing schools, health clinics or water and electricity infrastructure? These types of issues will also appear in a later chapter on cultural impact, and in an upcoming chapter on corporate social responsibility applied to more direct economic issues, such as labor relations, "sweatshops" and supply chain responsibilities. Readers might refer back to the connection continuum in Figure 4.1 to help assess the relationship between causality and capability factors in determining ethical MNE responsibility in those cases.

NOTES

1. J. Kline, "Political Activities by Transnational Corporations: Bright Lines Versus Grey Boundaries," *Journal of Transnational Corporations*, vol. 12, no. 1, April 2003, pp. 1–25.
2. Many publications cover the struggle against apartheid in South Africa. For a diversity of good reference sources, used in the preparation of this section, see United Nations, ECOSOC, "Activities of Transnational Corporations in Southern Africa: Impact on Financial and Social Structures," report of the Secretariat, 16 March 1978, E/C.10/39 78–05257; Interfaith Center on Corporate Responsibility (ICCR), "The Case Against US Investment in South Africa," ICCR Brief, May 1979; H. Schomer, "South Africa: Beyond Fair Employment," *Harvard Business Review*, May–June 1983, pp. 145–56; S. Unger and P. Vale, "South Africa: Why Constructive Engagement Failed," *Foreign Affairs*, winter 1985–6, pp. 234–58; W. Minter, "South Africa: Straight Talk on Sanctions," *Foreign Policy*, vol. 65, winter 1986–7, pp. 43–63; J. Kibbe and D. Hauck, *Leaving South Africa: The Impact of US Corporate Disinvestment*, Washington, DC: Investor Responsibility Research Center (IRRC), 1988; J. Kline, "Doing Business in South Africa: Seeking Ethical Parameters for Business and Government Responsibilities," *Pew Case Studies in International Affairs*, Case 511, New York: Carnegie Council on Ethics and International Affairs, 1991; S. Sethi and O. Williams, *Economic Imperatives and Ethical Values in Global Business: The South African Experience and International Codes Today*, Boston, MA: Kluwer, 2000.
3. T. Beauchamp, *Case Studies in Business, Society, and Ethics*, 2nd edn, Englewood Cliffs, NJ: Prentice Hall, 1989, p. 243.
4. Deontologically oriented decision makers can face difficult challenges on this viewpoint, especially for exported products that lack an obvious connection to apartheid's harm while producing benefits for the non-white population. For example, if the product exported to South Africa was medicine unavailable domestically, and if the medicine actually benefited the non-white population, a teleologist would argue for continuing such medicine exports as a beneficial outcome.
5. See A. Sparks, "A New South Africa: The Role of Sanctions," *The Washington Post*, 5 October 1993,

p. A19; K. Rodman, " 'Think Globally, Punish Locally': Nonstate Actors, Multinational Corporations, and Human Rights Sanctions," *Ethics and International Affairs*, vol. 12, 1998, pp. 19–41; and Minter, "South Africa," p. 55.

6. L. Sullivan, "Agents for Change: The Mobilization of Multinational Companies in South Africa," *Law and Policy in International Business*, vol. 15, no. 2, 1983, p. 434.

7. C. Stevens, "US Firms Divide on 'Lobbying' in South Africa," *The Wall Street Journal*, 15 February 1985, p. 1.

8. How far should MNEs go to overturn apartheid? In 1985, Rev. Sullivan urged US executives to "make a common front" with South African business leaders who had met outside South Africa with leaders of the outlawed ANC. Should MNE executives meet with an illegal rebel group attempting to overthrow the investor's host country government?

9. Shortly before Rev. Sullivan abandoned the Principles, the US government adopted essentially the same set of principles as standards that US firms doing business in South Africa must meet in order to qualify for US trade assistance programs. Significantly, however, the US government standards omitted the fourth amplification that called upon firms to undertake political activities against apartheid. Kline, "Doing Business in South Africa," pp. 14–16.

10. Most material in this section is drawn from T. Gladwin and I. Walter, *Multinationals Under Fire*, New York: Wiley, 1980, pp. 192–6. See also C. Powers, *People/Profits: The Ethics of Investment*, New York: Council on Religion and International Affairs, 1972, pp. 172–91.

11. G. Melloan, "Chevron's Problems with the Company It Keeps," *The Wall Street Journal*, 22 September 1987, p. 33.

12. Information in this section is drawn from R. Ullman, "Human Rights and Economic Power: The United States versus Idi Amin," *Foreign Affairs*, vol. 56, no. 3, April 1978, pp. 529–43; Gladwin and Walter, *Multinationals Under Fire*, pp. 182–4; C. May, "Amid the Agony of Uganda: The Puzzle of Obote," *The New York Times*, 21 September 1984, p. A9; S. Buckley, "Uganda, in Comeback, Attracts Investors," *The Washington Post*, 15 March 1995, p.A1; S. Raghavan, "A Decade of Peace; Hopes of Prosperity; Economic Reforms Help Restore Uganda," *The Houston Chronicle*, 15 August 1996, p. 1; Q. Peel, "Yoweri Museveni Tells Quentin Peel the Philosophy Behind Uganda's Success," *Financial Times*, 27 January 1997, p. 18; and M. Holman and W. Wallis, "A Tyrant-Buffoon Whose Reign of Terror Wrought Lasting Damage," *Financial Times*, 18 August 2003, p. 2.

13. Gladwin and Walter, *Multinationals Under Fire*, p. 184.

14. In addition to other articles cited in this section, material is also drawn from S. Mufson, "How Social is Trying to Avoid Cross Fire in Sudanese Dispute," *The Wall Street Journal*, 15 May 1984, p. 1; D. Ottaway, "US Eased Law on Terrorism to Aid Oil Firm," *The Washington Post*, 23 January 1997, p.A25; G. Bowley, "Talisman May Not Find Good Fortune from Sudan Oil," *Financial Times*, 19 November 1999, p. 7; "Sudan's Oil: Fuelling a Fire," *The Economist*, 2 September 2000, p. 62; and "War, Famine and Oil in Sudan," *The Economist*, 14 April 2001, p. 41.

15. K. DeYoung, "Over US Protests, Canada to Reopen Sudan Ties," *The Washington Post*, 15 February 2000, p. A24.

16. K. Vick, "Activists in Sudan Fear Loss of Western Oil Firms' Influence," *The Washington Post*, 24 June 2001, p. A15.

17. K. Warn, "Talisman Asset Sale 'Lower Its Defences'," *Financial Times*, 1 November 2002, p. 22.

18. C. Fried, "How States Are Aiming to Keep Out of Sudan," *The New York Times*, 14 February 2006, p. 5.

19. L. Beck, "China Urges to Sudan to Be More Flexible on Darfur Peace Plan," *Reuters*, 12 April 2007, p. A23.

20. The military government changed the official name of Burma to Myanmar.

21. Material in this section is drawn from: G. Millman, "Troubling Projects," *Infrastructure Finance*, February–March 1996, pp. 17–19; S. Prasso and R. Horn, "Freezing Out the Junta," *Business Week*, 22 April 1996, p. 53; T. Bardacke, "American Burma Boycotts Start to Bite," *Financial Times*, 6 February 1997, p. 10; P. Baker, "US to Place Trade Sanctions on Burma for Rights Abuses," *The Washington Post*, 22 April 1997, p. A1; R. Smith, "Burma's Army Keeps Its Grip," *The Washington Post*, 18 May 1997, p.A18; L. La Mure, "The Burma Pipeline," Harvard Business School Case Study 9-798-078, rev. 29 July 1998; Rodman, "Think Globally," pp.31–4; K. Grimsley, "Activists Press Burma Campaign," *The Washington Post*, 5 January 2002, p.E1; US Department of State, "Burma: Country Reports on Human Rights Practices, 2001," 4 March 2002, mimeo.

22. L. Urquhart and A. Kazmin, "Tobacco Group Pulls Out of Burma Under Pressure from UK

Government," *Financial Times*, 7 November 2003, p. 6. See also P. Montagnon, "Ministers Urge Premier to Quit Burma Project," *Financial Times*, 12 April 2000, p. 8; A. Parker, A. Ward and R. Corzine, " 'Ethical' Move on Burma Attacked," *Financial Times*, 13 April 2000, p. 8; and A. Parker and A. Ward, "Ethical Foreign Policy Halo May Be Slipping," *Financial Times*, 14 April 2000, p. 11.

23. E. Crooks, "Total Says Pulling Out Would Raise Hardship," *Financial Times*, 28 September 2007, p. 2.

24. M. Arnold, "Total Pays €5.2m in Burma Case," *Financial Times*, 30 November 2005, p. 22.

25. N. Boustany, "Burma Protests Draw Harsh Crackdown," *The Washington Post*, 12 September 2007, p. A14; P. Walker, "Burmese Junta Extends Aung San Suu Kyi's Detention," Guardian.co.uk, 27 May 2008, online, available at http://www.guardian.co.uk/world/2008/may/27/burma.cyclonenargis.

26. In an interview response to the question "What message do you have for investors who want to come to Burma?" Aung San Suu Kyi stated: "We want investment to be at the right time—when the benefits will go to the people of Burma, not just to a small, select elite connected to the government. We do not think investment at this time really helps the people of Burma. It provides the military regime with a psychological boost. If companies from Western democracies are prepared to invest under these circumstances, then it gives the military regime reason to think that they can continue violating human rights because even Western business companies don't mind." S. Prasso, "Take Your Investments Elsewhere, Please," *Business Week*, 30 March 1998, p. 52.

27. M. Arnold, "Total Chief Rejects Calls to Quit Burma," *Financial Times*, 18 May 2005, p. 22.

28. E. Alden, "US retailers back import ban on Burma," *Financial Times*, 16 April 2003, p. 12.

29. Material for this section is drawn from the following sources: G. Brooks, "Slick Alliance: Shell's Nigerian Oilfields Produce Few Benefits for Region's Villagers," *The Wall Street Journal*, 6 May 1994, p.A1; P. Beckett, "Shell Boldly Defends Its Role in Nigeria," *The Wall Street Journal*, 27 November 1995, p. A9; S. Buckley, "Nigerian Oil Spills: Pipelines to Poverty," *The Washington Post*, 27 December 1995, p. A1; W. Wallis, "Nigeria Protests Prompt Development Moves," *Financial Times*, 22 February 2001, p. 4; W. Wallis, "Shell Takes Action to Counter Criticism," *Financial Times*, 22 February 2001, p. 4; W. Newburry and T. Gladwin, "Shell and Nigerian Oil," case study, in T. Donaldson and P. Werhane, *Ethical Issues in Business*, Englewood Cliffs, NJ: Prentice Hall, 1999, 6th edn, pp. 539–64; and Rodman, "Think Globally," pp. 34–7.

30. Amnesty International and the Prince of Wales Business Leaders' Forum, "Shell: Linking Security to Human Rights in Nigeria," *Human Rights: Is It Any of Your Business?*, see note 1, London, April 2000, p. 94.

31. J. Mouawad, "Oil Industry on Trial," *The New York Times*, 22 May 2009, p. B1.

32. Mouawad, "Shell Agrees to Settle Abuse Case for Millions," *New York Times*, 9 June 2009, p. B1. Chevron also faced a lawsuit under the same Act for a 1998 incident in Nigeria. The company reportedly asked the Nigerian army to intervene and provided helicopters to transport troops to an offshore oil platform occupied by local protestors. Chevron claimed its platform workers were held for ransom and threatened with violence but had not intended and regretted that two protesters were killed during the incident. Chevron won that case in 2008. M. Peel, "Old Law Exhumed by Rights Fghters," *Financial Times*, 26 May 2009, p. 12.

33. L. Polgreen, "Blood Flows with Oil in Poor Nigerian Villages," *New York Times*, 1 January 2006, p 1; M. Green, "Nigeria Hopes to Learn from Shell's 'Mistakes' in Oil-Rich Region," *Financial Times*, 26 Mary 2009, p. 4; M. Green and D. Mahtani, "Grip on Restive Country Loosens," *Financial Times*, 31 June 2008, pp. 6; W. Conors, "State Finds (Or Buys) Some Peace in Nigeria," *New York Times*, 4 December 2008, pp. A12; D. Mahtani and D. Balint-Kurti, "Shell Signed Up Nigerian Companies Linked to Violent 2003 Insurrection," *Financial Times*, 27 April 2006; D. Mahtani, "Delta Militants Release Hostages," *Financial Times*, 27 March 2006.

34. Brooks, "Slick Alliance"; and H. Dawley and P. Dwyer, "The Latest Shell Shock," *Business Week*, 27 November 1995, p. 48.

35. Amnesty International, "Shell," pp. 95–6.

36. Material for this section is drawn from the following sources: D. Farah and D. Ottaway, "Watchdog Groups Rein in Government in Chad Oil Deal," *The Washington Post*, 4 January 2001, p. A14; M. Ottaway, "Reluctant Missionaries," *Foreign Policy*, July/August 2001, pp. 44–54; J. Useem, "Exxon's African Adventure," *Fortune*, 15 April 2002, pp. 102–14; "Useful Stuff, Maybe, for Once," *The Economist*, 14 September 2002, pp. 49–50; and R. Thurow and S. Warren, "In War and Poverty, Chad's Pipeline Plays Unusual Role," *The Wall Street Journal*, 24 June 2003, p. 1.

37. Thurow and Warren, "In War and Poverty."

38. L. Polygreen, "World Bank Ends Effort to Help Chad Ease Poverty," *The New York Times*, 11 September 2008, p 1.

39. Ibid.

40. Polygreen and C. Dugger, "Chad's Oil Riches, Meant for Poor, Are Diverted," *The New York Times*, 18 February 2008; L. Wroughton, "World Bank Pulls Plug on Chad Oil Pipeline Agreement," *Reuters*, 10 September 2008, http://www.alertnet.org/thenews/newsdesk/No9320796.htm (accessed 26 November 2009).

41. "Voluntary Principles on Security and Human Rights," statement released by governments of the United States and the United Kingdom, Bureau of Democracy, Human Rights and Labor, US Department of State, 20 December 2000, mimeo. See also B. Freeman and G. Hernandez Uriz, "Managing Risk and Building Trust: The Challenge of Implementing the Voluntary Principles on Security and Human Rights," in R. Sullivan (ed.), *Business and Human Rights*, Sheffield: Greenleaf, 2003, pp. 241–59.

42. This concept is drawn from J. Kline, "TNC Codes and National Sovereignty: Deciding When TNCs Should Engage in Political Activity," *Transnational Corporations* 14:3 December 2005, pp. 29–54.

43. This approach is reflected in the Extractive Industries Transparency Initiative and the "Publish What You Pay" campaign by NGOs. See J. Reed and C. Hoyos, "Angola Forced to Come Clean," *Financial Times*, 2 October 2003, p. 8. Also see N. Shaxson, "Voluntary Codes Alone Will Not Limit Corruption," *Financial Times*, 24 June 2004, p. 13, and C. Woolfson and M. Beck, "Corporate Social Responsibility Failures in the Oil Industry," in Sullivan, *Business and Human Rights*, pp. 123–4.

5

LABOR AND PRODUCTION STANDARDS

INTRODUCTION

Foreign production comprises an essential element of global business that helps build socioeconomic linkages among nations. The increased connections, forged through both FDI and trade, also amplify the range and nature of resulting ethical dilemmas. Although many issues have long existed, the 1990s' highly publicized debate over "sweatshops" gained unprecedented public attention, highlighting a new assertion that even retail firms, far removed from foreign production sites, bear an ethical "supply chain" responsibility for overseas employment practices and workplace conditions. This chapter explores the rationale for asserted "supply chain" responsibilities, using ethical analysis to examine whether or how business linkages affect judgments regarding who should do what, where and when, to address problems associated with foreign production processes.

The stakeholder concept can be employed to identify individuals or groups to whom a corporation may be responsible. Although employees generally constitute one of the most direct stakeholders, often ranked just after invested shareholders, foreign production also connects an enterprise to other groups, including suppliers, local communities, and host and home countries. Contractual relationships provide one way to identify relevant actors and assess relative degrees of responsibility. Formal legal contracts and informal social contracts both establish ethical obligations. Case-specific factors help determine a corporation's place in the subsidiarity chain of responsibility that may also include governments, international organizations, NGOs and consumers. Corporate FDI usually increases considerations of causality and proximity, but general trading relationships often involve sufficient buyer capability to create ethical duties in cases of critical need. The notions of minimal and maximal corporate social responsibilities offer a possible way to set general parameters for resultant ethical obligations.

The "sweatshop" debate represents an umbrella concept covering many separate but related issues. Most case experience derives from the manufacturing sector, although natural resource industries, particularly agriculture, as well as service sector activities can also entail abusive work conditions comparable to those encountered in more typical factory environments. Case scenarios examined in this chapter encompass a range of foreign production processes, generally but not always located in developing countries. An initial step in most cases requires assessing the nature and seriousness of identifiable problems. Individuals suffering harm, particularly violations of human rights, may be ethically due reparation, compensation or assistance from specific actors. Examination of case experience provides practice in answering the Who, Where, When and What questions associated with these determinations, along with the related Why rationale. The last chapter questioned whether corporations should set minimum standards for a country's political conditions before investing or only refrain from doing business where prohibited by law?

The central framing question of this chapter is: Should corporations produce in any way legally permissible (or should corporations follow voluntary ethical standards for labor, production processes and community responsibilities that must be met above and beyond legal requirements)?

PEEKING INSIDE A "SWEATSHOP"

Myriad stories emerged during the 1990s that offer insights into the dismal conditions confronting millions of workers each day. Specific elements of the story line alter with each telling, as the characteristics of individual workers vary in terms of age, sex, race, ethnicity, religion, education, location, family circumstances, etc. Hence, no "typical" story exists that fully captures the ethical issues raised by "sweatshop" production. Nevertheless, Exhibit 5.1 offers a quick peek inside one story, reported from Mexico in early 1991 as a wave of media coverage raised public awareness of foreign "sweatshop" conditions, sparking renewed attention and activism on these issues.

For Vicente Guerrero, life changed dramatically when he graduated from sixth grade at the top of his class. Introduced by his father to assembly line production of sneakers at the Deportes Mike factory, Vicente took his place among other young boys, or *zorritas* (little foxes), who helped cheaply staff the small company. After reading this case scenario, identify the various ethical issues raised in the story and assess their relative severity by rank-ordering them. One approach would be to relate Vicente's circumstances to possible violations of his human rights. (Because the last chapter focused heavily on civil and political (CP) rights, readers might want to review the economic, social and cultural (ESC) human rights contained in the UN Universal Declaration.) Do violations of some rights constitute a more serious harm (critical need) than violations of other rights? On a more subjective level, rank-order the issues according to your own personal "bother" scale, i.e. which issues connected most with you emotionally as unfair or unjust?

For example, how important is Vicente's age in this case? Child labor represents one of the most widely condemned "sweatshop" practices, but who should decide the definition of a "child" and when a young person can ethically be employed? Mexican law prohibited employing children younger than fourteen, two years older than Vicente, but between 5 million and 10 million underage Mexican children reportedly work, suggesting a significant difference between local law and local practice. An International Labor Organization (ILO) convention (No. 138) dating from 1973 establishes fifteen as the minimum working age (with fourteen permitted for developing countries), but estimates suggest that at least 125 million children aged five to fourteen work full-time in developing countries.[1] The plant superintendent's son, who is a year younger than Vicente, has already worked in the factory for three years. Vicente's own father, who began working in shoe factories when he was seven years old, considers Vicente "lucky" to have already enjoyed so many years of a "lazy" childhood.

Should Vicente's excellent performance and potential in school become a factor in determining whether or when he should work? If educational opportunities constitute an individual right, or a societal value, Vicente's personal potential and his possible contribution to Mexico's future development may go unrealized if his school books remain in the corner junk heap. On the other hand, if educational opportunity is a true human right, all individuals, regardless of their relative intellectual potential, deserve the right to some certain minimum education. Is Article 26 of the UN Universal Declaration being violated in this case? Consider whether compulsory elementary education represents an ethically mandatory minimum; where and when higher education opportunities should exist, and for whom; and whether a parental right to make educational choices for their children validates Patricio Guerrero's decision to terminate his son's education after the sixth grade (then the legally required minimum in Mexico, even though sixth-graders may still fall below the minimum legal working age of 14).

Potential workplace hazards confront the young boys laboring in Deportes Mike. Vicente smears sneaker soles with glue, ignoring toxic warnings and written cautions against exposure to minors. A doctor associates Vicente's illness with glue fumes that could cause long-term damage to his vital organs and central nervous system. Yet the factory owner considers that "These kinds of problems will help make a man of him." Should such workplace hazards rank higher or lower than Vicente's age as an ethical issue deserving attention? Perhaps combining the two factors strikes emotional chords that either, singly, would not touch: for instance, if a young child is employed in a safe work environment, or if only older workers undertake hazardous tasks. Consider whether one, or both, factors might be necessary to reach a level of critical need where external actors can be called upon for ethically obligated actions.

Financial compensation and family need reflect other case scenario factors that may affect ethical judgments regarding Vicente's employment at Deportes Mike. Vicente earns 100,000 pesos ($34) a week—less than an adult worker, which appeals to the factory owner. The article does not indicate how this wage rate compares to other standards, but Vicente does earn nearly as much as a local teacher (120,000 pesos). Additionally, his family's income recently suffered from the lay-offs of two relatives and his pay check enables the family to eat just a bit better. Some questions to consider on this issue are: could a specified wage rate or relative family need justify child labor (at any age)? Should pay scale be determined by factors such as age,

Exhibit 5.1 From Sixth Grade to the Shoe Factory

Underage Laborers Fill Mexican Factories, Stir U.S. Trade Debate

Vicente Guerrero, 12, Quits School for Footwear Plant; Dad: "We Eat Better Now"

By MATT MOFFETT
Staff Reporter of THE WALL STREET JOURNAL
Leon, Mexico

When Vicente Guerrero reported for work at the shoe factory, he had to leave his yo-yo with the guard at the door. Then Vicente, who had just turned twelve years old, was led to his post on the assembly line: a tall vertical lever attached to a press that bonds the soles of sneakers to the uppers.

The lever was set so high that Vicente had to shinny up the press and throw all his 90 pounds backward to yank the stiff steel bar downward. It reminded him of some playground contraption.

For Vicente this would have to pass for recreation from now on. A recent graduate of the sixth grade, he joined a dozen other children working full time in the factory. Once the best orator in his school and a good student, he now learned the wisdom of silence: even opening his mouth in this poorly ventilated plant meant breathing poisonous fumes.

Vicente's journey from the front-row desk of his schoolroom to the factory assembly line was charted by adults: impoverished parents, a heedless employer, hapless regulators, and impotent educators. "I figure work must be good for me, because many older people have helped put me here," says Vicente, shaking his hair out of his big, dark eyes. "And in the factory I get to meet lots of other boys."

Half of Mexico's 85 million people are below the age of eighteen, and this generation has been robbed of its childhood by a decade of debt crisis. It's illegal in Mexico to hire children under fourteen, but the Mexico City Assembly recently estimated that anywhere from five million to 10 million children are employed illegally, and often in hazardous jobs. "Economic necessity is stronger than a theoretical prohibition," says Alfredo Farit Rodriguez, Mexico's Attorney General in Defense of Labor, a kind of workers' ombudsman.

Child labor is one of several concerns about standards in the Mexican workplace clouding the prospects for a proposed US–Mexico free trade agreement. It is being seized upon, for example, by US labor unions, which oppose free trade and fear competition from Mexican workers.

Recently, Democratic Sen. Lloyd Bentsen of Texas, the chairman of the Senate Finance Committee, and House Ways and Means Committee Chairman Dan Rostenkowski of Illinois warned President Bush in a letter of the major hang-up: "the disparity between the two countries in . . . enforcement of environmental standards, health and safety standards and worker rights." Mr. Bush yesterday reiterated his support for the trade pact.

Free-trade advocates argue that investments flowing into Mexico would ameliorate the economic misery that currently pushes Mexican children into the work force. Partisans of free trade also point to the aggressiveness Mexican President Carlos Salinas de Gortari has lately shown in fighting lawbreaking industries: Mexico added 50 inspectors to regulate foreign plants operating along the US–Mexico border and shut down a heavily polluting refinery in Mexico City.

Little foxes. Young Vicente Guerrero's life exemplifies both the poverty that forces children to seek work and the porous regulatory system that makes it all too easy for them to find jobs. In the shantytown where Vicente lives and throughout the central Mexico state of Guanajuato, it is customary for small and medium-sized factories to employ boy shoemakers known as *zorritas*, or little foxes.

"My father says I was lucky to have so many years to be lazy before I went to work," says Vicente. His father, Patricio Guerrero, entered the shoe factories of Guanajuato at the age of seven. Three decades of hard work later, Mr. Guerrero lives in a tumbledown brick shell about the size and shape of a baseball dugout. It is home to twenty-five people, maybe twenty-six. Mr. Guerrero himself isn't sure how many relatives and family friends are currently lodged with him, his wife and six children. Vicente, to get some privacy in the bedroom he shares with eight other children, occasionally rigs a crude tent from the laundry on the clotheslines crisscrossing the hut.

School was the one place Vicente had no problem setting himself apart from other kids. Classmates, awed by his math skills, called him "the wizard." Nearly as adept in other subjects, Vicente finished first among 105 sixth-graders in a general knowledge exam.

Vicente's academic career reached its zenith during a speaking contest he won last June on the last day of school. The principal was so moved by the patriotic poem he recited that she called him into her office to repeat it just for her. That night, Vicente told his family the whole story. He spoke of how nervous he had been on the speaker's platform and how proud he was to sit on the principal's big stuffed chair.

After he finished, there was a strained silence. "Well," his father finally said, "it seems that you've learned everything you can in school." Mr. Guerrero then laid his plans for Vicente's next lesson in life. In a few weeks, there would be an opening for Vicente at Deportes Mike, the athletic shoe factory where Mr. Guerrero himself had just been hired. Vicente would earn 100,000 pesos a week, about $34.

At the time, money was tighter than usual for the Guerreros: Two members of the household had been laid off, and a cousin in the US had stopped sending money home.

After his father's talk, Vicente stowed his schoolbooks under a junk heap in a corner of the hut. It would be too painful, he thought, to leave them out where he could see them.

Last August Vicente was introduced to the Deportes Mike assembly line. About a dozen of the fifty workers were underage boys, many of whom toiled alongside their fathers. One youth, his cheek bulging with sharp tacks, hammered at some baseball shoes. A tiny ten-year-old was napping in a crate that he should have been filling with shoe molds. A bigger boy was running a stamping machine he had decorated with decals of Mickey Mouse and Tinker Bell. The bandage wrapped around the stamper's hand gave Vicente an uneasy feeling.

Showing Vicente the ropes was the plant superintendent's thirteen-year-old son, Francisco Guerrero, a cousin of Vicente's who was a toughened veteran, with three years' experience in shoemaking.

When a teacher came by the factory to chide school dropouts, Francisco rebuked her. "I'm earning 180,000 pesos a week," he said. "What do you make?" The teacher, whose weekly salary is 120,000 pesos, could say nothing.

Vicente's favorite part of his new job is running the clanking press, though that usually occupies a small fraction of his eight-hour workday. He spends most of his time on dirtier work: smearing glue onto the soles of shoes with his hands. The can of glue he dips his fingers into is marked "toxic substances . . . prolonged or repeated inhalation causes grave health damage; do not leave in the reach of minors." All the boys ignore the warning.

Impossible to ignore is the sharp, sickening odor of the glue. The only ventilation in the factory is from slits in the wall where bricks were removed and from a window near Vicente that opens only halfway. Just a matter of weeks after he started working, Vicente was home in bed with a cough, burning eyes and nausea.

What provoked Vicente's illness, according to the doctor he saw at the public hospital, was the glue fumes. Ingredients aren't listed on the label, but the glue's manufacturer, Simon SA of Mexico City, says it contains toluene, a petroleum extract linked to liver, lung and central nervous system damage. The maximum exposure to toluene permitted under Mexican environmental law is twice the level recommended by recently tightened US standards. And in any event, Deportes Mike's superintendent doesn't recall a government health inspector coming around in the nine years the plant has been open.

When Vicente felt well enough to return to work a few days later, a fan was installed near his machine. "The smell still makes you choke," Vicente says, "but *el patron* says I'll get used to it."

El patron, the factory owner, is Alfredo Hidalgo. "These kinds of problems will help make a man of him," Mr. Hidalgo says. "It's a tradition here that boys grow up quickly." Upholding tradition has been good for Mr. Hidalgo's business: Vicente and the other zorritas generally are paid less than adult workers.

Mr. Hidalgo doesn't see that as exploitation. "If it were bad for Vicente, he wouldn't have come back after the first day of work," he says. "None of the boys would, and my company wouldn't be able to survive."

"The system makes protecting the zorritas very, very difficult," says Teresa Sanchez, a federal labor official in Guanajuato state. The national labor code gives the federal government jurisdiction over only a limited number of industries that make up just 3 percent of businesses in the state. "The important industries, like shoes," she says, "are regulated by the states, and the states . . ." She completes the sentence by rolling her eyes.

At the state labor ministry, five child labor inspectors oversee 22,000 businesses. The staff has been halved in the decade since Mexico's economic crisis erupted, says Gabriel Eugenio Gallo, a sub-secretary. The five regulators make a monthly total of 100 inspections. At that rate it would take them more than two decades to visit all of the enterprises under state jurisdiction. Because child labor violations weren't even punishable by fines until very recently, state regulators say they have a hard time getting the tradition-bound employers they do visit to take them seriously. "Ultimately, the schools must be responsible for these kids," Mr. Gallo concludes.

Located just four blocks from where Vicente Guerrero labors, the Emperador Cuauhtemoc school employs two social workers to reclaim dropouts. (Children are required by law to stay in school through the sixth grade.) One-third of the students at Cuauhtemoc never finish the Mexican equivalent of junior high. With their huge caseloads, the two social workers certainly have never heard of Vicente Guerrero. "Ultimately, it's the

boy's own responsibility to see to it that he gets an education," says Lourdes Romo, one of the counselors.

Vicente is still getting an education, but it's of a different sort than he would be getting in school. On a factory break, the superintendent puts a zorrita in a headlock to act out the brutal murder of a member of a local youth gang. This pantomime is presented to Vicente and a rapt group of boys as a cautionary tale. "Boys who don't work in the factory die this way on the street," the superintendent warns.

Vicente hasn't missed work again, though he always has a runny nose and red eyes. "One gets accustomed to things," he says. It's lucky for him that he is adaptable. The plant was expanded recently and Vicente's window, once his source of fresh air, now swings open onto a sewing room where several new boys labor.

The zorrita tradition is unlikely to fade any time soon. "We eat better now that Vicente works," says Patricio Guerrero, watching his wife stir a skillet of chicken in sweet mole sauce. "And Vicente has few pesos left over so he can enjoy being a boy."

But Vicente doesn't have the time. Even though he's the captain, he recently missed an important Saturday match of his soccer team. A rush order of soccer shoes had to be filled at Deportes Mike. His friends tell him that "I stink as bad as the patch on a bicycle tire," he says. "But I know that's just the smell of work."

---

productivity, health hazards, legal rates or whatever wage rate market forces permit? Could older, laid-off family members seek to replace Vicente at the shoe factory, or should he work anyway because the family's economic condition appears so low?

Who in this case bears the most responsibility to protect Vicente's rights? The article suggests a number of possible candidates: his parents; the factory superintendent or factory owner; government labor inspectors; his schoolteachers, counselors or social workers; or Vicente himself? Specify the *why* rationale for rank-ordering these various actors along a subsidiary chain of ethical responsibility. For example, does the existence of only five child labor inspectors for 22,000 businesses indicate a lack of capability that reduces the government's responsibility, or should the government

An unidentified young boy prepares leather for the soles of shoes in a Mexico City factory. While Mexico and other countries have improved child protection laws, "sweatshop" conditions still exist in many factories in both developing and developed countries. Large retailers and brand-holders face pressure to use their purchasing power to set and enforce workplace standards in foreign factories. Photo by Albert Moldvay/National Geographic/Getty Images.

be held indirectly causally responsible for allocating insufficient revenue to enforce its law against child labor? Is the employer directly causally responsible for (illegally) hiring Vicente and exposing him to workplace health hazards, or is this small factory owner incapable of paying higher salaries or improving working conditions because market competition forces him to reduce costs, and on a cost/benefit basis Vicente and his family are better off with the extra salary than if he was not working and ended up in a local youth gang?

A notable aspect of the case scenario presented in Exhibit 5.1 is that the "sweatshop" examined does not appear connected to international business operations. One might suspect that the athletic sneakers produced at the factory may attempt to present an image associated with US products (after all, Deportes *Mike* is a bit unusual for a Mexican name), but no mention appears of foreign investment or exported products. In fact, the vast majority of child labor situations and general "sweatshop" conditions in developing countries bear no direct connection with international corporations. The World Bank estimates that less than 5 percent of child laborers in developing countries work in export industries.[2]

Nevertheless, the article's brief reference to a proposed free trade agreement between Mexico and the United States (later adopted, with Canada, as the North American Free Trade Agreement [NAFTA]) foreshadows globalization's expanding network of interrelated business ties. Increased economic interdependence among nations forces issues such as national labor standards and practices on to international political agendas. Simultaneously, governments in economically linked nations arguably possess greater ethical responsibility to address abusive labor practices and workplace conditions occurring in partner countries. International corporations that use intergovernmental agreements to forge new trade and FDI ties likewise become more closely linked (through increased potential causality, capability and proximity) to the foreign "sweatshop" conditions portrayed so publicly in the media since the early 1990s.

ASSESSING SUPPLY CHAIN RESPONSIBILITIES

Assigning ethical responsibilities to invested owners of foreign "sweatshops" constitutes a relatively simple and straightforward task. MNEs with ownership stakes in foreign production facilities are direct employers of the facilities' workers, at least to a degree corresponding to the percentage of ownership. The central bond between employer and employee creates a direct and important stakeholder relationship where the firm's role, proximity, awareness and capability carry both legal and social contract responsibilities toward its employees. The MNE can set labor and workplace conditions at fully or majority-owned foreign affiliates, within the parameters of local law. The MNE may also exceed legal minimum standards on issues such as wage rates or safety standards if local law falls below an ethical minimum, or the MNE chooses to follow a higher maximal corporate social responsibility standard.

The more novel and controversial application of corporate responsibility arises when trade rather than FDI connects a business enterprise to the workers involved in a foreign production process. In particular, importers and/or retailers in developed countries face increasing pressure to improve conditions for foreign workers, although the firms lack the proximity or employer role inherent in FDI ownership. Instead, civil society groups confront these firms, forcing an awareness of "sweatshop" conditions in factories where imported goods are produced, and then call upon the importers and retailers to use their capabilities to improve foreign labor practices and workplace conditions. Sometimes critics suggest direct complicity with worker abuse, asserting that the purchasing firms' low price demands or short delivery schedules lead to inadequate worker wages and forced overtime. More commonly critics charge importers and retailers with beneficial or silent complicity, reaping higher profits from low-wage foreign labor while ignoring the uglier aspects of their workplace conditions. (Refer to the last chapter's connection continuum in Figure 4.1 to portray these differences.)

The traditional corporate response to such complaints rests on the argument that buyers in one country cannot impose labor standards on producers in another country when no ownership ties exist. This rationale proved largely persuasive until the 1990s, when changing circumstances altered many opinions. Media stories increased public awareness of "sweatshop" conditions, fostering a sense of critical need. In assessing relative ethical responsibility for action, the immediate local employer seemed either incapable of funding improvements or inaccessible to direct pressure from foreign critics. Local governments often appeared ineffective or corrupt and unresponsive to criticism. Other national governments hesitated to interfere in the internal affairs of sovereign countries. Only the most egregious forms of labor abuse, such as prison or slave labor, or children employed as soldiers or prostitutes, reached the political level of diplomatic discussion in international forums.

Civil society groups then looked for the next most capable potential actor. Laying the subsidiarity chain of ethical responsibility alongside the international supply chain of most "sweatshop" industries, the groups found importers and retail firms. These enterprises lacked geographic and political proximity as well as ownership ties to the abusive conditions, but further analysis led many critics to conclude that importers and retailers nevertheless possess sufficient capability to press for ethical improvements. In contemporary international business, control need not rest on ownership. Indeed, analytical reports and international agreements increasingly refer to "low and non-equity" foreign investment.[3] In typical "sweatshop" industries, high-volume purchasers often exert demonstrable influence, even control, over foreign production processes. For example, product quality control requirements, often including overseas factory inspections, clearly demonstrate the capability to reach inside the factory and influence the production process. If purchasers can determine product quality standards, could/should they also determine the labor standards and workplace conditions where the products are produced?

Civil society activism on behalf of foreign "sweatshop" workers helped galvanize US public opinion behind the issue as one of critical need and focused attention on prominent US retailers as actors capable of bringing about improvements. One well-publicized example emerged around two young garment workers from Central America, Claudia Molina and Judith Viera, who traveled to the United States to tell stories that recall some of Vicente Guerrero's plight, while adding a few new dimensions of abusive treatment. On many labor issues, the factory owner appeared the most responsible actor, often based on causal connections. Both factories where Molina and Viera worked involved FDI links, but the Taiwanese and Korean investors, respectively, faced little ethical pressure from government or civil society groups in their home countries, and the governments in El Salvador and Honduras appeared to lack the resources and/or political will to enforce their labor laws in economically important foreign trade zones.[4]

By contrast, major foreign purchasers of the factories' garments, such as the

Gap, J. C. Penney and Eddie Bauer, might prove more responsive. These firms' competitiveness depends heavily on brand-name image, which can be vulnerable to critical public actions by civil society groups. Organized tours for the garment workers put a human face on "sweatshop" statistics. Anecdotal examples can leave powerful impressions, such as the difference between the $20 purchase price of a Gap T-shirt and the reported 16 cents earned by the worker who made the shirt. Surely someone possessed the capability to provide Molina with the extra 30 lempiras weekly ($3) that she considered fair, if first the abusive treatment stopped.[5]

Many importing firms indicate a willingness to investigate abuse charges, although their statements and actions vary regarding how clearly or fully they accept social responsibility for any "sweatshop" conditions, or just what the importing firms might do about such problems. Indeed, exactly *what* should be done raises other ethical questions. Should the importers terminate their purchases (and leave) or retain the buyer relationship but insist on improved conditions (stay and reform), perhaps even paying higher prices for the garments to provide extra funding to carry out the improvements (both assist and help protect)?

Sometimes foreign owners of "sweatshop" factories respond to criticism and pressure by simply shifting production to other locations. Such a move would not help the abused victims; in fact, unemployment would leave them in an even worse condition. A company's capital is more mobile than its workers, leaving employees vulnerable to lay-offs if they encourage public criticism of their employer's practices. The same calculation holds even more clearly for foreign companies that simply contract to buy a "sweatshop's" production without investing any equity in the factory. When exposed to public criticism and consumer pressure for selling "sweatshop" goods, these companies can easily shift their orders to another factory and/or country.

One such story emerged when Lisa Rahman visited Washington, D.C. in 2002 to tell about her experiences working in a factory in Dhaka, Bangladesh. The Shah Makhdum plant produced the Winnie the Pooh clothing line and other goods for the Walt Disney Company. She related that "I was crying all the time" because of poor working conditions at the plant, including 12-hour shifts and filthy conditions.[6] However, when worker complaints reached the media, the subcontractor used by Disney ceased purchases from the plant and it closed, leaving 200 workers unemployed. Disney may not have directed the subcontractor to terminate the relationship (an act of commission), but some critics might consider Disney's failure to encourage or assist positive reform (omission) as falling short of its corporate social responsibility. Alternatively, perhaps the subsidiarity chain of responsibility should stop before it reaches Disney, or support for labor reforms at the plant might be considered a discretionary maximal ethical action rather than an obligatory ethical minimum.

Figure 5.1 depicts the flow of production in one type of international supply chain arrangement where subcontracted foreign workers produce brand-name goods exported for final retail sale in other countries. The "sweatshop" campaign's asserted responsibility for worker conditions flows in reverse, arising from informed consumer pressure on retailers and brand holders that possess contractual leverage over foreign subcontractors. Consider who should have done what among supply chain

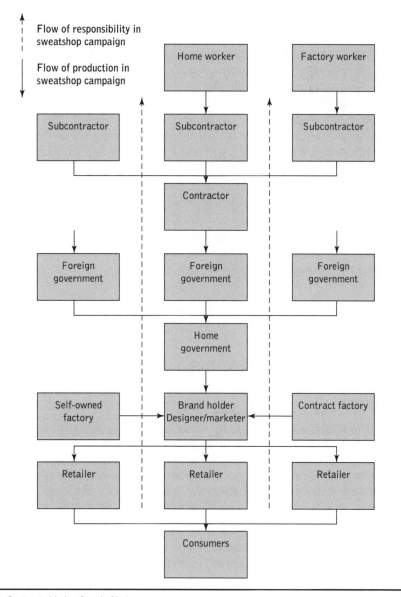

Figure 5.1 Contracted Labor Supply Chain.

actors more proximate to the "sweatshop" location before retailers might bear responsibility as actors of last resort.

The campaign against "sweatshops" recorded a series of notable successes, mainly based on stimulating the adoption of individual corporate and/or industry-wide codes of conduct. Affected production processes range from weaving rugs and stitching soccer balls to sewing clothing and producing athletic footwear.[7] Nike, Reebok, Adidas, Levi Strauss, Eddie Bauer, Phillips-Van Heusen and Liz Claiborne number among the largest and best-known companies with clothing and footwear brands that faced organized public pressure and responded with codes to govern labor conditions in factories producing their goods. In most cases, contracts with supplier firms require adherence to minimum code standards on issues such as contracted labor supply chain employee age, hours, wages and unionization.

Exhibit 5.2 reports on a "sustainability summit" held by Wal-Mart in China to announce new social and environmental standards for factories in its supply chain. Supplier agreements would require compliance with labor standards that ban child- or forced labor and require paying at least the local minimum wage. Environmental standards address issues such as air and water pollution and managing hazardous waste. The company pledged to keep close track of factories producing goods that Wal-Mart sells, "even if they pass through many hands." A mandatory three-level audit process would be carried out by the vendors, Wal-Mart and an outside party. Standards would be phased in, starting in 2009, and within three years suppliers must source 95 percent of goods for Wal-Mart from factories with the highest audit ratings. Wal-Mart will consider providing longer-term contracts to suppliers that invest heavily to improve operations to meet the new standards.

Exhibit 5.2　Wal-Mart Sets Chinese Supplier Standards

Wal-Mart to Toughen Standards

By STEPHANIE ROSENBLOOM

Wal-Mart plans to announce Wednesday in Beijing that it will require manufacturers supplying goods for its stores to adhere to stricter ethical and environmental standards, the latest effort by the big retailer to answer criticism of its business practices.

At a gathering of more than 1,000 suppliers, Chinese officials and advocacy groups, Wal-Mart executives plan to reveal a new supplier agreement that will require manufacturers to allow outside audits and to adhere to specific social and environmental criteria. The agreement will be phased in beginning in January.

The changes signal a move on the part of Wal-Mart, the world's largest retailer, away from intermittent transactions with many suppliers toward longer-term arrangements with a smaller group of manufacturers. Wal-Mart is betting that using its buying power this way can help keep prices low even as it keeps a closer eye on its suppliers.

Wal-Mart, long criticized for its treatment of workers in the United States and its ostensible willingness to overlook violations abroad, has in recent years offered a series of environmental and labor initiatives. A Beijing meeting now under way is the company's first "sustainability summit."

By next year, Wal-Mart will start keeping close track of the factories from which its products originate, even if they pass through many hands. By 2012, Wal-Mart will require suppliers to source 95 percent of their production from factories that receive the highest ratings in audits of environmental and social practices.

The agreement includes a ban on child and forced labor and pay below the local minimum wage.

"Meeting social and environmental standards is not optional," Lee Scott, Wal-Mart's chief executive, plans to say at the Beijing summit, according to his prepared remarks. "I firmly believe that a company that cheats on overtime and on the age of its labor, that dumps its scraps and its chemicals in our rivers, that does not pay its taxes or honor its contracts, will ultimately cheat on the quality of its products. And cheating on the quality of products is the same as cheating on customers."

To ensure suppliers are making changes, Wal-Mart said it would require three levels of audits: from the vendors themselves, from an outside party and from Wal-Mart, which will initiate more of its own random, unannounced audits.

Wal-Mart said the audits would assess factory working conditions as well as compliance by manufacturers with standards regarding air pollution, wastewater discharge, management of toxic substances and disposal of hazardous waste.

Environmental and labor groups that follow Wal-Mart said the retailer had a mixed history when it came to the environment and labor practices—and that sometimes the company's goals were lofty, while the measurable outcomes were less so. Through the years, Wal-Mart has been accused of various abuses.

In the 1990s it came to light that workers at factories producing Kathie Lee Gifford clothing for Wal-Mart were subjected to inhumane conditions. Last year two nongovernmental organizations said abuse and labor violations (including child labor) occurred at 15 factories that produce or supply goods for Wal-Mart and other retailers. In June the United States government and the state of Oklahoma filed a complaint in federal court claiming that Wal-Mart and other companies dumped hazardous waste in Oklahoma City. In Bangladesh, it was charged that factory workers were made to work 19-hour shifts, with some bringing home just $20 a month.

Michael Green, executive director of the Center for Environmental Health, a watchdog group in Oakland, Calif., said he believed Wal-Mart's effort to improve suppliers' practices began as a program to counter public-relations damage. "I think

what happened along the way is some people there actually got convinced," he said. "It became more than a sophisticated P.R. stunt, but something they believed in."

However, without knowing the specifics of Wal-Mart's new plan, Mr. Green said it would not be easy sledding. Suppliers under pressure to offer the company the lowest prices are likely to have an incentive to cheat, he noted, and outside auditors may not want to report violations for fear of losing a lucrative Wal-Mart contract. Additionally, tracing the origins of all the working parts that go into a single toy, for instance, is difficult because it involves multiple factories.

Still, groups that have criticized Wal-Mart are attending the Beijing summit to hear the company's plans.

In a telephone interview from Beijing Tuesday night, Mr. Scott said Wal-Mart may offer longer-term agreements to suppliers willing to make the big investments needed to live up to its environmental demands.

The company said that within China, a nation with major environmental problems, Wal-Mart would aim by 2010 to cut water use in half in all stores, design and open a prototype store that used 40 percent less energy, and reduce energy use in existing stores by 30 percent. "People will judge us," Mr. Scott said, "based on the results."

The Wal-Mart story gained attention for several reasons. The company was involved in an early protest against "sweatshop" conditions in factories that supplied branded Kathie Lee Gifford clothing for its stores. Wal-Mart also was a target of protests against US store practices, particularly related to labor rights and community relations, and was moving to improve its domestic reputation. By contrast, this high-profile initiative recognized the retailer's connection to the far end of its supply chain, confronting the conditions in China, a major source for Wal-Mart products but also a difficult country to impose outside standards and monitor implementation. Although Wal-Mart clearly intended to enhance its social responsibility image, a company executive also tied irresponsible production practices to quality control and consumer confidence issues (areas where Chinese-made goods had suffered recent problems). Groups critical of past Wal-Mart practices showed interest in the company's new standards but expressed some skepticism about how well the principles would be put into practice.

When companies and relevant civil society groups achieve general agreement on standards, debate often shifts to implementation issues, particularly monitoring in individual factories to assure written standards translate into altered practice. Contentious points involve who monitors compliance (the purchasing company or its contracted auditors versus independent auditors or local civil society groups), the transparency of the process, and sanctions for non-compliance (termination of contracts versus requirements for assisted reforms).[8] The Wal-Mart initiative will likely be judged on which outside party participates in the three-level audit of its supplier code on what actions the company takes in cases of non-compliance.

LIVING WAGE, DEBT BONDAGE AND UNION RIGHTS

Wage standards represent one of the most problematic labor issues in code of conduct debates. The wage debate revolves around the question of where to set an ethical minimum wage rate. Traditional choices involved either the local legal minimum wage or the local industry market wage (that may fall below the legal minimum where laws are not well enforced).[9] In many developing countries, neither choice appears ethically acceptable to civil society groups. Governments often set legal minimum wage rates low as an incentive to attract foreign investment and promote labor-based exports. In these countries, excess labor acts as a competitive economic factor endowment, meaning market forces of supply and demand also repress wage rates. Under these circumstances, either standard can leave workers with insufficient money to live, even well below the local poverty line.

The concept of a living wage attempts to address this issue by setting an ethical minimum wage rate based on a worker's survival needs rather than other possible distributive justice standards such as contribution (productivity), equality, seniority, etc. The normative argument draws on the employee's position as a central stakeholder to whom the firm owes a strong social responsibility. A major difficulty, however, lies in defining "living wage."[10] For example, while providing enough money for minimum survival requirements appears reasonable, agreement rapidly disappears as the list of included items lengthens: food, clothing, housing, health care, transport, education, savings, etc. If a list of items is agreed and priced by the local cost of living, troublesome questions still remain regarding, for example, whether a worker's salary should provide only for that person or also for family members (spouse, children/how many, extended family). Wage-related standards may also conflict; for instance, two workers, one single and the other the head of a large household, might require a different minimum living wage, but such a differential would conflict with an equal pay for equal work standard.

Many companies object to extending social responsibility beyond the direct employee relationship, particularly in cultures where large extended family ties are common and important. Living wage standards, particularly if liberally defined, could quickly push labor compensation far above local law or industry market levels, leaving the firm at a competitive disadvantage. Losing their low wage rate advantage could also drive investing or purchasing firms to look elsewhere for a production site, leaving the workers without any wages. Companies also argue that governments or other social institutions should be responsible for providing individual minimum income needs; employee wage rates should be set by market forces that respond to worker productivity (contribution to the production process).[11] The rejoinder from critics often relies on the Tavis thesis that corporate social responsibility becomes greater where market forces do not work efficiently and governments are ineffective or unresponsive to the needs of their people—circumstances that mark many developing countries.[12]

A central argument in setting the terms for an ethical minimum wage revolves around the issue of free choice. Employers contend that workers themselves should decide whether an offered wage improves their situation rather than setting some arbitrary rate above market conditions that may preclude possible job offers. Free market theory suggests that a worker will not accept a job that does not improve his or her condition. Free acceptance of an employment offer thereby constitutes evidence of an ethical wage rate because the worker considers it an improvement. Critics dispute this contention by asserting that workers do not have free choice unless viable alternatives exist that provide an effective choice. In countries with inefficient market forces and structurally high unemployment, acceptance of a job that pays below a living wage constitutes a desperate choice rather than a free and ethical choice.

Debt bondage represents an emerging labor relations issue for international corporations that combines a situation of desperate choice with hiring practices that exploit the vulnerabilities and relative powerlessness of impoverished workers in the least developed countries. This practice appears in countries such as Taiwan, South Korea and Malaysia that import workers from poorer neighbors (especially Vietnam, Thailand and the Philippines). By employing foreign workers at one-half to two-thirds the rate paid local employees, these countries can compete with China and other low labor cost regions. The debt bondage arises from labor brokers who fill open jobs by recruiting foreign workers—for a fee to be paid by the workers.

A *Fortune* article reported one example of such an arrangement where a woman from the Philippines borrowed funds to pay a local labor broker $2,500 for a job in Taiwan with a monthly salary of $460 (many times comparable pay in the Philippines, if work were even available). Upon arrival in Taiwan, another labor broker unexpectedly demanded $3,900 to complete the arrangements. As a result, the woman's pay check quickly disappeared before she could send money home to pay for her initial interest-bearing loan in the Philippines. From her $460 monthly salary, Taiwan's income tax deducted $91, the factory retained $72 for room and board, the labor broker in Taiwan wanted $215, and $86 went into a required savings bond redeemable only on completion of a three-year contract. This type of bond, sometimes termed "run-away insurance," helps keep the indebted worker tied to the job. Many employers also impose curfews and keep the passports of their foreign workers to assure even greater control.[13]

Surveying possible actors with an ethical responsibility in such a case reveals the most proximate, causally connected parties pursuing financial self-interest objectives at the woman's expense. However, in addition to the "free choice" argument, these actors could assert they lack the capability to offer improved conditions. Citing competition from China, Taiwanese employers can claim the jobs would not exist at normal local market wages. The national government shapes labor regulations to permit special exemptions and permits discriminatory treatment of foreign workers to facilitate export-oriented operations. If neither the local employer nor government takes corrective action, attention begins to shift along the supply chain to the next most capable, responsible party—the foreign purchaser.

For corporations that accept a social responsibility to improve conditions in over-seas "sweatshops," the debt bondage issue presents a logical but difficult extension of responsibility. For example, overseas subcontractors could offer their employees wage rates high enough to meet the code requirements of an MNE purchaser but then effectively offset the wages with deductions and expense charges. Should purchaser code standards and monitoring programs be expected also to investigate and control the roles played by labor brokers? If direct employers and local governments collude in the use of debt bondage practices, should supply chain ties impose subsidiarity chain responsibilities on a foreign importer to control labor broker practices in the Philippines in order to improve the labor conditions in subcontractor plants in Taiwan? The *Fortune* article suggests that production outsourcing by high-technology companies such as Motorola and Ericsson may now pose ethical challenges similar to those faced by Nike, and that an awareness of the debt bondage issue will increase their responsibility to address such problems.[14]

"Sweatshop" practices exist in many regions, not just in developing countries, even in their most extreme forms. For example, in 1995 state and federal officials raided a "sweatshop" in El Monte, a section of greater Los Angeles, where Thai workers were confined behind barbed wire in a garment factory, working 17 hours a day at wage rates as low as 60 cents an hour. Most workers faced debt bondage requirements to repay charges for transport and false travel documents. This incident sparked equally shocking media reports on the prevalence of US "sweatshops." California's apparel industry reportedly included 1,000 illegal factories, one-sixth of the total in the state. According to a 1994 government survey, one-half the legal firms paid less than minimum wage and 93 percent violated health and safety regulations.[15]

Robert Reich, US Secretary of Labor at the time of the El Monte raid, invoked the supply chain responsibility concept by publicly identifying large retail companies whose names appeared on boxes in the "sweatshop." Even though the retailers lacked legal responsibility, they agreed to a statement of principles calling on their suppliers to follow labor law standards. Responsibility for compliance with legal standards would seem to fall first on direct employers and then on the government, but there were only 816 US federal labor investigators to monitor 6.5 million companies. According to Secretary Reich, "We need to enlist retailers as adjunct policemen."[16] If the US government lacks the capability or political will to secure labor rights at garment factories in the United States and must seek voluntary retailer supply chain involvement, how much less capable would developing countries be to enforce labor laws against "sweatshop" conditions, even assuming the governments valued worker rights above corporate competitiveness or economic growth objectives?

A final labor relations issue often associated with the "sweatshop" debate concerns the right to collective bargaining, or independently organized labor unions. "Sweatshop" employers generally discourage workers from forming unions, using tactics that range from harassment and intimidation to firings and physical violence. The UN Declaration recognizes a right to organize trade unions in Article 23. Freedom of association is a condition for ILO membership and core ILO conventions 87 and 98 address these rights.[17] Despite these international standards, national laws vary in their treatment of unions, ranging from outright prohibition or government-connected unions to legal protection but lax enforcement. The potential for unions to serve as organizing bases for political activities makes this issue particularly sensitive in many nations. As discussed briefly in Chapter 4, actions by foreign corporations to alter organized labor practices in other countries can be seen as unwelcome political involvement or even improper interference in a nation's internal affairs.

Most corporate codes recognize workers' right to organize and pledge not to interfere with such efforts but defer to the primacy of local law, even where regulations inhibit labor-organizing activities. These codes essentially stop at the "do no harm" premise rather than helping to protect workers or assist them to attain their rights. Such a stance may be justified on the basis of societal role distinctions or lack of proximity or citizenship status, especially for non-invested enterprises that just purchase products from unaffiliated foreign factories.

The potential role of representative unions can encompass standard setting as well as implementation and monitoring functions. One approach to establishing minimum ethical standards for employment practices attempts to define the specific content of standards that would apply everywhere. Hence, debate occurs over which number to use as the minimum working age for children, the maximum number of hours for a working day, or the amount of pay that would constitute a minimum or living wage. An alternative, more process-oriented approach relies on unionization and collective bargaining to determine the best standards in each situation. Whichever specific standard emerges from collective bargaining would be accepted as ethically justifiable rather than attempting to define specific outcomes by legal fiat or corporate code. Support for unionization therefore becomes a priority objective for labor supporters who believe process rather than predefined outcomes will yield the best ethical work standards to address "sweatshop" conditions.

COMMUNITIES AND THE FOREIGN PRODUCTION PROCESS

Modern MNEs locate production processes in many nations, selecting investment sites offering the best competitive combination of factors such as wage rates, access to raw materials and markets, macroeconomic strength, low taxation and political stability. Corporations choosing to purchase from foreign subcontractors rather than engaging in FDI sacrifice some control over production but can more flexibly select and shift their sourcing decisions among many foreign locations. Although international business decisions generally refer to investment in or export from a nation, the actual production process occurs in specific local communities. These communities constitute important stakeholders for the enterprise. Not only will many employees and their families reside in the surrounding community, but local suppliers, service providers and many others hold a stake in (i.e. affect and are affected by) the production facility.

Two principal ethical issues arise from the integration of foreign production processes into a global business network. The first issue relates to business decisions that result in the serious downsizing or closure of a production facility. Laid-off employees bear the most direct cost of such actions, but the economic and social ripple effects spread throughout a local community, usually in proportion to the plant's size as a part of the local economy. Although such disruption and dislocations become diluted within a nation's broader economy, the impact on community life can be devastating. The ethical issues arise primarily from the geographic, social and sometimes cultural separation between the locus of distant corporate decision makers who accrue the benefits and the local decision takers who bear the costs. Although corporate relocation decisions are not new, global commerce seems to exacerbate the controversy by expanding the scope of possible sites and offering a potential "escape" from local or national political controls.

Foreign relocation issues arise in developed as well as developing countries. A review of the US debate over MNEs since the early 1970s reveals continuing charges of "run-away shops" and an "export of jobs."[18] The argument generally implies that a developed country's loss will result in a developing country's gain, where local communities there will benefit from the new or expanded production processes. Within the developing world, however, communities initially gaining production facilities can lose them as well, as corporations shift production or purchases to other communities or countries with even lower wages or other relative cost advantages. Without getting into the full economic debate over international comparative advantage that underlies business decisions, a relevant ethical question asks whether corporate social responsibilities exist toward communities harmed by business relocation.

Although communities would want the relocation decision reconsidered, a corporation could at least offer the community some involvement in the deliberations before a final decision has been reached. This step could help community leaders understand the basis for the corporate move and perhaps even consider adjustments that might retain the facility. If a move must occur, then the company could provide advance notice to give the community time to plan for necessary adjustments. The corporation could also offer various forms of adjustment assistance, financial or otherwise, perhaps parallel to "out-placement" services sometimes offered laid-off employees.

These suggestions raise three ethical questions regarding corporate social responsibility. Does the corporation owe less responsibility to a local community than to its employees? Considering whether the same types of assistance should be offered to both groups (one group a subset of the other) may help answer this question. Second, in evaluating the three suggested steps a corporation could take (involvement, time and assistance), would all three responses constitute discretionary maximal ethical actions or should any of them be considered a minimum ethical obligation? Third, does the form of the corporate connection to a community alter the firm's responsibilities? For example, does an invested MNE that owns the local facility hold a greater responsibility to the community than a foreign enterprise that only purchases from the local facility, but whose decision to source the product elsewhere results in the facility's closure?

A somewhat different element of corporate social responsibility toward stakeholder communities arises from an infamous case that has been called "the world's deadliest industrial accident."[19] In 1984 a gas leak from a Union Carbide plant in Bhopal, India quickly killed roughly 3,000 people living near the facility, while many others suffered serious health problems from which at least 11,000 more would later die. This case, a classic for many business ethics discussions, wound through tortuous legal proceedings in both India and the United States as courts sorted through various claims of responsibility and liability. Originally sued for $3billion by the Indian government, Union Carbide settled with the government in 1989 by paying $470 million into a compensation fund for victims. However, over 12 years later most victims had reportedly received only $500 from this fund. Some victims continued their legal suits against Dow Chemical, which acquired Union Carbide in 2001.

The facts of the Bhopal case remain contentious, with conflicting explanations and speculation leading to differing judgments about which parties bear proportional responsibility for the tragedy.[20] Contending explanations range from deliberate sabotage to corporate neglect or misconduct to inappropriate governmental requirements. Judgments on key factors might seem to increase or decrease Union Carbide's responsibility for the deaths. For example, Union Carbide retained majority control of its Indian subsidiary, but the Indian government may have required the production of dangerous chemicals and limited the company's ability to use US technicians. An MNE could refuse to participate in a potentially hazardous production process unless the company could effectively guarantee at least its own ethically minimum safety control standards. Of course, such a stand in the face of aggressive host government pressures might result in a massive loss of corporate investment. Should the risk to corporate capital be calculated relative to the risk to community inhabitants, i.e. how much is the life of an Indian neighbor worth compared to the loss of a factory? Indian courts reportedly have offered about $10,000 per victim in other historical cases, a rather paltry sum compared to compensation for accident victims in the United States.[21]

A similar case emerged from the British legal system in July 2000. The Law Lords of the upper chamber of Parliament ruled that the Cape corporation could be sued in British courts by the workers and residents near Cape's facilities in South Africa for asbestos-related illnesses. The court cases test a legal theory regarding whether parent corporations can be held responsible for actions of their foreign subsidiaries. The key elements revolve around factors of awareness, knowledge and capability to control foreign production processes that raise hazards for workers and community residents. This particular case was settled out of court in late 2001 when Cape reportedly agreed to provide $40million in compensation to South African asbestos victims.[22]

Regardless of determinations of legal liability under British law, the same questions can be posed for any international corporation in terms of ethical responsibilities. Do corporations have an ethical responsibility for their operations abroad, or does ethical responsibility depend on factors such as the nature of ownership ties? Perhaps a corporation can purposely structure its relationship with foreign subsidiaries so as to avoid legal liabilities; would such steps also excuse it from ethical responsibilities?

The extended saga of the Bhopal tragedy is presented in Exhibit 5.3. Over two decades later, the gas leak's aftermath still presents medical and environmental problems for people living in the surrounding community. Political opinion in India appears divided on both the merits of the case and its priority. Legal battles continue, hampered in part by the inability of Indian legal processes to reach American defendants. Dow Chemical contends it did not inherit any responsibility for Union Carbide's former Bhopal site when it acquired the firm. Is a corporation that acquires another firm free from ethical responsibility for the acquired firm's past actions, or does it acquire that firm's ethical responsibilities along with its assets? To whom can victims in the Bhopal community turn for assistance, both to address continuing health difficulties and for protection from the toxic remains that threaten to add new victims to the incident's already record-setting count?

Survivors of the Bhopal gas leak protest in New Dehli on 28 March 2008. They walked for 37 days to demand a meeting with the prime minister to seek a clean-up of toxic waste sill present at the site. Survivors also called upon Dow Chemical to take responsibility for the past actions of its Union Carbide subsidiary, a firm Dow acquired after the Bhopal gas leak. Photo by Manan Vatsyayana/AFP/Getty Images.

Exhibit 5.3   The Bhopal Gas Leak's Continuing Saga

Indians Pressure Dow on Bhopal Cleanup

By RAMA LAKSHMI
Washington Post Foreign Service

NEW DELHI, March 28—Twenty-three years after a Union Carbide chemical plant in India spewed poisonous gas in what remains the world's worst industrial disaster, survivors are demanding a cleanup of toxic chemicals at the abandoned factory site that have contaminated their groundwater.

On Friday, about 70 protesters arrived in New Delhi after marching 500 miles from Bhopal, the city whose name has become synonymous with the catastrophe. Organizers of the march said about 50 more people will arrive by train every day until their demands are met.

The marchers say Michigan-based Dow Chemical Co., which acquired Union Carbide Corp. in 2001, is responsible for cleaning up the site and paying the medical bills incurred after their exposure to the toxic water. They have also asked Dow to produce representatives of Union Carbide who have been charged with culpable homicide in the disaster.

"After 23 years, the neighborhood around the factory still shows a high rate of birth defects, cancer and other disabilities," said Nafisa Khan, 40, who marched from her home near the factory site to New Delhi. "The toxic chemicals buried in and around the factory have entered groundwater, and we use the contaminated water for drinking, cooking and bathing. First we were hit by the poisonous gas and then by this bad water that gives us skin diseases, chest pain and loss of appetite."

Khan was among hundreds of thousands of people who ran from the plumes of 40 tons of deadly methyl isocyanate gas that escaped from the Union Carbide pesticide plant shortly after midnight on Dec. 3, 1984. The leak killed at least 3,000 people in the first few days and led to 14,000 deaths overall from illness, according to the government. Survivors contend the toll is 23,000.

More than 100,000 people still suffer from chronic illnesses tied to the incident, including tuberculosis, depression, poor eyesight and gynecological problems. Khan, who was two months pregnant at the time of the disaster, had a miscarriage; three others in her family died.

Union Carbide settled out of court in 1989 and paid the Indian government $470million. But survivors have been fighting a seemingly endless battle to get help for the 30,000 people who continue to live in shantytowns around the factory.

The cleanup of the site, which contains about 8,000 tons of carcinogenic chemicals, has been blocked by court battles, official indifference and debates over corporate responsibility. Because the factory land now belongs to the Madhya Pradesh government, Dow says the state is responsible for cleaning it up. But the Indian government's Chemicals and Fertilizers Ministry has said in court that Dow should pay 1 billion rupees, about $25million at current exchange rates, to clean up the site.

"It is Dow's duty to clean up. Why should anybody else pay for it?" Khan said. "Until this is done, we will not allow Dow to rest easy and do business in India. We may be poor, but they have to value our lives."

Although the Chemicals and Fertilizers Ministry has supported the case against Dow, other parts of the Indian government have been more reluctant. Survivors from Bhopal will meet an official from Prime Minister Manmohan Singh's office Saturday to renew their long-standing demand for a national commission to provide social and economic rehabilitation and safe drinking water and to pressure Dow to clean up the site and produce Union Carbide representatives in Indian court. Survivors say they believe the government fears that pressuring the company would jeopardize future investment.

In an e-mail response to questions, a Dow official in Midland, Mich., said the firm did not inherit Union Carbide's liabilities when it acquired the company.

"Anyone who knows of this issue has deep sympathy for the victims of the tragedy in Bhopal. Today, we all ask the same question, 'Why isn't this site cleaned up?' " said Scot Wheeler, a Dow spokesman. He said Dow had "never owned or operated the former Bhopal plant site and this situation is not Dow's responsibility, accountability, or liability to bear," adding that Union Carbide is a separate subsidiary company.

A senior Indian government official familiar with the matter, Montek Singh Ahluwalia, said: "We have not taken any position on the issues before the court. Dow is aware that they have to defend themselves in court as best they can."

The wall of the Bhopal factory is covered with survivors' graffiti such as "Dow Chemicals Must End Toxic Terror in Bhopal" and "23 Years Is Enough, Bhopal Justice Now." Residents say that much of the site is unguarded and that children and animals often wander in. People also sneak in to steal scrap metal and copper coils for resale.

"The factory was a source of jobs for all of us, but it turned into a messenger of death," said Rashida Bee, 52, who lost six members of her family that night. "The compensation was a pittance. When the money was finally distributed among 570,927 survivors in 2005, most of the people got the equivalent of $1,280 each."

In 2001, when Dow purchased Union Carbide, Bee led the residents to Mumbai, where the group covered the walls of the Dow office with red paint, calling it "the blood of Bhopal."

Dow has operated in India for more than 50 years and manufactures pesticides, polymers and industrial adhesives. In the past six months, students at India's premier engineering school, the Indian Institutes of Technology, have resisted Dow's efforts to conduct job interviews on campuses and called for action on the Bhopal site.

An activist at the march Friday said that Dow has civil and criminal liability in India.

"We are not saying Dow is responsible for the gas tragedy in 1984," said Nityanand Jayaraman, a volunteer for the International Campaign for Justice in Bhopal. "But Union Carbide is a wholly owned subsidiary of Dow, so it has a criminal liability to produce Union Carbide representatives in Indian court. By not doing so, it is sheltering a fugitive. The responsibility to clean up the deadly factory site is Dow's civil liability."

Then he added, "Instead of a cleanup, all we get is coverup."

EMERGING EFFORTS TOWARD COMMON INTERNATIONAL STANDARDS

Foreign production processes raise numerous ethical issues that center on MNE responsibilities to important stakeholders, principally involving employees and host communities. Many of these issues have existed for decades and some received sporadic earlier attention. However, the emergence of the "sweatshops" debate in the 1990s drew related issues together in a more understandable manner that created public awareness and galvanized the sustained involvement of important civil society groups. Subsequent activities move toward evolving common international standards, although progress is sporadic and piecemeal in its application. Still, notable initiatives merit attention and ongoing evaluation of their results.

Active sectoral campaigns by civil society groups stimulated the development and adoption of numerous corporate and industry codes of conduct, including the pioneering application of the supply chain responsibility concept to non-producing corporate retailers.[23] The increased debate over monitoring issues sometimes obscures both growing acceptance of corporate responsibility for many overseas "sweatshop" issues and agreement on some defined minimum standards for ethical employee practices and workplace conditions. The main limitations on this movement stem from its dependence on public pressure tactics that apply primarily to well-known corporations with branded consumer products in developed countries. Corporations based in other countries or industries with minimal consumer name recognition are less vulnerable to marketplace pressures, unless connected through supply chain linkages with vulnerable targeted firms.

Several initiatives offer unusual examples of expanded social responsibility on "sweatshop"-related issues. A private sector initiative began in Franca, Brazil, where child labor has been endemic in the country's shoe industry. When shoe companies and their suppliers sign agreements to prevent child labor anywhere in the supply chain, the manufacturers can display a special logo on their product to certify it free of child labor. University teams inspect production facilities to ensure compliance. Three-quarters of local producers joined the program, stimulated in part by a desire to expand sales into export markets, although neither FDI nor trade relations played an important role in the creation of this program.[24]

Brazil also pioneered a public sector initiative, Bolsa Familia, which distributes cash to families in poverty if all their young children regularly attend school and receive health services. The payments aim to offset the need for poor families to withdraw young children from school and send them to work, often illegally, to provide needed income. Positive results show declines in children not attending school, in the illiteracy rate, in child labor, and in unemployment. In 1997 Mexico began *Oportunidades*, a similar program in rural areas that later expanded into cities. This initiative also recorded improvements, increasing secondary school enrollments for boys by 10 percent, for girls by 20 percent, and reducing drop-out rates. Inspired by these examples, nearly 20 other countries have begun similar programs, including Chile, Indonesia, South Africa, Turkey and Morocco.[25] These illustrations show how governments can tackle root problems of poverty that lead to the domestic incidence of child labor. Other efforts involve mixed public/private sector initiatives that address a broader range of "sweatshop" issues.

For example, trade was at the center of a Cambodian initiative to improve labor conditions in the garment industry, including but not limited to child labor. Prior problems led firms such as Nike to terminate contracts with Cambodian firms when media reports documented underage workers in supplier factories. The US government offered an 18 percent increase in a quota on Cambodia's garment exports to the United States if Cambodia improved its record on labor rights. Effective monitoring was required because existing Cambodian labor laws were not effectively enforced. With US financial assistance, the ILO established a monitoring program for the industry that identified individual firms failing to meet labor standards. For MNE purchasers, such as Nike, an ILO validation of factory labor standards offers some protection against social activist criticism. Nike placed a new order with a Cambodian factory two years after ending purchases from the country. Both Cambodian officials and private shoe association executives express hope the ILO-monitored program can increase the country's competitiveness by offering strong guarantees that garment exports do not involve violations of basic labor rights.[26]

The Cambodian program drew together many global elements to improve labor conditions: ILO standards and monitoring; US trade controls and financial assistance; civil society activism; media involvement; consumer interest and concern; MNE buyer standards; national government participation; local business cooperation. Certain aspects of the program were less desirable, particularly the restrictive US quota whose partial loosening provides an incentive, and the recognition that Cambodia's new competitive advantage arises only because other producing countries continue to violate labor rights.

This trade restriction element dissipated after the quotas imposed under a Multifibre Arrangement (MFA) expired in 2005. Subsequently, Cambodia's competitive advantage was linked even more closely to maintaining a reputation for garments produced under responsible labor conditions.

A different approach contemplates imposing minimum labor standards on all exporting countries through World Trade Organization (WTO) rules.[27] However, proposals to incorporate labor standards in WTO trade negotiations generate controversy and opposition. Developing countries fear developed countries will set high standards in order to negate low-cost labor advantages in the developing countries, thereby discouraging FDI and trade while protecting higher-cost jobs in the developed countries. The voluntary UN Global Compact garners broad support for its endorsement of core ILO standards, but many countries would resist enforcing these standards through WTO trade sanctions. Although the global community has moved toward common morality standards, insufficient detailed consensus exists on most labor rights issues to establish internationally enforceable rules. The resultant differences in national laws and practice leave room, and asserted responsibilities, for other actors to promote at least minimum ethical standards on labor relations and workplace conditions.

Applying ethical analysis to the case scenarios presented in this chapter can begin to determine the parameters for these actors' ethical responsibilities by answering the five "W" questions. Determining who should act involves identifying each relevant actor's place on a subsidiarity chain of ethical responsibility, weighing case factors such as causation, complicity, proximity, awareness, knowledge and capability. Governments, intergovernmental organizations, NGOs, MNEs, local producers, workers, communities, foreign importers and retailers, and consumers all appear arrayed along typical subsidiarity chains. Questions of when and where action should be taken involve assessing issues of national sovereignty and international business connections. A central issue concerns whether ethical responsibility for foreign production processes requires an FDI ownership link or if responsibility also extends through the supply chains of global trade relationships. Determining what action should be taken can seek minimum ethical standards on issues related to labor practices and workplace conditions or endorse process-oriented mechanisms such as collective bargaining by organized labor unions or the standards determined by local governments or market forces. Recognizing that foreign production processes raise a variety of ethical issues, answers to the "W" questions may vary depending on such factors as whether a particular issue reaches a critical need threshold. These distinctions can be drawn most clearly by exploring and developing the "why" rationale for answers given to the other four "W" questions.

NOTES

1. P. DeSimone, "Global Labor Standards," 2002 Background Report: A, Social Issues Service, Washington, DC: Investor Responsibility Research Center (IRRC), 2002, p. 23.
2. S. Buckley, "The Littlest Laborers," *The Washington Post*, 16 March 2000, p.A1.
3. This concept is recognized in the United Nations' *World Investment Report* and forms an important element in the debate over the definition of FDI in international negotiations, such as the draft text for the Multilateral Agreement on Investment in the OECD. See United Nations Conference on Trade and Development (UNCTAD), *World Investment Report 1999: Foreign Direct Investment and the Challenge of Development*, Geneva: United Nations, 1999, pp. 126–31, 465–6; and UNCTAD, *International Investment Instruments: A Compendium*, vol. IV, Geneva: United Nations, 2000, pp. 111–15.
4. A. Borgman, "Garment Workers Show US the Child Behind the Label," *The Washington Post*, 24 July 1995, p. D1. For more detail on this story, see the case summary provided in T. Beauchamp and N. Bowie, *Ethical Theory and Business*, 6th edn, Upper Saddle River, NJ: Prentice Hall, 2001, pp. 632–6.
5. Ibid.
6. K. Grimsley, " 'Already Old' in Bangladesh," *The Washington Post*, 25 September 2002, p. E1.
7. T. Moran, *Beyond Sweatshops*, Washington, DC: Brookings Institution, 2002, pp. 85–97.
8. A. Maitland, "Big Brands Come Clean on Sweatshop Labour," *Financial Times*, 10 June 2003, p. 8; A. Bernstein, "Sweatshops: Finally, Airing the Dirty Linen," *Business Week*, 23 June 2003, p. 100.
9. Another possibility sometimes suggested is the home country wage, but this alternative proves too extreme and would negate any wage-related reason for companies to invest or source abroad, reducing the ability of developing countries to attract FDI or build export industries.
10. For more background on this debate, see I. Maitland, "The Great Non-Debate Over International Sweatshops," in Beauchamp and Bowie, *Ethical Theory and Business*, pp. 593–604. Also see P. Varley (ed.), *The Sweatshop Quandary*, Washington, DC: IRRC, 1998, pp. 60–6; and DeSimone, "Global Labor Standards," pp. 24–6.
11. Despite this general corporate position, standards accepted as part of the Sullivan Principles in South Africa essentially adopted a "living wage" concept. "Companies that joined the Sullivan Principles program were expected to pay a minimum wage at least 30 percent above the poverty line for a family of five or six." DeSimone, "Global Labor Standards," p. 25.
12. Debate over the living wage concept also occurs in the United States, gaining momentum since the mid 1990s. By early 2003 over 100 US cities and counties, including New York, Boston, Chicago, Denver and St Louis, required that employees of city government and city contractors pay wage rates above the mandated national minimum wage. In adopting such self-imposed requirements, these governments essentially acted in their capacity as direct employers and purchasers, setting an ethical minimum living wage above both the local market and the national legal minimum. By contrast, when Santa Fe's city council debated a living wage bill, the proposed wage standard covered most private sector employers located in the city, whether or not they did business with the city government. In that case, the parallel with the government acting as a standard-setting employer breaks down and the action reflects the more normal public law function. See L. Hockstader, "Santa Fe Wrangles Over Broad 'Living Wage' Bill," *The Washington Post*, 26 February 2003, p. A3.
13. N. Stein, "No Way Out," *Fortune*, 20 January 2003, pp. 102–8.
14. Ibid.
15. W. Branigin, "Sweatshop Instead of Paradise: Thais Lived in Fear as Slaves in LA Garment Factories," *The Washington Post*, 10 September 1995, p. A1.
16. S. Chandler, "Look Who's Sweating Now," *Business Week*, 16 October 1995, p. 98.
17. DeSimone, "Global Labor Standards," p. 24.
18. M. Stanley, "The Foreign Direct Investment Decision and Job Export as an Ethical Dilemma for the Multinational Corporation," in M. Hoffman, A. Lange and D. Fedo (eds), *Ethics and the Multinational Enterprise*, New York: University Press of America, 1986, pp. 493–509; R. Barnet and R. Muller, *Global Reach*, New York: Simon & Schuster, 1974, pp. 303–33.

19. R. Lakshmi, "India Seeks to Reduce Charge Facing ex-Union Carbide Boss," *The Washington Post*, 18 July 2002, p. A12. Other information in this section was drawn from the following sources, which contain additional detail and discussion of the gas leak from the Union Carbide plant in Bhopal: M. Gladwell, "Settlement Won't Hurt Carbide," *The Washington Post*, 15 February 1989, p. D1; R. Koenig, B. Garcia and A. Spaeth, "Union Carbide, India Reach $470 Million Settlement in '84 Bhopal Gas Leak That Killed More Than 2,500," *The Wall Street Journal*, 15 February 1989, p. A3; M. Gladwell, "The Costly Outcome of Bhopal," *The Washington Post*, 19 February 1989, p. H1; S. McMurray, "India's High Court Upholds Settlement Paid by Carbide in Bhopal Gas Leak," *The Wall Street Journal*, 4 October 1991, p. B8; J. Carlton and T. Herrick, "Bhopal Haunts Dow Chemical," *The Wall Street Journal*, 8 May 2003, p. B3; and T. Donaldson, *The Ethics of International Business*, New York: Oxford University Press, 1989, chapter 7.

20. T. Jackson, "Bhopal's Awkward Truth," *Financial Times*, 5 September 2002, p. 11.

21. Gladwell, "The Costly Outcome of Bhopal." This disparity in court settlements explains why Bhopal victims sought legal action in US courts, and why corporate critics charge that MNEs engage in a "race to the bottom" by sending hazardous production processes to developing countries where both regulatory standards and penalties for violations are lowest.

22. J. Eaglesham, "S. African cases open door to claims against multinationals," *Financial Times*, 22 August 2000, p. 7; A. Sharma, "Victory for Asbestos Victims," *African Business*, 273, February 2002, p. 43.

23. See Moran, pp. 85–107; and Varley, pp. 399–476, 505–94.

24. G. Dyer, "Brazil Pushes on with Work in Effort to Eliminate Child Labour," *Financial Times*, 23 March 2000, p. 20.

25. "Brazil-Bolsa Familia: Changing the Lives of Millions in Brazil," online, available at <http://web.world-bank.org/WBSITE/EXTERNAL/COUNTRIES/LACEXT?BRAZILEXT> (accessed 26 May 2009); "Brazil-Lifting Families Out of Poverty-Bolsa Familia Program," online, available at <http://webworld-bank.org/WBSITE/EXTERNAL/COUNTRIES/LACEXT/BRAZILEX> (accessed 26 May 2009); R. Paes de Sousa, "Bolsa Familia Program Effects on Health and Education Services: Catching Unusual Suspects," Ministry of Social Development and Fight Against Hunger, October 2006; K. Lindert, A. Linder, J. Hobbs, and B. de la Briere, "The Nuts and Bolts of Brazil's Bolsa Familia Program: Implementing Conditional Cash Transfers in a Decentralized Context," SP Discussion Paper, No. 0709, The World Bank, May 2007; "Reducing Poverty, Sustaining Growth: Scaling Up Poverty Reduction," The World Bank, paper presented at the Global Learning Process Conference in Shanghai, 25–27 May 2004.

26. A. Kazmin, "US Sportswear Giant May Be Ready for a Cambodia Comeback," *Financial Times*, 18 June 2002, p.7; and Kazim, "Monitoring is Paying Off," *Financial Times*, 10 December 2002, p. III. Nike also received publicity surrounding a court case charging that company actions relating to a public relations campaign about conditions at overseas factories constituted false advertising. The suit was settled without resolving contentious issues regarding the line between free speech and commercial speech, after the US Supreme Court dismissed an appeal from a California Supreme Court ruling that would have permitted a trial. See A. Reddy, "Nike Settles with Activist in False-Advertising Case," *The Washington Post*, 13 September 2003, p. E1.

27. The rationale for this approach was laid out by then US Secretary of Labor Robert Reich in a 1994 editorial. See R. Reich, "Escape from the Global Sweatshop," *The Washington Post*, 22 May 1994, p. C1.

6

PRODUCT AND EXPORT CONTROLS

INTRODUCTION

Globally traded products require willing buyers and sellers as well as permissive intervening governments in both exporting and importing countries. Additional stakeholders may include international organizations, civil society groups, intermediate users, final consumers and affected communities. This chapter examines decision making about whether certain products should be traded internationally, particularly products whose use may be hazardous to some stakeholders. Whereas Chapter 4 assessed the country location of foreign production and sales, and Chapter 5 examined issues associated with the foreign production process, this chapter explores the nature of products themselves, asking what benefits (and potential costs) the products may bring, where and when, and who should decide on their international sale? These questions can be addressed through ethical analysis by testing alternative approaches to determine the best reasoning as to why products should or should not be traded internationally.

The focus of this chapter lies with traded goods that are subject to potential customs controls as they leave and enter national territories. International agreements can constrain or enhance national government capabilities to impose such trade controls. Although the global trading system's general bias favors freer trade, persuasive rationales may be presented for trade restraints, including potential harm from traded products. In a diverse global community, however, opinions differ on the nature and extent of a product's potential harm and on whether realized benefits may outweigh harm that does occur. This chapter therefore explores possible ethical principles and process mechanisms that might provide a foundation of common morality for global community action on issues involving product exports and trade controls.

The central framing question for this chapter is: Should corporations sell any product not banned by government authorities (or should corporations follow voluntary ethical standards on product safety and efficacy that must be met above and beyond legal requirements of exporting and importing governments)?

ACTORS AND DECISION TOOLS

Case experience represented below suggests that the most critical "W" questions for product export and trade control issues are: who should decide, and why? The most obvious responsible actor may be importing governments whose border trade controls should serve the best interests of their people. Difficulties arise where these governments either lack effective capability to prevent harmful imports or fail to pursue the public's best interest due to inefficiency, corruption or the absence of representative governance. In a global community, failure or inaction by importing governments might shift responsibility along the subsidiarity chain to other actors, such as exporting governments or intergovernmental organizations.

Exporting governments primarily promote their own national interests through increased sales, but such actions should not cause serious harm to other individuals, regardless of the victims' citizenship. Determining degrees of responsibility for exporting governments could involve considerations such as how directly the exported products caused the harm and whether the government knew such products might be harmful. One measure of such factors, apparent in many case scenarios, is whether the exporting country prohibits or restricts a product's sale in its own domestic market, which would indicate clear awareness of potential harm. The role of intergovernmental organizations, of course, largely depends on the ability of member governments to reach agreement on a normative standard to govern trade in potentially hazardous products.

In addition to public authorities, responsibilities may also fall on producing and/or exporting companies that can unilaterally decide whether or not to sell to certain countries. The ethical question in such cases asks whether a company may ethically sell abroad any product whose sale is not prohibited by governmental authority. An affirmative answer would effectively remove companies from the subsidiarity chain by placing full ethical responsibility on government actors. Arguments for corporate responsibility often assess factors such as a company's awareness, technical knowledge and causal connection to harm associated with their products.

Of course, consumers and other stakeholders should also be considered. By restricting export sales, governments and/or corporations deny potential consumers the ability to choose whether or not to purchase a product, essentially making a negative choice for them. The case scenarios will test individual choice principles by evaluating factors such as the knowledge and assessment capabilities of various actors, the calculation of cost/benefit measures, and the distribution of costs and benefits among relevant groups, including sellers, intermediate users, final consumers and affected communities. Allocating appropriate degrees of decision-making responsibility among these varied public and private sector actors requires establishing clear ethical rationales for the determination.

Assessments of decision tools can play a role in assigning responsibility among relevant actors. Cost/benefit calculations figure prominently in teleological approaches that focus on evaluating case outcomes. For example, debate over the export of agricultural pesticides involves identifying, measuring and comparing specific benefits from increased crop production versus associated harm to health from pesticide use. One consideration could be distributional impacts, such as whether general benefits for the utilitarian majority should prevail over concentrated harm suffered by a few individuals or minorities. Associated teleological issues would include specifying when to calculate the cost/benefit outcomes and where to measure the effects, i.e. whether national boundaries or citizenship make a difference.

Deontological decision methods could also be chosen, relying more on process, rules and individual rights. If the principle of individual choice prevails, market mechanisms relatively unrestricted by governmental controls could guide product purchase decisions. Justifications for limiting individual choice might arise if individuals lacked a capability to make fully informed decisions or if individual choices might result in harmful effects on others. In such cases, more expert and capable actors might intervene to provide additional information or restrict the range of choices available to individuals.

The major decision tool currently employed by the global community on product export and trade control issues involves a process of prior informed consent (PIC) as applied to trade in certain hazardous products. This mechanism calls for exporting governments to provide importing governments with pertinent product risk information before permitting a regulated product's export, thereby shifting final decision responsibility to the importing country's government. To a more limited extent, intergovernmental organizations also now prohibit or severely restrict trade in a few products widely agreed to produce significant and long-lasting harm. These intergovernmental mechanisms, however, depend on achieving a common morality standard broadly endorsed by most national governments, a difficult goal that also designates public authorities as the principal responsible actors. Individuals or groups dissatisfied with governmental actions may still call upon other actors in the subsidiarity chain, particularly corporations, to exercise their own decision-making power where official export and trade controls do not satisfactorily restrict product sales.

PRODUCT RISK FOR CONSUMERS

The ethical issues outlined above have fueled policy debates for over a quarter-century. Exhibit 6.1 reproduces an editorial appearing in *The Washington Post* on 27 February 1980, summarizing the contending arguments and ethical challenges posed by a number of contemporaneous cases involving the export of products banned or severely regulated for sale in the United States. Some progress on international standards has occurred since that time, shaping both national and international guidelines covering certain products. Reviewing the experiential results in several of these early cases, however, can help elucidate the issues and highlight key factors important to the decision-making process.

A classic early case involved children's pajamas that had been treated with Tris, a flame-retardant chemical. Introduced in the mid 1970s, the pajamas proved a

Exhibit 6.1 Exporting Goods Banned at Home

Unsafe in Any Country?

Should a substance deemed too dangerous for use in this country be licensed for export? An answer is still elusive despite years of study and debate, while exports of banned and untested substances have been growing. The key issues are these: Does the United States have a moral responsibility to prevent the export of a substance it knows—or thinks—is dangerous? Or does the making of such judgments constitute unacceptable intrusions on the sovereignty of other nations? And what effect would stricter controls have on an already shaky US balance of trade?

No single, simple control policy—for example, banning the export of anything that is banned domestically—will sensibly cover the complete range of exports that include such items as Tris-treated pajamas, pesticides, effective but risky medicines, toxic chemicals and dangerous toys for children. In each case the nature of the risk will be different, as will the degree of certainty about whether or not a risk actually exists. In some cases, alternatives to a dangerous product will be available, in others not.

In many cases the conditions in an importing country—rampant unemployment, exploding population growth, epidemics of insect-borne disease—make US standards of health or safety completely inappropriate. For example, Depo Provera, a long-lasting, injected contraceptive, has been banned in this country because of uncertain long-term risks. However, in a country whose number one problem is overpopulation, and the illness and mortality rates associated with it, the risk-versus-benefit judgment is different. And in fact, Depo Provera is licensed in more than seventy nations. Should US firms then be prohibited from selling it?

An apparently satisfactory way to balance ethical responsibility, practical economic considerations and respect for the right of others to make their own decisions is for the United States to require only that the importing country be fully aware of the potential risks. In practice, however, this approach has many drawbacks.

A serious notification policy, for instance, would require full publication of the thousands of regulatory actions—bans, suspensions, registrations, deregistrations, judicial injunctions, to name a few—occurring each year. A document from the government of the importing country indicating that it had received and considered the information would also be required. Masses of paperwork and thousands of additional man-hours would be needed. In this country all that would be possible, though unwelcome, but in many—if not most—others it would be impossible. Two years ago, for example, the Ministry for Environment in Nigeria (one of the larger and richer developing countries) consisted of the minister, one assistant and one secretary. A high level of scientific and technical expertise would also be necessary to evaluate the risk-benefit trade-offs posed by a possible import. And even if this step could be accomplished, many governments lack the procedures and the degree of central control necessary to set and implement standards for safe use.

Probably the only really workable solution lies in the creation of common international standards. But although some steps in this direction are being taken by a number of UN agencies, it will be many years, if ever, before they amount to much. Meanwhile, this country will have to find an acceptable set of standards for itself. The United States must accept *some* responsibility for its exports—that much is clear. But where the line comes between appropriate care and becoming the world's environmental policeman—against the will and wishes of importing countries with different priorities and standards and needs of their own—is not so clear. Finding the right balance will be a thankless task: for every developing country that objects to becoming a dumping ground for the industrialized world, there is another that objects even more loudly to having the developed world's standards imposed on it. Nevertheless, the task is worth the effort. Lethal pesticides, toxic chemicals and dangerous drugs all have a way of coming back to haunt their makers. Mixed in the volatile brew of international relations, they can become explosive.

popular item with safety-conscious parents until Tris was found to cause kidney cancer in children. The US Consumer Product and Safety Commission (CPSC) banned domestic sales in June 1977 and ordered a product recall to protect consumers. The affected clothing could be buried, burned or used as industrial wiping cloths. The CPSC, however, did not ban export sales until the following year, providing some producing companies a window of opportunity to prevent the complete loss of their investment. Other trading firms also stepped into the gap, buying Tris-treated pajamas for 10–30 percent of the wholesale price and shipping the goods overseas. An estimated 2.4 million pajamas were exported to other countries before imposition of the export ban.[1]

If companies can ethically sell any products whose sale is not prohibited by government regulation, then the pajama exporters cannot be judged any more harshly than the manufacturers selling Tris-treated products in the United States prior to the CPSC action. However, what if the manufacturers had originally known about the carcinogenic risk to children before the product was first sold and the companies marketed the product anyway; would knowledge of health risks impose ethical obligations on the companies to refrain from product sales, or at least require prior effective notification or warnings to governmental authorities and/or potential buyers? In such cases, awareness and knowledge factors may increase corporate responsibility regardless of government action, especially if only the company possesses such knowledge.

There is no indication in the pajama case that manufacturers knew about the Tris cancer risk before the first sales in the United States. There is no doubt that these companies were aware of the risk after the CPSC domestic sales ban and before the export prohibition. Unless all responsibility falls on governmental entities (exporting and importing country agencies), manufacturers exporting their products after the initial CPSC action could be seen as causal agents for kidney cancers in any foreign children who wore Tris-treated pajamas. Manufacturers selling discounted pajamas to intermediary agents who then exported the products may also be held indirectly responsible for harms suffered, if the manufacturers were aware (or should have been aware) that the products were being purchased for foreign sale. The awareness factor raises issues of willful ignorance, or how far a company should go in asking questions regarding its product's use, once aware of product risk. (A comparative case scenario in Chapter 4 might be Polaroid's assessment of its cameras' use in enforcing apartheid regulations.)

Much public revulsion over this case probably stemmed from the characteristics of potential victims and the seemingly clear cost/benefit calculation related to the product's sale. The image of vulnerable pajama-clad children exposed to carcinogenic chemicals evokes protective impulses that for many people can transcend considerations of a victim's nationality, creating a sense of shared responsibility that may not apply in other cases. The harm to personal health suffered by victims of kidney cancer also offers a more salient measure of serious cost compared to the economic benefits to corporations from continued product sales.

Perhaps an assessment of the pajamas' flame-retardant qualities would yield a more comparable benefit measure that also focuses on a child's health. The CPSC action suggests how US authorities evaluated this comparison, but the likelihood of cancer versus fire deaths in children could vary depending on conditions where the children reside, so a teleologically oriented decision tool might use national or even local cost/benefit projections to inform case-by-case determinations. Study results could be given to public authorities in importing countries or even provided to parents, who could then make more informed individual purchase decisions. Of course, the expense of more detailed studies would also likely raise product cost, unless subsidized by other entities.

Comparisons with other examples help illustrate the relative importance of various case factors. For instance, the vulnerability of children as potential victims often plays a key role in making certain product exports appear especially heinous, such as the dangerous toys mentioned in Exhibit 6.1, or the export of nearly one-half million pacifiers of a type that caused choking deaths.[2] These products appear to offer even less significant offsetting benefits for children than flame-retardant pajamas. Similarly questionable offsetting benefits to health risks appeared to mark an earlier case in 1969. Tests with cyclamate, an artificial sweetener, produced dangerous malformations in chick embryos, leading the Food and Drug Administration (FDA) to ban US sales of the product. Companies challenged the reasonableness of the FDA's risk criteria, however, and continued to export cyclamate to countries whose authorities did not restrict its importation and sale. The FDA never acted on a 1985 petition to reapprove cyclamate even though over 50 countries, including the United Kingdom and Canada, permit its use in consumer products.[3] The cyclamate example highlights difficult questions regarding how much confidence to place in scientific tests and, equally importantly, who should determine acceptable risk levels.

Many similar ethical considerations arose in a long-running controversy over potential health risks posed by silicone breast implants. Introduced by Dow Corning in 1963, this product faced subsequent charges that implant ruptures or leakage of silicone gel caused diseases such as lupus, rheumatoid arthritis or breast cancer.[4] Numerous lawsuits resulted, many alleging that Dow Corning ignored or concealed problems with the product. As media attention grew, the FDA called in January 1992 for a 45-day moratorium on implant sales and later ordered them off the market in the United States, except for women undergoing mastectomies.

Four US producers of silicone implants took contrasting actions following the FDA call for a sales moratorium. While all four companies stopped selling the product in the United States, only Dow Corning ended all sales. Bioplasty continued to export its product, contending it had not received an FDA request to stop such sales. Mentor and McGhan both stopped exports but Mentor continued sales abroad by using a two-month inventory of goods previously exported, while McGhan sold implants manufactured at its plant in Ireland. For Bioplasty, the immediate ethical question was whether the FDA's request for a domestic sales moratorium should be sufficient indication of a potential customer health risk that the company should also halt export sales, even if not requested by the FDA. For Mentor and McGhan, the issue revolves around whether suspending exports met their ethical obligation toward customer safety if foreign sales continue unabated through use of existing product inventory or new foreign production. If governments bear full responsibility for assuring product safety, then corporate compliance with regulatory requirements meets a minimal ethical standard; following voluntary FDA requests might even qualify as maximal ethical action. On the other hand, if companies owe ethical responsibilities to customers, regardless of governmental mandates, then the issue becomes whether FDA concerns should indicate a sufficient health risk to warrant stopping all sales, domestic and foreign.

Ending all sales could impose high costs on the companies, particularly the three small firms that depended far more than Dow Corning on implant sales. Most ethicists do not contend that individuals are ethically obligated to sacrifice their own life to save others. (Although such self-sacrifice may be deemed meritorious, it is not ethically required.) The same self-sacrifice limitation may not apply to corporations (as artificial legal persons). Even though a corporation's death (bankruptcy or dissolution) would inflict some harm on certain stakeholders (shareholders, employees, communities), continuing to sell products posing serious health risks for consumers would be judged unethical by deontological standards and, except in theoretically extreme cases, by most teleologically measured cost/benefit standards as well.

In general, the more important the ethical value at stake, the more costs ethical actors should be willing to bear. Preservation of life, and the prevention of serious physical injuries, usually ranks high on the priority list of human values. In the case of silicone breast implants, a key decision factor concerned evaluations regarding the level of consumer health risks posed by the implants. The case against silicone implants was also strengthened by the existence of a safer alternative (implants filled with a saline solution). In cases where nearly equivalent benefits can be obtained by using a significantly safer alternative, the ethical burden of proof becomes heavier on advocates for the riskier product.

Later developments highlight the sometimes unpredictable and even ironic twists that can occur in complex ethical dilemmas. Dow Corning, rather than its smaller competitors, declared bankruptcy, driven to this step in 1995 by thousands of lawsuits brought by women suffering various health maladies they attributed to the company's silicone implants. Then, in a rather startling turnabout, new reviews of silicone implant studies concluded in 2000 that the implants likely did not cause most serious health problems previously associated with the product, casting doubt on the FDA's earlier assessment. Inamed Corporation, McGhan's corporate parent, applied to the FDA to renew sales of silicone breast implants. (Both Inamed and Mentor had reportedly continued their overseas sales, despite the FDA's mandatory imposition of a domestic sales ban, since the final FDA action did not cover exports or foreign production. Lawsuits had forced Bioplasty into bankruptcy.)

Controversy continued over the scientific studies of longer-term health risks as well as the appropriate standard to evaluate the product's costs and benefits. In July 2003 a news article reported that, according to an FDA official: "the goal of the FDA is not to approve only those drugs and devices that are entirely safe. The agency, he said, has to weigh the risks and benefits of a product. If the potential benefits outweigh the risks, he said, then 'it is reasonable to let consumers decide if they want to take the risks for the potential benefit.' "[5] This approach clearly endorses the cost/

benefit decision tool, although the appropriate measurements or time frame remain unclear. Implicitly, this position does require the FDA to determine that potential benefits can (to some unspecified degree of certainty) outweigh costs before transferring the final decision to potential consumers.[6] In November 2006 the FDA finally lifted its ban on silicone implants but mandated follow-up studies. With recent evidence that many women still suffer ruptures or leakage, the agency also requires the manufacturers to inform women that "most recipients will need at least one additional surgery to remove or replace their implants."[7]

This case thus returns to the questions of who should decide, when, and where (i.e. should the US government preemptively control sales to foreign consumers; should the geographic location of potential consumers determine their degree of product choice?). Questions regarding what actions to take (such as voluntary or mandatory restrictions on production, exports and sales) depend largely on who will decide and the decision tools they will employ. Answering these ethical questions can be informed by scientific studies of factors such as product health risks, but this case suggests that such "objective" factors may change or be reinterpreted.[8] In the end, the answer to who decides should derive from a clear rationale for why that choice is made (i.e. which value standard guided the selection) based on shared societal values.

RISKS AND BENEFITS FOR MULTIPLE STAKEHOLDERS

Whereas consumers enjoyed the direct benefits and bore the principal health risks of products discussed above, the costs and benefits from other products fall more broadly among multiple stakeholders. These products may also face domestic sales restrictions or prohibitions if governments determine they cause significant harm to their citizens. In such cases, similar ethical issues arise regarding whether to impose export and trade controls on the products in order to protect foreign populations or to leave such decisions to the discretion of exporting companies, importing governments or other foreign groups and individuals.

Pesticides represent the classic example of products typifying this kind of ethical issue.[9] An article in the November 1979 edition of *Mother Jones* magazine spawned a follow-up piece entitled "The Circle of Poison" that set out the initial concerns and stimulated early debate on this topic.[10] The concept traces the circuitous route that can evolve from the use of potentially hazardous products. For example, pesticides banned from domestic operations by US regulators were still exported to developing countries for application to improve agricultural harvests. Along the way, such pesticides can cause serious illness or death among farm workers exposed during field applications, as well as residents in surrounding communities poisoned by pesticide run-off into nearby streams or through consumption of tainted produce. The described "circle of poison" is closed when pesticides return to the United States as residue on the growing import of agricultural produce, placing US consumers at risk.

One way to explore the debate over pesticide exports would be to start with elements that raise ethical responsibility issues, such as the harm suffered by particular individuals. After examining the causes and assessing responsibility for the harm, including ways to reduce pesticide hazards, offsetting benefits might be considered.

This analysis should lead to conclusions regarding who should do what, when and where in these types of cases.

Examining potential harm to consumers offers a comparative assessment that tests whether ethical responsibilities should depend on the citizenship of at-risk consumers. Companies creating, producing and selling a product are held responsible for some level of due diligence regarding their product's safety. Governments often assess corporate safety tests to check their accuracy and the reasonableness of evaluation standards. Sophisticated regulatory systems in the developed countries address most product safety concerns, although mistakes still occur. Prohibitions on domestic use of certain hazardous pesticides arise from a determination that initially approved products actually cause unacceptable harm to a nation's citizens.

Governments that consider health risks too high to permit domestic pesticide use may still permit exports of the same pesticides that could place foreign consumers at risk. If a government's ethical responsibility ends at its territorial border, then such action could be justified. Of course, with international travel, a nation's citizens might still be at risk as temporary consumers in foreign countries. However, the test becomes clearer when the circle is fully closed and pesticide residue returns on agricultural produce imported and consumed in the exporting country. Should a government control exports of hazardous pesticides if residue on imports threatens their citizens (the same rationale for banning domestic use) but not if the threat to health falls only on non-citizens living in other countries?

Relative ethical responsibilities increase when actions (promoting exports) or even inaction (failing to prohibit exports) connect a party to the physical harm suffered by pesticide victims in other countries. Risk awareness, knowledge and capability factors all reinforce the causal connections applying to corporate and government actors who could decide not to sell or export hazardous pesticides, regardless of the re-importation risk.

Prohibitions on domestic pesticide use also help protect other domestic stakeholders, including farmers and residents of surrounding communities. Permitting pesticide exports places vulnerable counterpart groups in other (especially developing) countries at risk. In fact, foreign groups and individuals arguably run even higher risks because they possess lower awareness, knowledge and capability to deal with hazardous products. Chemical companies avow their products' safety if used in proper concentrations and with protective equipment. However, investigations have revealed that few men, women or children applying pesticides to crops in developing countries use protective clothing or even know about the risks. Even pesticides permitted and used safely in the United States or other developed countries may pose higher health risks abroad, where safe-use capabilities are lower.

A safe-use standard raises different ethical considerations than safe-consumption concerns, recalling the type of worker safety issues discussed in the previous chapter's examination of foreign production processes. Figure 6.1 depicts the pesticide supply chain as described in the "circle of poison" argument. Compare this depiction to the contracted labor supply chain portrayed in Figure 5.1 in the last chapter. In the pesticide case, the assertion of potential supply chain responsibilities begins earlier and moves forward, from the manufacturer of pesticides (an intermediate product)

An unidentified (and essentially unprotected) youth sprays pesticide in a field near Chaina, India on 23 April 2008. Local residents may also be at risk due to pesticide run-off in streams and residue on local produce. A study revealed cancer rates 45 percent higher among people living close to this area compared to a nearby region with lower pesticide contamination. Photo by Pedro Ugarte/AFP/Getty Images.

to the pesticide user (farmers), rather than backward from the retailer or consumer of the final product (food). The question posed asks whether pesticide producers (or intervening government authorities) have ethical responsibilities to assure safe use of their products on the farms and, if so, what types of actions might be required.

Minimal ethical action may require at least providing available knowledge to foreign governments, importers, intermediate users, ultimate consumers or other parties who would otherwise be left unaware, uninformed and unprotected. Warning labels affixed to hazardous products, containing information both on health risks and

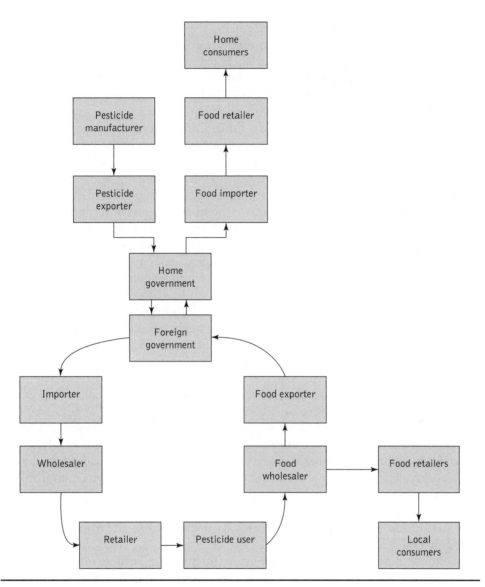

Figure 6.1 Pesticide Supply Chain.

safe-use requirements, might fulfill such an ethical obligation and could be required by government regulation. For internationally traded products, however, the efficacy of warning labels can involve complex and potentially costly adjustments.

A first step would be printing labels in the local language wherever the product is sold, but exporters often utilize bulk containers, shipping pesticides overseas in enormous barrels. Is an exporter responsible for assuring that importers, wholesalers and retailers, who may or may not be affiliated with the producing company, also apply appropriate warning labels to smaller, repacked pesticide containers before sale to farmers? Purchasing farmers often rely on hired field workers to actually apply the pesticides. In such cases, the individuals facing the greatest health risk are probably the least aware, knowledgeable and capable of using the products safely. Even if still affixed in the local language, warning labels may be incomprehensible to illiterate field workers and attempts to rely on symbols encounter cross-cultural difficulties.[11] Even if informed of risks, the workers may lack proper training or equipment to apply the pesticide in a safe fashion.

Few training programs exist to help inform and protect field workers. Ethical analysis would ask whether (or which) actors along the supply chain should provide such training. If the most proximate farmer/employer (comparable to the "sweat-shop" factory owner in the previous chapter) lacks the ability or will to satisfactorily protect the workers, how far back should subsidiarity responsibility extend along a chain that includes the pesticide retailer, wholesaler, importer, importing country government, exporting country government, exporter and producer? If end-points are identified where certain actors' responsibility terminates, specific factors should be identified to establish why that actor no longer carries any ethical connection to the physical harm suffered by field workers. If responsibilities are asserted, then questions of what action to take can be addressed, including either positive measures (warnings or training) or negative steps (stopping imports, exports or product sales).

From a contemporary perspective, arguments might suggest that actors who come after the field workers' place on the supply chain might also carry ethical responsi-bilities, including agricultural produce retailers or consumers (making the case more comparable to the "sweatshop" issue). A review of Figures 6.1 and 5.1 can help illus-trate this comparison. For example, grocery chains or consumers might refuse to buy agricultural goods not certified as grown with safe-use practices for field workers. In reality, actions at this end of the supply chain, as buyers begin to seek pesticide-free produce, have thus far been driven almost exclusively by consumer safety con-cerns. Such buying preferences may serve indirectly to reduce pesticide exposure for farm workers as well, but these consumer-based actions differ in motivation from the steps taken to protect workers in the anti-"sweatshop" campaigns.

Preventing or minimizing potential harm from hazardous pesticides addresses only part of this issue's ethical complexity. Particularly from a teleological perspec-tive, potential offsetting benefits should also be considered, perhaps including their distribution among affected parties. Consider the plight of farmers who feel trapped between the promised production benefits and the potential health costs of using haz-ardous pesticides. Quantifiable costs emerge from estimates of a million annual severe pesticide poisonings, from which thousands die. On the other hand, pesticides can increase agricultural output, providing substantial benefits for both individual farm-ers and the national economy. More food could be available for local consumption as well as export, enhancing economic development objectives.

Cost/benefit calculations require evaluating rather dissimilar value measures, dis-tributed unequally across disparate groups. While farm workers bear most of the health costs in return for meager wages, farm owners and pesticide companies realize proportionately larger financial benefits with less or no real health risk from the product's use. Consumers broadly benefit from increased agricultural output, while potential health costs fall more narrowly on the unlucky individuals who consume unsuspected pesticide residue. Local communities enjoy the spin-off benefits from visibly improved farm harvests while facing unseen risks from pesticide run-off.

Pesticide opponents and proponents both challenge the validity of many cost/benefit assessments. Opponents contend pesticides upset the ecology, fostering uncounted environmental damage that will reduce or negate benefits for individual farmers and national economies over the longer term. Alternative production methods could avoid this damage, but less hazardous pesticides are often higher-priced while a shift to pesticide-free production methods may reduce crop yields, raising questions about when to measure outcomes. Pesticide proponents often challenge the level of estimated health risks, especially reports on pesticide-related deaths. One university expert claimed only a quarter of pesticide deaths resulted from work-related applications, with the vast majority attributable to suicides, where pesticides provide a cheap and available method in developing countries.[12] Although such a claim may seem exaggerated, a reported World Health Organization estimate suggested that 2 million people annually purposely ingest pesticides, resulting in some 200,000 successful suicides.[13]

Clearly, the pesticide issue is complex, with legitimate rationales available to support a range of responses. Yet in real-world situations difficult decisions must be taken by both private and public sector actors regarding whether to sell and/or regulate hazardous products. For the ethical dilemma presented by foreign pesticide sales, select a "best choice" decision that indicates who should do what, when and where. Identify the most important factors that influence your decision, explaining why those elements shape the most persuasive ethical rationale for this case.

PRODUCT USE AND ABUSE

The suicide contention raises a final ethical issue regarding product end use that will also appear in the next chapter on marketing practices, i.e. whether, or to what extent, a company or government bears responsibility for harm resulting from the abuse of a product. For pesticides, the debate generally involves how to measure health costs rather than assertions that pesticide-related suicides require a cessation of exports or extraordinary steps by producers to prevent such willful misuse of their product. However, similar arguments emerged, with somewhat different assessments, in a widely cited case that explores the toxic impacts of product abuse involving glue-sniffing in Central America.

According to accounts of this case,[14] a subsidiary of the H. B. Fuller Company began selling adhesives in Latin America in the early 1980s, using the brand name Resistol. In 1983 Honduran newspapers began reporting arrests of street children who were sniffing glue, often labeling them *resistoleros*, whether or not the glue being abused was the Fuller product or another brand. Chemical fumes from solvent-based glues induced stupors in the children and could lead to hearing loss, nervous system damage, liver failure or even cardiac arrest. Similar product abuse appeared elsewhere in Latin American, particularly in neighboring Guatemala. Organizations working with the street children urged Fuller to withdraw its product, add noxious agents to discourage sniffing or switch to safer water-based alternatives.

Noted for its social responsibility actions in the United States, Fuller investigated the charges and decided the core problem lay with the street children's poverty and desperation rather than with the company's product. Believing that abuse of other products would substitute for glue-sniffing if Resistol sales ended, Fuller decided to promote educational efforts and support organizations that worked with the street children. After controversy continued to damage the company's image, Fuller also reportedly switched to using a somewhat less toxic but still hazardous ingredient in Resistol and announced a decision to end retail sales of the product in Honduras and Guatemala. Initially hailed by company critics, this announcement backfired when Resistol remained available in those countries through sales to commercial and industrial users. In 2000 Fuller announced a termination of Resistol sales in most of Latin America while reaching an understanding with industrial customers in two countries that would guard against the possible resale of its product. Other manufacturers reportedly had switched to water-based glues for their Latin American sales.

This case illustrates some of the ethical issues raised by harm resulting from product abuse rather than use. Fuller did not intentionally or directly harm street children, but once aware of harm resulting from abuse of its product, the firm's potential capability to help protect the children arguably left it responsible for some action to minimize or prevent the harm. When local governments failed to take effective action, what additional steps, if any, should Fuller have taken, and why? Among the actions considered or taken, decide which constitute an ethically required minimum response and what steps could be considered discretionary maximal ethical actions.

INTERNATIONAL TRADE IN HAZARDOUS WASTE

Developed and industrializing countries generate growing amounts of industrial and municipal waste, much of which can be toxic, persistent or otherwise difficult to manage. As these same nations adopt stricter domestic safety and environmental standards to regulate waste disposal, the society confronts a challenging and increasingly costly not-in-my-back-yard (NIMBY) dilemma. Technological advances in waste treatment and improved recycling programs address some of the problem, but waste can also become a commodity that shifts geographically between countries according to least-cost principles. At that point, the global community confronts ethical questions regarding whether market mechanisms or other value principles should govern international trade in hazardous waste.

One type of problem arises when the economics of waste disposal lead to illegal dumping from developed countries into developing countries or transitional economies where regulatory enforcement is less effective. This issue surfaced when the formerly closed economies of Eastern Europe opened their doors to trade with Western Europe, generating stories about the tons of distasteful garbage hidden among the truck traffic that flowed primarily from West to East. In 1992 Poland alone intercepted over 1,300 improper shipments of waste from Western Europe while many more loads certainly went undetected. Included among the illegal waste were items such as "hazardous smelting dust, sludge, rubble, bloody hospital syringes, amputated limbs, expired chemicals and paints."[15]

Boys in Ghana search among dumped computers and TVs for any parts that can still be salvaged. Burning plastic insulation off computer wiring produces toxic smoke but frees copper strands that may be sold for scrap. Most electronic waste comes from developed countries and is shipped, often illegally, for cheaper disposal in developing countries where "recycling" methods create hazards to both human health and the environment. Photo by Peter Essick, Aurora Photos.

More currently, recyclers in developed nations use middlemen to ship old computers to developing countries where high-technology wastes create serious problems. Heavy metals in old computers make recycling costly and dangerous for individual health and the environment. Estimates suggest that 70 percent of computers collected by recyclers get shipped to Asia, where disposal amounts to one-tenth the cost in the United States. Reports describe an unregulated process where children and unemployed persons essentially scavenge the dumped computers for reusable scrap, suffering injuries and causing land and water pollution from lead, mercury and other agents that lead to higher birth defects, blood diseases and serious respiratory problems in surrounding communities. Although China strengthened its ban on such imports in 2003, payments to customs officials in smaller ports reportedly help evade the controls.[16]

Increased enforcement in one country may simply shift the hazards to other poor and less regulated countries. Exhibit 6.2 vividly describes the "recycling" activities, often carried out by young children, at a computer dump heap in Ghana. Burning toxic insulation off computer wires to recover resalable copper can provide meager short-term income at a longer-term cost. Who is most responsible for the health and environmental consequences? Consider the scavengers at the dump, the importer and

Exhibit 6.2 Scavenging Dumped Computers in Ghana

High Tech Trash

Will your discarded TV end up in a ditch in Ghana?

By CHRIS CARROLL
National Geographic Staff

June is the wet season in Ghana, but here in Accra, the capital, the morning rain has ceased. As the sun heats the humid air, pillars of black smoke begin to rise above the vast Agbogbloshie Market. I follow one plume toward its source, past lettuce and plantain vendors, past stalls of used tires, and through a clanging scrap market where hunched men bash on old alternators and engine blocks. Soon the muddy track is flanked by piles of old TVs, gutted computer cases, and smashed monitors heaped ten feet (three meters) high. Beyond lies a field of fine ash speckled with glints of amber and green—the sharp broken bits of circuit boards. I can see now that the smoke issues not from one fire, but from many small blazes. Dozens of indistinct figures move among the acrid haze, some stirring flames with sticks, others carrying armfuls of brightly colored computer wire. Most are children.

Choking, I pull my shirt over my nose and approach a boy of about 15, his thin frame wreathed in smoke. Karim says he has been tending such fires for two years. He pokes at one meditatively, and then his top half disappears as he bends into the billowing soot. He hoists a tangle of copper wire off the old tire he's using for fuel and douses the hissing mass in a puddle. With the flame retardant insulation burned away—a process that has released a bouquet of carcinogens and other toxics—the wire may fetch a dollar from a scrap-metal buyer.

Another day in the market, on a similar ash heap above an inlet that flushes to the Atlantic after a downpour, Israel Mensah, an incongruously stylish young man of about 20, adjusts his designer glasses and explains how he makes his living. Each day scrap sellers bring loads of old electronics—from where he doesn't know. Mensah and his partners—friends and family, including two shoeless boys raptly listening to us talk—buy a few computers or TVs. They break copper yokes off picture tubes, littering the ground with shards containing lead, a neurotoxin, and cadmium, a carcinogen that damages lungs and kidneys. They strip resalable parts such as drives and memory chips. Then they rip out wiring and burn the plastic. He sells copper stripped from one scrap load to buy another. The key to making money is speed, not safety. "The gas goes to your nose and you feel something in your head," Mensah says, knocking his fist against the back of his skull for effect. "Then you get sick in your head and your chest." Nearby, hulls of broken monitors float in the lagoon. Tomorrow the rain will wash them into the ocean.

People have always been proficient at making trash. Future archaeologists will note that at the tail end of the 20th century, a new, noxious kind of clutter exploded across the landscape: the digital detritus that has come to be called e-waste. . . .

"We in the developed world get the benefit from these devices," says Jim Puckett, head of Basel Action Network, or BAN, a group that opposes hazardous waste shipments to developing nations. "But when our equipment becomes unusable, we externalize the real environmental costs and liabilities to the developing world."

Asia is the center of much of the world's high-tech manufacturing, and it is here the devices often return when they die. China in particular has long been the world's electronics graveyard. With explosive growth in its manufacturing sector fueling demand, China's ports have become conduits for recyclable scrap of every sort: steel, aluminum, plastic, even paper. By the mid-1980s, electronic waste began freely pouring into China as well, carrying the lucrative promise of the precious metals embedded in circuit boards.

Vandell Norwood, owner of Corona Visions, a recycling company in San Antonio, Texas, remembers when foreign scrap brokers began trolling for electronics to ship to China. Today he opposes the practice, but then it struck him and many other recyclers as a win-win situation. "They said this stuff was all going to get recycled and put back into use," Norwood remembers brokers assuring him. "It seemed environmentally responsible. And it was profitable, because I was getting paid to have it taken off my hands." Huge volumes of scrap electronics were shipped out, and the profits rolled in.

Any illusion of responsibility was shattered in 2002, the year Puckett's group, BAN, released a documentary film that showed the reality of e-waste recycling in China. *Exporting Harm* focused on the town of Guiyu in Guangdong Province, adjacent to Hong Kong. Guiyu had become the dumping ground for massive quantities of electronic junk. BAN documented thousands of people—entire families, from young to old—engaged in dangerous practices like burning computer wire to expose copper, melting circuit boards in pots to extract lead and other metals, or dousing the boards in powerful acid to remove gold.

China had specifically prohibited the import of electronic waste in 2000, but that had not stopped the trade. After the worldwide publicity BAN's film generated, however, the government lengthened the list of forbidden e-wastes and began pushing local governments to enforce the ban in earnest. . . .

China may someday succeed in curtailing electronic waste imports. But e-waste flows like water. Shipments that a few years ago might have gone to ports in Guangdong or Zhejiang Provinces can easily be diverted to friendlier environs in Thailand, Pakistan, or elsewhere. "It doesn't help in a global sense for one place like China, or India, to become restrictive," says David N. Pellow, an ethnic studies professor at the University of California, San Diego, who studies electronic waste from a social justice perspective. "The flow simply shifts as it takes the path of least resistance to the bottom."

It is next to impossible to gauge how much e-waste is still being smuggled into China, diverted to other parts of Asia, or—increasingly—dumped in West African countries like Ghana, Nigeria, and Ivory Coast. At ground level, however, one can pick out single threads from this global toxic tapestry and follow them back to their source.

In Accra, Mike Anane, a local environmental journalist, takes me down to the seaport. Guards block us at the gate. But some truck drivers at a nearby gas station point us toward a shipment facility just up the street, where they say computers are often unloaded.

There, in a storage yard, locals are opening a shipping container from Germany. Shoes, clothes, and handbags pour out onto the tarmac. Among the clutter: some battered Pentium 2 and 3 computers and monitors with cracked cases and missing knobs, all sitting in the rain. A man hears us asking questions. "You want computers?" he asks. "How many containers?" . . .

Ultimately, shipping e-waste overseas may be no bargain even for the developed world. In 2006, Jeffrey Weidenhamer, a chemist at Ashland University in Ohio, bought some cheap, Chinese-made jewelry at a local dollar store for his class to analyze. That the jewelry contained high amounts of lead was distressing, but hardly a surprise; Chinese-made leaded jewelry is all too commonly marketed in the U.S. More revealing were the amounts of copper and tin alloyed with the lead. As Weidenhamer and his colleague Michael Clement argued in a scientific paper published this past July, the proportions of these metals in some samples suggest their source was leaded solder used in the manufacture of electronic circuit boards.

"The U.S. right now is shipping large quantities of leaded materials to China, and China is the world's major manufacturing center," Weidenhamer says. "It's not all that surprising things are coming full circle and now we're getting contaminated products back." In a global economy, out of sight will not stay out of mind for long.

Source: Chris Carroll/National Geographic Stock. *National Geographic*, January 2008, pp. 64–80. Reprinted with permission.

exporter of the old computers, the importing and exporting governments, the computer manufacturer, and the computer user who discarded the equipment. Who should take what actions; why? Perhaps the contaminants finding their way back into the United States in jewelry imports are the beginning of a newer "high tech" version of the "circle of poison" described earlier for international trade in dangerous pesticides.

Moving beyond the struggle to prevent illegal waste imports, the central ethical questions really concern who should determine whether trade in hazardous waste is right or wrong, legal or illegal, and which value principles should govern such decisions. For example, consider an inverse case. If the prevailing governments in Poland or China (or Moldova, Congo, Burma or North Korea) do not prohibit imports of hazardous waste, can any waste products be ethically shipped to those countries? Ethical analysis might suggest the need to assess issues such as the country's capacity for managing safe disposal and the potential impact (cost and benefit distribution) on the local population. Ineffective, unrepresentative or corrupt governments can make sole reliance on a country's official import regulations ethically problematic. In such cases, responsibilities might fall on alternative actors, including MNEs, exporting governments and international organizations.

As repulsive as it might sound, strictly market-driven economic calculations could conclude that the comparative international trade advantage for some poor developing countries lies in their use as a disposal site for the hazardous waste generated in richer, more advanced economies. Establishing some international floor for safe management and disposal practices requires an appeal to minimum human value principles that incorporate more than economic factors in such cost/benefit assessments. Again, the central issue becomes deciding which actor(s) should determine the value standards, and why. Until recently the traditional answer came from international agreements that favored free and open trade flows. Exceptions required initiatives by the importing country to specifically determine that a particular commodity's cost/benefit outcome for the nation was unfavorable enough to warrant imposing official import restrictions. Most developing countries lacked the information as well as the financial and technical resources to initiate, evaluate and administer such individual import assessments.

Rather than beginning with an importing government's responsibility for conducting teleological cost/benefit calculations, some commentators suggest a contrasting deontological standard that places primary ethical responsibility on supply-side actors, such as waste-generating companies and exporting countries.[17] One argument for this approach draws on capability factors, citing the superior knowledge and technical capabilities possessed by the companies who created products generating the waste and developed country governments experienced in formulating and administering trade regulations. If greater capabilities bring corresponding responsibilities, these private and public suppliers of hazardous waste exports should at least take steps to minimize potential harms resulting from such trade.

Another contention asserts an unfair imbalance in how different types of costs, as well as cost/benefit outcomes, are distributed among the affected parties. Waste-generating companies and countries typically enjoy the main standard-of-living benefits from produced goods while bearing the financial costs of exporting hazardous waste by-products. Developing countries gain financial benefits for receiving the waste products, with the financial gain typically distributed among already powerful elites, while non-financial health and environmental costs fall primarily on disenfranchised populations in the importing country's poorest regions. Distributive justice principles might argue that waste-generating producers should accept responsibility for disposing of hazardous waste products within their own country, which enjoys the product's principal benefits, possesses technical knowledge important to safe disposal and, subject to local political governance, can be held more effectively accountable for public costs or risks that may result from waste disposal procedures.

THE MOVEMENT TOWARD GLOBAL STANDARDS

The international community made significant if incomplete progress over the 1990s in negotiating common standards and procedures covering many export and trade control issues presented in this chapter. The main initial standard relies on PIC (prior informed consent) procedures that invest exporting companies and countries with responsibility to inform international organizations and foreign governments regarding certain export product risks, but importing governments still carry the central decision-making role. To a lesser degree, some international agreements have also begun to develop an agreed list of especially dangerous products that should be banned from international commerce and eventually eliminated entirely. A review of these steps toward a global common morality position on export and trade controls involving hazardous products can help update and elaborate some of the previous case discussion.

The stories of pesticide poisonings sparked initial movement in the 1980s, in particular with a voluntary code of conduct and information exchange system adopted through the UN Food and Agriculture Organization (FAO). Under the 1985 FAO International Code of Conduct on the Distribution and Use of Pesticides, any pesticide banned or severely restricted in a country should not be exported without the agreement of the importing country. Following experience with this voluntary mechanism, the international community adopted a convention in 1998 to make the PIC procedures mandatory and enhance information dissemination. Participating countries initially agreed to cover over two dozen hazardous products, with the intention to expand this list in the future. The PIC procedure may also be applied to pesticides that could be hazardous when used under prevailing conditions in developing countries, even if the product is not severely restricted in its country of origin. By 2004, enough countries had ratified this convention on the Prior Informed Consent Procedure for Certain Hazardous Chemicals and Pesticides in International Trade (Rotterdam Convention on PIC) to give it legal force, covering over 125 parties by 2009.

Another international agreement, the Stockholm Convention on Persistent Organic Pollutants (POPs), targets highly toxic, persistent chemicals whose movement can impact areas thousands of miles from the point of use. The Stockholm Convention initially identified a "dirty dozen" products covering eight pesticides, two industrial solvents and two chemicals, including PCBs (polychlorinated biphenyls), dioxins and other products linked to birth defects and cancers. While containing some notification requirements and trade restrictions, this accord actually seeks to restrict production and use, moving toward eventual elimination of the products. Adopted in

May 2001, the Stockholm Convention quickly acquired over 150 signatory countries and received enough subsequent ratifications to enter into legal force on 17 May 2004.

Trade in hazardous waste was restricted under the Basel Convention on the Control of Transboundary Movements of Hazardous Wastes and their Disposal, adopted in 1989 and entered into legal force in May 1992. This agreement aims to halt hazardous waste exports from developed to developing countries and economies in transition. The Basel Convention's original PIC procedure was strengthened to prohibit most hazardous waste exports from developed OECD members to non-OECD countries. The challenges of effectively enforcing the tougher ban are reflected in Exhibit 6.2. Additional attention focuses on principles that seek to minimize waste generation and locate waste disposal as close as possible to where it was generated.

Reviewing these international agreements on export and trade control issues, a proponent of global common morality principles might feel cautiously optimistic. The activity reflects an international community with an expanding recognition of shared responsibilities and an incipient willingness to move beyond reliance on unilateral national political action or inaction. Still, these achievements by no means mark a solution to the problems. Even after agreements have secured sufficient ratifications to enter into force, the conventions are binding only on participating nations. The documents reflect the present status of agreed value principles and procedures for common global action on these issues, similar to many ILO conventions on labor rights, but coverage is not universal and enforcement is not automatic.

Even for countries covered by the conventions, effective implementation remains a challenge. For example, while the Rotterdam PIC Convention covered 26 pesticides and 5 industrial chemicals in 2002, over 77,000 different chemicals were being marketed worldwide, with 1,500 new ones introduced each year.[18] Wide areas remain where corporations and other actors still face ethical judgments regarding which value principles will guide potential export and sale decisions for unlisted but potentially hazardous products.

The Stockholm Convention may most clearly reflect new progress in the challenge of developing global common morality principles. In final discussions on the accord's content, negotiators from 122 countries reached agreement on two points that addressed particularly difficult and complex ethical dilemmas. One issue stemmed from the control of DDT, a pesticide banned in the United States since 1972, whose continued export was already subject to PIC guidelines under the Rotterdam Convention. Although this product's persistent toxicity slates it for eventual elimination, special provisions permitted continued DDT use in developing countries for public health reasons.

When countries such as Sri Lanka and South Africa had previously banned DDT use, malaria infections skyrocketed. Continued spraying for mosquito control appeared essential in many regions, such as sub-Saharan Africa, where malaria kills one in every twenty children. A South African official reportedly acknowledged the pesticide's long-term health threat, saying: "it will kill us—but it will take twenty, thirty years. Malaria will kill you tomorrow."[19] With malaria annually killing about one million people, most African children under age five, the WHO reversed its policy in 2006 to support DDT use in regions where malaria was a major health problem.[20] This example shows one rationale for using the PIC procedure rather than a global ban, based on teleological cost/benefit calculations that consider the timing, distribution and severity of potential harms resulting from DDT use versus its prohibition. Limited use of DDT is therefore permitted until safe, affordable and effective alternatives become available.

The reference to affordable alternatives indicates another issue where the Stockholm negotiations employed an international principle with potentially important implications for future global accords. Developed nations agreed to help poor countries meet expenses to implement the convention and switch to alternative product. In taking this step the developed nations accepted additional responsibilities reflecting their greater financial capabilities, helping offset the disproportionate adjustment costs (measured relative to ability to pay) that developing countries face in switching to alternative products and establishing effective enforcement mechanisms. Developing countries received $360million to support implementation of the Stockholm Convention but estimated needs in 2010–2014 could exceed $5billion, especially after nine more chemicals were added to the "dirty dozen" in May 2009.[21] Financial transfers to poorer nations to meet globally agreed standards represent a core issue for many international negotiations, particularly in the environmental area that will be covered more fully in Chapter 9.

A TRIPLE DILEMMA FOR PHARMACEUTICALS

Pharmaceutical products present a triple dilemma of ethical choices relating to exports and trade control issues that covers foreign drug testing, export sales and intellectual property protection. These elements represent different components of the pharmaceutical industry's involvement in global commerce, but all three relate to international trade policies that reflect value decisions made by corporations, governments and other societal actors. Ethical issues regarding trade in pharmaceuticals merit particular attention because of the products' central relationship to human health. Trade decisions affecting the international availability and use of life-enhancing or life-saving drugs address values of vital importance that provide stark tests of when to employ deontological principles, such as individual human rights, or teleological approaches weighing case-specific cost/benefit calculations.

The international issues surrounding drug testing relate to potential new pharmaceutical products exported from research-based laboratories in developed countries for use in clinical trials in developing countries. This practice increased after 1980, when the FDA began accepting results from foreign research trials to support applications to approve new drugs for sale in the United States. Drug tests conducted in developing countries offer many advantages, including large numbers of people with a high incidence of untreated diseases who are willing to join drug trials as a means to obtain medical care. Clinical trials abroad also offer lower costs, quicker results and often reduced regulatory controls.

A major six-part investigative series published by *The Washington Post* in December 2000 documented the growth in overseas drug tests and offered illustrations for their rationale.[22] By 1999 over one-quarter of new FDA drug applications contained results from foreign tests, triple the figure recorded in 1995. The number of foreign researchers registered with the FDA to conduct tests on drugs for US approval leaped after 1991 in most developing country regions, rising from 5 to 453 in South America; 1 to 429 in Eastern Europe and 2 to 266 in southern Africa. The director of a firm that locates sites for drug tests reported over 1,000 tests under way in Latin America, predicting a tenfold increase in that number by 2005.

The cost advantages were evident. Tests for drugs to be sold in the United States require an average of 4,000 people. Contrasting expenses showed one complex test cost $10,000 per patient at a site in Western Europe versus $3,000 per patient in Russia. Pharmaceutical companies often pay doctors to recruit participants for the studies. A Hungarian psychiatrist reported earning a normal salary of $178 a month but receiving $1,000 to $2,000 for every patient he recruits for drug tests. These types of incentives can induce misbehavior and undermine the presumptive standard of patient participation on the basis of informed consent (a concept difficult to measure or enforce in conditions such as mental hospitals or countries with strong authoritarian traditions). The threat of potential abuse in patient recruitment and testing emerges from lower foreign regulatory controls. For example, Hungary relied on one full-time inspector who annually visited only about 30 of some 200 test locations in the country. Even if abuses were found, the inspector lacked the power to fine or bar researchers from the tests. Still, an environment conducive to speed in finding patients and completing testing attracts pharmaceutical companies, which reportedly can lose $1.3million in unrealized US sales for each day a major drug is delayed in reaching the market.

The principal ethical issue in this chapter's examination of foreign drug testing relates to whether test standards required in a drug maker's home country and/or principal target market should accompany any export of the drugs being tested. Comparative cost factors or disease prevalence could still favor testing in foreign locations, but important questions have arisen regarding differences in the treatment of test patients. The essential value question asks whether there should be a minimum ethical floor governing patient treatment and, if so, what standard should be used. To facilitate ethical analysis, this discussion will focus primarily on the level of medical treatment given test participants and the calculation and distribution of costs and benefits arising from the drug tests.

Exhibit 6.3 discusses two cases in Thailand where tests on AIDS-related drugs employed patient treatment standards different from methods required in the United States and most other developed nations. The cases involve a higher use of placebos and, in one test, a decision to use placebos rather than a proven drug as a comparative test standard. Higher placebo use means fewer test participants benefit from improved health if the drug proves effective; the choice to use a placebo over a proven drug more certainly biases the outcome against placebo recipients and, in this reported case scenario, likely resulted in a number of preventable HIV-positive births.

As the article reports, an international voluntary statement of principles on drug experiments has existed since 1964. Sparked by outrage over reports of tests such as the ones in Thailand, the World Medical Association adopted revisions to the statement in what resembles an evolving common morality standard within the

Exhibit 6.3 Drug Tests and Infected Babies in Thailand

Life by Luck of the Draw

In Third World Drug Tests, Some Subjects Go Untreated

By MARY PAT FLAHERTY *and* DOUG STRUCK
Washington Post Staff Writers

. . . At a spartan drug clinic in the heart of Bangkok, heroin addicts lined up on a recent morning to receive an experimental HIV vaccine produced by an American company. Drawn by small payments and offers of free rice, they signed on for a test in which they had a greater chance of receiving a placebo—or dummy shot—than would Americans taking part in the same research in the United States.

In Bangkok's two largest maternity wards, pregnant women infected with HIV, the virus that causes AIDS, enrolled in an American test aimed at reducing AIDS transmission from mothers to children. But half the Thai women were given placebos instead of a proven drug, and thirty-seven babies who might have been spared were born HIV-positive.

Set against a staggering AIDS epidemic, the Thai cases highlight the unequal bargains underlying the recent boom in overseas drug testing by both private and public medical researchers: rich countries have the drugs and hypotheses, while poor countries have vast numbers of patients. Yet the trade-offs made in experiments do not always distribute burdens and benefits evenly.

Medical progress has always depended on some individuals bearing personal risk for society's benefit. Placebos give researchers a clearer view of which experimental therapies work and which do not, many scientists contend. Passive studies that track how a disease moves unimpeded through a population can provide insights into treatment and prevention.

But those long-standing research methods have become more complicated and controversial as scientists from wealthy nations increasingly work amid poverty in developing countries. Such tests have spurred angry debate on review boards of American universities, in the halls of African and Asian health ministries and in chambers of the World Health Organization.

Among the questions: When Western researchers travel to impoverished countries to set up drug experiments, which country's ethical guidelines should apply? While working with poor test subjects, must researchers provide the best treatment available in wealthy countries? Or are they free merely to provide the best local care available—which in some medically deprived settings may mean some test subjects get no treatment at all?

With 800,000 adults of its 61 million residents carrying the virus, Thailand's vast HIV-infected population has spent the last five years on these ethical and scientific frontiers. Open, increasingly democratic and cooperative with the West, Thailand discovered a scourge of AIDS in its midst a decade ago and turned emphatically to its wealthy allies for help.

In 1991, the WHO designated Thailand as a country ripe to test AIDS vaccines, sowing the seeds of research still underway. In 1994, WHO issued a second challenge, encouraging researchers to help developing countries find an affordable, practical alternative to the costly Western method of reducing the transmission of HIV from pregnant women to their infants.

After each appeal, researchers armed with new drugs and theories fanned out through the country. Testing new treatments against placebos, as many did, generated fast answers. But for the men, women and children recruited into such tests, the approach meant the luck of the draw determined who received care and who wound up with nothing.

Many in Thailand tried to "look at the bright side and accept that when you are a poor people you may have the choice between getting some treatment and care in a study or having none," said Vichai Chokevivat, until recently the vice chairman of Thailand's central ethics committee for human research.

Yet others in Thailand chafe at a system that allows Western researchers to present foreign test subjects with choices that provide less care and protection than those same researchers would be obliged to give subjects back in their own countries.

"It seems like every time this is the way things happen in Thailand," said Ratchanee Tunraka, a social worker with Siam Care in Bangkok, a charity that works with needy families, including some who participated in American research projects.

Why, she wondered aloud, are the studies brought to her country set up "to give someone nothing before we all can get a little something?" . . .

Ethical firestorm. The "race to the bottom" is how some medical ethicists have described drug researchers' moves into developing countries. But public health researchers, including some from developing countries, denounce as "ethical imperialism" the notion that Western standards of care always must prevail.

"The easy thing to accuse [international drug testing] of is Yankee exploitation, of taking advantage of disadvantaged populations," said Robert H. Rubin, professor of health sciences and technology at Harvard Medical School and a clinical trial pioneer in the United States. "Frankly, that's nonsense."

"It has to be done right, and appropriately, [but] if you believe as fervently as I do that there is benefit to society . . . then all society should bear some of the burdens" of developing new drugs.

The opposing viewpoints clashed sharply this fall as the World Medical Association met to revise the 1964 Declaration of Helsinki, the statement of principles that has guided ethical decisions in drug experiments around the world. With representatives from forty-five countries, including developing nations that have become hotbeds for drug research, the conference voted to clarify language on the use of placebos, making it unethical to use dummy medicines on some subjects in trials where proven treatments may be available. The declaration does not have the force of law in the United States, but it wields considerable moral clout.

Outrage over American experiments on pregnant women in Thailand and sub-Saharan Africa was a driving force behind the change.

Public and private researchers in the United States are still unsure how they can comply with the strong international mandate while trying to tackle the treatment and prevention of life-threatening disease. The National Bioethics Advisory Commission, a presidentially appointed panel that is drafting ethical guidelines, has struggled with both the placebo issue and questions about what researchers owe local populations once an experiment is completed.

"Clearly, this is an evolving issue," said Helene Gayle, director of the Centers for Disease Control and Prevention's National Center for HIV, STD and TB programs. "Through research, we cannot change the reality that there are inequities and there is poverty in the world. We should, as citizens of the world, attack that reality, but not through constraining research."

But ultimately, the West's anguished ethical debates occur far from the ordinary, struggling families swept along in the global drug testing boom. . . .

global medical community. However, the revised standard appears to respond only to certain cases using placebos rather than proven drugs and remains voluntary in its application. Some researchers may still favor placebo use to obtain clearer, more efficient test results. Health costs falling on some individual participants might be justified by achieving faster effective tests results that could speed drug approval for use by many more patients (as well as better financial returns to the company).

Such an argument for continued placebo use apparently was involved in an

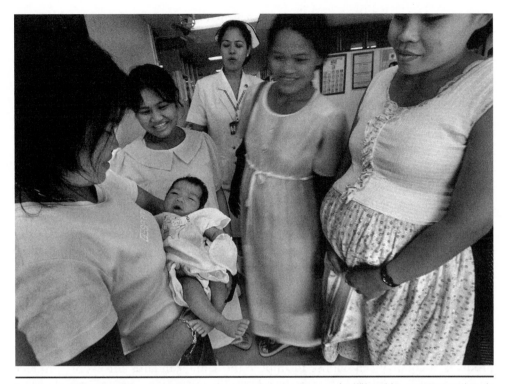

A mother presents her newborn baby to other members of a support group for HIV-positive expectant mothers in Bangkok, Thailand. HIV-positive babies were born to mothers given placebos rather than existing medicine during a drug trial aimed at reducing mother-to-child AIDS transmission. Photo by Lois Raimondo/*The Washington Post*/ Getty Images.

application by a US laboratory for FDA recognition of planned drug tests in Latin America that would deviate from US standards, and from planned methods for tests in Europe. In Latin America the company reportedly proposed using placebos in tests involving infants with a serious lung disease for which proven treatments were already available, asserting benefits from tests that could bring a more effective drug to market a year and a half sooner. The firm's president is quoted as saying it would be unethical not to conclude the tests as quickly as possible. In addressing potential health costs to infants on placebos, the company argued that the test infants would not normally have access to currently available drugs and medical treatment anyway.[23]

The tests would not technically violate a "do no harm" principle, because even infants receiving placebos would be no worse off than if they did not participate in the test. In fact, the tests might meet a "help protect" standard by improving health care for test participants, even those getting placebos, because all test participants would benefit from ventilators and antibiotics not available without the test. A more active "provide assistance" standard could be achieved, for large numbers of people, if the test drug proved successful. Of course, the likelihood of a successful test result varies with each case and projected outcomes are subject to strong uncertainty factors.

This example extends the cost/benefit calculation issue further by also raising distributional questions regarding who would benefit from a more effective new drug. If potential test participants in Latin America normally cannot afford four existing drugs for the lung disease, then the countries whose citizens would bear the test's principal health costs would also likely be excluded from enjoying the possible health benefits if the tests are successful. In response to such criticism, the company suggested the final drug could be made available at a reduced price for citizens of those countries in which the tests took place. For government officials oriented to utilitarian cost/benefit calculations, such an outcome might promise benefits for enough of the population to justify the likely health costs to a few test participants. For a deontologist, uncertain benefits for the many would not justify the violation of individual rights represented by using even a few infants as placebo patients. The choice of alternative value approaches might thus yield quite different results in terms of public policy decisions to permit the importation and use of drugs for the planned testing.[24]

These cases again raise questions regarding who should decide, as well as which decision standard should be used. The company initiates and shapes proposed tests.[25] Government agencies can regulate methods used in local tests and influence methodologies through market approval standards for test results. Because drugs used in international tests must pass through border controls, both exporting and importing governments can set standards for trade approval. As with potentially hazardous products, a country can choose to impose the same standards for export product sales and use as employed at home or rely on the importing government's decision making. The medical profession and other healthcare actors can also attempt to influence test standards through voluntary codes and public moral suasion.

A second ethical dilemma related to pharmaceutical products centers on their export for sale in foreign markets. These exports, perhaps ironically, pose many of the same ethical questions confronted in the case discussions on pesticides. Pharmaceuticals represent inherently beneficial but potentially hazardous products if used inappropriately. Therefore, ethical issues tend to revolve around whether export and trade controls should incorporate any standards regarding safe use of these products. Specifically, most debate involves whether to restrict exports of drugs not approved for use in the producing country and whether to impose safe-use labeling standards on exported drugs.[26]

The export restriction issue arises from different testing and approval procedures and standards in various countries. One decision relates to permitting exports of unapproved drugs for use in clinical tests abroad, as discussed above. A separate issue concerns whether to permit exports of unapproved drugs for general sales in other countries whose regulations do not restrict the product's use. In some cases the foreign government may affirmatively approve the drug for sale; in other countries the government may simply not prohibit its use or may just lack effective enforcement. The ethical question asks how far the pharmaceutical company and/or exporting government's responsibilities extend in trade situations where an importing government appears ineffective at independently regulating drug imports. One factor that could influence the level of responsibility might be whether the exporting country has officially approved the drug's use in its own market or, conversely, whether it severely restricts or bans its sale. Consider what other factors in the discussion of pesticide exports might also apply to an ethical evaluation of pharmaceutical exports.

The other major export sales issue, again reminiscent of the pesticide discussion, examines the extent of corporate and exporting government responsibilities to disseminate information important to safe use of pharmaceutical products. For pharmaceuticals, such information can include descriptions of indications (when a drug can be used beneficially) as well as contraindications (when a drug should not be used due to various risk factors). Without high standards of accuracy and truthfulness, drug sales could be increased by promoting uses (indications) for which there exists little or no proof of effectiveness. This outcome may result in wasted financial costs to the consumer. Inaccurate or omitted warnings (contraindications) could result in serious damage to the consumer's health.

If information relating to effective and safe drug use should be disseminated along with exported pharmaceuticals, then applied questions become: who should get what information, where, when and why? A PIC standard would focus on the importing government, transmitting information for that country's regulatory decision and action. A more active ethical notion could extend responsibility farther along the business chain to the actual consumer, requiring appropriate information labels affixed to pharmaceutical products at point of retail sale. As with pesticides, practical considerations will arise, such as printing labels in each local language and assessing whether consumers can effectively understand the instructions and warnings. (Anyone attempting to read many package inserts in US drugs may be sympathetic with the dilemma of deciding how much information to include and how to inform consumers with widely different educational backgrounds.) One approach could be to require drug sales through prescriptions from a medical professional, essentially transferring responsibility to those individuals for assuring patient understanding of effective and safe use instructions. However, the low level of medical care available in many developing countries, particularly in rural areas, realistically limits this approach.

The third ethical dilemma relating to pharmaceutical products involves the role of intellectual property rights (IPRs) in trade controls that effectively restricts the availability of useful medicines in many parts of the world. Populations in poor countries cannot afford the high prices of patented pharmaceuticals and IPR trade regulations restrict the sale of many alternative generic drugs. Although the debate over drugs used to fight HIV/AIDS reflects the most widely publicized example of this issue, similar considerations arise with pharmaceutical products used against other diseases such as malaria, tuberculosis, cancer and heart disease. Rather than policies to promote export sales, the ethical issues involve decisions where corporate pricing strategies effectively limit drug sales to high-income populations, utilizing trade controls to prevent sales of cheaper competing generics so that high-income consumers have restricted product choice while lower-income populations effectively have none.

A focal point for the AIDS dilemma reportedly emerged at a 1991 meeting in Geneva when World Health Organization (WHO) officials met with top executives from 18 pharmaceutical MNEs.[27] The WHO Director General described the objective as assuring the development and production of AIDS-fighting drugs at costs all could afford. He predicted that by the end of the century 40 million people would be infected by the HIV virus, with over 90 percent of the victims residing in developing countries—projections that proved reasonably accurate. Already available new drugs had improved survival rates in some developed countries but their costs, reaching over $10,000 a year, placed them beyond the resources of victims in poor countries where per capita annual incomes can average $250. The WHO head challenged the pharmaceutical MNEs to employ more flexible international pricing systems, charging near production-cost levels in poor countries whose consumers could not afford patent-protected market prices.

Opposing views on this AIDS debate stalled effective action for most of the decade. Pharmaceutical MNEs contended that continued costly research into new medicines required high returns from profits on patented drugs. Offering lower prices in poorer countries could result in the cheaper drugs being re-exported to developed countries as well as a consumer backlash in markets where high prices were maintained. While recognizing the tragedy of untreated AIDS victims in developing countries, the firms urged increased public funding for international assistance programs to purchase and provide the needed drugs. Even if drug prices were lowered, companies asserted that other problems could prevent effective AIDS treatments, including the lack of medical personnel and facilities in developing countries needed to manage the administration and follow-up to drug treatments.

International trade aspects of this issue took center stage as a new agreement on Trade Related Aspects of Intellectual Property Rights (TRIPS) extended patent protections worldwide as part of the creation of the World Trade Organization (WTO) on 1 January 1995. Although developing countries could phase in compliance with its provisions, the TRIPS accord promised to restrict the production or import of cheaper generic alternatives to patented products, including some available AIDS-related medicines. Even as the international trade regime was changing on patented products, the United States threatened trade sanctions against countries such as Brazil and South Africa that permitted and even promoted generic drugs to address their populations' health crises. These publicized trade disputes increased debate about the ethical value choices reflected in such policies and actions. The seeming clash between value priorities was posed in 1998, when a World Health Assembly executive board meeting endorsed a position on drugs giving public health priority over commercial interests, and a UN paper on "Globalization and Access to Drugs" declared that drug patents conflicted with a human right to equal health care.[28]

Most pharmaceutical MNEs subsequently moved to drop prices on AIDS-related drugs in some developing country markets, although approaches varied by firm regarding how widely or narrowly to target their discount pricing schemes. International organizations also increased cooperative programs to promote AIDS prevention and treatment efforts in developing countries, backed by greater financial support from some developed countries. Still, the AIDS pandemic raged, causing over 8,000 deaths a day in 2000 as the increase in new infections spread from a concentration in sub-Saharan Africa to more populous areas including China and India.

The dispute over whether or how trade controls should restrict generic drug production and imports took center stage at WTO trade negotiations in Doha in November 2001. A global common morality consensus appeared to emerge around a policy that would permit developing countries to declare national health emergencies which could exempt them from TRIPS requirements for AIDS-related drugs. However, an obstacle arose when debate turned to implementation details, including how broadly this principle should apply to drugs that treat other serious health problems. This reformulated ethical dilemma dealt with exports and trade controls on patented pharmaceutical products. The proposed WTO policy exception for TRIPS enforcement aimed to respond to public health crises on AIDS and certain other serious infectious diseases. Disagreement arose over whether the exception should be broadened to cover other diseases that also threaten developing countries with healthcare epidemics. The ethical dilemma appeared to center around the concept of critical need, i.e. what level of potential harm justifies the use of a TRIPS exception.

The principle cited above in UN documents and World Health Assembly action suggests that health care is a human right that takes precedence over pharmaceutical patent rights. However, the UN Declaration on Human Rights also recognizes a right to private property, setting up a deontological clash of human rights principles. If health care should always take priority, without qualification, then intellectual property rights in the pharmaceutical field become ineffectual. On the other hand, if generational interests are considered, future health care may suffer if the loss of revenue from patent protection seriously impairs research by the pharmaceutical industry that has developed current drugs and continues the search for new medicines. The concept of critical need offers a potential compromise where the most serious healthcare crisis overrides normal IPR protections. The practical dilemma remains with defining and applying the concept.

For example, the US government took a position in late 2002, reportedly in line with pharmaceutical industry urgings, which would have limited the TRIPS exception policy to 20 infectious diseases such as HIV/AIDS, malaria, and tuberculosis. Twenty qualified exceptions appear significant and establish that the action springs from a value principle rather than isolated, unique circumstances surrounding AIDS. However, for many medical personnel in developing countries the list of covered diseases appeared frustratingly limited and perhaps somewhat arbitrary. If healthcare needs are defined by deaths, then heart disease kills more Africans than malaria, while cancers, digestive ailments and diabetes outrank some other more exotic but covered diseases such as hepatitis and schistosomiasis.[29] Of course, if the value principle standard relies on a deontological notion of individual human rights, rather than teleological or utilitarian outcomes meant to benefit the majority, then a poor African patient with diabetes may wonder why his or her life is valued less than a similarly poor African malaria victim, or a richer AIDS patient in the United States.

This third ethical dilemma involving pharmaceutical products offers a complex but interesting test of global value principles. Protection of intellectual property rights through patent restrictions represents a societal decision to deviate from the operation of market forces. The justification for granting a temporary monopoly to a company rests with a cost/benefit calculation that values continued research for new medicines over immediate financially accessible treatment for more individuals. When applied through international trade regulations, such policy decisions should reflect the value priorities of a global society. Who should decide what international policy actions to take, and why?

In one respect, this debate on the trade-offs involved with pharmaceutical intellectual property rights mirrors a broader healthcare dilemma that deals with distributive justice questions in a global community with supposedly limited resources. During the AIDS-related drug debate in 1997, the World Health Organization commissioned an illustrative chart to depict potential trade-offs on how $10,000 might be spent to save lives threatened by major world health problems. Using comparative drug costs at the time, the bar graph showed how $10,000 could help save 9,000 dehydrated children, hundreds of pneumonia and tuberculosis patients or a single AIDS victim.[30] What ethical principles should govern the allocation of available resources, or influence the level of resources made available, to address such healthcare needs? Priority might be given to saving the largest number of people, or special consideration could be given to saving children. Should the geographic location or national citizenship of victims also influence their claim on assistance funds?

Another instructive example of cost/benefit decision making also emerged during the debate on AIDS-related drugs. A World Bank executive developed a "disability-adjusted life year" measure to calculate productive years lost to illness or death. The concept can be used to estimate how various healthcare expenditures would affect national wealth.[31] For example, spending $1,000 annually to save the life of a person who earns $750 a year represents a net economic loss for the nation. Considering that one-half the world's population live on incomes under $2 per day, strictly economic calculations would not justify significant assistance for most individuals suffering from AIDS, malaria or other serious diseases. But then, exactly how should one measure the value of a single human life; and is one life, current or future, worth more than another?

In August 2003 negotiators reached a compromise agreement that did not restrict the diseases that could define a national health emergency but did suggest limits on which countries should invoke the TRIPS generic import exception. Very poor developing countries without domestic drug producers could import inexpensive generic medicines, while most high-income developed countries would "opt out" from invoking this provision. The issue then refocused on how middle-income countries should respond and whether generic drug exporters would aggressively exploit permitted exceptions to improve their market strength through expanded international sales. The negotiated compromise addressed these concerns by exhorting countries not to abuse the TRIPS exception, subject to general monitoring oversight. Generic drug exporters also should clearly differentiate their product from the original drug through shapes or labeling that discourage the re-export or diversion of generic medicines to developed country markets where patents still apply.[32]

These steps represent progress toward constructing a global policy to deal with the clash of deontological principles in this third ethical dilemma relating to pharmaceutical products. The agreement expands potential access to affordable medicines for desperately ill and impoverished populations while retaining a role for private property rights that promote future medical advancements. However, disagreements persist on whether a proper balance was struck and many other related issues will remain on the international agenda. Many patents on first-line AIDS drugs have lapsed, bringing large price reductions, but patients who live longer can develop resistance to initial medicines, requiring newer second- and third-tier drugs still under patent protection that can be 10 times as expensive. Although the rate of infection has slowed in some regions, UNAIDS estimates that just providing AIDS drugs to 80 percent of people needing the medicines by 2015 will cost nearly $20 billion a year, with related health services more than doubling the cost.[33]

Placed within a broader context, the pharmaceutical patent issue also represents just one subset of the broader distributive justice question regarding how the world community deals with global health crises. Even as international organizations, national governments and private sector groups mobilize resources to confront the AIDS pandemic, individuals who suffer from other diseases may wonder why the global community judge their cases to be less ethically compelling of follow-up attention and response.

NOTES

1. W. Shaw, *Business Ethics*, 3rd edn, Belmont, CA: Wadsworth, 1999, pp. 33–6; and C. MacKerron, "Does 'Made in the USA' Mean 'Let the Foreign Buyer Beware'?" *National Journal*, 18 April 1981, pp. 649–51.

2. Shaw, *Business Ethics*, p.34.

3. T. Beauchamp and N. Bowie, *Ethical Theory and Business*, 5th edn, Upper Saddle River, NJ: Prentice Hall, 1997, pp. 655–6, and E. Whelan, "The Bitter Truth About a Sweetener Scare," *The Wall Street Journal*, 26 August 1999, p. A18.

4. This case discussion draws on information from R. Rose, "Breast Implants Still Being Sold Outside U.S.," *The Wall Street Journal*, 4 March 1992, p. B1; J. Byrne, "Informed Consent," *Business Week*, 2 October 1995, pp. 104–16; M. Kaufman, "Implants Settlement Reached," *The Washington Post*, 21 September 2002, p. A7; and M. Kaufman, "Silicone Implants Reconsidered," *The Washington Post*, 21 July 2003, p. A2.

5. Kaufman, "Silicone Implants Reconsidered."

6. The number of potential US consumers has grown substantially. While 32,000 women had breast enlargements in 1992, over 237,000 women underwent the procedure in 2002 (not counting 70,000 women who received implants after breast surgery). This number is expected to increase if silicone implants become available. See Kaufman, "Silicone Implants Reconsidered."

7. D. Brown and C. Lee, "FDA Ends Ban on Silicone Implants," *Washington Post*, 18 November 2006, p. 1.

8. Another irony in the Dow Corning case arises from the tragic personal circumstances relating to the director of Dow Corning's heralded business ethics program and his wife's personal experience with breast implant surgery. For a presentation of this story, see Byrne, "Informed Consent," *Business Week*, 2 October 1995, pp. 104–16.

9. Information for this section was drawn from material that includes: B. Meier, "As Food Imports Rise, Consumers Face Peril from Use of Pesticides," and Meier, "Farm Workers in Third World Face Major Health Threat from Pesticides," *The Wall Street Journal*, 26 March 1987, pp. 1 and 26; B. Lambrecht, "Misused Farm Chemicals Poisoning Poor Nations," *St Louis Post-Dispatch*, 24 October 1993, p. 1; "US Pesticide Exports and the Circle of Poison", hearing before the Subcommittee on Economic Policy, Trade and Environment, House Foreign Affairs Committee, 103rd Congress, 2nd Session, 26 January 1994; and D. Schemo, "US Pesticide Kills Foreign Fruit Pickers' Hopes," *The New York Times*, 6 December 1995, p. A12.

10. D. Weir and M. Schapiro, *Circle of Poison: Pesticides and People in a Hungry World*, San Francisco, CA: Food First/Institute for Food and Development Policy, 1981. See also the same authors' earlier article, "The Boomerang Crime," *Mother Jones*, vol. 4, no.6, November/December 1979.

11. For example, Meier, in "Farm Workers," reports that the Western skull-and-crossbones danger symbol was used as a trademark for a branded pesticide in Southeast Asia; using the color red to signal danger could be interpreted in China to signal happiness.

12. Meier, "Farm Workers."

13. B. Lambrecht, "Third World Solution to Life's Pain: Suicide by Pesticide," *St Louis Post-Dispatch*, 24 October 1993, p. A14.

14. Material on this case is drawn primarily from the following sources: N. Bowie and S. Lenway, "Case Study: H. B. Fuller in Honduras: Street Children and Substance Abuse," in T. Donaldson and P. Werhane, *Ethical Issues in Business: A Philosophical Approach*, 4th edn, Englewood Cliffs, NJ: Prentice Hall, 1993, pp. 24–38; D. Kurschner, "Product Liability: Is Resistol Too Sticky for H.B. Fuller to Handle?" *Business Ethics*, vol. 9, no. 4, July–August, 1995, pp. 20–1; and D. Henriques, "Black Mark for a 'Good Citizen'," *The New York Times*, 26 November 1995, p. F1; D. Henriques, "Suit Against Fuller Over Death of Guatemalan Youth Dismissed," *The New York Times*, 25 September 1996, p. D5; and "Glue Company H. B. Fuller Finally Succumbs to Outside Pressures and Withdraws Toxic Products from the Latin American Market," *Casa Alianza*, 19 January 2000, online, available <http://www.casa-alianza.org/EN/1mn/docs/20000119.00367.html> (accessed 11 July 2003).

15. S. Coll, "Free Market Intensifies Waste Problem," *The Washington Post*, 23 March 1994, p. A1.

16. P. Goodman, "China Serves as Dump Site for Computers," *The Washington Post*, 24 February 2004, p. 1.

17. For an excellent explanation of this view as applied to pesticides, see L. Paine, "Regulating the International Trade in Hazardous Pesticides: Closing the Accountability Gap," in Beauchamp and Bowie, *Ethical Theory and Business*, 4th edn, pp. 547–56.

18. F. Williams, "UN Calls for Export Ban on Asbestos and Three Pesticides," *Financial Times*, 22 February 2002, p. 7.

19. J. Jeter, "Global Ban on 12 Toxic Substances Approved," *The Washington Post*, 12 December 2000, p. A42.

20. D. Brown, "WHO Urges Use of DDT in Africa," *Washington Post*, 16 September 2006, p. A9.

21. Earth Negotiations Bulletin, 11 May 2009.

22. Most material in this section is drawn from the series on "The Body Hunters" from *The Washington Post*, including J. Stephens, "Where Profits and Lives Hang in Balance," 17 December 2000, p. A1; M. Flaherty, D. Nelson and J. Stephens, "Testing Tidal Wave Hits Overseas," 18 December 2000, p. A1; S. LaFraniere, M. Flaherty and J. Stephens, "The Dilemma: Submit or Suffer," 19 December 2000, p. A1; J. Pomfret and D. Nelson, "An Isolated Region's Genetic Mother Lode," 20 December 2000, p. A1; K. DeYoung and D. Nelson, "Latin America Is Ripe for Trials, and Fraud," 21 December 2000, p. A1; and M. Flaherty and D. Struck, "Life by Luck of the Draw," 22 December 2000, p. A1 (Exhibit 6.3).

23. M. Flaherty and J. Stephens, "Pa. Firm Asks FDA to Back Experiment Forbidden in US," *The Washington Post*, 23 February 2001, p. A3.

24. In this case, the company reportedly dropped the use of placebos in April 2001 after talks with the FDA. See J. George, "Drug Firm Nixes Plan to Use Placebos," *Philadelphia Business Journal*, 2 April 2001, online, available <http://www.bizjournals.com/philadelphia/stories/2001/04/02/story1.html> (accessed 6 August 2003).

25. Companies may use contract research organizations (CROs) to conduct drug research trials, raising issues (similar to those addressed in Chapter 5 on overseas production processes) regarding how business structures and contractual relations may affect the allocation of ethical responsibilities. Low costs and the abundance of potential clinical trial patients draw many CROs to India, another country where the ethical standards for drug testing are being debated. See R. Marcelo, "India Beckons as a Testbed for Western Drug Companies," *Financial Times*, 14 October 2003, p. 20; and J. Slater, "India Emerges as New Drug Proving Ground," *The Wall Street Journal*, 19 February 2004, p. B1.

26. For more information and discussion on these and related pharmaceutical issues, see Office of Technology Assessment, US Congress, *Drug Labeling in Developing Countries*, Washington, DC: US Government Printing Office, February 1993; L. Tavis and O. Williams, *The Pharmaceutical Corporate Presence in Developing Countries*, Notre Dame, IN: University of Notre Dame Press, 1993; and G. Gereffi, "The Global Pharmaceutical Industry and its Impact in Latin America," in R. Newfarmer (ed.), *Profits, Progress and Poverty*, Notre Dame, IN: University of Notre Dame Press, 1985, pp. 259–97.

27. Material for this section is drawn primarily from the following sources: "Death Watch: AIDS, Drugs and

Africa," a three-part series of articles in *The Washington Post*, including B. Gellman, "An Unequal Calculus of Life and Death," 27 December 2000, p. A1, and "A Turning Point that Left Millions Behind," 28 December 2000, p. A1; and B. Brubaker, "The Limits of $100 Million," 29 December 2000, p. A1; K. Vick, "African AIDS Victims Losers of a Drug War," *The Washington Post*, 4 December 1999, p. A1; D. Pilling, "Patently Overpriced," *Financial Times*, 31 July 2000, p. 18; S. Buckley, "US, Brazil Clash Over AIDS Drugs," *The Washington Post*, 6 February 2001, p. A1; "A War Over Drugs and Patents," *The Economist*, 10 March 2001, pp. 43–4; D. Pilling and N. Innocenti, "A Crick in the Resolve of an Industry," *Financial Times*, 19 April 2001, p. 15; A. Faiola, "Brazil to Ignore Patent on AIDS Drug," *The Washington Post*, 23 August 2001, p. A20; V. Marsh, "Cheap Drugs Deal for Poor Boosts Trade Talks," *Financial Times*, 16–17 November 2002, p. 2; G. Dyer, E. Luce and J. Kynge, "China and India are on the Edge of an Aids Epidemic," *Financial Times*, 27 November 2002, p. 12; and G. Dyer, "How Do You Price Aids Treatment?" *Financial Times*, 26 March 2003, p. 10.

28. Gelman, "An Unequal Calculus."
29. R. Thurow and S. Miller, "As US Balks on Medicine Deal, African Patients Feel the Pain," *The Wall Street Journal*, 2 June 2003, p. 1
30. Gelman, "An Unequal Calculus."
31. Ibid.
32. G. Dyer, "A Drugs Deal for the World's Poorest: Now the Fight Over Patents and Cheap Medicine is in Middle-income Countries," *Financial Times*, 2 September 2003, p. 11.
33. D. Brown, "AIDS Funding Binds Longevity of Millions to U.S.," *Washington Post*, 26 July 2008, p. 1; UNAIDS 2008 Report on the Global AIDS Epidemic.

7

MARKETING MOTIVES AND METHODS

INTRODUCTION

Marketing shapes the relationship between sellers and buyers, generally companies and consumers, in a process that can be both cooperative and competitive. Market forces emphasize efficiency in resource allocation and maximize utility as measured by the satisfaction of consumer preferences. Market theory asserts that transactions entered into by willing sellers and buyers yield benefits as desired by both parties. A key ethical issue associated with marketing relates to free choice principles, particularly how business actions to promote the sale of products and services affect a buyer's decision to purchase and their resulting welfare gain or loss. Essentially, ethical analysis asks whether companies, or other stakeholders, bear any responsibility for adverse impacts resulting from a product's purchase or use, particularly where advertising or other promotional techniques influence the buyer's preference and behavior.

The last chapter's focus on exports and trade controls covered first-step marketing decisions to sell a product internationally, including some related safe-use issues. This chapter's discussion of marketing motives and methods relates to follow-up actions that determine the format and content of a company's communication with potential buyers regarding a product's characteristics, qualities and possible drawbacks. The producer/seller possesses information important to a potential buyer's purchasing decision. Advertising and other promotional techniques communicate product information to the consuming public. Case scenarios in this chapter explore when or whether corporate marketing should follow some set of normative standards, addressing values such as accuracy, truthfulness, fairness, completeness and safety.

The global marketplace introduces significant quantitative and qualitative differences into an assessment of marketing ethics. Not surprisingly, differences are most pronounced where MNEs employ techniques honed in advanced developed country markets to promote the same or similar products in developing countries. Governments and other potential actors in developing countries play a less prominent role in asserting consumer protection goals. Most importantly, populations in developing countries comprise generally less educated, less informed and more potentially vulnerable consumers compared to developed countries. The case scenarios will test whether differences in product, region or consumer characteristics should affect business marketing motives and methods.

The central framing question of this chapter is: Should corporations market/advertise in any way legally permissible (or should corporations follow voluntary ethical standards on marketing and advertising that must be met above and beyond legal requirements)?

CHOICES FOR MARKETING STANDARDS AND VALUES [1]

Marketing promotes the sale of goods and services. In exploring whether ethical norms should guide marketing motives and methods, one possible response would be to deny any ethical relevance and simply rely on the principle of *caveat emptor*, i.e. let the buyer beware. Under this approach, the seller can seek to maximize self-interest gains by using the most cost-efficient and profit-effective methods of increasing product sales. Governments or other potential actors would bear no subsidiarity responsibilities to intervene on behalf of potential consumers, who would be fully responsible for making purchasing decisions in their own self-interest. In economic market theory, such free interplay might result in maximum efficiency gains for all parties. In real-world practice, market failures occur when seller and buyer operate on very different levels of knowledge and competence, generating calls for compensating actions to promote more just, fair and even more economically efficient outcomes.

Most ethical controversies related to international marketing center on charges that corporate practices limit or distort the application of free choice principles. Other qualifying terms can be added to this general concept in order to provide more specific criteria to determine whether a particular consumer or groups of consumers are exercising free choice decisions in their purchases. These additional criteria include:

Rational free choice;
Informed free choice;
Understood free choice;
Free choice *with alternatives*; or perhaps
Rational, informed, understood free choice, *with alternatives*.

Ethical analysis can use case scenarios to explore such applications by examining the interrelated effects of three factors: the characteristics of a target audience, the marketing techniques employed, and the nature of the product involved. These factors help establish the value basis for ethical concerns, the impact of particular marketing practices and the level of critical need presented by a case.

Consider the extreme case of a mentally incompetent person purchasing a product. *Caveat emptor* assigns no necessary responsibility to the seller to be concerned about the buyer's welfare. A free choice standard likewise carries no seller responsibilities as long as the buyer is not coerced into the purchase. Under *rational* free choice, a seller should at least consider the nature of the product and, at an ethical minimum, refrain from promoting sales that are certain or highly likely to cause serious physical harm to a mentally incompetent buyer. A higher maximal ethical standard might encourage sellers to assess whether the buyer could actually realize some benefit from the purchase.

However, individuals can make irrational purchasing decisions without being mentally incompetent. Hence, adopting a rational free choice standard involves deciding whether to assess a potential buyer's general competence or the rationality of each sales transaction for each buyer. The seller's level of ethical responsibility also might vary depending on the nature of the product and its potential to cause harm to an irrational purchaser. Ethical imperatives to "do no harm" or "help protect" appear especially clear when dealing with irrational purchasing decisions that threaten immediate physical injury. When a seller and buyer employ more nebulous criteria for measuring costs and benefits, relating possible outcomes to a standard of rationality becomes correspondingly more difficult.

Informed free choice essentially presumes a rationality standard in order for information to make any difference in a purchasing decision. Information is central to marketing motives and methods because the seller normally possesses substantially more relevant product information than potential buyers and employs techniques, such as advertising, to communicate information that will promote greater sales. Ethical issues involve judgments regarding what information is communicated and what is not, considering both the information's quantity and quality. Recognizing that the purpose of marketing is to promote sales, meeting a standard of informed free choice sometimes requires transmitting information that does not serve, or might even undermine, that purpose.

One way to evaluate how marketing information affects informed free choice would be to array various examples along a continuum such as that indicated in Figure 7.1.[2] The impacts on consumer choice range from rational persuasion to a created compulsion. Between these extremes appear various forms and levels of manipulation as marketing techniques present, withhold, misrepresent, embellish or otherwise alter product-related information to promote sales. The specific labels represent general tendencies rather than precise points on the continuum, as interpretations will vary regarding the significance or impact of particular advertising techniques. However, the further a particular technique falls to the left side of the continuum, the more certainly the marketing practice can be judged to violate an informed free choice principle.

| Created compulsion | Deception | Concealment | Exaggeration | Imagery | Rational persuasion |

Figure 7.1 Marketing Continuum.

Created compulsion represents the antithesis of informed free choice where a consumer's ability to decline a product becomes impaired or even lost, perhaps best illustrated in cases of addiction. *Deception* implies actively using information or misinformation to mislead, while *concealment* signifies an effort to suppress availability or access to information. *Manipulation* stands at the center point above the continuum because it denotes an umbrella concept that encompasses terms on both sides, reflecting ways marketing techniques use information to promote product sales. *Exaggeration* stretches basic information into forms of overstatement. *Imagery* attempts to link a product's marketing with generally desirable symbols or concepts whose association with the actual product may range from conceivable to preposterous. (Examples of imagery include advertising that associates a product with popular lifestyles, personality types or even cartoon characters.) *Rational persuasion* involves communicating objective information needed to facilitate purchasing decisions that would maximize consumer benefit. In discussing this chapter's case scenarios, evaluate where various marketing techniques would be located along the continuum in terms of their impact on consumer free choice.

A possible "rule of thumb" to evaluate the quantity and quality of marketing information would test how well particular practices match up against the standard used in a court of law. Does the information communicated by a marketing method tell the truth? The whole truth? And nothing but the truth? All marketing practices need not meet the high test of a sworn legal statement, but this interrelated three-part standard provides a revealing way to understand and apply more common norms, such as the accuracy of marketing information. In testing the truthfulness of product advertisements, one standard would measure the accuracy of the information provided. A somewhat higher standard goes beyond the information provided to ask whether anything important were omitted, testing whether the whole truth was presented. The third component in this standard evaluates whether the marketing practice also incorporated unneeded elements that might serve to camouflage or otherwise distort the impact of the truthful information, thereby inhibiting informed free choice.

Understood free choice involves assessing how well marketing information matches the characteristics of a target audience. Both the substantive content and the method of communication influence how well potential consumers will comprehend the information provided. Key audience characteristics include factors such as age, literacy, education, familiarity with advertising techniques and general life experience. Ethical issues can arise when target audiences rank low on any of these indicators, leaving them relatively unprepared to process and evaluate some forms of sophisticated marketing information and therefore vulnerable to greater manipulation, intentional or unintentional.

Children represent an audience especially susceptible to manipulation because their youth also signifies limited levels of education, life experience and general maturity. In countries with low public literacy and education, broader groups of potential consumers appear similarly at risk. Marketing methods employed effectively in developed countries can exert differential and potentially damaging impacts unless adjusted to match the local population's characteristics. The challenge becomes especially problematic where companies promote products priced for elite, upper-income groups by using mass marketing techniques whose appeal reaches a much broader audience.

One illustration of this differential impact arises when marketing information includes warnings of possible injury from product use or misuse. Ethical marketing should employ communication methods that assure all potential customers can understand potential risks and recommended safe-use procedures. More broadly, marketing techniques utilizing exaggeration or imagery also impact differently on diverse audiences. Even in developed countries, not all consumers become inured to exaggerated advertising claims or product lifestyle associations common in media marketing campaigns. Similar use of exaggeration and imagery in countries less familiar with such methods may affect consumers more powerfully, perhaps shifting the techniques' evaluation farther left on the Figure 7.1 continuum, moving it closer to deception.

Free choice *with alternatives* tests the practical meaning of a consumer's purchasing decision. The buyer should be free from compulsion or coercion, able to select an alternative product or no product at all. Marketing addictive products may meet initial free choice standards, but the consumer's freedom of choice for future purchases diminishes with each use. In this chapter's examination of the infant formula controversy, providing free initial samples to new mothers was one marketing technique criticized for undermining free choice. Many mothers did not realize that, by using the free formula instead of breastfeeding, the mother could lose her ability to lactate and therefore lose any alternative to future purchases of more formula.

Restrictions on free choice may be psychological as well as physical. Ethical marketing concerns can arise when techniques create a perceived need that convinces potential consumers a product purchase is required for their own health or well-being. Often involving deception, such marketing can also introduce elements of psychological compulsion that limit the perception, if not the reality, of consumer free choice. When combined with audience characteristics that indicate consumer vulnerability, these marketing methods can induce powerful pressures that drive purchasing decisions. Linking an individual's feelings of self-worth or peer acceptance to particular athletic sneakers or personal grooming products, for example, can create near-compulsive behavior among some population groups, even in developed countries. The most objectionable cases occur in circumstances where consumers expend limited income to satisfy wants or desires created by marketing campaigns, forgoing alternative purchases that would meet pre-existing real needs.

Free choice value standards adopt an essentially deontological approach, accepting whatever result emerges from a process of free choice as the best decision. Deciding which qualifying terms should be attached to the (*rational*) (*informed*) (*understood*) free choice (*with alternatives*) concept provides a way to evaluate whether free choice exists in a particular case. Under a fully deontological approach, if free choice values rank foremost among priority rules, any form of marketing manipulation would be judged unethical. More typically, marketing standards are assigned varying degrees of ethical obligation, often dependent on case-specific "critical need" judgments involving the nature of the product and characteristics of the relevant audience. This mixed approach uses teleological projections to evaluate when and how strenuously to enforce deontological marketing rules against manipulating consumer choice.

For example, the more vulnerable the potential consumer, the more stringent could be the protections against manipulative marketing. The greater the potential for significant harm to the consumer (risking violations of a "do no harm" rule), the more anti-manipulation precepts might be required. As teleological outcome evaluations become more important, the deontological imperative decreases. If mentally competent individuals make purchasing decisions deemed irrational (and therefore failing a free choice standard), those judgments rely heavily on case-specific outcome evaluations. Similarly, an outcomes-based approach could ethically justify using marketing methods that consciously and purposely manipulate consumer choice if such actions lead to the best possible results for the individual or (for utilitarians) the majority. For instance, marketing might employ exaggeration or even deception to persuade children to eat nutritious food rather than sugary treats as an exercise in "ethical" manipulation of consumer choice.

The following case discussions examine international marketing motives and methods covering a range of products, techniques and relevant audiences. Assessing the factors most important to ethical evaluations in each case and comparing ethical judgments across the various cases can help identify concepts and approaches to guide ethical decisions on international marketing issues. Attention to the role played by various actors may also suggest general assumptions regarding who should do what, when and where, to promote ethical marketing practices in a growing global community.

INTERNATIONAL MARKETING OF TOBACCO

The marketing of tobacco products, represented principally by cigarettes, clearly illustrates a case where free choice issues involve arguments related to the nature of the product, the characteristics of the audience and the marketing techniques employed.[3] Informed by a growing body of scientific evidence, product safety concerns about adverse health impacts from cigarettes dominate discussions of the product's nature. Gro Harlem Brundtland, former Director General of the World Health Organization (WHO), offered a blunt description of tobacco when she said: "It is the only product which, when used as intended, will kill one half of its consumers."[4] Cigarette smoking causes at least several million deaths every year, a figure the WHO projects will climb to 10 million annually by 2020, with most deaths occurring in poor nations.[5] The geopolitical location and socioeconomic characteristics of consumers, and the associated techniques used to promote cigarette sales, shape assessments of this product's international marketing motives and methods.

Health concerns related to smoking have led to declining sales in the United States and other traditional developed country markets. Expanded marketing campaigns by tobacco MNEs aimed at developing countries and transitional economies help offset lower profits in developed countries, where tobacco products face growing public opposition and increased government regulation. Applying marketing methods successfully honed in advanced economies, MNEs reportedly transform local markets, creating new demand and increasing cigarette sales, particularly among women and youth.

One estimate suggests that two teenagers in China start smoking for every US smoker who quits. According to a director of the US Office on Smoking and Health, consumers in developing countries are "attracted to anything American, and promoting the Western lifestyle and linking these cigarettes to the United States makes them particularly attractive."[6] By contrast, supporters of cigarette exports characterize marketing efforts as a competition for sales to existing smokers. A president of the US Cigarette Export Association argued that the "issue is whether those smokers will

Two secondary school girls about 12 years of age share a cigarette along a Hong Kong back street in January, 1999. An advertising campaign that featured a wildly popular pop singer was withdrawn after fears it would encourage his young followers to try smoking. Photo by Michel Porro/Getty Images Sport/Getty Images.

have the liberty to choose an American product or be restricted to smoking only those made by a protected . . . local industry."[7]

The tobacco industry received significant help from US government efforts to open foreign markets for US cigarette exports, including pressure to permit corporate marketing practices that would promote new brands in the foreign market. Although some government agencies viewed tobacco as a health issue and acted to reduce smoking among US consumers, other government agencies treated tobacco exports as solely a trade issue and assisted the marketing drive by US MNEs to expand cigarette sales to foreign consumers. Former US Surgeon General C. Everett Koop regretted this policy, saying: "I feel the most shameful thing this country did was to export disease, disability and death by selling our cigarettes to the world. What the companies did was shocking, but even more appalling was the fact that our own government helped make it possible."[8]

Different values obviously guided different applications of US policy on tobacco products. The US government chose to regulate cigarette marketing within its territorial borders to help protect public health. Does the active promotion of cigarette exports fail to similarly protect foreign consumers? When the US government pressures foreign governments to remove restrictions on cigarette marketing practices, including some advertising techniques banned in the United States, does such action violate a minimal "do no harm" value standard?

Many foreign governments have operated tobacco monopolies and gained revenue from cigarette sales, giving them a vested interest in restricting competing imports. Policy based on fair trade principles applied to company or country interests might therefore support the US trade actions. However, if consumer health ranks as a higher value than company profits or country export competitiveness, US trade policy jeopardizes the higher individual value. A report by the National Bureau of Economic Research estimated that cigarette exports rose by 600 percent to countries targeted by US trade actions in the early 1990s, while the increased advertising and competition expanded per capita cigarette consumption nearly 10 percent.[9]

As in the United States, a priority concern regarding cigarette marketing overseas pertains to its potential to attract new smokers, particularly among youth. The tobacco industry denies targeting young people with advertising and emphasizes goals relating to brand competition for sales to existing smokers. This industry contention could be judged from several perspectives, including whether particular marketing methods appear aimed at young people, whether the techniques may influence youth smoking, and whether such effects are intentional. Critics have reported the following examples of cigarette marketing apparently aimed at a youthful audience.[10] Consider which advertising techniques might be most influential in stimulating youth smoking and whether it is reasonable to infer that young people are an intended audience for such marketing methods.

- Cigarette logos on kites, notebooks, earrings and chewing gum packages in Thailand.
- Clothing with cigarette brands distributed to children in Kenya and Guatemala.
- Free cigarettes provided during lunch recess at a high school in Buenos Aires.

- Sponsoring a rock concert by a teen idol in Taiwan, with five empty cigarette packs as the only admission ticket; ten packs for a free souvenir sweatshirt.
- Distribution of free cigarettes at rock concerts and discos in Eastern Europe, with sunglasses given to anyone accepting an immediate light.

A WHO survey found that one-fifth of young people in developing countries and transitional economies begin smoking by 13 to 15 years old. Particularly for these youth, Mrs Brundtland challenged the view that smoking involves freedom of choice to use a legal product, stating: "Most people get addicted when they are young, long before we can discuss freedom of choice." She also challenged contentions that smokers in general know the risks and deliberately choose to smoke, asserting that the dangers of smoking are not widely known or understood in developing countries. Mrs Brundtland tied the health hazards of smoking directly to the industry's marketing methods when she "described smoking as a 'communicable disease'— communicable through advertising."[11] A WHO report in 2008 documented a shift in tobacco-related deaths to developing countries, saying it "results from a global tobacco industry strategy to target young people and adults in the developing world, ensuring that millions of people become fatally addicted every year."[12]

Tobacco marketing became the focus of WHO efforts to address the adverse health effects of smoking, beginning with hearings held in late 2000. After several years of contentious debate, the WHO's World Health Assembly adopted the Framework Convention on Tobacco Control in May 2003. Key provisions support a ban on advertising by tobacco companies as well as sponsorship of television programs and entertainment events. The convention also urges that warning labels cover at least 30 percent of the packaging on all smoking products. National governments are further encouraged to strengthen indoor air quality laws, impose higher taxes on tobacco products and enforce measures against cigarette smuggling.[13] China, with an estimated one-third of the world's total smokers, signed the convention; subsequent ratification reportedly could lead to restrictions on advertising and other anti-smoking actions.[14]

The convention marks a significant statement of global common morality standards on marketing methods involving tobacco products. The primary provisions center on aspects of informed free choice, mandating substantial warnings (although not specifying the content) and restricting advertising most likely to reach younger audiences (although not prohibiting all methods, such as products with logos). The convention also illustrates, however, the current limit of intergovernmental consensus, which does not deal with broader marketing or fully address several issues related to advertising techniques.

Despite the millions of deaths each year attributed to smoking, the WHO did not severely restrict or ban trade in tobacco products, as it has done in conventions discussed in the last chapter dealing with certain dangerous pesticides and hazardous waste. If the products were measured from a teleological cost/benefit perspective, many pesticides and products that produce hazardous waste can claim productive economic benefits, even though the calculated overall effect may be negative. By contrast, benefit claims for smoking center largely around short-term individual psychological impacts that are overwhelmed in aggregate calculations by the economic, health and even longer-term psychological costs arising from smoking-related illnesses and death. The deontological principle of individual consumer choice therefore appears to represent the key value difference in explaining why trade in tobacco is not banned. On the other hand, the possible effects of second-hand smoke on non-smokers may complicate this application. If tobacco smoke harms individuals who did not choose to smoke, the ethical issues resemble more closely the effects of pesticides or hazardous waste that harm unsuspecting consumers and residents in communities near the hazards' locations.

The consumer free choice principle on cigarettes is usually qualified by the key consumer characteristic of age, with young people considered more vulnerable to marketing manipulation, thereby justifying restrictions on some forms of advertising. However, the current WHO consensus does not extend to setting a minimum age for a consumer choice to smoke, as the ILO has done in setting a minimum age for child labor. WHO requirements for prominent warning labels on packages reinforce informed free choice values by prohibiting concealment of safety information. However, without agreement on the content of mandated warnings, the actual information presented (or withheld), as well as the tone and urgency of the message, may permit some degree of continued manipulation, even if not to the continuum extreme of concealment.

The WHO Framework Convention on Tobacco Control thus offers an opportunity to examine the global community's response to some of the ethical issues raised by the international marketing of cigarettes. Identify which issues are addressed by the convention and which issues remain unresolved at the international level. If significant issues remain unresolved, who (which actors) should do what, when and where? Consider the appropriate role responsibilities for intergovernmental organizations such as the WHO; national governments, including their use of trade controls and even extraterritorial regulations; NGOs, especially health care and development-oriented organizations; and MNEs, particularly tobacco firms and advertising agencies.

Exhibit 7.1 presents another relevant application of these questions and illustrates the effective limits of the WHO's marketing standard. The European Union adopted regulations requiring that health warnings cover 30 percent of packages for smoking products, the same standard contained in the new WHO convention. EU rules also prohibit the use of terms such as "mild" and "light" in advertising cigarettes because such phrases might mislead consumers by suggesting that some cigarettes are less harmful than other brands. In upholding this restriction on advertising, the European Court of Justice explained: "The purpose of that ban is to ensure that consumers are given objective information concerning the toxicity of tobacco products."

If charted on the marketing continuum of advertising techniques, the use of "mild" or "light" might be considered exaggeration or perhaps imagery. The EU action, however, appears to evaluate the technique's impact as closer to deception, finding it so misleading about health risks as to be declared illegal. In practice, the standard will restrict marketing of certain US and Japanese cigarette brands in EU countries, but the restriction does not apply to cigarettes marketed by EU MNEs in

Exhibit 7.1   No "Mild" Cigarettes in the European Union

Ruling on cigarette labelling marks victory for exporters

By FRANCESCO GUERRERA
in Brussels

Cigarettes produced in the European Union can be labelled as "mild" or "light" provided they are sold outside the Union, the European Court of Justice ruled yesterday.

The decision is a victory for manufacturers such as British American Tobacco and Imperial Tobacco, which export a substantial part of their EU-made cigarettes to the fast-growing Asian and Middle Eastern markets.

However, the Luxembourg-based court confirmed that terms such as "mild" or "light" will be outlawed within the EU from October next year, as demanded by a new European law. As a result, popular brands such as Philip Morris' Marlboro Light and Japan Tobacco's Mild Seven will have to be renamed and repackaged in the EU.

The court ruling ends a fifteen-month legal battle between the UK government and the European Commission on one side and BAT, the maker of Lucky Strike cigarettes, and Imperial, the company behind Lambert & Butler, on the other.

The two companies challenged the EU's tobacco products directive, which imposes tough rules on the sale and marketing of cigarettes. They argued the UK government should not abide by the law, approved by EU governments in 2001, because its provisions were excessive and legally invalid.

But the court ruled the EU ban on the use of terms suggesting that some cigarettes are less harmful than others was justified to avoid misleading consumers and encouraging smoking.

"The purpose of that ban is to ensure that consumers are given objective information concerning the toxicity of tobacco products," the court said. The court also ruled that other aspects of the directive, such as a requirement to have health warnings covering 30 percent of packets, were valid.

However, the judgment said terms such as "mild" and "light" could be used on cigarettes sold outside the EU, as European law does not extend beyond the Union.

"The prohibition . . . applies only to products marketed within the community," the court said.

BAT and Imperial welcomed this part of the decision but criticized the rest. Imperial said it was "most disappointed that all other aspects of the directive have been ruled valid."

BAT said the ruling meant consumers would suffer from "the fall-out of the Commission's crusade against the tobacco industry."

The company exports 90 percent of the 50 billion cigarettes it produces in the UK outside the EU. Over the past few years, tobacco manufacturers have shifted their focus from Europe and the US to Asia, where cigarette consumption is rising more quickly and legislation is less strict. The Commission welcomed the court decision.

Source: © *Financial Times*, 11 December 2002, p. 3. Reprinted with permission.

---

non-EU countries. As the article points out, there will be no effect on expanding marketing campaigns in Asia and other regions where laws are less restrictive. Would such advertising be equally misleading, with similar harmful effects, in developing country markets?

The US government also acted against similar advertising by tobacco companies, charging them with "racketeering and fraud for deceiving the public about the dangers of smoking." In a 10-year case upheld on appeal in 2009, the court ruling banned labels such as "light" and "mild" because they were no safer than other cigarettes.[15] About 40 countries have adopted policies to ban misleading descriptors in tobacco packaging, but large variations in national regulations and regional coverage leave most countries unregulated. There is similarly uneven adoption of broader restrictions on tobacco marketing advocated in the WHO Convention and only about a dozen nations apply their regulations to cross-border advertising that originates from their territory. The WHO reports that "International collaboration to combat cross-border advertising would certainly promote elimination of this form of marketing."[16] Should individual consumers make their own unregulated free choice decisions, or should a common advertising standard be applied to all markets by voluntary corporate codes, NGO pressures, national laws, EU extraterritorial regulations or the WHO convention? Trace the subsidiarity chain of responsibility in this instance as far as justified by an evaluation of the case's critical need.

ADVERTISING ALCOHOLIC BEVERAGES

An emerging international discussion of ethical marketing issues related to alcoholic beverages presents the opportunity for a comparative analysis of alcohol and tobacco products. Many similarities exist, with some differences in degree of application, regarding the role of consumer free choice values, concern over marketing impacts on youthful (and sometimes illegal) consumers, and critical need factors involving adverse health impacts, addiction, and potential secondary harm to unrelated individuals (such as through drunk driving incidents). A summary of factors motivating international concern with alcohol marketing appear in the WHO's *Global Status Report on Alcohol* issued in June 2001. According to that report:

- Alcohol consumption is declining in most of the developed countries, and rising in many of the developing countries and the countries of Central and Eastern Europe.
- Alcohol causes as much death and disability as measles and malaria, and far more years of life lost to death and disability than tobacco or illegal drugs.
- Production of beer and distilled spirits for export is concentrated in the hands of a few large companies mostly based in developed countries.
- These corporations spend heavily on marketing to stimulate demand for alcoholic beverages, and to maintain high barriers to entry into the alcohol trade.
- With the decline in consumption in developed countries, these companies have intensified their efforts to establish new markets in developing countries and countries in transition, and among constituencies such as women and young people who have traditionally abstained or drunk very little.[17]

In 2001 the WHO also initiated an international review investigating the relationship between alcohol marketing and youth. In addition, many national governments, critic groups and industry associations are exploring the nature of these issues as well as possible approaches to address potential or actual problems. As some national governments consider tougher marketing standards, and in advance of the WHO research findings, the president of the International Center for Alcohol Policies reportedly urged the industry to adopt a more moderate marketing strategy. The proposal suggested advertisements emphasizing the simple social pleasures of responsible drinking rather than "edgy" depictions of "raucous binge drinking and sexual innuendo."[18]

The initiative responded to groups, such as the Center for Science in the Public Interest, that criticize alcohol advertisements aimed at teenagers. According to press reports, the president of the Beer Institute asserted that consumers love the advertisements and dismissed claims that such marketing will cause young people to drink, a contention seconded by the head of the Distilled Spirits Council, Peter Cressy. In a marketing assessment similar to the argument advanced by cigarette executives, Mr Cressy reportedly said: "Advertising, whether someone is of age or not, affects what they might choose to drink, not whether they drink."[19]

Former US FDA commissioner David Kessler perceives parallels between tobacco and alcohol advertising, suggesting it can play a "crucial role" in the desire of young people to drink. Alcohol marketers had established voluntary guidelines to prevent television advertising on programs where young viewers constitute a majority of the audience. Serving as an advisor to the Center on Alcohol Marketing and Youth, Dr Kessler suggested the voluntary guidelines were not followed and urged placing much lower limits on the youth composition of program audiences.[20] In September 2003 the National Academy of Sciences (NAS) released a report contending that alcohol marketing does reach young audiences, and recommended a national campaign to reduce underage drinking, including funds from increased alcohol taxes. By contrast, a Federal Trade Commission (FTC) report released concurrently concluded that the alcohol industry followed its voluntary advertising standard, finding no evidence of targeting underage consumers. The Beer Institute used the occasion to announce that the voluntary standard on media advertising was being lowered from an expected audience composition of 50 percent youth to a limit of 30 percent.[21]

Although much of the debate over alcohol marketing has focused on television commercials, the promotion of alcoholic beverages also employs many marketing methods used by tobacco companies. When the United States and some other nations prohibited television advertising for cigarettes, those other marketing techniques assumed greater importance. Therefore, a discussion of ethical marketing standards for alcoholic beverages that begins with television advertisements might also examine the full range of marketing methods. Compare ethical marketing issues related to these two products, including similarities or differences in the nature of the product involved, the characteristics of the target audience(s) and where particular marketing techniques would fall on the manipulation continuum.

In anticipation of further WHO debate on marketing alcoholic beverages, especially to youth, one approach for ethical analysis would be to assess how well the marketing standards contained in the Framework Convention on Tobacco Control would address the ethical issues raised with regard to alcoholic beverages. For example, a teleological cost/benefit assessment of alcohol could measure economic, health, social and individual psychological factors to determine whether the outcome supports a rule utilitarian decision to adopt societal controls over alcohol consumption. The deontological value for free choice decisions might weigh whether the incidence of alcoholism as a disease affects free choice similarly to nicotine addiction. Appropriate criteria for evaluating free choice decisions could be established, including whether minimum age or information (warning label) requirements are needed. These determinations would then receive practical application in decisions on whether to adopt WHO or other international marketing standards for alcoholic beverages and, if so, what specific marketing methods should be covered.

INTERNATIONAL CODES FOR MARKETING INFANT FORMULA

Despite very evident differences between tobacco, alcohol and infant formula, the three products share some commonalities related to ethical assessments of their international marketing motives and methods. The debate over infant formula marketing actually occurred first, resulting in a pioneering WHO marketing code nearly two decades before action on tobacco or alcohol. In examining the infant formula controversy, key elements again are the nature of the product, the characteristics of the audiences involved, and the degree to which specific marketing techniques manipulate consumer purchasing decisions.

Concern over the marketing of infant formula arose as MNEs expanded promotional practices in developing countries in the mid to late 1960s, when the growth potential in traditional developed country markets stagnated due to declining birth rates and entrenched competition.[22] The seminal event occurred in 1974 with the publication of research critical of infant formula marketing in a pamphlet titled *The Baby Killer*. A popularized German translation of this work reportedly altered the title to *Nestlé Kills Babies*, provoking a lawsuit from the corporation but inextricably linking Nestlé to the issue as the most prominent MNE under attack for marketing infant formula in developing countries.

Concerned by a decline in breastfeeding, some developing country governments and civil society groups attempted to encourage mothers to nurse their babies rather than expending scarce income on infant formula. Unless a mother confronts medical problems, all parties to the controversy agreed that breast milk provides babies with the best nutrition as well as beneficial antibodies from the mother's immune system. Disputes arose over whether Nestlé's marketing practices encouraged mothers to choose infant formula over breastfeeding or simply met demand for a product selected by a mother's free choice.

Compared with tobacco and alcohol, the nature of this product raises few problems. If used properly, infant formula can provide babies with nutrition benefits exceeding most alternatives except breast milk. Ethical complications arose instead from a change in key characteristics of the consumer audience, linked with the impact of particular marketing techniques. As infant formula marketing spread from relatively high-income consumers to poorer populations within developing countries, the new consumers' socioeconomic characteristics jeopardized the product's safe use. When a supply of infant formula can consume a significant portion of a poor family's income, mothers become tempted to dilute the formula to stretch the supply. Not only does dilution reduce the nutritional quality, but contaminants in the water supply available in low-income neighborhoods can lead to diarrhea, disease and infant death. In short, this potentially beneficial product requires demanding conditions for safe and effective use. Marketing the product to audiences essentially lacking basic safe-use conditions appeared ethically questionable.

Particular marketing techniques exacerbated the potential for problems arising from inappropriate infant formula use. Accepting that mothers would not intentionally inflict harm on their babies, critics questioned why poor mothers would freely choose to purchase infant formula that they could not use safely. The two most common answers evolved into charges that the marketing methods used by MNEs (1) left the mothers unprepared to exercise fully informed and understood free choice, and (2) manipulated or even deceptively coerced mothers into purchasing infant formula.

Early disagreements arose over whether MNE marketing methods promoted infant formula as a better choice than breast milk for an infant's well-being. Most companies eventually adjusted their marketing to acknowledge the superiority of breast milk while still promoting their own infant formula for mothers who decide to select that alternative, perhaps for health, convenience, prestige or other individual choice reasons. More broadly, MNE marketing often simply failed to convey in an understandable fashion the income, sanitation and other conditions required for safe and effective use of infant formula, thereby leaving mothers uninformed in weighing the product's likely costs and benefits. Even without an intention to conceal, the failure to fully inform consumers about safe-use requirements could be considered an act of ethical omission.

Acts of commission sprang from MNE marketing methods that employed imagery and even deceptive techniques to induce greater infant formula sales. Advertising associated infant formula use with both healthy babies and modern mothers who enjoy the freedom to work, socialize or otherwise organize their day without being tied to a home nursing schedule. Marketing distribution channels provided another form of imagery. Hospitals and clinics received free supplies of infant formula to give to new mothers, associating the product with the medical profession even without an explicit doctor's endorsement. So-called mothercraft or "milk nurses" in white uniforms were employed to visit expectant or new mothers in urban hospitals or in rural villages that lacked healthcare facilities. The "milk nurses" possessed varying degrees of healthcare skills but their basic function was clearly to promote sales, a point reinforced when they were paid on commission. These marketing practices might be considered deceptive if they inappropriately portrayed infant formula as recommended by medical professionals. As mentioned early in this chapter, the distribution of free infant formula samples also could be viewed as deceptive or even coercive, especially if mothers are not fully informed they may be physically unable to lactate by the time the free formula runs out, taking away their choice to breastfeed and requiring future purchases of infant formula.

The controversy over infant formula marketing garnered unusually widespread attention and action. Led by the Infant Formula Action Coalition (INFACT), NGOs submitted shareholder resolutions, urged governmental action and organized a consumer boycott against Nestlé products, attempting to pressure the company to change its marketing of infant formula in developing countries. Many MNEs joined together in the International Council of Infant Food Industries (ICIFI), a self-regulatory association that developed a voluntary Code of Ethics and Professional Standards for Advertising, Product Information and Advisory Services for Breast-Milk Substitutes. Critic groups largely rejected the ICIFI code as deficient in content and lacking enforcement credibility.

Some national governments enacted marketing regulations or sponsored campaigns to promote the benefits of breastfeeding. The issue also worked its way on to the WHO agenda, attracting enough concern to stimulate first resolutions endorsing breastfeeding and then negotiations to develop a global marketing standard for infant formula products. The large number of actors in this subsidiarity chain who accepted some degree of responsibility on this issue likely stemmed from two critical need factors. Quantitatively the harm was significant, with estimates of as many as one million deaths annually associated with inappropriate bottle feedings. Likely most important, the victims were babies, sparking emotive outrage that seemed to demand action by all capable parties, regardless of their proximity or causal connection to the problem.

The resultant WHO International Code of Marketing of Breastmilk Substitutes broke new ground in setting global standards for the marketing of a specific product. Adopted on 21 May 1981, the code established non-binding recommendations to governments, providing guidelines for infant formula marketing regulations that could be enforced at the national level. Provisions addressed the need for information that stressed the superiority of breastfeeding, warned of dangers associated with inappropriate feeding methods, and provided instructions for the safe preparation and use of infant formula. Free samples, mothercraft nurses, idealized imagery in advertising and promotion to the general public counted among the marketing methods recommended for restriction.

Despite overwhelming support (the United States cast the sole negative vote), many governments were slow to pass implementing legislation and sometimes lacked the resources or will to enforce new regulations. NGOs continued to investigate MNE marketing methods, publicizing practices that violated WHO code guidelines, and applying public pressure for voluntary adoption of the standards by the companies. With Nestlé moving first, most MNEs gradually brought their marketing methods into conformance with the code, although disagreements remained over some definitions and interpretations. Sporadic reports still surface regarding alleged violations of code standards, even in countries where binding regulations have been adopted.[23]

Historically, the perceived imperative to protect helpless babies from manipulative marketing that endangered their lives led to ground-breaking action in terms of internationally coordinated NGO pressure on MNE marketing activities and the potential to forge a broad consensus in intergovernmental organizations on marketing standards for specific commercial products. Consider the similarities and differences in this infant formula case and the emergence of international standards for tobacco marketing and the discussion of marketing standards for alcoholic beverages. Reflecting back on the last chapter's examination of pharmaceutical products, think about whether drugs resemble infant formula as products with clear benefits that can also lead to health hazards when used improperly. Should a set of international marketing standards be developed for pharmaceutical products, particularly regarding their packaging, distribution, labeling and provision of information on indications and contraindications?[24]

GENERAL INTERNATIONAL MARKETING TECHNIQUES

A variety of international marketing techniques can be arrayed along the continuum displayed in Figure 7.1. Specific practices elicit greater opposition as their degree of manipulation increases to the point where imagery, exaggeration and deception appear "unfair" to target audiences. In a globalizing economy, standardized marketing norms evolve both by regulatory design and through the homogenizing effects of MNE business practices. Although most restrictions appear first as national regulations in developed countries, the actual "unfairness" of marketing techniques may be as great, or even greater, in developing countries that lack the political attention or societal resources to adopt similar national restrictions. As regional economic agreements harmonize business regulations, especially within the expanding European Union, questions arise as to whether similar criteria should be applied extraterritorially or through a negotiated global convention that establishes minimal ethical standards for general international marketing techniques.

For example, televised advertisements targeting or involving children have been subject to regulation in various European nations, often requiring changes to commercials that air unrestricted in other countries. Reported past examples have included: a prohibition in Austria on using children in commercials, leading some firms to employ dwarfs or use animation; children similarly could not endorse products on television in France; toy soldiers could not be shown carrying weapons in German commercials; and candy advertisements in the Netherlands had to show a toothbrush.[25] Some countries prohibit direct comparisons that result in competitive claims between products, while other countries approve this type of comparative advertising as a way to provide information useful for consumer choice. Until recently, national historical and cultural traditions shaped the area and manner of government intervention, but the drive toward regional harmonization has reached the field of marketing techniques.

European Union proposals advocated a ban on "unfair practices" as part of enhanced consumer protection. For EU regulators, the proposals represent another step toward internal market reforms that eliminate divergent and confusing regulations which discourage cross-border purchases. In many respects, the proposals mirror the EU action described earlier that banned the descriptive use of "mild" or "light" in cigarette advertisements as misleading to consumers. A news report[26] summarized the following areas as targets for new EU restrictions:

- Falsely stating products will be available for a short period.
- Promoting a product in the media without stating it was a paid "advertorial."
- Making persistent phone calls/home visits.
- Staging a "liquidation sale" when the shop is not closing down.

- Targeting consumers who have suffered a bereavement or illness with products linked to those events.
- Using artificially high prices as the basis for discounts.
- "Inertia selling"—demanding money for products sent to consumers who did not request them.
- Implying that a product will help children to be accepted by their peers.
- Refusing to show advertised products to consumers.
- Pyramid schemes.

Most (but not all) of these practices were included in the EU's Directive on Misleading and Comparative Advertising, adopted in May 2005.[27] Which practices should not be regulated as "unfair"? Consider whether any of the restrictions should be enforced extraterritorially, or incorporated in a global code of conduct for general international marketing techniques.

An applied exercise to evaluate marketing techniques could involve reading the advertisements in a popular magazine to analyze both the visual and the written messages being conveyed. Do the pictures and narratives tell the truth, the whole truth and nothing but the truth, or should they? Consider whether an assessment should vary depending on the nature of the product being promoted, or the presumed characteristics of the anticipated audience. Or, walk through the aisles of a grocery store and read the labels on various food products. Although some government regulations increasingly mandate listing a food product's ingredients as well as nutrition-related facts, the information still may not be completely "truthful." For example, carefully read the average serving size used to calculate calories or fat content on the nutrition labels, particularly for "snack food." With extensive market research, companies should possess good data on product use. Does the stated average serving size reflect the average consumption for you or your friends? Examine other promotional techniques and evaluate the quality and utility of information provided when a product is trumpeted as "new" or "improved," "healthy" or "low" fat or "great" tasting.

OBESITY AND THE MARKETING CONNECTION

The WHO warned in 2005 that a staggering increase in obesity will lead to a deadly rise in chronic diseases, especially heart disease, strokes and type 2 diabetes.[28] Fundamental causes of the obesity crisis stem from both decreased physical activity and dietary shifts to food high in fat and sugars but relatively low in nutrients. While many actors play a role in this development, a central debate focuses on food marketing, particularly for so-called "junk food" that is often targeted at youth.

One issue relates to the impact of advertising on food purchases and whether marketing can be judged a "cause" of obesity. In 2005, a congressionally requested study by the Institute of Medicine, a part of the US National Academy of Sciences, challenged arguments that no proven, direct link exists between TV advertising and the food children eat. The study found "strong evidence that television advertising influences the food and beverage preferences and purchase requests of children aged two through 11 years old and affects their consumption habits" that establish later eating patterns. The study's authors advocated voluntary industry action to shift the emphasis in advertising on children's programming away from high-calorie, low-nutrient products to healthier foods, and called for legal mandates if voluntary efforts failed.[29]

Some individual companies such as Kraft Foods had already moved to stop or restrict advertising of less nutritious products to children. Faced with prospects for legal action in both the United States and Europe, more companies joined cooperative efforts. One new program, called the Children's Food and Beverage Advertising Initiative, pledged in 2006 to promote healthier foods or lifestyle in at least half of advertising directed at children, refrain from advertising in elementary schools, reduce using cartoon characters to promote junk food, and advocate nutritious foods in interactive games. Critics pointed to definitional loopholes and expressed skepticism about the success of self-regulation. Pressure continued to mount for legal regulation, with the American Academy of Pediatrics calling for a ban on junk food ads during children's programming. Kellogg Company broke new ground in June 2007 by announcing it would either reformulate or stop marketing half its products to children, including cereals such as Fruit Loops.[30]

Exhibit 7.2 reflects another step in the self-regulation process. Through a new marketing code sponsored by the International Council of Beverage Associations (ICBA), adherent companies pledge to end advertising directed toward children under age 12 on all paid media outlets including television, radio, print, internet and cinema. Of particular significance is the code's global reach. The ICBA is an international umbrella group for the beverage industry and the new marketing standards will apply to company operations worldwide. Past voluntary restrictions arose mainly in the United States and Europe where companies faced active threats of mandatory regulation. Establishing a global code commits the industry to apply the same standards even in countries where domestic pressures on obesity issues are weak or absent. Movement toward a common morality norm may prove especially beneficial in developing countries. As the WHO has noted: "Once considered a problem only in high-income countries, overweight and obesity are now dramatically on the rise in low- and middle-income countries, particularly in urban settings."[31]

Of course, problems of obesity will not be solved by one industry's marketing code or even by restrictions on all types of beverage and food advertising. Progress will require the collaboration and sustained commitment of many stakeholders, including both public and private sector actors. Parents and school teachers must emphasize healthy eating habits and regular exercise. Governments must provide healthy food options at public schools. Nevertheless, according to the WHO: "Initiatives by the food industry to reduce the fat, sugar and salt content of processed foods and portion sizes, to increase introduction of innovative, healthy, and nutritious choices, and to review current marketing practices could accelerate health gains worldwide."[32]

What should be the nature and extent of business ethical responsibility to address obesity problems? Are corporations responsible to alter behavior only when their

Exhibit 7.2   Stop Soft Drink Ads for Kids

Coca-Cola and PepsiCo vow to
stop ads aimed at children

By ANDREW BOUNDS
in Brussels

Coca-Cola and PepsiCo, the world's largest beverage companies, plan to stop targeting under-12s with advertising by the end of the year, in response to rising worries over child obesity.

Other international soft drinks makers are also likely to endorse a new marketing code to be unveiled today by the International Council of Beverage Associations, the industry's umbrella group.

The US groups are expected to make a pledge to implement the code worldwide by the end of 2008 at this week's World Health Assembly, the annual meeting of the World Health Organisation in Geneva.

The WHO and government regulators have been pressing the food and drink industry to address fast-rising obesity among youngsters. With 400m people dangerously overweight, today's generation is the first forecast to live shorter lives than their parents.

While companies in many countries, particularly in the European Union, have brought in voluntary curbs, the code is the largest commitment yet.

"Adopting robust guidelines . . . broadens our industry's commitment to providing meaningful leadership around the world," Alain Beaumont, secretary general of the group representing European soft drinks companies, will say.

"As partners and grandparents ourselves, we recognize that children may be more susceptible to marketing campaigns and may not always be able to make the right dietary choices for themselves."

Drink and food companies fear they could become as demonised as the tobacco industry if they are seen to be pushing unhealthy products to children.

Under the ICBA guidelines, companies agree to eliminate the marketing of beverages, including carbonated soft drinks, to any audience comprising predominantly children under 12.

The policy covers paid media outlets such as television, radio, print, the internet, phone messaging and cinema, and includes product placement. It does not cover water, juices and dairy-based beverages.

Consumers International, a consumer watchdog, said the code did not go far enough. "We need globally agreed restrictions that hold the entire food and drink industry to account, not piecemeal self-regulation," said Emily Robinson, CI's campaigns manger.

Tim Armstrong, a physical activity expert at the World Health Organization, welcomed the move, especially its global reach. Health regulation is often weaker in poor countries.

Source: © *Financial Times*, 20 May 2008, p. 2. Reprinted with permission.

---

marketing is definitively proven to directly cause obesity? Should advertising be restricted only when targeted at children and is age 12 the appropriate cut-off point? Should a food or beverage company seek to minimize only ingredients like fat and sugar that could "do harm" or should a company seek to "do good" by emphasizing healthy and nutritious product offerings? How would you design an ethical voluntary marketing code for the global food and beverage industry?

RACIAL, ETHNIC AND SOCIOECONOMIC MARKETING ISSUES

When product promotion campaigns span diverse countries and cultures, MNE marketing motives and methods may encounter ethical issues that stem from varying societal perceptions and sensitivities. In such circumstances, MNEs will confront marketing decisions that involve value choices regarding whether or how to adjust products and promotional techniques for different markets. In effect, social standing can be employed in marketing techniques as well as linked to actual product use. The ethical issues raised by social-related marketing become evident in exploring international marketing applications that deal with race and ethnicity.

Some MNE marketing campaigns have incorporated racial or ethnic characteristics as an advertising technique to increase product sales. Exaggerated racial and ethnic stereotypes were sometimes used in an attempt at humor but provoked criticism for their perceived denigration of the represented groups. Confronted with the protests, MNEs and their advertising agencies generally withdrew or altered the offensive material. Ethical analysis may help identify key factors in such cases that could clarify the proper use of value principles and choices involved in such marketing decisions.

For example, a Kellogg cereal advertisement reportedly drew on established comic book art popular in France. In a strip of cartoon-like scenes, black African cannibals with wildly exaggerated features were preparing to cook a white hunter in a boiling pot until they tried the Cracky Nut cereal from his backpack, after which he was worshipped on a throne. If the decision to stop using the comic figures in a marketing campaign for cereal reflects a position that exaggerated racial stereotyping violates important value principles, should the same principle apply equally to other products, such as commercial comic books or long-established classics that might be considered comic art? A Kellogg spokesman said the ads "weren't meant to offend anyone—just appeal to the French."[33] Consider whether a racially based appeal to humor is wrong on a global scale or whether a firm that markets only within one nation can ethically choose products or marketing techniques that use racially based humor. This broader question of societal and cultural differences will be dealt with more extensively in Chapter 8 on "Culture and the Human Environment," but aspects of this issue clearly relate to ethical international marketing decisions and standards as well.

An international advertising firm developed a marketing campaign for Kirin beer that used ethnic parody to market Japanese beer in Great Britain. Accompanied by geisha girls, a samurai confesses: "My karaoke singing used to sound rike fowsand howring banshee but now I sing rike spawo and hafe recod contract with Wonco [after drinking Kirin Beer]." Focused on a British beer-drinking audience, one creator of the ad related: "We thought a Japanese character who spoke the way a Japanese person might speak would be funny—certainly more interesting than putting a beer bottle in front of Mount Fuji."[34] The Japanese media and Kirin executives were not amused and the ad was stopped. However, what if Japanese executives either did not find the parody offensive or anticipated that the potential for expanded sales could trump the ethnic offense? Should ethical norms permit ethnic-based humor in a self-parody to promote products in other countries and cultures?

A related issue concerns whether marketing visuals should be manipulated to adjust racial or ethnic composition to match a target market's audience. For an ad meant only for Poland, Ford Motor Company changed a factory photo to replace the faces of Indian workers with white employees. A company spokesperson explained: "There are no colored people in Poland, and because of that, there was a thought that the photo should be altered."[35] Without knowing the reasoning behind this "thought," one might speculate on a discussion among company executives regarding this marketing technique. What could be some possible reasons to alter the picture? To make the Polish audience feel more comfortable or associated with the company and its product? To pretend the company or product is not associated with "colored people"? Would the product be less appealing to Polish consumers if the picture were not altered? What principles should guide the company's decision on whether, or how, to use this marketing technique?

Is there any ethical difference between altering the picture, as was done, and taking a new picture where individuals are deliberately selected to reflect a preferred racial and ethnic composition (a technique prevalent throughout the advertising and entertainment industries)?[36] In one sense, the deliberate omission of specific groups of people may be less offensive than their deliberate inclusion for purposes of parody. On the other hand, the motive for deliberately excluding certain racial or ethnic characteristics from an advertisement must stem from a belief that such action will enhance the ad's effectiveness in selling the product (or else why do it?). Would such motivation and method implicitly, if not explicitly as with parodies, involve denigrating the excluded groups?

The article reprinted in Exhibit 7.3 raises somewhat different ethical issues regarding race. In this reported case, the product as well as the marketing motives and method explicitly relate to the way a society perceives and responds to racial differences. Hindustan Lever sells a skin-whitening product in India. Seeking expanded sales in the face of new competition, the company adopted an aggressive marketing strategy that suggested a causal relationship between women using the skin-whitener and finding a good job and a husband. Among the ethical questions raised by this case are whether the marketing methods respond to, reinforce or help create racial prejudices, and what value standards should guide MNE marketing decisions in such situations.

One advertising executive defends the marketing method by contending the "advertising industry reflects rather than moulds wider social values." Certainly India's historical and cultural traditions, including the caste system's social stratification, contain race-based elements that constitute part of the country's contemporary reality. Perhaps marketing that associates success with lighter skin just reflects the prevailing societal sentiment and responds to existing demand, as suggested by the commercial with the father distraught about the prospects of marrying off his dusky-complexioned daughter until she becomes an "eligible beauty" by using a skin-whitener. The Hindustan Lever executive reportedly believes such advertising simply shows the transformation of a negative to a positive, "with romance and a husband the pay-off." This type of marketing assertion might be considered a form of lifestyle association through imagery or perhaps an example of advertising exaggeration.

Exhibit 7.3   Promoting Skin-Whiteners in India

India orders ban on advert saying fairer equals better for women

Advertisers are alarmed at government intervention in campaigns, write **Khozem Merchant** *and* **Edward Luce**

Indian sensibilities on core issues of caste and colour have been stirred by a government ban on a television commercial that says a bestselling skin whitener will help dark-skinned women find a better husband and job.

The crackdown on the advertisement made by Hindustan Lever, part of the Anglo-Dutch Unilever group, highlights a progressively interventionist approach towards advertising that officials believe breach public decency.

This month, officials told broadcasters to remove commercials for condoms, following an earlier controversial decision to withdraw a publicity campaign to raise awareness about HIV-AIDS. Sushma Swaraj, minister for health, said that the publicity had offended the moral sensibilities of most Indians.

Ravi Shankar Prasad, information and broadcasting minister, said last week that his decision to ask broadcasters to withdraw commercials for Hindustan Lever's Fair & Lovely skin whitener did not signal a change of policy towards self-regulation in the advertising industry.

"Self-regulation is the only way," he said, but he warned that he would not hesitate to act again against offensive advertising. "I will not allow repellent advertisements such as this to be aired," he said.

Official interventions have alarmed the Advertising Standards Council of India, a self-regulatory body that vets commercials but only on the basis of a complaint. "We have an 80 percent compliance record, which we believe shows that self-regulation works," said Ravi Kant of ASCI, which upheld the complaint of offensiveness against Fair & Lovely.

In India, skin colour is closely identified with caste and is laden with symbolism. Bollywood glorifies conventions on beauty by always casting a fair-skinned actress in the role of heroine, surrounded by darker extras. Hindustan Lever's

research says 90 percent of Indian women want to use whiteners because it is "aspirational, like losing weight". A fair skin is, like education, regarded as a social and economic step up. Newspapers carry matrimonial adverts asking for "graduates with wheat skin complexion".

Hindustan Lever, the biggest personal products company in India and the largest advertiser, with a budget of Rs14billion ($29million, €27million, £18million) a year, is unrepentant. It says the Fair & Lovely commercials were about "choice and economic empowerment for women".

One commercial shows a sad father wishing he had a son and not a daughter, whose dusky complexion, he believes, diminished her prospects of attracting a good husband, a big dowry and a well-paid job. She uses Fair & Lovely and becomes an eligible beauty. Another shows a dark girl using Fair & Lovely and landing a job as an air hostess.

Arun Adhikari, executive director for personal products at Hindustan Lever, said historically Fair & Lovely's "thoroughly researched" advertising depicted a "before and after effect". The current commercials "show a negative and positive situation. We are not glorifying the negative but we show how the product can lead to a transformation, with romance and a husband the pay-off".

Pramila Pandhe, of the All-India Democratic Women's Association, says she has no issue with skin whiteners. AIDWA objected to the explicit causal relationship in Hindustan Lever's campaign, replacing what was an ambiguous association between the cream and good fortune in romance and work. "The campaign portrays a low-grade status of women," she says.

Hindustan Lever says the protests of women's activist groups bear no relationship to the popularity of Fair & Lovely, the best-selling brand in India's Rs6.91billion skin whitener market.

The Fair & Lovely issue has divided the Rs100

billion advertising industry. Piyush Pandey, group president of Ogilvy & Mather in Bombay and an award-winning director, says: "India's young advertising industry reflects rather than moulds wider social values." Meenakshi Madhavani, who runs Carat India media agency, said the campaign was "offensive because it says if you're dark you're doomed".

Analysts say the Fair & Lovely campaign was hardened in response to a sluggish market for skin-care products. Hindustan Lever's dominance is under threat from new rivals.

Fair & Lovely sales are rising 15 percent a year in a flat market, according to Hindustan Lever, but penetration levels are still short of targets, say analysts. Skin whiteners account for half of India's Rs13.69 billion skin care products market.

Source: © *Financial Times*, 20 March 2003, p. 8. Reprinted with permission.

However, the executive claims the depiction is "thoroughly researched" and, within the context of India's cultural caste system, such before-and-after scenarios may have some basis in fact. Such a contention might reduce the degree of manipulation present in the marketing method, but would that make it ethically "right"?

Considering the subsidiarity chain of potential actors in this case scenario, who should take what action, when and where? The Indian government asked Hindustan Lever to withdraw the new commercials as "repellent advertising" that breached public decency, and an industry self-regulatory body similarly upheld complaints against the commercials. Both actions apparently depended on the company's voluntary compliance. This approach relies on case-by-case judgments by local institutions embedded within the Indian society, where racial prejudices associated with the caste structure still wield strong social powers, even though many governmental policies aim to reduce the caste system's impact. For the global Unilever group, should non-Indian norms help guide Hindustan Lever's marketing practices?

When a product demand is based on racial prejudice, can demand be ethically met? Demand certainly exists in India for skin-whiteners, but should a corporation produce a product to meet a market demand that is based on racial prejudice? If so, then the impact of different marketing methods should also be evaluated and selected to meet varying expectations and objectives—fulfilling existing demand; reinforcing demand and stimulating expanded consumption among existing consumers; or creating new demand to expand the number of potential consumers. Review the advertising examples discussed in the article and evaluate whether the marketing motives and methods used would likely respond to, reinforce or help create racially based product demand.

The commercial success of skin-whitening products for women inspired a male companion. Sales exploded for a new product, Fair and Handsome, mainly among lower middle-class men who "want to have their skin lightened and attract fairer-skinned brides who often come with larger dowries in this largely dark-skinned country."[37] The cream usually costs $1, or half a day's wage for many Indians, so some companies market their product in tiny packages for poorer Indians.

The use of racial stereotypes in marketing is not confined to skin-whitening products nor does it appeal only to lower-class consumers. Caucasian models are increasingly prevalent in print and electronic advertisements, with a modeling

A salesman in New Delhi arranges a shelf of "fairness" products for men in September, 2007. In a new commercial, a famous Bollywood actor advised a young man to use the cream to gain women's attention. Protestors objected that such products strengthen long-time prejudices equating fair skin with good looks, reinforcing racial elements of India's discriminatory caste system. Photo by Manan Vatsyayana/AFP/Getty Images.

agency reporting customers who ask: "Do you have white girls who are Indian-looking?" Models from Iceland, Hungary, and Slovenia appear in advertisements dressed in exquisite saris or wedding clothes draped with traditional Indian jewelry. The fashion editor of *Vogue*'s Indian edition reportedly suggested that putting a white model in Indian clothes is "a cultural exchange." She went on to say: "Of course, it also caters to the general feeling that 'fair' and 'beautiful' go together. For a rickshaw-puller who earns $2 a day, seeing a fair-skinned woman is an escape, a fantasy."[38]

Vogue India also claimed headlines with advertising that took a strikingly different approach. In its August 2008 issue, the magazine offered a 16-page presentation of expensive purses and umbrellas, modeled by average, poor Indians for whom the products are clearly unaffordable. One columnist denounced the spread as "distasteful" and an "example of vulgarity." A *Vogue* editor defended the presentation, urging critics to "Lighten up" and suggesting that with fashion, "Anyone can carry it off and make it look beautiful." The editor explained that: "We weren't trying to make a political statement or save the world." Other commentators point to the challenge of marketing luxury goods to a rising affluent class in areas that are still dominated by abject poverty. Underlying the critics' view may be a feeling that the *Vogue* presentation uses the poor individuals photographed with props in a demeaning or dehumanizing way that exploits their poverty. Should companies market their products in any way legally permissible or should there be some voluntary minimum ethical standard for advertising, particularly for luxury products advertised in deeply impoverished areas or in how advertisements gain attention by using the plight of individuals suffering poverty?

MARKETING THROUGH BRIBERY AND FACILITATING PAYMENTS

The topic of bribery could be examined under several categories relating to business ethics in a global political economy. Fueled by revelations in the mid 1970s that US MNEs had engaged in extensive bribery of foreign government officials, early controversies highlighted political involvements.[39] Follow-on attempts to define and legislate against bribery brought out varying cultural dimensions of payment practices in different countries and regions. Fundamentally, however, bribery serves as a marketing tool to promote increased sales, directly in specific contracts or indirectly through securing favorable treatment. Although commercial bribery between private entities raises some similar ethical concerns, this section focuses on corporate bribery involving foreign government officials in order to capture the international political economy dimension of the issue.

Bribery raises several ethical concerns. Essentially, bribes constitute an unfair method of marketing whose motive is to circumvent accepted legal rules of business competition to assure self-interested commercial gains. In a specific transaction, bribery unfairly disadvantages companies that lose potential sales. More generally, the practice undermines the theory of market competition where the seller offering the best product or service at the lowest price should win the sale. When bribery of government officials affects public contracts, the extra cost of the bribe also generally passes on to the taxpaying public through a sales price higher than under normal competition. Over time, such practices can undermine confidence in governmental processes and institutions. On the Figure 7.1 continuum of manipulative marketing, bribery generally involves both concealment and deception, falling close to the pole of created compulsion. When bribery causes a government official to choose a particular product, the procurement process loses all aspects of free choice on behalf of the real consuming and taxpaying public.

Bribery presents a curious ethical issue for the global community because the laws of nearly every nation already outlaw the practice, albeit using various definitions. Despite such broad conceptual agreement, reality proves markedly different, as many national legal prohibitions lack effective enforcement, particularly in countries with limited resources or essentially corrupt administrations. Historically, individual cases occasionally captured public attention, but international bribery emerged as an important ethical issue when investigations into the US Watergate political scandal revealed over 500 US companies with secret overseas accounts used for bribes or other improper purposes. Congressional hearings led to the passage of the Foreign Corrupt Practices Act (FCPA) in 1976, requiring accurate record keeping and extending US law extraterritorially to permit criminal prosecution of US companies and individuals involved in bribing foreign government officials.

Although some policymakers envisioned similar steps by other countries and the adoption of international agreements against bribery, two decades passed before further significant action occurred. The Organization of American States (OAS) approved the Inter-American Convention against Corruption on 29 March 1996 that addressed prohibitions and punishments for "Transnational Bribery" in Article VIII. Subsequent Conventions against corruption were adopted by the OECD, the Council of Europe, the African Union, and the United Nations. The UN Convention Against Corruption, adopted in 2003 and entered into force in 2005, is notable because it includes corruption between private sector companies as well as corruption involving government officials.

These agreements led some nations to pass anti-bribery laws covering their MNEs' foreign activities and increased international cooperation among national legal authorities. In the late 1990s the IMF and World Bank also adopted policies to discourage bribery, with the Bank pledging to "blacklist" guilty companies and bar them from participation in future projects. The UN Global Compact also added a tenth anti-corruption principle in 2004, calling on companies to establish policies and programs to combat corruption.

Most of these documents define corruption broadly, such as offering or accepting an undue advantage that distorts the proper performance of public duties. Usually bribery is specifically named, but more precise definitions are needed when national legislation is required to implement the international Conventions. The broad common morality consensus against bribery and other forms of corruption can break down particularly in efforts to draw distinctions between bribery and "facilitating payments." In general, bribes denote large payments made to high government officials for the purpose of securing a contract, influencing policy or inducing an illegal action. Facilitating payments usually represent small payments made to lower government bureaucrats to persuade them to expedite the performance of their legitimate duties. Laws and policies often acknowledge this distinction, penalizing bribery while permitting or ignoring facilitating payments. The justification argues that facilitating payments involve minor transactions and reflect customary practices in many cultures that would be practically difficult to regulate.

Exhibit 7.4 recounts the growing global consensus against bribery while posing the remaining question regarding how to treat facilitating payments or "petty corruption." Few governments have moved vigorously against facilitating payments and some countries commonly recognize that such income supplements the low salaries received by public employees. Company policies must conform to legal strictures against bribery, but MNEs can usually decide whether or not internal policies should also prohibit facilitating payments, as illustrated in the differing decisions reached by BP and Shell. Consider who (governments or companies) should take what action on facilitating payments, when, where (applied globally or nationally) and why (the normative rationale).

As the article suggests, bribery and facilitating payments appear to violate the same deontological principle. Viewed in terms of teleological outcomes, the payments differ in scale but both types may prove objectionable. Facilitating payments can become systemically corrosive to market competition and representative government institutions. Although individual facilitating payments appear insignificant, their cumulative effect could be substantial. Even single facilitating payments can yield unfair competitive outcomes. For example, the distinction between bribery

Exhibit 7.4   Debating Standards for "Petty Corruption"

Petty corruption set to move up agenda for multinationals

Many companies accept small-scale bribery as a fact of life. **John Mason** *suggests this view will soon change.*

You work for a well-run multinational company that strives to behave decently, within the law and abide by all the current wisdoms of good corporate governance. Your board genuinely warms to the idea that global companies should embrace their wider social responsibilities.

The problem is—you are stuck in a one-horse town in a far-flung country where a lowly bureaucrat is threatening not to process your paperwork unless you slip him a fair few dollars. A large contract worth millions could disappear unless you open your wallet and pass over a handful of notes.

Such dilemmas surrounding petty corruption crop up in most, if not all, parts of the world as a live issue for many companies.

Unilever and BP confessed to a House of Commons committee this week that they sometimes approved the payment of small bribes or "facilitating payments". With distaste, and under controlled circumstances, they argued that such things were necessary to commercial survival. Payments were discreetly recorded in annual reports under "petty disbursements".

Petty corruption is very different to the large scale bribery where leading exporters, notably from the arms and construction industries, have historically paid 10 percent or more of a contract's value to a senior official to win the business.

Such "grand corruption" is currently high on the international agenda and is being addressed by legal and economic initiatives from organisations such as the Organisation for Economic Co-operation and Development and the World Bank.

However, petty corruption such as the paying of facilitating payments is often regarded as of secondary importance. It is widely accepted as a fact of life. The view of companies such as Unilever is that customs officials and others in many

countries have to be paid extra to persuade them to do their jobs. Making such payments is not grand corruption, they argue, since the sums are far smaller and they do not leave companies at a competitive advantage in winning business.

David Murray, deputy chairman of Transparency International, the anti-corruption pressure group, says to impose macro-legislative solutions on petty corruption would be unrealistic, impossible to enforce and only discredit attempts to tackle larger scale bribery.

However, most TI members would like to see the issue given equal importance, he says. Grand and petty corruption were not so different in principle and thrived together in practice.

John Bray, a policy consultant with Control Risks, the corporate security group, agrees. He says petty corruption can be as damaging to a society as the grand version. Not only do the small payments add up, but corruption is usually very systematic, with powerful links from the top to the bottom of social hierarchies.

Both advocate a tough policy that no bribes, no matter how small, should be paid. This finds echoes in the commercial world too. Shell takes a more rigid line on the issue than BP. Its policy is to pay no bribes whatsoever. It admits it is having to introduce this policy over time, educating employees and leaving individual Shell companies to devise their own strategies.

Anecdotal evidence suggests it may be working—according to John Bray, in some countries, police no longer stop Shell employees and accuse them of fictitious motoring offences because they know that Shell won't pay bribes.

Petty corruption may be a lesser priority for governments than its grander cousin. However, it is still likely to move up the agenda for many international companies.

Source: © *Financial Times*, 11 January 2001, p. 13. Reprinted with permission.

and facilitating payments usually involves both method (size of payment) and motive. But size is a relative concept. The article describes a typical facilitating payment case where a "fair few dollars" or "handful of notes" can convince a "lowly bureaucrat" to process paperwork whose delay threatens a multi-million-dollar contract. However, such a facilitating payment should not be viewed in competitive isolation. A "fair few dollars" to an MNE with a multi-million-dollar contract at risk may actually represent a large sum of money to other affected parties, including the bureaucrat and other (perhaps smaller local) companies whose own paperwork now may be pushed to the bottom of the pile unless they similarly pay an amount that, for them, represents a large payment. In such a case, the MNE's "small" facilitating payment can affect broader competitive outcomes just as surely as a "large" bribe.

Consider whether the size of a payment or the motive involved represents a more important factor in distinguishing between an unethical bribe and a perhaps ethical facilitating payment. Just as an MNE might make a "small" payment that appears "large" to other companies to "expedite" a legitimate action, MNEs might also make a relatively "small" (for them) payment to accomplish the purposes of a bribe: to secure a contract, influence policy or induce an illegal action. If normative distinctions are to guide public policy and legal criteria for determining proper and improper activities, then the ethical rationale for distinguishing between bribes and facilitating payments should be clear. Similarly, if internal company policies permit facilitating payments, the definitions used to distinguish such payments from bribes, and the way such payments are recorded on corporate ledgers, should also reflect a clear normative basis for drawing such a distinction. Consider how you would formulate an internal corporate policy covering "petty corruption," deciding whether and why "facilitating payments" are permissible marketing techniques in certain parts of the world.

NOTES

1. Material for this section was drawn primarily from the following sources: A. Goldman, "Ethical Issues in Advertising," in T. Regan (ed.), *Just Business: New Introductory Essays in Business Ethics*, New York: Random House, 1984, pp. 235–69; T. Gladwin and I. Walter, *Multinationals Under Fire*, New York: Wiley, 1980, pp. 330–74; T. Beauchamp and N. Bowie, *Ethical Theory and Business*, 6th edn, Upper Saddle River, NJ: Prentice Hall, 2001, pp. 455–526.
2. This continuum concept is adapted from the framework used in T. Beauchamp, "Manipulative Advertising," in Beauchamp and Bowie, *Ethical Theory and Business*, pp. 476–84.
3. Material for this section was drawn primarily from the following sources: P. Sethi and P. Steidlmeier, *Up Against the Corporate Wall*, 6th edn, Upper Saddle River, NJ: Prentice Hall, 1997, pp. 357–75; S. Mufson, "Cigarette Companies Develop Third World as a Growth Market," *The Wall Street Journal*, 8 July 1985, p. 1; H. White, "Thailand, Bowing to Foreign Pressure, Will End Its Ban on Cigarette Imports," *The Wall Street Journal*, 12 October 1990, p. B4g; J. Guyon, "Tobacco Companies Race for Advantage in Eastern Europe While Critics Fume," *The Wall Street Journal*, 28 December 1992, p. B1; S. Efron, "Lighting Up World of Smokers," *Los Angeles Times*, 8 September 1996, p. A1; "Big Tobacco's Global Reach", four-part series by *The Washington Post*, including: G. Frankel, "US Aided Cigarette Firms in Conquests Across Asia: Aggressive Strategy Forced Open Lucrative Markets," 17 November 1996, p. A1; G. Frankel, "Thailand Resists US Brand Assault," 18 November 1996, p. A1; J. Rupert and G. Frankel, "In Ex-Soviet Markets, US Brands Took On Role of Capitalist Liberator," 19 November 1996, p. A1; and G. Frankel and S. Mufson, "Vast China Market Key to Smoking Disputes," 20 November 1996, p. A1.

4. W. Giles and J. Thornhill, "Gloves Off in WHO Tobacco Campaign," *Financial Times*, 22 September 2000, p. 3.
5. A. Langley, "World Health Meeting Approves Treaty to Discourage Smoking," *The New York Times*, 22 May 2003, p. A11.
6. M. Levin, "Targeting Foreign Smokers," *Los Angeles Times*, 17 November 1994, p. A1.
7. Ibid.
8. Frankel, "US Aided Cigarette Firms."
9. Ibid.
10. "Tobacco Marketing to Young People," INFACT, 1994, online, available <http://www.infact.org/youth.html> (accessed 1 December 2003).
11. Giles and Thornhill, "Gloves Off."
12. "Reports of the Parties Received by the Convention Secretariat and Progress Made Internationally in Implementation of the Convention," World Health Organization, 14 October 2008.
13. Langley, "World Health Meeting."
14. Associated Press, "China May Ban Ads For Cigarettes as Part Of UN Agreement," *The Wall Street Journal*, 18 November 2003, p. B10.
15. N. Pickler, "Landmark Case Against Tobacco Firms Upheld," *The Miami Herald*, 23 May 2009.
16. "Reports of the Parties received by the Convention Secretariat and progress made internationally in implementation of the Convention," World Health Organization, 14 October 2008.
17. World Health Organization (WHO), a summary of "Global Status Report on Alcohol," WHO/NCD/MSD/2001.2, June 2001, mimeo.
18. N. Ives, "Advertising: A Trade Group Tries to Wean the Alcohol Industry from Full-figured Twins and Other Racy Images," *The New York Times*, 6 March 2003, p. C7.
19. Ibid.
20. V. O'Connell and C. Lawton, "Curbs Sought on TV Alcohol Ads," *The Wall Street Journal*, 18 December 2002, p. B2.
21. N. Ives, "The Media Business: Advertising," *The New York Times*, 10 September 2003, p. C3; and J. Becker, "Don't Merely Punish Adults," *USA Today*, 24 September 2003, p. 20A.
22. Material for this section was drawn primarily from the following sources: P. Sethi and J. Post, "The Marketing of Infant Formula in Less Developed Countries," in M. Hoffman and J. Moore, *Business Ethics*, New York: McGraw-Hill, 1984, pp. 427–37; B. Hewson, "Influencing Multinational Corporations: The Infant Formula Marketing Controversy," *International Law and Politics*, vol.10, no.125, 1977, pp. 125–70; and J. Brooke, "Criticism Mounts Over Use of Baby Formulas Among World's Poor," *The Washington Post*, 21 April 1981, p. A15.
23. For example, see A. Lichtarowicz, "Baby Milk Marketing Breaks Rules," BBC News World Edition, 17 January 2003, online, available: <wysiwyg://40/http://news.bbc.uk/2/hi/africa/2667401.stm> (accessed 17 January 2003). Nestlé captured headlines again in 2004 with a US advertising campaign for Nan, its leading brand of infant formula in Latin merica, reportedly targeting Hispanic immigrants who might associate infant formula use with socioeconomic status. The company did not advertise in countries such as Mexico that followed the WHO code. Although the United States finally signed the code, no laws were passed to enact its provisions, leaving the code dependent on voluntary observance by companies. See M. Jordan, "Nestlé Markets Baby Formula to Hispanic Mothers in U.S.," *The Wall Street Journal*, B1, 4 March 2004.
24. In fact the WHO explored developing a marketing code for pharmaceuticals shortly after adoption of the infant formula code. Action was deferred when the International Federation of Pharmaceutical Manufacturers' Associations (IFPMA) adopted a voluntary marketing code. The issue still emerges periodically, with some NGOs contending the IFPMA code is insufficient and ineffective. See J. Kline, *International Codes and Multinational Business*, Westport, CT: Quorum Books, 1985, pp. 93–5.
25. R. Alsop, "Countries' Different Ad Rules Are Problem for Global Firms," *The Wall Street Journal*, 27 September 1984, p. 33.
26. F. Guerrera, "Business Angry at 'Unfair Practices' Proposal," *Financial Times*, 5–6 April 2003, p. 7.
27. European Council and Parliament Directive 2005/29/EC, "Unfair Commercial Practices Directive."
28. F. Williams and J. Grant, "WHO Warns of 'Staggering' Increase in Obesity Problem," *Financial Times*, 23 September 2005, p. 9.
29. J. Grant, "Appetite for Junk Food Linked to Ads," *Financial Times*, 7 December 2005, p. 1.
30. C. Mayers, "TV Ads Entice Kids to Overeat Study Finds," *The Washington Post*, 7 December 2007, p. D1;

A. Bounds, "Food Groups Urged to Join War on Obesity," *Financial Times*, p. 10 November 2006, p. 8; A. Martin, "Leading Makers Agree to Put Limits on Junk Food Advertising Director," *The New York Times*, 15 November 2006, p. C3; J. Birchall, "Food Makers Tighten Code to Avoid Ads Ban," *Financial Times*, 18 July 2004, p. 4.

31. Fact sheet N311, World Health Organization, September 2006.

32. Ibid.

33. A. Faiola, "To Many, the Overseas Pitches Are Foul," *The Washington Post*, 9 November 1996, p. H1.

34. Ibid.

35. Ibid.

36. A comparable but contrasting question can also be posed that might help clarify whether ethical concern is directed at the technique used or the objective it is meant to achieve. Should company advertisements (or entertainment programs) deliberately alter or adjust their racial or ethnic composition to reflect greater diversity than exists in the surrounding society? The answer to this question may reflect whether the relevant society is defined on a local, national, regional or global scale.

37. E. Wax, "In India, Fairness Is a Growth Industry," *The Washington Post*, 4 May 2008, p. A17.

38. R. Lakshmi, "In India's Huge Marketplace, Advertisers Find Fair Skin Sells," *The Washington Post*, 27 January 2008, p. A14.

39. Material for this section was drawn primarily from the following sources: N. Jacoby, P. Nehemkis and R. Eells, *Bribery and Extortion in World Business*, New York: Macmillan, 1977; Y. Kugel and G. Gruenberg, *International Payoffs*, Lexington, MA: Lexington Books, 1977; M. Pastin and M. Hooker, "Ethics and the Foreign Corrupt Practices Act," and K. Alpern, "Moral Dimensions of the Foreign Corrupt Practices Act," in Hoffman and Moore, *Business Ethics*, pp. 463–75; T. Donaldson and T. Dunfee, "When Ethics Travel: The Promise and Peril of Global Business Ethics," in Beauchamp and Bowie, *Ethical Theory and Business*, 6th edn, pp. 579–86; K. Pennar, "The Destructive Costs of Greasing Palms," *Business Week*, 6 December 1993, p. 133; D. Milbank and M. Brauchli, "How US Concerns Compete in Countries Where Bribes Flourish," *The Wall Street Journal*, 29 September 1995, p. A1; P. Blustein, "IMF Takes Tough Stance Toward Corrupt Regimes," *The Washington Post*, 8 August 1997, p. A25; P. Blustein, "Big Firms Accused of Bribery in African Dam Project," *The Washington Post*, 13 August 1999, p. E1; "The Short Arm of the Law," *The Economist*, 2 March 2002, pp. 63–5; J. Finer, "World Bank Focused on Fighting Corruption," *The Washington Post*, 4 July 2003, p. E1; T. Catan and J. Chaffin, "Bribery Has Long Been Used to Land International Contracts: New Laws Will Make that Tougher," *Financial Times*, 8 May 2003, p. 11.

8

CULTURE AND THE HUMAN ENVIRONMENT

INTRODUCTION

Culture reflects and helps sustain a society, manifesting the pattern and product of human interaction among a group of people. The growth of a global political economy facilitates but does not dictate the emergence of a global society and culture. Ethical analysis can assist in examining how globalization affects existing cultures and clarify potential choices regarding whether an evolving world community could or should develop a common global culture.

Cultural relativism represents the antithesis of global culture. Under a relativistic ethical view, existing cultural beliefs and practices in various societies should not be judged or overridden by conflicting external standards. For instance, placed in the context of earlier chapters, cultural practices in particular societies would not be subject to broader notions such as the concept of universal individual human rights. Hence, one aspect of examining culture and the human environment relates to deciding whether core values exist that provide a basis for rejecting cultural relativism, perhaps defining common morality principles upon which a global society could develop.

In examining the "W" questions, where relates to identifying the societal boundaries associated with a particular culture. Legal, political, ethnic, geographic and other characteristics help shape cultural patterns whose effective limits are often not coterminous with national borders. Questions of when raise issues concerning the impact of time on culture. From one perspective, any existing culture merits a certain respect as an evolved pattern of human values, a viewpoint that tends to emphasize preservation and protection. However, change occurs with the passage of time, even in isolated cultures. Time-related issues therefore concern primarily factors that influence the rate and direction of cultural change rather than attempts to maintain a cultural status quo, *ad infinitum*.

Issues that pose what questions deal with a culture's substantive content. Culture represents a composite concept that often appears greater than the sum of its individual parts. However, because many value dilemmas concern issues associated with cultural change, ethical analysis requires identifying the elements essential to a culture's continuance as well as the priority relationships among those elements. This step permits an assessment of how change to a particular component may affect the entire culture. The who questions essentially seek to identify the most appropriate individuals or groups that should guide and determine the pace, direction and magnitude of cultural change; and why?

The central framing question of this chapter is: Should corporations adopt local culture, adapt to local culture but maintain minimum corporate standards, or seek to change local culture (especially elements that conflict with international norms)?

CULTURAL CHANGE IN A GLOBAL POLITICAL ECONOMY

A society's culture changes as the elements comprising that culture evolve. Normally, internal political and social mechanisms help regulate the degree and rate of change, facilitating societal adjustments. However, when cultural change stems largely from external forces, a society's traditional regulatory mechanisms may be bypassed or overwhelmed. The multifaceted pressures exerted by the emergence of a global political economy create countless impacts on distinctive cultures around the world. MNEs constitute uniquely efficient vehicles for transmitting global forces, embedding external influences deeply within a society by operating simultaneously as both a foreign and a domestic enterprise.

Imports of foreign products introduce some external influence to a society, but that impact pales in comparison to the broader, integrated effects that accompany modern MNE operations. Private international corporations bring an entire ethos that may differ significantly from traditional societal norms, especially for non-Western societies. The MNE business culture emphasizes efficiency and productivity, measuring business performance on a monetary basis of profitability while emphasizing individual values associated with the acquisition of personal property and wealth. MNEs reward sales and management skills that deliver results in a market-based economic system. Drawing on their extensive network of affiliated international resources, MNEs possess business options and leverage unavailable to domestic firms, translating into greater influence for the operational modes and values manifested by foreign-based enterprises. These norms are then dispersed more broadly into the host society through direct employees, suppliers, buyers, competitor imitation and other related multiplier effects.

The increased societal interdependence that accompanies global economic integration affects all countries, but developing nations and transitional economies experience relatively greater disruption of traditional norms compared to the more developed nations from which most MNEs originate. Although some ethical dilemmas arise from shared transactions within the Triad of North America, Europe and Japan, many more issues appear when MNEs from largely Western industrialized nations increase their activities in Southern and Eastern regions with lower levels of economic development and often strikingly different cultural traditions.

A nation's choice of development strategies, including the role designated for international trade and investment, will shape the impact foreign influences exert on national culture. Development policy decisions affect the direction and speed of societal change as well as distributional consequences on population groups within the nation. Chapter 2's introductory case of Tambogrande in Peru illustrates how this type of development issue can impact cultural values. From a political perspective, a national government's representative quality and administrative effectiveness would generally determine how foreign forces affect local culture. However, the proliferation of international economic agreements increasingly limits national political discretion, particularly regarding the use of regulations that might restrict foreign imports or restrain the entry and operation of MNEs within the country.

Assessed from a deontological perspective, the emergence of a global political economy raises normative issues about the rules or process by which policy decisions are taken that affect culture and the human environment. As global forces alter or override traditional political and social mechanisms that regulate cultural change, key questions become: "Who should decide the direction, degree and rate of change?" and "What component elements of a culture should undergo change?" An associated issue would explore the normative principles that are chosen to guide cultural change, examining the extent to which external or global principles may differ from local norms and why the selected principles take precedence.

Alternatively, a teleological approach would examine the outcomes for each case of cultural change. Ethical analysis would seek to determine when to measure the outcome on an affected culture (where), as well as what important cultural components to assess. Perhaps the key issue again involves a who question, seeking to identify the group of people for whom the best cost/benefit outcomes should be sought. In the context of culture and the human environment, this step involves considerations such as whether to seek optimal outcomes for an indigenous people's local culture, or for the larger majority of population groups defined by national, regional or global characteristics.

SYSTEMIC DIMENSIONS OF CULTURAL CHANGE

The most dramatic cases of global economic impact on culture and the human environment arise when large natural resource MNEs invest heavily in exploiting oil or mineral deposits in small, least developed countries. In many such cases the host countries lack good alternative methods of development, leaving them relatively weak compared to the negotiating leverage wielded by global MNEs. Some host governments also appear ineffective or unrepresentative, failing either to utilize or fairly allocate revenue benefits derived from the foreign investment. Because many unexploited natural resources lie in economically undeveloped areas, large disparities may appear between the incoming MNE and existing local cultures. Projects can lead to incursions on to the traditional land of indigenous peoples whose culture may even differ significantly from that of the prevailing national authority. In such instances, policy decisions can involve calculations of development gains versus a loss of cultural integrity, where public and/or private sector actors external to the local culture essentially determine the appropriate rate and magnitude of resulting cultural change.

Reports over the last several decades from Papua New Guinea (PNG) offer classic examples of this type of systemic cultural change.[1] MNE engineers discovered valuable mineral deposits in various locations around the country, often in the vicinity of distinct tribal populations, some "one step from the Stone Age."[2] Many of these indigenous peoples were geographically, economically, socially and culturally isolated from national political authorities centered in the capital of Port Moresby. The PNG government exercised little presence in remote regions where the economy relied on traditional hunting and gathering activities and tribal customs determined the effective social and political structure. Although MNEs negotiated foreign investment contracts with the national government, the companies also needed to forge arrangements with local populations. This task often confronted the firms with ethical dilemmas that raised issues of significant cultural impact.

A review of natural resource projects in PNG reveals a series of similar difficulties. Local cultural traditions often rest on communal use of land rather than ownership of private property, contrasting both with MNE desires to purchase or lease land rights to extract natural resources and with the distant national government's contractual agreement with MNE investors. The concept of fair compensation for land or mineral rights creates challenges, especially in largely non-monetary cultures, that can easily lead to exploitation of local populations, intended or unintended. When MNEs seek discussions with local leaders, tribal authority lines and approval processes also prove difficult for outsiders to discern and follow.

Indigenous populations often lack basic education and their relative isolation from the outside world creates substantial obstacles to communicating the intent and potential impact of investments. In one reported story, the local chief's first encounter with white men came when geologists arrived by helicopter, appearing as "spirits riding a great bird."[3] Even when MNEs obtain project approval from identifiable local leaders, as well as national authorities, ethical questions occur as to whether the local agreement took place under conditions of fully *understood* free choice. Most village chiefs would find it difficult to comprehend either the when or the what issues surrounding proposed mining projects, expecting the outsiders to go up the mountain, get the valuable rocks they seek, and leave. A project's magnitude and duration come as a surprise, spawning a network of roads or even the creation of new towns populated by several times the number of people many local villagers would normally encounter in their lifetime.

Large natural resource projects generate significant and sometimes irreversible consequences for the natural environment that is integrally linked with most indigenous cultures. Game animals disappear, toxic mine wastes threaten fishing, and Western clothing begins to replace traditional local styles. On the other hand, some men can receive training for jobs at the mine, children may attend mine-supported schools and outside medicine brings the promise of extended local life spans. Who should evaluate the projected gains and losses to local tribes and decide the appropriate direction, degree and speed of cultural change they will face? What will the local population do when a mine closes? Have the villagers consciously and knowingly chosen this path of cultural change?

Historical cases of MNE mining ventures encountering Stone Age tribes arguably portray an extreme type of cultural impact that, while real, could be limited in application. Over time, fewer isolated tribes exist and MNEs can improve their approaches to dealing with indigenous populations. Enhanced controls could also reduce problems created when projects degrade the natural environment in ways that exacerbate adverse impacts on the local human environment.

Nevertheless, similar cultural issues can emerge in contemporary cases, even where MNEs follow socially conscious investment strategies and their projects cause limited damage to the natural environment. Exhibit 8.1 examines some of the ethical dilemmas encountered in PNG when a British state enterprise with a mandate "to promote the well-being of local communities" invested in palm oil plantations.

This case scenario centers on the traditional role of land in Borowai villages, where customary clan ownership and informal communal practices clash with the formal contractual approach employed by CDC Capital Partners. The UK firm recognized the need to reach agreement with local communities but confronted difficulties in identifying representative authorities to negotiate and sign the contracts. The central dispute concerns whether the villagers did, or could, give fully informed and

Seeds of palm oil are harvested at a plantation on Sumatera Island, Indonesia in August, 2005. The impact of MNE agribusiness, mining and other natural resource investments can dramatically alter community life, especially in relatively isolated regions where local culture has evolved slowly. Photo by Dimas Ardian/Getty Images.

Exhibit 8.1   Community Contracts in Papua New Guinea

When contrasts fall foul of local culture

Michael Peel looks at how a company that set out to help communities develop their resources and to treat them fairly has been accused of misleading villagers.

It is approaching noon in a village in Borowai, eastern Papua New Guinea, and the atmosphere inside the communal long-house is intense. As a dog and a small child sleep to escape the hottest part of the day, twenty or so villagers detail why they are unhappy with the British government.

One old man criticises CDC Capital Partners, the state-owned UK business that invests in the less industrialised world, for failing to provide the benefits villagers expected in return for leasing their land to the company. "What they promised they have not done," he says. "We wanted something good to come from the land."

It is not the only complaint against CDC. Across PNG's palm oil plantations, in which CDC invests, tensions have arisen between western notions of commerce and property rights and local traditions, under which almost all land is owned customarily by clans.

Many multinational investors fall foul of the communities in which they operate. What makes CDC special is that despite having a government-imposed mandate to treat landowners fairly, it has still clashed with the people of PNG. If a company with a mission to promote the well-being of local communities falls out with them, what hope is there for companies whose first duty is to shareholders?

Enlightened foreign investment of the sort advocated by CDC stands to benefit few countries more than PNG. Most of its citizens live in poverty in the midst of abundant natural resources. In spite of rich reserves of minerals and ideal conditions for tropical agriculture, PNG had a 1998 average annual income per person of less than $1,000 (£700). Infrastructure and social services are almost nonexistent in many of the rural and remote areas that characterise the nation.

CDC says its investment offers much-needed extra income. It is involved in palm oil through a 76 percent stake in Pacific Rim Plantations, which operates landholdings in three PNG locations: New Ireland, Popondetta and Milne Bay, which includes Borowai. An advertisement in the airport at Port Moresby, PNG's capital, declares palm oil is "PNG's fastest-growing agricultural success story."

PacRim operates about 23,000 hectares of plantation land and is expanding. The company, which has traditionally used territory leased from the PNG government, last year began for the first time to rent land held under the traditional ownership of clans. PacRim signs contracts with land-owner groups to make periodic rental payments and to give shares of royalties from the sales of palm fruit.

The rental agreements between Milne Bay Estates, a PacRim subsidiary, and the Borowai villagers are typical. One contract shows that PacRim has agreed to pay local currency equivalent to £3,500 for a 20-year lease on an area the size of sixty football pitches.

The document shows that PacRim has disbursed money for petrol, housing loans and cash advances, in addition to making quarterly rental payments equivalent to £45.

Alice Chapple, manager of the unit responsible for social and ethical aspects of CDCs business, argues that PacRim is more socially responsible than many other palm oil producers would be.

In 1999 PacRim launched a three-year house-building programme in Milne Bay to deal with overcrowding. The company continues to invest in communities when economic conditions might lead other companies to stop funding social programmes.

But the villagers are unhappy. One of their complaints is that PacRim is reluctant to forward them money to use for business development. They say they are perplexed by the company's apparent arbitrariness in giving cash advances for some purposes but not others. "They said: 'What ever you want us to do, we will do it for you,' " says one woman. "They misled us."

Pressure groups raise the question of whether the contracts between landowners and PacRim are inherently unfair.

Brian Brunton, forests specialist for Greenpeace Pacific, argues that people are signing deals without fully understanding the commitments involved. The transactions are loaded because of the contrast in the sophistication of the parties and the villagers' lack of access to legal advice, he says.

There is more to this than a lack of commercial experience: it also has a cultural dimension. Papua New Guineans have traditionally taken an informal approach to land use, with families frequently lending territory to one another according to need. "Local people can get a legal agreement [on land use] and think they are happy with it," says Ian Poole, a Milne Bay resident who emigrated from Australia many years ago. "But when the other side adheres strictly to the agreement the villagers find it very hard—very cold."

CDC admits oil palm farming raises big social and environmental problems. It has not helped that world commodity prices are depressed and emerging markets in turmoil. The benchmark Rotterdam rate for Malaysian palm oil is below $400 a tonne, compared with $800 in 1998. CDC says this makes it harder for it to meet demands for cash from villagers and communities.

Ms Chapple says that it is also "horrendously difficult" to ensure that landowners are aware of the implications of the contracts they sign. PacRim is continually trying to resolve complaints from villagers who feel hard done by. "It's no good my passing on a leaflet [to local people]," she says. "You can't often give them an indication of whether this change is going to be good for them or bad for them."

One difficulty, she says, is the lack of representative structures within landowner groups. This means that people with whom PacRim deals often lack the authority to speak on behalf of the community. The situation is further complicated by the internal politics of villages, leading to deals behind the scenes of which the company is unaware.

CDC says it is trying to deal with people's complaints. It argues that the solution is to become more involved with landowners and their problems rather than withdrawing from potential areas of conflict. "In every country where we invest there are people we need to engage with and often perhaps are not engaging [with] thoroughly enough," says Ms Chapple, "That's certainly an area we can improve on."

Yet the social programmes highlighted by CDC seem unlikely to resolve the central questions raised by its critics. Landowners and pressure groups will continue to argue with the company over whether villagers have been misled.

Ms Chapple acknowledges: "It's very difficult to say whether [an agreement] was informed consent or a manipulated consent—or whether it was something that was extracted from them under duress."

But it is not difficult to gauge the depth of feeling among landowners in the Borowai longhouse. People explain how the land has for many generations occupied a central position in the lives of clans, providing a source of essential items such as house-building materials and agricultural produce.

As one man, who owns a plot near the village, puts it: "We have got resources and minerals, we have got pride—we have got everything in that land."

Source: © *Financial Times*, 30 July 2001, p. 7. Reprinted with permission.

---

understood consent to contractual conditions regarding the lease of their lands. CDC makes specified rental payments and royalties while supporting housing projects and providing some loans. But villagers feel misled, expecting a more flexible and generous response to requests for loans to aid local business development. NGO representatives suggest a general conclusion from the case—that villagers face inherent disadvantages and unfair outcomes when legal contracts are used to define the relationship between such culturally and economically dissimilar parties.

As a role-play exercise, examine this case scenario from the perspective of a member of CDC's social and ethical affairs business unit, managed by Alice Chapple. Identify the cultural elements in this case that appear to lead to misunderstanding or dissatisfaction between Borowai villagers and CDC. Consider how communication gaps might be bridged more effectively to avoid some of these conflicts. Assess whether other points of disagreement or discontent appear unrelated to cultural differences. Speculate on areas of local cultural change that may arise from a continuation or expansion of this business venture. Overall, assess whether this investment project does or can meet CDC's deontological mandate to "treat landowners fairly" and "promote the well-being of local communities." Prepare a list of talking points for a meeting between Alice Chapple and Brian Brunton of Greenpeace Pacific. How might a teleologist define and measure cost/benefit outcomes (what, when and for whom) in this case scenario?

The PNG case provides a useful scenario for testing the tools and skills of ethical analysis on issues of cultural change. Stark contrasts emerge between the methods and norms employed by global MNEs and the relatively homogeneous lifestyle and values practiced in local tribal cultures. More difficult assessments arise when globalization intrudes upon more economically and socially developed regions marked by less glaring but still substantial differences. For example, consider a story[4] reported from northern Argentina on the eve of the new century (establishing the initial where and when parameters for this analysis). The most difficult ethical questions in this case relate to determining what elements constitute the culture impacted by external globalization forces and who should decide the guiding principles or desired outcomes sought from Argentina's open market reforms.

Argentina stood at the forefront of countries adopting free market policies after the Soviet Union's demise seemed to discredit state-controlled or directed economic systems. Although not communist in its orientation, Argentina had followed a largely state-centric economic model, particularly since the time of Juan Peron when state enterprises, such as the Aceros Zapla steel and mining company, comprised the central actors in the country's economic development plans. During the government of Carlos Menem in the 1990s, Argentina reversed course and privatized most state enterprises, including sales to MNEs, and liberalized economic policies by reducing barriers to imports and foreign investment. This opening to globalization forces initially thrust the country vigorously ahead on many macroeconomic indicators but left some regions of the country falling behind. By the end of the decade, and the century, the Argentine economy failed, leading to deep recession and a political collapse that witnessed the installation of five new Presidents within a two-week period at the end of 2001.

As Argentina rapidly opened to global economic forces, the workers and families associated with Aceros Zapla found their lives profoundly altered when a private venture, including foreign investors, bought the company and rapidly reduced employment by nearly three-quarters. For workers used to the job security of state enterprises the shock was considerable. Entire villages experienced disruption of their community life as social and cultural patterns that had prevailed over the past 40 years suddenly changed because facilities run by Aceros Zapla closed, altering people's employment, home life, expectations and dreams. In analyzing the impact of globalization forces on Argentina, should cultural change be defined and evaluated at the national, regional, provincial or village level? Should these changes, reportedly brought on by the new pressures of global competition in an open economy, be examined differently because of their link to international forces?

Economic change often plays an important role in the evolution of local cultures. In assessing the Argentine case, the particular impact of globalization may lie primarily in the magnitude and speed of the change. From a teleological perspective, an ideal cost/benefit analysis would compare and evaluate cultural impact with and without the open market policy reforms. Unfortunately, this ideal measurement requires counterfactual analysis, i.e. what would local life have been like around the Aceros Zapla facilities if the Menem government had not embraced market liberalization and privatization? Even employing various economic projection techniques, such a calculation would be highly speculative. More important, from the standpoint of the people affected, change is felt on a factual before-and-after basis rather than in some hypothetical with-or-without circumstance.

If the introduction of external globalization forces will broaden the magnitude and increase the speed of cultural change within Argentina, who should decide on the appropriate direction, degree and rate of probable change? An elected democratic government adopted the new economic policies, although the regime's representative character suffered persistent charges of official corruption, particularly surrounding the privatization sales of state enterprises. Policy reforms removed many regulatory controls, enabling private business owners, including MNEs, to rapidly dismantle worker protection standards and terminate employees or shut down entire facilities. Should NGOs or other external groups be as concerned about the changes occurring in Argentina as they were with the effects in Tambogrande, Peru or in the tribal areas in PNG? Why, or why not?

CLASHES BETWEEN LOCAL CULTURE AND GLOBAL VALUES

Along with the type of systemic cultural change discussed above, globalization can lead to more focused clashes between particular components of a local culture and external values guiding global actors. Specific "flashpoints" often materialize around MNE operations that seek to respect and adapt to local culture while maintaining the advantages and integrity of the enterprise's foreign or global culture. The adage to "Think global, act local" fails to capture the ethical dilemmas encountered in such situations. As citizens of an incipient global society, an MNE's local actions attract growing scrutiny from diverse stakeholders who increasingly challenge the older adage "When in Rome, do as the Romans do." As universal values define and guide the growth of a global society, situations arise where local and global values clash, raising significant ethical questions regarding what set of values should constitute minimum conditions principles that should guide MNEs or other actors in any local culture.

An especially difficult ethical dilemma emerges in situations where local culture involves the interpretation and practice of religious traditions that may clash with values endorsed by global society, particularly principles enunciated in the UN Universal Declaration of Human Rights. A core challenge for the evolution of a global community based on common morality principles lies in confronting the deontologist's problem of assigning priorities among fundamental value principles. Freedom of religion counts among the UN Declaration's enshrined rights, including the freedom to manifest religious beliefs in practice.[5] This broad right must sanction the wide array of religions as evolved in diverse cultures around the world. Yet, as with other recognized human rights, the right to religious practices may not be absolute, especially when clashes occur with other similarly fundamental human rights.

Recurring examples of this tension emerge at UN conferences, particularly during clashes between women's rights and various cultural applications of religious principles. The fourth World Conference on Women, held in Beijing, China, in 1995, adopted an extensive document aimed at promoting equality and preventing abuses against women. A subsequent conference held in 2000 to assess progress toward those goals generated heated debate over how such principles should apply to particular cultural practices. Some delegates pressed for resolutions endorsing birth control while also urging stronger laws against forms of sexual violence (such as female genital mutilation and spousal rape). Other delegates, largely from Islamic nations but backed by Catholic representatives, objected to some of these initiatives, asserting that "Western industrial nations were trying to force their 'cultural standards' on the rest of the world."[6]

The debate over so-called "honor killings" reflects an extreme example of how local culture can clash with global values. Although sometimes associated with religious fundamentalism, this practice stems more from long-standing ethnic traditions and beliefs that sanction punishment, including murder, of family members perceived to have brought shame upon the family. Most commonly, females believed to have engaged in adultery, premarital sex or sometimes even non-sexual relationships against parental or spousal approval may be deemed to have disgraced a family's honor. Legal statutes now generally outlaw these killings in most nations, but many laws lack vigorous enforcement, and convictions often bring only minimal penalties in regions where such practices enjoy a long cultural tradition. Although not always a high priority among human rights activists who focus on government actions rather than inaction, "honor killings" arguably clash with several human rights principles, including the fundamental rights to life and security of the person.[7]

Similar, if less extreme, value clashes can occur around other religious practices related to the treatment of women under interpretations of Muslim beliefs. In Exhibit 8.2, editorialist Colbert King discusses some manifestations of religious practices in Saudi Arabia regarding the treatment of women. The writer crystallizes the issue by juxtaposing current charges of discrimination against women with the historical conflict over South Africa's discrimination against its non-white population. He likens South Africa's practice of racial apartheid to practices amounting to "gender apartheid" in Saudi Arabia.

Two interrelated, reverse-image ethical issues emerge in this argument. One issue concerns whether external actors should foster change in local cultural practices by seeking to protect or promote non-discrimination standards for women. The reverse-image issue questions whether foreign actors should themselves respect local culture by complying or conforming to local practices that may involve discrimination against women. Both issues come together when applied to how MNEs and other foreign actors operate in Saudi Arabia.

The editorial describes situations involving the Saudi Arabian operations of well-known US restaurants. Charges relate to the use of different eating areas to segregate the sexes, the relative quality of the comparative facilities, and other discriminatory treatment of women. If such practices violate minimum common morality principles for a global society and if those norms take priority over local cultural traditions, even if based on interpretations of religious beliefs, then the MNEs should not conform with discriminatory local practices. To explore this issue, assess the apartheid comparison suggested by Colbert King. Would the same local practices be ethically acceptable if based on race rather than gender? Would it make a difference if a group asserted that their religious beliefs required segregation based on race? Should an MNE develop a set of minimum condition "Sullivan Principles" for gender-based treatment of employees and/or customers in Saudi Arabia, and withdraw from the country if unable to maintain operations based on those principles?[8]

Another point of ethical analysis for this case scenario might explore the role of local laws and customs as guiding standards for MNE operations. Although Saudi law requires some gender-related discrimination, such as prohibitions against women driving, the editorial portrays many of the practices employed by the US firms as conforming to custom rather than legal mandates. Illustrating this point is the comparative reference to a local Dunkin' Donuts establishment where men and women can eat at adjoining tables in an open seating area. The McDonald's spokesperson also reportedly attributed company practices to the need to "respect and observe local customs." Ethical analysis would ask what elements of local culture should be observed and who decides both the requisite content of customary practice and to whom it should apply. If not required by local law, where should an MNE look for cultural practice guidelines; and should local guidelines apply to relations with all MNE stakeholders (foreign as well as local managers, staff and customers)?

An incident in February, 2008 shows that customers can be affected by how these questions are answered.[9] A US businesswoman was arrested at a Starbucks in Riyadh for sitting in the family section with an unrelated male. Men from the Commission for Promotion of Virtue and Prevention of Vice (also known as the "Mutaween" or religious police who enforce dress codes, sex segregation and prayer observance) took her to jail where she was reportedly strip-searched, threatened and forced to sign a confession. A judge told her she was sinful and would burn in hell. Her husband, a prominent businessman, used political connections to trace his wife and secure her release the next day.

The woman had been living in Jeddah for eight years and was a managing partner at a finance company that had just opened an office in Riyadh. When the electricity went out at the office, she and her colleagues (all male) visited a nearby Starbucks that had wireless internet connection. This explanation did not satisfy the Mutaween who approached and questioned her and deemed her conduct sinful. Although denying

Exhibit 8.2   Fast Food and "Gender Apartheid" in Saudi Arabia

Colbert I. King

Saudi Arabia's Apartheid

In response to last week's column concerning treatment of women in the Middle East, an American official who just completed a tour of duty in Riyadh, Saudi Arabia, wrote: "As a husband and as a father of a teenage daughter, I can assure you that life even for Western women in Saudi Arabia is every bit as bad as you describe. Saudi official assurances that non-Muslims need not follow Muslim codes of dress and behavior are utter nonsense, and the very real threat of punishment or abuse for not wearing abbayas [head-to-toe black cloaks] or for going out unaccompanied leaves most Western women in Riyadh to live lives of silent depression."

He said he and his wife were amused to read early press reports from Afghanistan about the oppression of women and religious minorities. "Virtually everything described there was taking place in Saudi Arabia, with the exception that at least the Taliban permitted other religions to exist in their country. This is absolutely forbidden in Saudi Arabia."

Then he threw in this grabber: "One of the (still) untold stories, however, is the cooperation of US and other Western companies in enforcing sexual apartheid in Saudi Arabia. McDonald's, Pizza Hut, Starbucks, and other US firms, for instance, maintain strictly segregated eating zones in their restaurants. The men's sections are typically lavish, comfortable and up to Western standards, whereas the women's or families' sections are often rundown, neglected and, in the case of Starbucks, have no seats. Worse, these firms will bar entrance to Western women who show up without their husbands. My wife and other [US government-affiliated] women were regularly forbidden entrance to the local McDonald's unless there was a man with them."

He said the only exception to their humiliation was Dunkin' Donuts, "which had an open seating area in which men and women freely ate at adjoining tables just as in the West."

"This willing compliance with apartheid on the part of US firms was perhaps the most galling." I was in Riyadh and Jeddah in Saudi Arabia during the 1980s; the forced seclusion of women from public life is nothing new. But Riyadh didn't have a McDonald's at the time. The kingdom got its first Mickey D's in 1993. Therefore, I don't pretend to know whether McDonald's or US restaurants have a policy of aiding and abetting sexual apartheid. But something told me the McDonald's Corp. in Oak Brook, Ill., would have the answer.

So I called the McDonald's communications office this week and got Ann Rozenich. She checked around and called back to say: "All restaurants in Saudi Arabia, no matter what kind— formal or quick service—have two dining areas. McDonald's, like other quick-service restaurants—for example, Kentucky Fried Chicken and Burger King—all have two designated areas: one for families and the other for singles, all males. The restaurants also have two separate entrances."

Rozenich said McDonald's, like other companies operating in Saudi Arabia, must respect and observe local customs. Which calls to mind an old 1940s lyric: "It seems to me that I have heard that song before, with that same old familiar score."

Ah, yes. South Africa.

Once upon a time, that country also had a longstanding official policy of strict segregation. As with Saudi Arabia today, South Africa maintained a system in which a huge segment of its society faced discrimination in all walks of life and was under the authority of men wielding power without any fear of being held accountable for their actions. The only difference: South Africa's victims were black; in Saudi Arabia, they're women.

As with Saudi Arabia, white-ruled South Africa viewed external criticism as a violation of its sovereignty and interference with its internal affairs. And US corporations in South Africa, as with their Saudi Arabian counterparts, pleaded that they had no choice but to defer to the local "culture."

But something happened in apartheid South Africa.

In 1971, a Philadelphia Baptist preacher named Leon Sullivan joined the board of directors of General Motors, an investor in South Africa. Sullivan used his GM post to apply pressure on the racial apartheid system. He first lobbied GM to pull out of South Africa. Next, Sullivan drafted a set of work-place principles in 1977 that essentially required US companies to practice corporate civil disobedience against apartheid. The first principle on the list: "Non-segregation of the races in all eating, comfort and work facilities."

Two years later, a dozen top US corporations in South Africa had bought into the Sullivan principles, refusing to tolerate apartheid under their roofs. But that country's white minority government resisted broader demands to improve the quality of life for black South Africans, and to eliminate laws and customs that impede social, economic and political justice. So Sullivan led a divestment campaign. By 1979, more than 100 businesses had withdrawn from South Africa, other businesses were avoiding new ventures in the country, international banks were refusing to lend there, and universities and pension funds where withdrawing their investments.

The rest, as they say, is history.

The question is whether Americans are as concerned today about US corporate support of gender apartheid in Saudi Arabia as the late Leon Sullivan and a host of others in the anti-apartheid movement were disturbed by the obedience of American businesses to racist apartheid policies in South Africa.

The Feminist Majority Foundation led the public outcry over the Taliban's human rights abuses against women and girls in Afghanistan. What do they and other opponents of gender discrimination think of the complicity of America's fast-food joints in Saudi Arabia? Or do American businesses, the golden arches, and American quick service purveyors of hamburgers, fries, pizzas and fried chicken in the Saudi kingdom get a free pass?

Source: From *The Washington Post*, 22 December 2001, p. A23 © 2001 *The Washington Post*. All rights reserved. Used by permission and protected by the Copyright Laws of the United States. The printing, copying, redistribution, or retransmission of the Material without express written permission is prohibited.

---

allegations of a strip-search and forced confession, the Commission vigorously defended their actions, accusing the woman of "wearing make-up, not covering her hair and moving around suspiciously while sitting with her Syrian colleague."[10] The Commission underscored its position that men and women should not mix at workplaces and that "the family sections at coffee shops and restaurants [the only seats where men and women are allowed to mix] are meant for families and close relatives."[11]

Actions of the semi-autonomous religious police complicate the challenge of matching human rights standards, national law, religious interpretations and customary practices in Saudi Arabia.[12] Several local columnists and groups protested the Mutaween's actions, including the National Society for Human Rights (NSHR). In a statement, the NSHR reportedly questioned why the Commission members had no police escort when arresting the woman, how she was forced into a taxi, and why she was not turned over to proper police officers in accordance with an Interior Ministry policy. When a reporter asked a US embassy official about the incident, the reporter was told it was being treated as "an internal Saudi matter," refusing further comment. If asked, what should Starbucks say about the incident? Is the company ethically complicit in a human rights violation for failing to "help protect" its customer? Should it at least protest the woman's arrest?

Another case raises similar issues involving a different foreign actor with operations in Saudi Arabia—the US military.[13] After unsuccessful efforts to seek internal reforms, Lieutenant Colonel Martha McSally, one of the first American women to fly combat planes, sued the US Secretary of Defense in December 2001, charging that US policy requirements in Saudi Arabia discriminated against women and violated their religious freedom. The principal policy at issue required female military personnel traveling off base in Saudi Arabia to wear the *abaya*, a head-to-toe gown with matching headscarf. Related regulations prohibited women from driving, specified they ride in the back seat, and required a male escort at all times.

The *abaya* policy appeared most objectionable because it required a woman to wear clothing related to a particular religious faith. Ironically, the clothing dispute recalled a related practice by the Taliban, widely criticized in the United States, mandating that Afghan women cover themselves with a head-to-toe *burqa*. The military policy reportedly stemmed from a desire to respect local cultural and religious practices but did not constitute requirements under Saudi law. In fact, neither female US State Department officials nor the wives of military personnel stationed in Saudi Arabia were forced to wear the *abaya*.

Congressional legislation in 2002 prohibited the US military's *abaya* requirement. By contrast, British Midland Airways reportedly adopted a corporate policy in 2005 that required its stewardesses flying to Saudi Arabia to wear an *abaya* and walk behind male counterparts in the airport and other public areas. One stewardess who objected asked not to be scheduled for such flights, despite an effective cut in her pay, and refused to go when assigned to fly to Saudi Arabia. She appealed a subsequent suspension but a labor tribunal upheld the company's requirements as based on "the need to conform to local customs, practices and law." Although an official Saudi dress code from 1979 requires foreign women to dress conservatively, there is no requirement to wear an *abaya*.[14] Should MNE policies force female employees to wear *abaya*s when in Saudi Arabia as a way to respect local culture?

These case scenarios focus primarily on how discriminatory practices affect non-Saudi women, leaving a question about whether, or to what extent, non-discrimination rights apply to individual Saudi women as well, i.e. should a woman's nationality, or religion, make a difference in how she is treated? Law and custom prevent Saudi women from exercising political power, but if they could, it is possible that the majority of those women might support religious interpretations that inspire many of the discriminatory practices embedded in the local culture. Consider whether a political or religious majority opinion should determine the standards for the treatment of all women in Saudi Arabia (or other countries and cultures), or whether certain minimum anti-discrimination standards exist as an *individual* human right that should not be abridged, even by majority rule, in any country or under any regime.

Showing respect for local culture does not mean adopting a position of cultural relativism that rejects the possibility for global norms to override local cultural practices if values clash. Ethical dilemmas require careful assessment to decide what cultural components should be respected, and why. Not all cultural practices may merit respect, even when based on asserted religious beliefs. When in Rome, one should not always do as the Romans do (or did).

In fact, the old adage might even be reversed. When in ancient Rome, one should not engage in certain local customs, such as the practice of feeding Christians to the lions. Foreign vendors who maintained food stands near the coliseum might even be criticized for benefiting from unethical complicity in the practice. The same judgment could be drawn regarding the Spanish inquisition's practice of torturing and executing persons deemed heretics by the interpreted beliefs of the Roman Catholic Church. Certain customary practices of early American Puritans included similarly objectionable rituals not endorsed by all ministers. For example, persons accused of conspiring with the devil and practicing witchcraft could face a water test, where the accused is bound and thrown into the water. Sinking (but possibly drowning) proved innocence while floating offered proof of guilt (the pure water would reject an impure person, as they rejected Christian baptism), leading to potential execution.[15]

The factual existence of these various historical practices as a religiously connected part of local culture does not mean they were normatively "right." The same issues may be posed today as different cultural practices and traditions, some linked to professed religious beliefs, encounter the ethical scrutiny of an evolving global society. Determining ethical minimum conditions principles sometimes requires starting with extreme cases and working inward until more difficult dilemmas blur the setting of clear normative priorities among competing value principles. With reference to cases already discussed, consider whether "honor killings" should be proscribed as a minimum ethical standard, even if endorsed by a country's religious majority. After reviewing the various discriminatory practices discussed above related to race, gender, religion or some combination of these elements, identify what other standards might comprise part of a minimum common morality guideline for a global society.

For MNEs and other external actors that interface with a local culture, responses can vary along a continuum, from adopting local values and practices to seeking an accommodation with local customs without sacrificing core standards, to supporting active change in practices where local culture clashes with global values. Business generally selects one of the first two approaches. An example of the adoption of local values appears in the last chapter, reflected in MNE marketing campaigns in India that promote skin-whitener products as a way to attract a desirable husband, improve social status and attain wealth. The second approach of cultural accommodation within acceptable normative bounds recalls initiatives in countries such as Bangladesh and Taiwan to establish certain minimal standards on such issues as child labor and debt bondage where MNEs own or contractually influence local factories.

MNE actions may also actively support changes in local cultural values, but such impacts are generally indirect, unintentional or at least unacknowledged. The actions against South Africa's apartheid policies represent one of the few instances where some MNEs openly campaigned to change a country's dominant (if minority) cultural system. A class discussion exercise could examine similar ethical issues raised by clashes between local culture and global values as applied to practices embedded in the caste system in India. Grounded in Hindu religious beliefs and customs, for

1,500 years the caste system has segregated Indians into groups with distinct political roles and socioeconomic privileges. With each person's place in society determined by birth, the culture left little room for substantial individual growth or improvement. India's 1950 constitution forbids caste discrimination, and quota policies reserve a proportion of national and state legislative seats, civil service positions, and university admissions for the lowest class of Untouchables or Dalits. Nevertheless, many caste system practices endure as a part of Indian culture and continue to shape and define important elements of India's political, economic and social life.[16]

General Electric confronts a cultural challenge in India where it sells ultrasound machines. These devices assist doctors with diagnoses of pregnant patients and can alert rural healthcare workers to potential childbirth problems that require transporting an expectant mother to a distant hospital. The machine's ultrasound images can also be used to determine the sex of a fetus, possibly leading to abortions. Indian culture has long sustained a family preference for boys as higher income earners and, especially among the poor, to avoid the financial burden of providing a dowry for girls at marriage. Female infanticide, killing newborn girls, has been a recognized social problem, but critics charge that increasing abortions of female fetuses, perhaps hundreds of thousands a year, are linked to wider use of ultrasound machines.

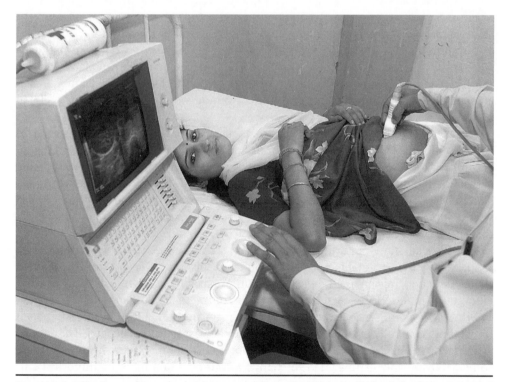

An expectant mother four months pregnant undergoes an ultrasound test to monitor the developing fetus at a hospital in New Dehli, India. The machines improve healthcare information, including in rural villages, but tests can also reveal the sex of a fetus, facilitating a cultural bias for sons. Photo by Prakash Singh/AFP/Getty Images.

Exhibit 8.3   GE Confronts Fetus Bias

India's Skewed Sex Ratio Puts GE Sales in Spotlight

By PETER WONACOTT

INDERGARH, India—General Electric Co. and other companies have sold so many ultrasound machines in India that tests are now available in small towns like this one. There's no drinking water here, electricity is infrequent and roads turn to mud after a March rain shower. A scan typically costs $8, or a week's wages.

GE has waded into India's market as the country grapples with a difficult social issue: the abortion of female fetuses by families who want boys. Campaigners against the practice and some government officials are linking the country's widely reported skewed sex ratio with the spread of ultrasound machines. That's putting GE, the market leader in India, under the spotlight. It faces legal hurdles, government scrutiny and thorny business problems in one of the world's fastest-growing economies.

"Ultrasound is the main reason why the sex ratio is coming down," says Kalpana Bhavre, who is in charge of women and child welfare for the Datia district government, which includes Indergarh. Having a daughter is often viewed as incurring a lifetime of debt for parents because of the dowry payment at marriage. Compared to that, the cost of an ultrasound "is nothing," she says.

For more than a decade, the Indian government has tried to stop ultrasound from being used as a tool to determine gender. The devices use sound waves to produce images of fetuses or internal organs for a range of diagnostic purposes. India has passed laws forbidding doctors from disclosing the sex of fetuses, required official registrations of clinics and stiffened punishments for offenders. Nevertheless, some estimate that hundreds of thousands of girl fetuses are aborted each year.

GE—by far the largest seller of ultrasound machines here through a joint venture with Indian outsourcing giant Wipro Ltd.—has introduced its own safeguards, even though that means forsaking sales. "We stress emphatically that the machines aren't to be used for sex determination," says V. Raja, chief executive of GE Healthcare

South Asia. "This is not the root cause of female feticide in India."

But the efforts have failed to stop the problem, as a growing economy has made the scans affordable to more people. The skewed sex ratio is an example of how India's strong economy has, in unpredictable ways, exacerbated some nagging social problems, such as the traditional preference for boys. Now, some activists are accusing GE of not doing enough to prevent unlawful use of its machines to boost sales.

"There is a demand for a boy that's been completely exploited by multinationals," says Puneet Bedi, a New Delhi obstetrician. He says GE and others market the machines as an essential pregnancy tool although the scans often aren't necessary for mothers in low risk groups. . . .

Vivek Paul, who helped build the early ultrasound business in India, first as a senior executive at GE and then at Wipro, says blame should be pinned on unethical doctors, not the machine's suppliers. "If someone drives a car through a crowded market and kills people, do you blame the car maker?" says Mr. Paul, who was Wipro's chief executive before he left the company in 2005. Mr. Paul is now a managing director at private equity specialists TPG Inc., formerly known as Texas Pacific Group. . . .

India has long struggled with an inordinate number of male births, and female infanticide—the killing of newborn baby girls—remains a problem. The abortion of female fetuses is a more recent trend, but unless "urgent action is taken," it's poised to escalate as the use of ultrasound services expands, the United Nations Children's Fund said in a report this year. India's "alarming decline in the child sex ratio" is likely to exacerbate child marriage, trafficking of women for prostitution and other problems, the report said. . . .

Boys in India are viewed as wealth earners during life and lighters of one's funeral pyre at death. India's National Family Health Survey, released in February, showed that 90% of parents with two sons didn't want any more children. Of those with two daughters, 38% wanted to try again. While there are restrictions on abortions in this Hindu-majority nation, the rules offer enough leeway for most women to get around them. . . .

Without discussing specific sales tactics, Mr. Raja, of GE Healthcare South Asia, acknowledges the company is "aggressive" in pursuing its goals. But he points out that ultrasound machines have broad benefits and make childbirth safer. As the machines become more available, women can avoid making long trips into cities where health care typically is more expensive, he says.

Indian authorities have tried to regulate sales. In 1994, the government outlawed sex selection and empowered Indian authorities to search clinics and seize anything that aided sex selection. Today any clinic that has an ultrasound machine must register with the local government and provide an affidavit that it won't conduct sex selection. To date, more than 30,000 ultrasound clinics have been registered in India.

GE has taken a number of steps to ensure customers comply with the law. It has educated its sales force about the regulatory regime, demanded its own affidavits from customers that they won't use the machines for sex selection, and followed up with periodic audits, say executives. They note that in 2004, the first full year it began implementing these new measures, GE's sales in India shrank by about 10% from the year before. The sales decline in the low-end segment, for black-and-white ultrasound machines, was especially sharp, executives say. Only last year did GE return to the sales level it had reached before the regulations were implemented, according to Mr. Raja.

Complying with Indian law is often tricky. GE can't tell if doctors sell machines to others who fail to register them. Different states interpret registration rules differently. GE also is under close scrutiny by activists battling the illegal abortion of female fetuses. Sabu George, a 48-year-old activist who holds degrees from Johns Hopkins and Cornell universities, crisscrosses the country to spot illegal clinics. . . .

A visit to the clinic in Indergarh, a town surrounded by fields of tawny wheat, shows the challenges GE faces keeping tabs on its machines. Inside the clinic, a dozen women wrapped in saris awaited tests on GE's Logiq 100 ultrasound machine. The line snaked along wooden benches and down into a darkened basement. On the wall, scrawled in white paint, was the message: "We don't do sex selection."

Manish Gupta, a 34-year-old doctor, said he drives two hours each way every week to Indergarh from much larger Jhansi city, where there are dozens of competing ultrasound clinics. He said even when offered bribes he refuses to disclose the sex of the fetus. "I'm just against that," Dr. Gupta said.

But he is not complying with Indian law. Although the law requires that clinics display their registration certificate in a conspicuous place, Dr. Gupta's was nowhere to be seen. When Dr. George, the social activist, asked for the registration, he was shown a different document, an application. But the application was for a different clinic: the Sakshi X-ray center. Dr. Gupta said the proper document wasn't with him, adding: "I must have forgotten it at home."

Asked by The Wall Street Journal about the clinic, the local chief magistrate of Datia district called for Dr. Gupta's dossier later in the day. When a local official arrived, "Sakshi X-Ray center" had been crossed out on the application. In blue pen was written the correct name, "Sheetal Nagar," the part of Indergarh where the clinic is located.

It's not clear how Dr. Gupta procured the GE machine. Dr. Gupta said he bought it from a GE company representative, but he declined to show documents of ownership. GE says it doesn't comment on individual customers.

Like the rest of India, the Datia district government has taken a number of steps to try to boost the number of girls in the district. For girls of poor families, the local government provides a place to live, free school uniforms and books. When they enter ninth grade, the government buys bicycles for them. Yet the low ratio of girls born hasn't budged much over the past decade, according to Ms. Bhavre, the district government official.

Ultimately, says Mr. Raja, head of GE Healthcare in South Asia, it's the job of the government, not companies, to change the prevailing preference for boys. "What's really needed is a change in mindsets. A lot of education has to happen and the government has to do it," he says.

India's Ministry of Health, which is now pursuing 422 different cases against doctors accused of using ultrasounds for sex selection, agrees. "Mere legislation is not enough to deal with this problem," the ministry said in a statement. "The situation could change only when the daughters are not treated as a burden and the sons as assets."

Source: *The Wall Street Journal*, 18 April 2007, p. A1. © 2007 by Dow Jones & Co. Inc. Reproduced with permission of Dow Jones & Co. Inc. via Copyright Clearance Center.

In this case, the Indian law prohibits doctors from revealing the gender of a fetus and requires clinics using ultrasound machines to register. GE adopted its own safeguards, educating salespeople about government regulations, requiring customers to sign affidavits not to use the machines for sex selection, and carrying out periodic audits. However, the resale of GE machines is difficult to track and Indian state governments can interpret regulations differently. Reflecting on the last chapter's discussion of marketing motives and methods, has GE met or exceeded minimum conditions for ethical marketing in this case scenario? Are their additional steps you believe the company should take to meet its responsibilities (including terminating sales)?

In terms of this chapter's focus on culture, the case reflects a situation where corporate actions complement national government efforts to change a local cultural practice. Does a coincidence between government regulations and corporate actions validate GE's decision to oppose its product's use in a long-standing local practice? Or, to pose the ethical dilemma more starkly, what if India's government did not have a law against using ultrasound machines to reveal the gender of a fetus? Should GE still place the same restriction on the sale of its equipment, or refrain entirely from marketing the product in India? Is India's cultural tradition of male preference, manifested through the abortion of female fetuses, wrong under international norms that GE should follow, or do a respect for local culture and a belief in cultural relativism require that GE refrain from imposing its judgments on a local practice?

CHALLENGING CULTURAL TRADITIONS: MUSIC, MOVIES AND MALLS

Changes to culture and the human environment do not always reflect systemic transformations or result from high-profile clashes between local and external values. Many times cultural change arises from a combination of broader and more disparate external challenges to local traditions. While singularly less impressive, the cumulative impact from these multiple challenges can significantly affect the direction, degree and speed of cultural change. The growth of influences associated with globalization suggests a trend toward the potential homogenization of cultures, promoted particularly by MNE commercial interests. In light of the predominant, though declining, role played by US-based MNEs, these homogenization effects sometimes appear as an "Americanization" of world cultures, rather than the emergence of a truly global culture.

The worldwide spread of US-based popular culture has been a recurring theme, often portrayed as a threat, for several decades. Spawned by aberrant US political and

economic dominance following the devastation of World War II, portrayals of affluent American life attracted attention and imitation in widely diverse countries and
cultures. Drawing initially on energy and images generated by youth-oriented movements in the 1960s, American icons soon covered the globe via commercialization
channels opened by the spread of US MNEs. Particularly through music, movies and
malls, components of US culture invaded other countries, challenging local cultural
traditions while reaping economic profit for US firms.

Music ranks as a leading example of globalization forces impacting local cultures.
From the enthusiastic response given rock bands on early trips behind the Iron
Curtain to the contemporary reach of MTV, popular music has especially captivated
young people from virtually all countries and cultures. Theater screens dominated by
Hollywood movies transmitted more detailed images of US ideas and values, whether
or not the stories reflected an accurate depiction of actual US life. Television programming reinforces US cultural impacts through the rebroadcast of many American
television serials, again selected for potential audience appeal rather than their accurate societal representation. Malls constitute a third transmission channel for challenging cultural traditions, hosting retail outlets that, whether or not foreign-owned,
generally promote trendy foreign (often American) consumer products with recognizable brand names. As discussed in the previous chapter, MNE marketing campaigns help build local demand for these products, often through lifestyle advertising
that promotes a foreign-fashioned image and idea as much as the actual product.

Publications critical of globalization trends often compile virtual catalogs of
real-life examples depicting the prevalence and implying the impact from MNE
promotion of entertainment and consumer goods. One book offers the following
passage to link these developments to the potential disruption, and reaction, in local
cultures. "The cultural products most widely distributed around the world bear the
stamp 'Made in the USA,' and almost any Hollywood film or video is bound to
offend traditional values somewhere. Scenes depicting independent women, amor-
ous couples, and kids talking back to parents upset all sorts of people across the globe
as assaults on family, religion and order."[17] Although the nature and seriousness of
the challenge to cultural traditions posed by these globalization forces will vary with
different countries and cultures, the perception of such a threat has motivated governmental responses in a number of countries, including purveyors of their own
cultural exports.

Canada probably feels the weight of US cultural influence more than any other
nation, with its comparatively small population concentrated along the country's
southern border with the United States. In an effort to preserve its own cultural
identity, Canada has subsidized local television and film projects while promulgating
restrictions that limit foreign textbook sales, magazine ownership and advertising,
and the amount of non-Canadian music played on radio stations. The government declared its right to take cultural exception to dismantling commercial trade
barriers under US–Canada bilateral accords as well as the North American Free Trade
Agreement (NAFTA). Canada's heritage minister, Sheila Copps, also hosted a meeting of 20 culture ministers from various countries aimed at forming a network to
prevent "national cultures from being steamrolled by global trade and economic

forces" such as reflected in the WTO. As she expressed the concern: "Globalization is a fact of life. But it has come on us so rapidly that on the cultural side we don't have any institutional instruments to deal with it."[18]

France represents both an historical transmitter of national culture to other countries and an aggressive defender of French cultural traditions from threats posed by more recent "Americanization" influences. Despite somewhat grudging acquiescence in the construction of a Euro Disneyland theme park outside Paris, France imposes restrictions on the amount of screen time that can be devoted to US productions both on television and in movie theaters. Concerned about the way adoption of American phrases could corrupt the French language, a government commission seeks to protect French culture by restricting the growing use of anglophone terminology associated with the internet and commercial advertising.

By law, civil servants in France should use French in communications. The government commission directed replacing "e-mail" with *le courriel* and "hacker" with *le fouineur*.[19] "Start-up" should give way to *jeune-pousse*, meaning "young bud." But the general campaign for linguistic purity, as determined by the Academie Française, faces popular resistance. As observed by Gilles Perles, director of the British American Institute in Aix-en-Provence: "It's the fact that we're in Europe, it's globalization, and it's the Internet." The resultant pressure on the French language and culture appears everywhere.

> A bulletin board for Mr. Clean cleaning products shouts out: "Serial Cleaner," a play on the phrase "serial killer," which is well known here from American movies. Nissan advertises its new sport-utility vehicle by pointing out that it has plenty of "*le* familyspace." A fashion supplement in the newspaper *Liberation* features the latest American trend in office-casual clothes, "*le* Friday wear." A popular radio station boasts 20 minutes of music "nonstop."[20]

India, whose Bollywood studios can surpass Hollywood in the number of movies produced annually, employs regulations that restrict the distribution of American films to be shown in local theaters. India earns substantial revenue from foreign distribution of its films, particularly in the large overseas communities of Indian expatriates. Nevertheless, the government joins many other developing countries in opposing new international trade agreements that would restrict a nation's right to regulate foreign imports in order to maintain national culture. These countries see giant US entertainment MNEs poised to overwhelm local companies if regulations are removed, risking the preservation of local culture along with the costs to local jobs and sales that might arise from increased imports.

In 2005 the UN Educational, Scientific and Cultural Organization (UNESCO) debated "the first international treaty designed to protect movies, music and other cultural treasures from foreign competition," also described in a news article as "a referendum on the world's love-hate relationship with Hollywood, Big Macs and Coca-Cola."[21] The Convention on the Protection and Promotion of Diversity of Cultural Expressions was approved by an overwhelming vote of 143–2, with only the United States and Israel dissenting. US officials protested the measure's potential use for unfair trade protection, but a delegate from Benin contended: "Not all countries are equal—some need to be protected."[22] The Convention does not override existing treaties so it's practical impact is unclear, particularly with regard to potential conflicts with WTO free-trade rules.

Exhibit 8.4 discusses an American product that might easily be found in the company of music, movie and mall exports. Although already sold in 18 other Beijing locations, the opening of a Starbucks outlet at the museum within China's historic Forbidden City sparked lively debate over the perceived challenge to Chinese culture and traditions. More than an oddity where local culture includes drinking tea, Starbucks's commercial coffee ventures, particularly the one in the Forbidden City, offended some Chinese as an affront to their country's long historical traditions and a seemingly blatant example of American imperialism. Other local residents and visitors perceived nothing more than a potential economic opportunity or just a "cool" place to hang out with friends.

A later article on Starbucks's Chinese operations referred to a local media report that 70 percent of people surveyed opposed the Forbidden City store and would not patronize it. The company took other steps to lower its profile, such as reducing its logo size, but remained there and pursued plans to open hundreds of new cafés across China. The controversy reignited in early 2007 when a Chinese

A Starbucks Coffee shop window reflects palaces in Beijing's historic Forbidden City, once reserved for China's emperors and now among the world's great heritage sites. Protested by some Chinese as a cultural affront, the shop remained open for nearly 7 years as the controversy raised the new company's profile, both negative and positive. Photo by Cancan Chu/Getty Images.

Exhibit 8.4   Selling Starbucks in the Forbidden City

Tempest Brews Over Coffee Shop

U.S. Chain Stirs Ire in Beijing's Forbidden City

By JOHN POMFRET
Washington Post Foreign Service

Beijing, November 22. A Starbucks has opened in the Forbidden City and it's causing a stink in Beijing.

It could be called globalization run amok and bad taste, even American cultural imperialism. It is certainly an irritant to Chinese nationalists. Or it may be just a nice place to get a mellow macchiato on a cold fall afternoon. But the opening last month of the nineteenth Starbucks outlet in the Chinese capital, smack in the middle of the ancient home of China's emperors, has sparked a tempest in a coffee mug.

"I'm against it," said Duan Fei, a gruff, middle-aged officer in the People's Liberation Army who visited the sprawling 500-year-old confines of the Forbidden City Museum today with his wife and son. "This is an American product. It's imperialism. We should kick it out."

"It's fantastic," said Huang Bing, a twenty-something part-time model from Shanghai, traveling to Beijing for the first time with her boyfriend. "Coffee is cool now. The Forbidden City can be cool, too."

Dozens of Chinese newspapers have reported on the issue, focusing on complaints about what nationalists regard as barbarian infiltration of the hallowed halls of China's past. It is also a hot topic in China's Internet chat rooms. Beijing's government, ever vigilant, wants the controversy to blow over soon. And the folks at the Forbidden City and Starbucks wonder what hit them.

"We had no idea there would be this kind of reaction," said Chen Junqi, the head of the director's office of the Forbidden City Museum, who has become the shell-shocked point man in the affair. "Let's just say this is an exploratory deal."

He said the museum board will meet soon to discuss what to do about the controversy. Starbucks is lapping it up faster than the foam off a latte.

"What we really like is all the exposure," said Brian Sun, the Chinese-born boss of Starbucks in Beijing, who has been giving nonstop interviews to Chinese reporters. "Right now, any exposure is good. It gets our name known in the market. Before, people said, 'What the heck is Starbucks anyway?' Now they know."

Beijing's reaction to Starbucks underscores some timeless issues for China, notably its conflicted response to Western goods and its love–hate relationship with its own history. The shop has touched a nerve in particular because Starbucks is strongly identified as an American brand, and because it is hawking coffee in a land of tea drinkers. It highlights what many here feel is the victory of commerce and kitsch over a culture that, everyone in China will tell you, is 5,000 years old.

Central to that culture is the Forbidden City, whose only equivalent in the West could be Versailles or Buckingham Palace. First planned in the early fifteenth century, the 8 million-square-foot complex of 800 golden-roofed buildings was home to two dynasties, the Ming and the Qing, China's last. The door frame on one entrance, the Gate of Supreme Harmony, starts out square, indicating the earth, and ends up round, signifying that all who enter are now in the realm of heaven.

At one time, foreigners were rarely allowed inside the Forbidden City. It was only opened to Chinese tourists in 1949, following the Communist revolution. Today the palace is also one of the world's great museums, containing 1 million paintings and objects d'art. Unfortunately, only a tiny percentage are ever seen because the museum lacks the space to show its treasures and the museum's managers—unlike those who built the Shanghai Art Museum in 1996—have never really backed the idea of a museum for the masses.

Last month, Starbucks opened its shop just to the east of the Gate of Heavenly Purity deep inside the emperor's palace, on the corner of a massive square. Barely bigger than a closet, it contains an espresso machine, a counter and two tables with six chairs. It serves about 300 people a day.

Starbucks' new home is in a building called Jiuqinfang in Chinese, meaning "place of many sleepers," a dozing den for court officials—a bit ironic for a merchant of caffeine. Right next to the Starbucks kiosk is a store hawking cheesy porcelain replicas of Chinese antiques.

"We like them here," said one shopkeeper. "It means more foreigners come. And foreigners have lots of money."

The appearance of commercial outlets in the center of China's cultural landmarks is almost de rigueur in China these days. The Forbidden City itself is already home to dozens of shops, selling fans, film, stale cookies and Coke.

There is a Starbucks look-alike with a huge garish sign in the middle of the Summer Palace on the outskirts of Beijing, where China's emperors used to beat the heat. The Great Wall in the suburb of Badaling looks like a Wild West brothel at Christmas, festooned with colored lights, and with touts selling bottled water at outrageous prices. At the Great Wall at Mutianyu, the PA system on the chairlift to the top blasts out one song: "I'm a Barbie Girl in a Barbie World."

Part of the reason for this is China's lust for development, a desire that has both awed and amazed foreigners for years.

"It took some adjusting, just twenty years ago, for me to get used to the National People's Congress being rented out for multinational banquets," said Jerome Cohen, an American lawyer with the longest tenure in Beijing.

Cohen recalled a banquet at the Great Hall of the People in 1980 when the news broke in New York that John Lennon had been murdered, stunning the diners. "When he felt it was his turn to say something appropriate," Cohen said, "the vice minister of foreign trade sitting next to me shook his head sadly and said: 'That man earned a lot of foreign exchange for his country.' "

During the Cultural Revolution, teams of Red Guards crisscrossed the country, smashing temples and pagodas and burning books. Today, Chinese bulldozers have flattened most of Beijing's old neighborhoods, replacing them with cement-block buildings in the name of modernization.

All these issues resonate in the Starbucks debate.

"Opening a coffee shop in the Forbidden City is like splattering black paint on the portrait of Chairman Mao on Tiananmen Square. Chinese people won't stand for it!" one angry Beijing resident wrote on a local Web site.

"What's all this stuff about protecting Chinese culture?" countered another. "Are we supposed to get the women to re-bind their feet? That just won't happen."

The issue becomes even more complicated because China continues to have a love–hate relationship with the United States.

"Some people believe this is US imperialism," said Chen of the Forbidden City Museum. "They have powerfully strong ethnic feelings. I don't think we should criticize them. We should protect them. They are very lovable. Like wolves who pee around their dens, they are protecting their homeland."

But Chinese are not the only ones uncomfortable with the coffee shop. Orville Schell, dean of the journalism school at the University of California at Berkeley, said he also sees a pattern of Western imperialism in Starbucks' foray into the Chinese palace.

But another reason involves China's troubled view of its own history. For decades, even centuries, intellectuals here have lambasted their history, their glorious past and what Chinese today call their feudal roots. These roots are both a source of tremendous pride and obvious pain for many Chinese. Dinner conversations with Chinese intellectuals often turn into maudlin affairs—with the intellectuals, deep in their cups, alternatively bemoaning and exalting China's past and lambasting and glorifying the West.

"Part of what makes Westerners Westerners is that unique Promethean energy that makes them want to go where they cannot get, and, indeed, are often not wanted. Whether the Amazon, Tibet, Antarctica or Mecca, there has long been a perverse desire to penetrate the inner sanctums of the most remote, sequestered and reluctant places on the globe," he said. "The *ne plus ultra* of 'forbidden' places must be the Forbidden City."

But Schell continued: "I have never been one to eschew a nice frothy cappuccino."

television personality provoked nationalist sentiments with an internet posting that denounced Starbucks's Forbidden City branch, saying: "This is not globalization, but abuse of Chinese culture."[23] Starbucks finally closed this outlet in July, 2007 reportedly after officials decided the coffeehouse had to operate under the brand of the Palace Museum. By year's end, the company had 230 coffeehouses throughout China.[24]

In reality, Starbucks appeal aims at the growing Chinese middle class rather than the entire population, most of whom cannot afford the product's high cost relative to local standards. In many cases, the attraction is not the taste of the Starbucks coffee but rather the image associated with its very public consumption. The regional manager for the J. Walter Thompson advertising firm suggests that Starbucks's Chinese customers "go there to present themselves as modern Chinese in a public setting," typically spending extended periods of time lingering over their drink. A customer in Shanghai reported that he preferred the taste of tea, which he drinks at home, but buys coffee from Starbucks because "It's an attitude"—one of "relaxed affluence."[25]

A Starbucks outlet in the Forbidden City would not cause the abandonment or collapse of Chinese culture. However, is Starbucks's entry into China only symbol, or substance as well, in terms of posing a challenge to cultural traditions? Consider the emerging cumulative impact of hundreds of Starbucks cafés spread across China, combined with other food and fashion outlets. Add to this picture the Great Wall of China trimmed with Christmas lights while a nearby chairlift treats passengers to the song: "I'm a Barbie Girl in a Barbie World." At some point, do seemingly small and relatively innocuous foreign pieces of music, movies and malls become a more significant collage of external cultural influences that can change local culture? Who should decide whether the direction, degree and speed of that change are desirable?

For China, the opening to global forces comes through explicit government decisions with active attempts to exercise regulatory control over the operations of foreign MNEs. For example, the government acted to ban a Nike television commercial that used a video game-style battle showing US basketball star LeBron James defeating a kung fu master and a pair of dragons, considered a sacred symbol in Chinese culture.[26] Nevertheless, even this centrally planned and controlled economy faces monumental challenges to manage foreign nuances through multiple layers of regional and local governments across business sectors being transformed under the dynamic of growing market forces. China's entry into the World Trade Organization places even more constraints on the government's ability to impose nationalistic restrictions. To complicate matters further, the external forces that appear ready to progressively alter Chinese society stem from multiple and diverse foreign sources, with easily identifiable US influences actually playing a relatively minor role.

Despite the conception that "globalization" and "Americanization" are nearly synonymous, at least in the world's popular culture, reality presents a distinctly more varied and nuanced mosaic. US MNEs no longer dominate global commerce, as European, Japanese and a growing number of enterprises from other countries have bought or overtaken many prominent American brands. As observed in the book *Global Dreams*, which critiques the growth of MNE commercial influences in general, "It is now obvious that you do not have to be American to sell American culture."[27] As the authors observe, Japanese or European MNEs have purchased major US music and movie studios, or surpassed traditional US labels in capturing global markets. Is it still American culture if peddled or adapted by non-American ownership?

BLENDS AND CONTRASTS IN CORPORATE CULTURE

The reality of modern business strategy increasingly blurs the nationality of MNEs, their products and even their workforce. Cross-investments, joint ventures, mergers and a vast array of intercorporate alliances mix and match business organizations and operations, especially across the Triad of North America, Europe and Japan. As a corollary result, cultural components and associations within these business units also mix and evolve. An MNE must blend the customary values of a managerial staff and workforce comprising thousands of individuals drawn from scores of countries with distinctively different cultural traditions. Link that enterprise to several other similarly challenged MNEs through strategic alliance arrangements and the task of managing this multinational, multilingual, multicultural Tower of Babel comes more clearly into focus.

MNEs seek to foster a common corporate culture to facilitate the coordination of essential functions, although the resulting blend increasingly reflects a multinational hybrid more than any single national model. Most MNE operations retain dominant traits drawn from developed home country cultures, including the slower incorporation of Japan's more distinctive business traditions. Cultural challenges still emerge from contrasts in the developed countries between MNE and local business styles and priorities, including the ordering of relationships among corporate stakeholders.

For example, US management practices prioritized return to shareholder value over the interests of other stakeholders. By contrast, traditional European approaches often incorporated management, labor and government interests through tripartite dialogues that reflected a broader array of societal interests. The Japanese culture of consensual decision making recognized labor security as an important management objective, along with responsiveness to government leadership on actions required to meet Japan's developmental needs. These varying approaches shaped different roles for business within their societies, affecting the broader matrix of cultural traditions. Nevertheless, shifting patterns of competition and collaboration among MNEs from all three regions increasingly mute these historical differences through the impact of global business strategies.

Cross-investments and strategic alliances raise issues of how much to adjust or adapt an MNE's traditional business culture to a new national environment, with resulting impacts on the host country's culture as well. US MNEs in Europe encountered societal criticism for insufficient sensitivity to employee welfare in large corporate lay-offs or plant closures.[28] Japanese MNEs with company union traditions faced the prospect of more adversarial negotiations with independently organized labor unions in the United States, sometimes choosing to locate plants in non-union states instead. Japanese and US differences emerged regarding the role of intellectual property in serving private versus community interests, as illustrated in a business dispute involving IBM and Fujitsu.[29]

Despite such differences in corporate practices among the developed countries, resultant challenges to cultural traditions can be mediated by relatively strong government institutions capable of regulating most undesirable impacts. By contrast, when MNEs operate within many developing countries and transitional economies, business cultures differ more widely while host governments possess less effective regulatory powers and options. A host government's mediation task proves especially difficult when MNE operations pose no direct challenge to official policies but exert diffuse, cumulative impacts on cultural traditions. Ethical analysis can examine such cases to evaluate the relative degree of responsibility different actors hold to assess and guide this type of cultural change.

For example, many Latin American countries exhibit embedded cultural practices that reflect traditions associated with both paternalism and *machismo*. The region's common Spanish heritage helped shape a patriarchal structure and personalized leadership style that marked the socioeconomic dominance of local family *grupos*.[30] When MNEs sought joint-venture partners to enter these countries, the *grupos* generally comprised the relatively small number of firms well enough established, both economically and politically, to constitute attractive allies for the foreign investors. Once conjoined, these commercial partners faced numerous challenges as they sought to either blend or choose between various aspects of their distinct business cultures, with potential resulting impacts on the surrounding host country's cultural traditions as well.

In the area of labor relations, privately held local companies sometimes approached employee issues the way landed elites dealt with rural workers, with the *patron* expecting personal loyalty while assuming paternalistic responsibilities toward his workers. By contrast, many US MNEs entering Latin America brought a more formal, institutional approach to labor relations, managed under the guidance of professional human resource executives. Gender issues also emerge when dealing with local *machismo* traditions and attitudes. The local hierarchy of predominantly male managers and business customers can create issues of authority and fair treatment for female employees in jointly run operations, including expatriate women raised and trained in the MNEs' home country culture.[31]

In another region of the world, Thomas Singer offered an early example of the ethical dilemmas MNEs confront in different cultures when he discussed Kaiser Aluminum's operations in Ghana during a conference on international business ethics in 1978. Among many labor relations challenges, he related how offering local workers traditional US-style medical coverage created conflicts with the local social structure. As he described the situation: "A Ghanaian worker may have more than one wife and is forced to choose which one should be covered by the company plan."[32] The Ghanaian concept of extended family also presented other sociocultural issues, such as how benefits from company disability or death insurance should be distributed among the many relatives.

The issue of employee benefit coverage for polygamous workers can still pose ethical questions for MNEs, especially where local cultural and sometimes religious traditions clash with most home country norms. Indonesia presents a contemporary test. Although not illegal, polygamy was discouraged for nearly two decades under the Suharto regime. More recently, polygamy is reportedly on the increase, with even an Indonesian vice-president openly maintaining three wives. Some advocates point to passages in the Koran that support the practice, with conditions, while other Islamic scholars argue for an interpretation in light of contemporary social conditions.[33] While the practice is declining overall in South Africa, polygamy remains socially acceptable and especially prevalent among Zulu and Swazi tribes. Indeed, Jacob Zuma, elected President of South Africa in 2009, remains an ardent supporter of polygamy and has several wives himself.[34] Would MNE subsidiaries or joint ventures simply be respecting local culture and religious practice by covering all wives and all children under employee benefit plans, or would the MNEs be encouraging polygamous practices that, at least in many home countries, may be perceived as a violation of ethical norms and women's rights? To which stakeholders should the MNEs respond, and which principles should guide their actions?

These business culture issues of blends and contrasts relate to broader globalization challenges to local culture because an evolving business culture will inevitably impact the surrounding host society. An MNE's presence within a country's economy transmits far more cultural influence than the mere importation of foreign goods. An MNE's reaction and responses to host country traditions can shape the direction, degree and pace of cultural change. From the standpoint of ethical decision making, the key decision choices when business cultures differ are: What cultural approach is "better," and who decides? Teleologists would want to assess selected cost/benefit measures for each decision case. Deontologists would seek to apply priority principles of fairness and justice. Consider how each approach might be used in evaluating cultural traditions such as paternalism, *machismo* and polygamy, and then evaluate the appropriate role and relative influence of different actors (local and foreign business partners, governments, civil society groups) in deciding how to respond.

Other international organizations, including intergovernmental institutions and NGOs, also face cultural change issues as they multinationalize or denationalize their staffing. Most UN institutions reflect the concept of an international civil service, while some EU institutions promote a similar approach on a regional level. The outlook, values and decisions taken by such officials can lead to cultural change just as surely, if perhaps not as directly or visibly, as MNE activities. The critical difference is that such international organizations are perceived legitimately to transcend individual national or cultural boundaries and hence appeal to common core standards, whereas MNEs remain wedded to the duality of both a global and a local personage, presenting more of a dilemma of choice. Do private MNEs carry less responsibility than other international organizations to follow the emerging value standards of a global community? Who should decide what cultural standards MNEs should adopt—where, when and why?

NOTES

1. For example, see G. Brooks, "Giant Mining Project in Papua New Guinea is Beset by Calamities," *The Wall Street Journal*, 24 April 1985, p. 1; K. Witcher, "Australian Mining Firm Meets Its Match as Tribesmen Invade Papua Gold Find," *The Wall Street Journal*, 29 December 1988, p. 1; C. McCoy, "Chevron Tries to Show It Can Protect Jungle While Pumping Oil: But Papua New Guinea Tribes Grow Restless Over Pact for Pipeline and a Road," *The Wall Street Journal*, 9 June 1992, p.1 (Exhibit 9.1); M. Shari, "Gold Rush in New Guinea," *Business Week*, 20 August 1995, pp. 66–8; and K. Richburg, "Mining Company Fills a Hole," *The Washington Post*, 30 November 1998, p. A19.
2. Witcher, "Australian Mining Firm Meets its Match."
3. Brooks, "Giant Mining Project."
4. A. Faiola, "Argentina's Lost World," *The Washington Post*, 8 December 1999, p. A1.
5. UN Universal Declaration of Human Rights, Article 18.
6. C. Lynch, "Women's Rights Dispute Rages," *The Washington Post*, 10 June 2000, p. A20. A similar clash arose during the World Summit on Sustainable Development in September, 2002 in discussions over the provision of women's healthcare services. Conservative groups attempted to omit references to "human rights and fundamental freedoms" that are generally used to counterbalance calls for consistency with "cultural and religious values" when agreements deal with issues that can relate to birth control and abortion. See K. Weiss, "Women Claim a Victory at UN Summit," *The Los Angeles Times*, home edn, 4 September 2002, p. A3.
7. R. Husseini, "Murder as Misdemeanor," *Ms*, vol. 13, issue 3, fall 2003, p. 36; M. Rizvi, "Honor Killings Persist Despite Gov't Claims," *Global Information Network*, 20 June 2002, p.1; L. Pervizat, "In the Name of Honor," and Z. Arat, "A Struggle on Two Fronts," *Human Rights Dialogue*, Carnegie Council on Ethics and International Affairs, series 2, no. 10, fall 2003, pp. 30–2.
8. Amnesty International in the United Kingdom offered a document with a suggested checklist and recommendations for corporate policies to manage situations involving potential human rights violations in Saudi Arabia. See Amnesty International UK Business Group, "Saudi Arabia: Business Briefing," London, June 2000, mimeo.
9. Information on this incident is drawn primarily from S. Verma, "Religious Police Arrest Mother for Sitting in Starbucks with a Man," *The Times* (London), 7 February 2008, p. 40; Verma, "Starbucks Mother Flouted the Law, Say Religious Police," *The Times* (London), 20 February 2008, p. 39; and A. Al-Zahrani, "Virtue Commission Defends Arrest of Businesswoman," *Arab News*, reported by BBC Worldwide Monitoring, 19 February 2008.
10. Verma, "Starbucks Mother Flouted the Law, Say Religious Police."
11. Ibid.
12. In an extreme clash of values not sanctioned by the Saudi authorities, earlier reports blamed the Mutaween for the death of 15 teenage girls when fire swept a school and students were prevented from fleeing, or bystanders from helping, because the girls lacked *abaya*s and could not be seen in public without them. See M. Eltahawy, "They Died for Lack of a Head Scarf," *The Washington Post*, 19 March 2002, p. A21.
13. A. Gerhart, "The Air Force Flier in the Ointment," *The Washington Post*, 7 January 2002, p. C1.
14. Editorial, "Not Buying the Abaya; British Airline Enforces Saudi Customs on Employees," *The Washington Times*, 14 May 2009, p. A18.
15. C. Hansen, *Witchcraft at Salem*, New York: Braziller, 1969, pp. 48–9, 157. I. Mather, *Remarkable Provinces*, repr. New York: Arno Press, 1977, pp. 198–204.
16. T. O'Neill, "Untouchable," *National Geographic*, vol. 203, no. 6, June 2003, pp. 2–31.
17. R. Barnet and J. Cavanagh, *Global Dreams*, New York: Simon & Schuster, 1994, pp. 15–16.
18. J. Geddes, "Canada's Culture Clash," *Maclean's*, 13 July 1998, vol. 111, issue 28, pp. 26–7. See also J. Weber, "Does Canadian Culture Need This Much Protection?" *Business Week*, 8 June 1998, p. 37.
19. C. Bremmer, "Gallic Language Police Repulse Anglo-American Spam Assault," *The Times* (London), 10 July 2003, p. 21.
20. K. Richburg, "French Snared in Web of English: Language Eroded by Globalization," *The Washington Post*, 17 September 2000, p. A19.
21. M. Moore, "U.N. Body Endorses Cultural Protection," *The Washington Post*, 21 October 2005, p. A14.
22. Ibid.

23. M. Dickie, "Starbucks' Forbidden City Outlet Has China Steaming," *Financial Times*, 19 January 2007, p. 15.
24. E. Judd, *Good Guanxi: Managing Government Relations in China*, Foundation for Public Affairs, 2008, p. vi.
25. G. Fowler, "Starbucks' Road to China," *The Wall Street Journal*, 14 July 2003, p. B1.
26. A. Ang, "China Bans Nike Television Commercial," *Associated Press*, 6 December 2004.
27. Barnet and Cavanagh, *Global Dreams*, p. 26.
28. For early examples where US MNE policies toward laid-off employees were criticized as violations of good corporate citizenship standards promoted by the OECD Guidelines, see J. Kline, *International Codes and Multinational Business*, Westport, CT: Quorum Books, 1985, pp. 78–80.
29. J. Badaracco, "The IBM–Fujitsu Conundrum," in Hoffman, M., Kamm, J., Frederick, R. and Petry, E. (eds), *Emerging Global Business Ethics*, Westport, CT: Quorum Books, 1994, pp. 79–88.
30. J. Kline, "Business Ethics in Chile: Foreign Practices and Domestic Traditions," in M. Hoffman, et al. (eds), *Emerging Global Business Ethics*, Westport, CT: Quorum Books, 1994, pp. 3–13.
31. For a case discussing issues that might confront a US female employee working at a US subsidiary in Mexico, see T. Beauchamp and N. Bowie (eds), *Ethical Theory and Business*, 6th edn, Upper Saddle River, NJ: Prentice Hall, 2001, pp. 627–9.
32. T. Singer, "Experiences of a Multinational Corporation with Respect to Adapting Overseas Operations to Cultural, Educational and Work Practices in Ghana and Jamaica," in Council of Better Business Bureaus, *Responsibilities of Multinational Corporations*, vol. I, Washington, DC: Council of Better Business Bureaus, 1978, pp. 77–88, 99–100.
33. E. Nakashima, "Debating Polygamy's Resurgence," *The Washington Post*, 28 November 2003, p. A1. Also see T. Mapes, "Table for Five? Chicken Magnate Puts Polygamy on Menu," *The Wall Street Journal*, 24 November 2003, p. A1.
34. K. Bruillard, "Which Mrs. Zuma Will be South Africa's First Lady?," *The Washington Post*, 8 May 2008, p. A1.

9

NATURE AND THE PHYSICAL ENVIRONMENT

INTRODUCTION

The concept of nature encompasses the myriad of elements that surround and sustain life, including essential resources in the physical environment that permit the maintenance and continued evolution of human life. As with culture and the human environment, change constitutes an integral part of nature and the physical environment. Critical normative questions arise from the unique type of interaction that occurs between humans and their physical environment. While all life adapts to changes in nature, humankind evolved unique capabilities to alter significantly its physical environment through intentional as well as unintentional actions. The capacity to affect the direction, degree and speed of change in the physical environment presents both dangers and opportunities. In essence, this capability involves the potential for conscious choice. Ethical analysis can help clarify the value implications of potential alternative actions and provide a guide to reasoned decision making.

The twentieth century saw exponential growth in human capacity to alter the physical environment, with accumulating evidence of adverse and potentially far-reaching damage to air, water and land resources. Globalization trends spread the scope of these impacts and sped their transmittal around the world through transnational business operations. Increasing debate focused on whether private enterprise calculations that drive most MNE activities can properly weigh the public good aspects of potential harm to the physical environment. Although governments should safeguard such public interests, many countries lack institutions sufficiently effective or responsible enough to control environmental degradation. Furthermore, the impact of adverse environmental actions taken in one country often spread to other countries and regions, because air and water pollutants do not recognize nor respect the political boundaries drawn by human authorities.

The global span of environmental issues shapes responses to the "W" questions posed by ethical analysis. The border-spanning reach of many environment problems complicates an assessment of questions regarding where such assessments should take place. Although some cases, such as oil pipeline ruptures, may present relatively contained impacts within a specific land area, issues such as damage to the earth's ozone layer or depletion of ocean fishing stock threaten truly global effects. These issues require examination of complex, interdependent relationships among many countries and cultures. Similarly, "when" questions involve a potentially longer time dimension than some other ethical issues. Responsibilities to future generations merit consideration when evaluating actions that can alter the sustainability of earth's essential physical resources.

The incorporation of broad geographic and generational elements leads to a correspondingly wide inclusion of many public and private sector actors in considering who possesses ethical rights and responsibilities. On one dimension, trade-offs will exist between various human groups distinguished by their generation, geography or level of socioeconomic development. From another perspective, issues may involve trade-offs between human and non-human life on the planet, raising somewhat different relative value considerations. Questions regarding what actions should be taken depend partly on the inherent versus instrumental value attributed to nature and the physical environment. Potential goals could seek environmental protection and preservation, restoration or enhancement, or exploitation with varying limits to meet sustainability concerns. The normative criteria used to choose answers to these questions will respond to the ethical question, why?

The central framing question for this chapter is: should corporations alter the environment in any way legally permissible (or should corporations follow voluntary ethical standards that minimize their environmental impact above and beyond legal requirements)?

CONCEPTUALIZING THE HUMAN RELATIONSHIP WITH NATURE

Questions regarding what actions should be taken, guided by reasoned ethical choice, raise contrasting decision approaches that are dependent, in part, on prior answers to the where, when and who questions. For instance, teleological calculations might first require defining whether to weigh cost/benefit outcomes for their impact on the physical environment *per se*, or for how the physical environment can serve the needs of humankind. This choice can be described as a contrast between a Naturalistic and a Humanistic or anthropocentric ethic.[1] The former approach casts humans as respectful stewards or trustees of nature and the physical environment; the latter view emphasizes ownership and property rights, essentially treating nature as a collection of physical resource commodities to be bought, sold and used to serve human objectives.[2]

If teleological cost/benefit assessments clearly favor human welfare, decisions still require determining whether possible outcomes should advance the interests of the majority, the least developed, the most powerful, or other distinct groups among human populations. Intergenerational trade-offs also arise in projecting the costs and benefits of actions that may, for example, require sacrificing some economic growth and poverty alleviation now to preserve physical environment resources for unborn future generations.

Deontological principles provide possible alternative guideposts for decision making. For example, valuing nature and the physical environment could mean seeking environmental protection, restoration and/or enhancement, signifying increasing levels of duty and obligation. Causality could be used to allocate some responsibility, with parties causing harm to the physical environment incurring requisite duties to restore the damage done (i.e. the "polluter pays" principle).

Responsibilities toward the environment might also be apportioned according to capability, with actors (countries and/or companies) possessing the most capacity to protect nature's resources bearing proportionate obligations to do so. Evaluating a party's degree of control over actions impacting the environment suggests one way to help operationalize principles dealing with causality and capability, such as assessing the level of ownership or influence a corporate entity holds in a joint business venture.

Relevant deontological guidelines might also be conceptualized in the context of international human rights principles. The UN Universal Declaration of Human Rights does not address rights linked specifically to nature and the physical environment, but broad environmental principles have emerged from UN forums such as the landmark 1992 Earth Summit in Rio de Janeiro. Perhaps there should be an individual human right to a clean and safe environment, and a corollary duty to protect such an environmental right for future generations.[3] Alternatively, rather than focusing on rights of the individual, environmental principles might begin from a recognition of complex interdependence between human and non-human life, evolving within the common surrounding sphere of nature and the physical environment. Conceptualized thus, a common morality ethic might develop to match the direction and needs of an emerging and sustainable global community.

PROTECTION, RESTORATION AND SUSTAINABLE DEVELOPMENT

Over the past several decades, rising concern about increased damage to the earth's physical environment sparked remarkable growth in the time, attention and priority accorded environmental issues by governments, business and NGOs. Few advocates populate the extreme positions that argue for either unconstrained exploitation of environmental resources or absolute preservation policies that would negate potential human development. However, vigorous debate takes place across the intervening spectrum where diverse public and private sector actors pursue agendas that reflect some combination of environmental protection, restoration and sustainable development goals.

Natural resource projects in developing countries provide some of the most prominent and useful examples for ethical analysis. As illustrated in earlier chapters, these projects often involve interrelated political, cultural and environmental concerns, as portrayed in case scenarios on MNE investments in Nigeria and Papua New Guinea. Countries with relatively ineffective government institutions run the greatest risk of adverse environmental (and political and cultural) impacts from such large natural resource investments.

A long-running controversy over environmental damage associated with the exploitation of oil reserves in Ecuador[4] poses a series of important questions for ethical analysis. This precedent-setting dispute led to a court case filed in New York based on assertions of environmental damage caused during a quarter-century of oil development by a joint-venture operation involving US-based Texaco. One question asks when project performance should be evaluated and whether contemporary or prior environmental standards should be used to judge the business venture's activities. Texaco's president argued that the business venture "complied not only with Ecuadorian laws and regulations but also with prevailing international industry standards," asserting further that most oil spills resulted from natural disasters rather than operational shortcomings.[5] Other Texaco officials compared operations in Ecuador to "the way the oil patch was operated in the US twenty years ago," protesting the use of standards evolved in the early 1990s to judge the company's work dating from 1967.[6] By the time the court case was filed, Texaco's involvement in the Ecuadorian project had ended.

The question of who has responsibilities in this case becomes linked to issues of timing as well as control and capability. The government of Ecuador not only set the prevailing legal regulations for business activities but actually participated directly in developing an oil sector that became a principal component of the country's economy. The state oil company, Petroecuador, was Texaco's joint venture partner in the project, Texpet. Texaco held a minority ownership position with 37.5 percent of the joint venture but exercised operational control through a contract with the government of Ecuador. The operating contract expired in 1990, two years before Texaco sold its share and three years before the court case was filed. Consider how these various factors might be used to allocate relative responsibility between Texaco and the government of Ecuador for actions undertaken by Texpet.

Decisions on when to evaluate factors in this case also affect the identity of who is involved, since the composition of both business and government actors evolved over time. When Texaco sold its shares in Texpet the company's existence as a legal person in Ecuador changed, leaving the US parent corporation as the targeted respondent for public criticism or legal action. As the court case dragged on, a 2001 merger created a new entity, ChevronTexaco. Corporate representatives contend that the new enterprise cannot be sued or held responsible for actions taken by a company that no longer exists.[7] The government of Ecuador also experienced transformations in its leadership, character and position during this dispute. After initially opposing the attempt to file a case in New York courts, the government changed its position when a different political faction took control. Then, in 1995, the government reached and certified an agreement whereby Texaco reportedly spent $40million to help clean up some toxic wastewater pits in rough proportion to its former ownership share. However, both local and foreign critics attacked this agreement and it was voided by the next Ecuadorian administration.[8]

This case set new legal precedents when the New York court sent the case to Ecuador for trial in 2002, but ruled that the foreign court's decision would be binding on the US parent company. Exhibit 9.1 provides an updated discussion of this long-running story. The court case in Ecuador yielded competing studies and expert testimony regarding asserted damage to the environment and human health as well

In May 1999, a local resident sits in front of an oil pit left by Texaco, some 200 yards from his home in Ecuador. While environmental damage is clear, a landmark lawsuit is struggling to determine how much compensation is due, from whom, to whom, and whether an Ecuadoran or US court should decide. Photo by Justin Ide/Getty Images.

as disputes over which actors bear what level of responsibility. The article depicts a pending judicial decision, but further legal and political delays appear inevitable after bias and bribery charges led the judge to recuse himself from the case.[9] Whatever the legal outcome, what ethical assessments should be made in this case scenario, based primarily on which key factors?

One approach might seek to determine whether Texaco's responsibility should be evaluated teleologically by its operational impact on the environment and human health or deontologically by specific operational process standards (such as local legal regulations or industry practice, at the time or now). Readers might compare these assessments with the Bhopal gas leak scenario in Chapter 5. Should corporations employ the best safety and environmental standards in operations throughout the world or is it sufficient to comply with local regulatory requirements? Should a joint-venture partnership with a state enterprise such as Petroecuador affect which standards are followed?

Political factors also may be important in assigning levels of corporate responsibility. The current President of Ecuador called Texaco's earlier cleanup a "charade" and initiated legal proceedings against former government officials who approved, asserting that their action did not relieve ChevronTexaco of responsibility. Although Chevron's lawyers initially asked the US court to move the trial to Ecuador and rely on the "professionalism of the Ecuadoran judicial system," an adverse ruling in

Exhibit 9.1   Ecuador and Chevron/Texaco Dispute Oil Damage

In Ecuador, High Stakes Against Chevron

JUAN FORERO; *Washington Post Foreign Service*

Deep in the northern Ecuadoran rain forest, next to pits filled with noxious sludge, a lawyer on his very first case argued that a U.S. oil company had deliberately fouled a swath of jungle nearly the size of Delaware during two decades of production.

Wearing a straw hat for the recent outdoor hearing, Pablo Fajardo was delivering the final arguments in a lawsuit that began in New York in 1993 against Texaco but is wrapping up here against Chevron, which bought Texaco in 2001. The stakes are high—and so tinged with nationalism that Ecuador's President Rafael Correa has openly sided with the plaintiffs, 48 individuals representing tens of thousands of people in the region.

If the judge rules against Chevron, the company could face the largest damages award ever handed down in an environmental case, dwarfing the $3.9 billion awarded against ExxonMobil for the 1989 spill in Alaska.

A report by a court-appointed team last year concluded that pollution caused mainly by Texaco's Ecuadoran affiliate, Texaco Petroleum, had led to 1,401 cancer deaths in this stretch of Amazonian jungle. The team's leader, Ecuadoran geologist Richard Cabrera, reported finding high levels of toxins in soil and water samples near Texaco's production sites and assessed damages at up to $27.3 billion.

"This is a simple case,'" said Fajardo, 37, a former oil worker. "We ask, is there damage or not? If there is damage, who pays? And if there is payment, how much and to whom?"

For Fajardo and his team, two 20-something lawyers financed by a Philadelphia law firm, the blame rests squarely with Texaco and, now, Chevron. They say that for 18 years, from the time Texaco started full-scale production in Ecuador in 1972, the company unloaded drilling mud and wastewater into hundreds of unlined pits or directly into waterways. They accuse Texaco of choosing savings over safety, and say the company botched a highly publicized cleanup of its production sites in the 1990s.

Chevron argues that Texaco complied with Ecuadoran law and that the case is driven more by emotion than science. A cornerstone of its defense is that Ecuador's government relieved Texaco of responsibility after the $40 million, three-year cleanup, which ended in 1998. Chevron also blames Texaco's successor and former partner, Petroecuador, saying that the state oil company is responsible for hundreds of oil spills since it took over operations in 1990.

Attorneys for Chevron call Cabrera's report a sham and say he was cozy with the plaintiffs. The company has issued its own expert reports to support its assertion that there is no link between oil and cancer in this swath of jungle.

Judge Juan Nuñez said he will begin reviewing about 145,000 pages of evidence after reports on the effects of the discharges on fishing and agriculture are completed.

"This trial should finish this year," he said, speaking in his bare office here in Lago Agrio, a dusty oil town named for Sour Lake, Texas, where Texaco got its start in 1903. "This has taken too long."

The case has attracted the attention of energy companies worldwide and, closer to home, the interest of Ecuador's 46-year-old populist president.

Correa, who took office in 2007 and has frequently tangled with oil companies, has said that Texaco's "savage exploitation" of oil "killed and poisoned people." He has also called Texaco's cleanup a charade, in which the company simply covered polluted sites with dirt, and labeled Chevron's Ecuadoran attorneys "sellouts."

Last April, Correa called for criminal investigations of former government officials who had signed off on Texaco's cleanup in 1998. In September, the attorney general indicted two Chevron attorneys and seven former government officials—two years after prosecutors had dismissed a similar criminal complaint against the same people.

That is not the way Chevron had hoped events would unfold when its lawyers filed motions in federal court in New York earlier this decade vouching for the professionalism of the Ecuadoran judicial system and asking that the trial be moved here. In 2003, proceedings began, alternating between Lago Agrio's ramshackle courthouse and visits to oil production sites and waste pits. But nearly six years later, Chevron's rosy assessment has given way to a sobering recognition that it may lose the case.

"We're concerned that no court in Ecuador is going to be able to hear or rule freely," said James Craig, a Chevron spokesman. "Clearly, the thumbs of politics are weighing heavily on the scales of justice in Ecuador, and the president has played a major part in that."

During the trial's latest stage, the "judicial inspections" of aging waste sites, local Cofan Indians in traditional garb and residents who say Texaco's operations left them ill showed up to watch the opposing lawyers spar. Judge Nuñez, a baseball cap worn low over his forehead, listened intently.

Among those who came on a recent day was Gabriel Ruales, who recounted how his family used to bathe and fish in a nearby river. He had brought along a 15-year-old son who suffers from a mental disorder and was seated in a wheelchair. "The water was completely salty, poisoned," Ruales said.

Carmen Isabel Bone, a nurse's assistant, also said the local drinking water had been poisoned. "I ask the authorities to give us justice," she said, blaming Texaco for ailments ranging from the flu and skin rashes to cervical cancer.

Diego Larrea, a Quito-based lawyer for Chevron, argued that no medical or scientific evidence has been presented to back such claims. "What we have here is the myth of the jungle," he told Nuñez.

Fajardo shot back, reading from a 1977 letter to state energy officials in which Texaco admitted to a serious leak from a waste pit. An internal 1972 memo, also in Nuñez's hands, instructed Texaco officials in Ecuador to report only spills that attracted the attention of the news media or regulators.

In another letter submitted in court, from 1980, Texaco officials told state energy officials that lining pits—a precaution against leaks that is common in the United States—would be prohibitively expensive. "It was cheaper to pay the fines than make the improvements," Fajardo told the judge.

Chevron says such documents were taken out of context and has submitted its own documentation to show that Texaco responded to accidents.

If there is a rare point of agreement in the trial, it is that Petroecuador is not blameless. Company and government officials acknowledge that the state firm also dumped waste into waterways after it assumed control, and that there were spills from its pipelines.

But for 26 years, Texaco was the sole operator, and the plaintiffs say that the waste the company left behind continues to leach into groundwater. The plaintiffs and the Ecuadoran government also argue that Petroecuador has upgraded equipment left by Texaco and modernized disposal of waste, for instance re-injecting wastewater into the ground.

The plaintiffs said that much of their strongest evidence lies in the waste pits surrounding the 356 wells that Texaco put into operation from 1967, when the company first struck oil, until 1990, when Petroecuador took over.

Chevron acknowledges that Texaco used unlined pits but argues that the use of such holding ponds is standard in the industry, including in the United States, according to Craig, the spokesman.

Unlined pits are indeed common in Texas, according to the Texas Railroad Commission, which oversees land use by oil firms. But commission officials said that in Texas, such pits are used to hold mud and heavy metals temporarily, before they are re-injected into the ground or otherwise disposed of.

The plaintiffs say Texaco did not re-inject the waste in Ecuador but instead used the shoddily designed pits for permanent storage. In 2001, Ecuador's General Controller, an office that investigates malfeasance, said that waste had oozed from pits and that Texaco's cleanup had fallen short. The plaintiffs also say that the cleanup covered only a few of the polluted sites and did not include groundwater or streams.

Kent Robertson, a Chevron spokesman, said that government inspectors later found flaws in the controller's report but that the report was never corrected. Chevron says the government-mandated cleanup it carried out at 161 pits and seven spill sites was effective, entailing removal of oil from soil, incineration of debris and revegetation.

These days, the ponds at the center of the

debate have drawn Donald Moncayo, an activist who works with the plaintiffs. His specialty is taking visitors on what he calls "toxic tours."

After a walk along a forest trail, he stopped at a pool that had been used by Texaco and poked a long stick into the black sludge. Waste also dripped out through a drainage pipe and ran down to a creek below. "As you can see, there is no protection," Moncayo said. "All these waters wind up in the rivers."

Among those who have spent their lives next to wells, waste pits and polluted waterways is Carmen Chamba, 54, who said she has suffered four miscarriages.

Chamba happens to live near an installation now operated by Petroecuador. But it was Texaco that first ran production near her home, so she says the U.S. company is liable.

"They need to pay me for my loss," she said.

Ecuador would likely lead the company to argue the proceedings were unfair and US courts should not enforce the decision. The company already reportedly backed lobbying efforts to bring US government trade pressures on Ecuador related to the case.[10] What would be the ethical basis for a US government response? Should US standards of judicial "fairness" apply to a case decided by the Ecuadoran judicial system?

PRESERVATION VERSUS DEVELOPMENT—WHO PAYS AND HOW?

For oil production projects, potential deforestation impacts represent a side effect of construction activities or an unintended follow-on consequence of building access roads. Examined more directly, business activities in the forestry sector present a fundamental challenge to the management of human relations with nature and the physical environment. The majority of all plant and animal species reside in forests, along with diverse groups of indigenous people. Forests also act as a natural "sink" for carbon-based gases related to global warming. Yet the world has lost over one-half its tropical forests, mainly during the twentieth century.[11] The most common choice posed on forestry resources casts preservation goals versus development activities through logging. Core ethical issues center on who decides, who benefits, and who pays.

For example, the government of Suriname faced a difficult choice in 1995.[12] Confronting serious economic problems, Suriname's government viewed the exploitation of its tropical forest resources as perhaps the only available development option. The government invited bids from timber companies and received proposals from Indonesian and Malaysian MNEs that sought logging rights to nearly one-quarter of the country. Despite some domestic protests, the legislature was poised to accept MNE investment proposals, but environmental NGOs, international organizations and the US government entered the debate, arguing against the proposed deals and offering alternative economic inducements.

Much of the debate over Suriname's decision revolved around teleological assessments of whether timber company proposals or the environmentally focused alternatives promised the better cost/benefit outcome. The MNEs' proposals contained measurable monetary terms, including an aggregate investment of $262 million with multiplier benefits through job creation for a new sawmill and factory. The government would receive $3 per acre annually for logging rights, generating perhaps $8.8million from just one of the firms, Malaysian-based Berjaya.

One criticism claimed that this revenue should be larger, arguing that it would amount to less than one-half the firm's expected profit from the deal. A second criticism promoted alternative uses for forest resources that could be lost if the timber companies won. Conservation International and other environmental NGOs suggested a three-part plan to develop ecotourism, seek medicinal plants and manage the forestry industry locally rather than using MNEs. The NGOs could seek international donors to support these steps and the head of the Inter-American Development Bank (IADB) offered an unspecified aid package if Suriname delayed approving the logging contracts.

This cost/benefit debate occurred almost entirely in monetary terms, reflecting the country's desperate economic situation. Largely absent from the discussion were other potential impacts that were difficult to monetarize. For example, the forest homes of three indigenous tribes would be disrupted by logging and the loss of more rain forests could increase global warming. Naturalists might even argue that the preservation of intact forests has unquantifiable but nonetheless real value. Issues of timing and the certainty of projected outcomes also affect cost/benefit calculations. The pressure for new revenue to meet current economic needs prioritized the up-front monetary benefits of annual fees for logging rights and the stimulus of new business and jobs. By contrast, potential environmental degradation and the disruption of tribal life were less immediately apparent and measurable, and the environmentalists' three-part plan offered uncertain financial results in an equally uncertain time frame.

Suriname's government possesses politically sovereign authority over the country's natural resources, but should nature and the physical environment be treated only as a commodity to be bought or sold as determined by a country's prevailing government? Suriname's previous Dutch colonial rulers possessed such sovereign authority at one time and might have stripped the country's resources without considering the welfare of the residents. A decision by Suriname's current government to sell the forests could result in cost/benefit distributions that sacrifice indigenous minorities to the majority, or the majority to a group of political and business elite.

Even assuming Suriname's leaders pursue legitimate national interests representative of their citizens' desires, foreign groups may seek to override those interests for the "greater" good of the world's citizens or the earth's future. What are the rights and role responsibilities of foreign actors in national policy decisions that could adversely affect nature and the physical environment? In practice, the world community might seek to prevent national economic development projects that could result in environmental degradation by pursuing a "carrot" or a "stick" approach. No discussion of possible "sticks," such as political, economic or even military sanctions, appeared in the Suriname case. Instead, foreign actors offered a "carrot" by suggesting financial inducements to offset anticipated revenue from logging, hoping Suriname would voluntarily choose the more environmentally friendly policy.

Ultimately, Suriname decided against selling extensive logging rights to foreign MNEs. In fact, the government announced in 1998 the establishment of a nature reserve that would cover over 4 million acres, or about 10 percent of the country. Supporting this decision, Conservation International secured private philanthropic funding to establish a $1million trust to manage and protect the reserve. The Dutch government signed a $30million accord with Suriname, backed by the UN Food and Agriculture Organization (FAO), to create mobile inspection units to monitor logging activities that would be permitted.[13] The IADB also approved $1.38million to help Suriname explore ecologically sound development strategies.[14]

The support offered Suriname to preserve its rain forests reflects the best side of the international community's growing awareness and concern about deforestation problems. Unfortunately, international financial assistance may prove insufficient to meet and sustain the multiple battles against deforestation pressures in developing countries. For example, in Suriname's neighbor, Guyana, attempts to develop ecologically friendly alternatives to extensive logging were falling short of becoming financially sustainable. Backed by $3million in UN funding, the country created Iwokrama, a 3,700 km^2 (1,400 square mile) rain forest preserve, to help demonstrate sustainable forestry. Despite a decade of projects promoting ecotourism, forestry research and training, and forestry products such as modeling with sap-based rubber, Iwokrama failed to achieve financial self-sufficiency. More broadly, a significant drop-off occurred in the interest and commitment of governments and international organizations to programs aimed at combating deforestation. Foreign assistance agencies in the United States, Canada and Switzerland reduced forestry personnel while international aid organizations faced the complexities of achieving sustainable forest management. A report on these problems quotes a World Bank official as growling, "Forestry—1 percent of the lending and 90 percent of the headaches."[15]

Exhibit 9.2 offers a case scenario from Guyana that presents a more recent stage in the preservation versus development choice, including who might pay and how. The President of Guyana offered to exchange management of his country's rain forests for foreign aid and investment, appealing initially to former colonial ruler Great Britain. His plan viewed rain forests as a "global asset in the fight against climate change," where "poor nations need to be compensated for the economic costs of avoided deforestation," using the preserved rain forests as "eco-collateral."

The plan reportedly took most people by surprise and sparked reactions from confused domestic constituencies that ranged from scorn to cautious support. The political opposition objected to Britain's involvement as creating a "new form of serfdom." Local and foreign logging companies were concerned how the plan might affect their commercial interests. Supporters saw a potential to tap revenue from carbon credit trading to replace reduced international aid for forestry preservation, particularly as Guyana faced new threats of expanded resource development.

The head of a local village, who serves as a birding guide in the Iwokrama Forest Reserve, did not know much about the President's plan. However, he knew about the adverse impacts of logging elsewhere in Guyana on forests and on local communities. Some 16 Amerindian communities help manage the Reserve as part of "Iwokrama's commitment to Amerindian development and stewardship." Initial foreign funding

Exhibit 9.2   Guyana's Rain Forest Proposal

Guyana's Modest Proposal

A South American president surprised his people when he offered to let foreign conservationists manage rain forests in return for aid. A new way to reconcile development and the environment, or a new eco-colonialism?

CHRISTOPHER FREY *reports*

Fairview, Guyana. It's the first time anyone has asked Bradford Allicock his opinion about the bold new plan for the rain forest he calls home. Late last year, Guyana's President, Bharrat Jagdeo, told Britain that he would turn over environmental management of the forests in return for aid and investment. A month later, the first journalists and TV cameras arrive in Fairview, the Amerindian village where Mr. Allicock is the *toshau* (village captain).

Stepping away from the Pentecostal service occurring in the shade beneath his stilt-raised house, he says he first heard about the offer in the media. Locally, there has been talk about carbon offsets and carbon sinks. Even though his people weren't consulted, he welcomes Mr. Jagdeo's proposal, saying it is better than the alternative.

"I see the footage of what the big timber companies are doing to other places in Guyana. And I've spoken with other communities who've shared their bad experiences. Our forest is still here. It's still standing. So let's ensure the future generations will benefit."

Mr. Jagdeo's offer surprised everyone. Describing the rain forest as a "global asset in the fight against climate change," he appealed to the British government and non-governmental organizations to assist Guyana in safeguarding it through bilateral investments in conservation and sustainable development.

Poor nations need to be compensated for the economic costs of avoided deforestation (the political term for such forest protection), he argued. They need technology transfers to help build a green economy. With his country's standing rain forest as eco-collateral, he wants to be paid not to follow the same path that made the developed world wealthy.

It could become a test case for how the world deals with the conflict between economic growth and environmental responsibility in developing countries. Critics worry that Guyana's model might undermine the sovereignty of struggling countries and engender a new form of colonialism in which poor nations hand over crucial decisions about their future in return for a cheque.

Meanwhile, rich governments will be looking to the emerging carbon-credit markets to help finance such schemes, even though it has not yet been proved to reduce greenhouse emissions.

English-speaking Guyana still possesses 50 million acres of virgin rain forest, part of the Guiana Shield that reaches into Venezuela, Suriname, French Guiana and Brazil. It is among the four largest tropical rain forests on Earth still relatively intact.

Mr. Jagdeo's proposition came sandwiched between Sir Nicholas Stern's landmark report on climate change in early November—which recommended avoided deforestation as an inexpensive step toward climate stability—and the United Nations Climate Change Conference in Bali, convened to begin negotiations on a successor agreement to the Kyoto Protocol.

Limits to deforestation were not included in Kyoto, although cutting of tropical forests accounts for 20 per cent of greenhouse-gas increases (second only to the energy industry). The final communiqué at Bali talked of exploring "policy measures and positive incentives" to encourage avoided deforestation.

How is Britain reacting to Mr. Jagdeo's proposal? According to Fraser Wheeler, the British High Commissioner in Guyana, "We're looking at it and we're very interested."

In the country whose rain forests are at issue, however, the proposal has been met with mixed confusion, scorn and cautious support. Guyana's politics are notoriously polarized—allegiances are often tied to race, and a legacy of corruption ensures a strong dose of public skepticism. The government has yet to fully explain its plan through a discussion paper or convene a meeting of stakeholders.

Local loggers and the large Malaysian and Chinese-owned forestry companies want to know what it means for their existing concessions. And while much of Guyana's standing forest may be uncut, it is part of a vast, largely unpoliced frontier.

The opposition is especially rankled at the president's decision to appeal exclusively to the U.K., Guyana's former colonial master, rather than pursue a multilateral approach. Even advocates for conservation have expressed disappointment that there was no public consultation first.

Robert Corbin, the leader of the opposition People's National Congress Reform, has likened the direct pitch to Britain as a return to colonialism. He calls the deal "a new form of serfdom in the 21st century."

But Dane Gobin, acting director of the organization that manages the Iwokrama Forest Reserve, presently Guyana's most prominent protected area, says there were pragmatic reasons to approach Britain as a partner—the U.K. has been one of the leading movers of debt relief for developing countries, its consumers are perceived as pioneers of fair-trade shopping and London has already become the world centre for the carbon-trading market.

Mr. Gobin even sees the lack of consultation in a positive light. "I think it might have been strategic in terms of dropping a bombshell, in that it raises immediate awareness," he says. "The media is coming here, so Guyana is getting huge mileage from it."

The red road
This talk of avoided deforestation, and achieving value from it, arrives at a critical juncture in Guyana's development. With 90 per cent of its 750,000 people living along the Atlantic coastline, there is little population pressure on the rain forest. But the globalizing world economy is another matter. Transnational logging, mining, gas and oil companies are increasingly turning their attention to the resources locked away in the country's densely forested interior.

Meanwhile, a joint effort with Brazil is under way to upgrade and pave the narrow, rugged belt of road that traverses the country from the capital, Georgetown, to the south. The highway would give the northeastern Brazilian province of Roraima, on the cusp of a boom in timber, tourism and mining, convenient access to Guyana's deep-water coastal port for shipping. But it would also dramatically transform the Guyanese frontier, reducing travel times, improving safety and opening its hinterland for future development, sustainable or otherwise.

For the time being, though, the clay-packed road still dyes everything that travels over it an ochre red. In the Iwokrama Forest Reserve, Ron Allicock stands in the back of a pickup truck sloshing along that artery after a rainstorm, its spray staining clothing and skin.

Mr. Allicock is a birding guide from the Iwokrama field station and Bradford Allicock's nephew. As the truck speeds beneath the outstretched canopy of green, he identifies the many birds circling or darting overhead—red-billed toucans, jabiru storks, king vultures. Jaguars occasionally survey the road through a crack in the forest wall, like sentries of its stunning biological diversity.

The forest and its waterways harbour arapaima, the world's largest freshwater fish, and endangered species such as the giant river otter, black caimans, giant river turtles and the rare harpy eagle—the strongest and most efficient avian predator.

Mr. Jagdeo has said he would like Iwokrama to serve as the model for the rest of Guyana's standing rain forest.

Mr. Allicock is a product of Iwokrama's commitment to Amerindian development and stewardship. The studious-looking 29-year-old, a native of Surama Village, is part of a process that begins with children's nature clubs and continues with opportunities in ranger training, guiding and forest management.

"When the researchers first came," he says, "they needed people to help them find the birds, the mammals, the fish, whatever they were looking for. I never realized that 10 years later that's what I would be doing with my life. And that I could make money from it."

The million-acre reserve has grown into an internationally recognized research station and slowly nurtured an ecotourism business that attracts about 1,000 visitors a year, many of them birders. It is home to 16 Amerindian communities that are directly involved in the reserve's management and economic initiatives.

While Iwokrama received substantial foreign funding in the decade after its inception in 1989, it has struggled in recent years as donor agencies have prioritized funds away from the environment and toward poverty reduction and HIV/AIDS initiatives. When it recently started a sustainable logging operation within the reserve, it was greeted with shock. But Mr. Gobin insists Iwokrama was never intended to be purely an act of conservation—it was an experiment in sustainable development.

It appears to be an intriguing model for other countries. Partly in thanks to the reserve, local Amerindian communities collaborate on business initiatives. But sustainable development is costly. It requires investment in training, capacity building and proper extraction techniques.

Iwokrama's small logging operation is trying to secure Forest Stewardship Council certification, which requires social and environmental measures that will put its lumber above the world market price. If it succeeds, it will be the only FSC-compliant timber operation in Guyana. But there starts the challenge—finding buyers willing to pay extra for knowing where the wood came from.

A fair trade?

But there is another worry, one that goes to the heart of the mechanisms being contemplated in the battle against climate change.

Last April, the arrival of Swedish-British businessman Johan Eliasch in Georgetown triggered speculation about what was in store for Guyana's rain forest. The owner of the sporting goods manufacturer Head and an adviser to the British Conservative Party on environmental issues, Mr. Eliasch turned heads in 2006 when he purchased 400,000 acres of Amazon rain forest in Brazil from a logging company.

The transaction, he insisted, was purely in the interests of conservation. But critics have pointed to his support for carbon-trading markets and suggested he could stand to gain financially. According to Mr. Wheeler, the British High Commissioner, talks between his office and the

Guyanese government on avoided deforestation began shortly after Mr. Eliasch's visit, including discussion of carbon markets.

There are questions, though, about the efficacy of using a market-based mechanism to reduce emissions. The system enables companies to gain credits when they reduce emissions or invest in green-technology projects. They can also buy credits from others. The credits can be used to gain leeway to exceed legal emissions limits in other operations. The system has high-profile supporters, including the World Bank and Conservation International.

The final Bali communiqué emphasized using the carbon market as a source of financing for avoided deforestation and alternative development. The fact that it does not require large investments by governments certainly makes it politically expedient.

"We have a problem that has been called the greatest market failure man has ever known, namely climate change, and the major solution being put forward to address this solution is a market solution," says Daphne Wysham of the Institute for Policy Studies in Washington. "The forest becomes a commodity you can buy and sell. It's a market in hot air, an invisible gas that no one can completely ensure is doing what it's supposed to be doing."

While talk of putting forests on the carbon market is relatively new, Ms. Wysham has been tracking how the scheme is working in other areas. She says the markets are typically riddled with "perverse incentives" that encourage dirty industries to play the system.

Coal-fired plants in India, for example, earn credits for producing cinderblocks from its waste fly ash, because they are reducing emissions that would otherwise be created by firing clay bricks in a kiln. Credits are also earned from diverting the highly toxic fly ash from dumps. In this case, the market only encourages the power plants to use more coal to make more cinderblock.

"People think of regulation and command and control as this bogeyman," Ms. Wysham says. "But governments can be more efficient and more involved and more targeted than a free market in something like carbon."

Mr. Corbin, the Guyanese opposition leader, says he has been approached in the past by British businessmen about his country's willingness to put its rain forest on the carbon market. He doubts such schemes will help Guyana.

"I think that we would be more concerned about the bottom line of such programs," he says. "Whether the people of Guyana and the country will derive some benefit from the lack of utilization of our forest resources. . . . Will the people of Guyana still suffer because the whole process has been subjected to the old market forces of trade?

I'm very skeptical when it becomes just a matter of trading. The question of Guyana's environment, global warming and rising sea levels become secondary to people making money."

Source: *The Globe and Mail (Canada)*, 19 January 2008, p. F8. © Christopher Frey. Reprinted with permission.

that sustained this "model" was diminishing, however, just as a major road-building project was poised to open access to much of the country's interior, a prospect drawing the attention of MNE logging, mining and other business interests.

This case scenario poses several value choice questions related to Guyana's policy options. First, should the country's forestry preservation be linked to carbon credit projects?[16] The Kyoto accord did not include deforestation and carbon credit trading is still at an early stage, with no single global price and 80 percent of credits arranged in bilateral trades or direct trades from sellers.[17] Critics charge that reliance on market mechanisms will also "encourage dirty industries to play the system", while countries such as Guyana realize little development benefit.

If links to carbon credit markets do not evolve, a second set of questions is whether Guyana's rain forests still have sufficient value to be preserved; how that value should be measured and assessed; and who should pay? These questions revert back to the same teleological cost/benefit calculations and issues raised when Iwokrama was first created and when Suriname opted for the alternative financial plans of foreign environmentalists. However, those early funding alternatives now appear insufficient to sustain the forestry reserves unless greater importance is attached to non-monetary environmental values (such as red-billed toucans and jaguars) or other new schemes prove successful (such as higher lumber prices from a Forest Stewardship Council certification—a process explained more in the next chapter.)

The final question revolves around distributive justice issues inherent in the potential trade-offs between environmental preservation and development. Does protection of the world's forest resources constitute such an important shared value for the global community that the subsidiarity chain of responsibility should eventually tap the public treasuries of countries most financially capable of sustaining such efforts? Movement toward this principle appeared to result from the 2007 Bali Conference with the creation of a Forest Carbon Partnership Facility (FCPF) that became operational in mid 2008. Nine developed countries initially pledged nearly $82million, with 14 developing countries (including Guyana) chosen as potential recipients. In 2009 another 12 developing countries became eligible (including Suriname, whose President had also strongly backed the initiative).[18] Unfortunately, funding disbursements were slow and developed country financial support did not keep pace with expanded proposals, leaving many developing countries with a familiar dilemma—preservation or development.

Consider the possible alternatives to logging and propose a "best choice" approach and reasoned advocacy proposal on forestry preservation to present to potential public and private sector supporters. Rather than the deontological principle of the "polluter pays" for environmental restoration, should the world community adopt a common morality principle that the most financially capable preservationist pays for the environmentally sustainable management of forest resources? Can payments best occur through foreign aid; a carbon credit market; higher consumer prices for certified, environmentally sustainable lumber; or other mechanisms?

MARKET MECHANISMS AND GLOBAL WARMING

Industrialization activities are a principal cause for increases in carbon dioxide and other so-called greenhouse gases that constitute a growing threat to nature and the physical environment. Debate continues over some issues, including the role of natural climate change and both the speed and the magnitude of perceived problems. Nevertheless, growing scientific evidence points to human activities, including industrial processes, as the more significant causal factors in rising global temperatures. Reports issued in 2001 from the US National Academy of Sciences and an Intergovernmental Panel on Climate Change reinforced earlier studies that projected damage from rising sea levels, more severe storms, agricultural disruptions and increased tropical disease.

Al Gore's well-received but controversial 2006 documentary, *An Inconvenient Truth*, graphically depicts these potential environmental consequences and offers stark predictions of their effects on the human population. The documentary suggests that rising sea levels will flood the coasts, destroying urban centers and eventually creating over 100 million refugees.[19] Deaths from global warming could reach 300,000 within 25 years. By mid century, such impacts could depress economic growth in many countries and, as one monetary measure of costs, result in insurance losses totaling $300 billion annually.[20] More fundamentally, but difficult to value financially, a new study of global warming effects on habitats around the world estimates that one-quarter of all plant and animal species face extinction by mid century.[21]

International recognition of the growing threat posed by global warming led more than 150 nations to support adoption of the Kyoto Protocol 1997. This accord set a goal to reduce greenhouse gas emissions by 5 percent by 2012. To enter into force, the treaty required ratification by enough large nations to represent 55 percent of industrial emissions from developed countries, a step not reached until late 2004. The US government, whose economy produces nearly one-quarter of greenhouse gas emissions, objected to implementation proposals and the Bush administration formally withdrew the United States from participation in 2001. A voluntary US plan announced the following year aimed at lowering the rate of growth rather than achieving absolute reductions in greenhouse gas emissions. Many US MNEs opposed the Kyoto Protocol, suggesting that the threat was exaggerated, the requirements for country actions were unfairly distributed (exempting some fast-industrializing developing countries), and the restrictions would severely retard US economic growth.[22]

A split developed among major US MNEs between the signing of the Kyoto Protocol and the US withdrawal. Some key companies left the Global Climate Coalition, which had backed a $13million advertising campaign against the Kyoto Protocol, to join the Pew Center on Global Climate Change, which accepted most global warming studies and supported business involvement in designing activist responses.[23] While perhaps persuaded by the mounting scientific evidence, the change in corporate position also derives from other motivations as well. Do motivations matter (deontologically) or only the resulting outcome (teleologically)? An understanding of corporate motivations, causally linked to operational changes, could help guide the strategies pursued by governments and/or civil society groups in efforts to alter corporate behavior.

Anticipating the development of government regulations, some companies took proactive steps to reduce harmful gas emissions, perhaps hoping to avoid more restrictive mandatory measures or achieve an early competitive edge over firms that responded reactively. Voluntary actions might also attract favorable publicity, yielding public image benefits for corporations, especially for enterprises whose past activities had drawn environmentalist criticism. Additionally, some companies advocated establishing a market system that capped total greenhouse gas emissions and allowed trading "shares" of the permitted emissions. Similar to a system used to curb sulfur dioxide emissions linked to acid rain in North America, this market mechanism would enable firms reducing below their emission allocation to offset some costs or even realize profits by selling their excess "shares" (sometimes called pollution or emission credits) to companies that exceeded their emission limits.

Disagreements arose between the United States and the European Union over proposals to establish a market for trading emission credits. Subsequently, Britain and Denmark set up government-regulated schemes while the European Union Greenhouse Gas Emission Trading System (EU ETS) began operating in 2005. The US government encouraged voluntary corporate arrangements but refused to set a mandatory cap on emissions. Some US firms pursued private sector arrangements, for example through developing the Chicago Climate Exchange to facilitate trading emission credits. The international scope of MNE operations generally provides additional incentives for proactive behavior on greenhouse gases. MNEs with facilities in countries likely to develop regulations supporting the Kyoto Protocol may voluntarily adopt similar changes in countries less likely to require specified emissions reductions in order to gain competitive advantage in profits and/or improved public image.[24]

DuPont helped spearhead voluntary MNE efforts while seeking to profit from the new market mechanisms. The company reported that its greenhouse gas emissions in 1990 represented the equivalent of 86 million tons of carbon dioxide, but nearly two-thirds of this total came from nitrous oxide, a gas with over 300 times the global warming effect of carbon dioxide. Machinery to reduce these emissions at each of five relevant DuPont plants (producing adipic acid for nylon production) cost $10million to $20million to install and over $1million annually to maintain. In

1999 the company established an office to promote emission trading policies and manage DuPont's own trading efforts. Over the next several years, the company engaged in nearly two dozen trades, primarily in Canada and the United States. The financial return from selling its emission credits likely fell far short of the cost DuPont incurred from operational changes to reduce its greenhouse gases, but the company also valued the corollary improvements in its environmental public image.[25]

DuPont's concern about its environmental image probably stemmed not only from its initial skepticism about global warming, but also from the firm's link to an earlier issue involving the production of chlorofluorocarbons (CFCs), a family of gases found to deplete the ozone layer that protects the earth from harmful ultraviolet radiation. After initial controversy and debate about the issue, a scientific and political consensus developed around the need to reduce and eventually eliminate CFCs, which were used as low-cost coolants in refrigerators and air conditioners, as well as for other industrial applications. Under the 1987 Montreal Protocol on Substances that Deplete the Ozone Layer, developed countries phased out most CFC use by the mid 1990s, while developing countries were to freeze emission levels by that time and then reduce use, with full elimination scheduled for 2010.[26]

DuPont, as the world's largest CFC supplier, received criticism for resisting early warnings about possible damage to the ozone layer. Once scientific studies validated the concerns, the company confronted difficult issues in ending its CFC production. Because developing countries would reduce use more gradually than developed nations, a market remained for the low-cost refrigerants. While encouraging the use of somewhat higher priced but less environmentally damaging alternative products, DuPont maintained some CFC exports (permitted under the protocol), but refused to sell its CFC technology for use in new developing country plants. This approach reduced the incentive for other countries to begin their own CFC production while still permitting DuPont responsibly to phase down and then end its own production operations.[27]

The differential in CFC phase-out commitments between developed and developing countries illustrates one way to answer normative questions about distributive justice in deciding who should do what in allocating the costs of a global public good outcome that will benefit everyone. Developing countries believed immediate CFC restrictions would unfairly penalize them for problems caused by earlier CFC use that had benefited the developed countries. Because higher-cost alternative products could retard economic development, developing countries sought both a longer phase-out period for CFC use and financial assistance to cover adjustment costs. A Multilateral Fund was established under the Montreal Protocol, expending $1billion in reducing CFCs and other harmful substances in 110 developing countries during the 1990s, with another $440million committed through 2002.[28] Similar distributive justice issues arise in assessing causation and allocating cost burdens on other global environmental issues, including the broader issue of greenhouse gas emissions linked to global warming. If harmful emissions are capped or reductions required, should the resulting "shares" be apportioned by industry, country, economic development level, or responsibility for damage already caused? Perhaps ethical analysis of the CFC experience can improve the normative criteria used to distribute the costs of addressing the global warming challenge.[29]

Expanded international cooperation on global warming appeared possible after elections in 2008 opened the door for a new US policy position and talks on a new international accord opened in 2009. However, efforts to move beyond the Kyoto Protocol face complex negotiations, particularly on the allocation of responsibilities and costs to be borne by developed countries that should reduce greenhouse gas emissions and developing countries that should restrain their increase of emissions arising from economic growth. What value principles should guide distributive justice decisions on such allocations among countries? Should global MNEs follow the same operational guidelines everywhere or adhere to whatever are the local country's legal requirements?

GOALS FOR WATER RESOURCE MANAGEMENT

Water resources essential to sustain life constitute another element of the natural environment increasingly managed, or mismanaged, to suit particular human needs and desires. Although integrally linked with other parts of the ecosystem, water is often treated as an independent commodity to be owned, sold and distributed according to shifting national economic and political priorities. Dams represent a major component of the human effort to harness and redirect fresh water resources, with resulting impacts on the surrounding natural and human environment. Although some dams reduce potential flooding, many projects aim primarily to supply the agricultural irrigation, hydroelectric power and metropolitan water needs demanded by national development programs. Such benefits can be quantified more easily than possible accompanying disruptions to discrete parts of the ecosystem. Ethical issues relate to the predominant use of cost/benefit decision methodologies, the distribution costs borne by minority populations and the non-human environment, and emerging attempts to promote international environmental standards for application to national water projects.

For example, a dam project was undertaken to generate revenue for impoverished Lesotho by selling water to the Johannesburg region of neighboring South Africa. Termed "white gold" in a news article,[30] water sales from the project account for a quarter of the country's exports while fostering related water, electricity and other improvements within Lesotho. Critics point to flooded valleys, displaced people and forgone conservation steps while grouping this project with other dams that threaten a "loss of freshwater biodiversity." Some problems, such as satisfactory compensation for 30,000 residents adversely affected by the dam, were more easily susceptible to monetary resolution than the magnitude of the difficulties created by much larger projects, such as the million-plus people displaced by the Three Gorges dam in China. The creation of two nature reserves and a minnow preservation effort in Lesotho also attempt to balance out the land, plant and animal loss caused by diverting so much of the Orange river's natural flow. The crucial aspect of ethical analysis in this case example rests on evaluating the adequacy of environmental measures and, most critically, who decides on both the measures and the correctness of the resulting balance.

The development and application of international environmental standards to major dam projects has developed primarily through conditions attached to financial assistance from foreign governments or international financial institutions. Of course, environmental impact constitutes just one among many criteria used to decide on possible financing packages, including political and socioeconomic considerations, and projects constructed without such financing strings generally face only diffuse verbal criticism.[31] Although most nations with water resource capacity covet the potential economic development benefits from dam construction, environmentalist pressures in the United States sparked movement toward removing some existing dams to restore natural river flows. Significant dams already breached include the Edwards dam in Maine (1999) and the Embrey dam in Virginia (2004), with a larger debate swirling around four dams on the lower Snake river, a major tributary of the Columbia river in the Pacific Northwest.[32] What role should concern for the natural environment play in the management of freshwater resources, and should a national government be able to dam, divert, and dispose of any water located (at least temporarily) within its territorial boundaries, without limitation by international environmental concerns?

A parallel water resource issue arises from growing overexploitation of important world fisheries. After World War II, technological applications of radar, acoustic fish finders and on-board freezers expanded the catch of many vessels. Beginning in the mid 1970s, excessive fishing led to the collapse of cod stocks near New England and Canada, while fisheries off Europe and elsewhere faced increased pressure. Jurisdictional issues arise because 90 percent of fish caught in the world's oceans depend for their growth on biological mass found on narrow continental shelves that fall largely within the exclusive economic zones of specific nation states.[33] Key issues involve management of the political and economic pressures for fishing access to these areas, where problems can be exacerbated by the use of huge "factory" vessels as well as illegal entry to protected fishing grounds.[34] Expanding aquaculture can provide increases of high-priced fish (such as salmon and sea bass), mainly for sale in developed countries, but such operations require large fishmeal supplies that actually consume more fish than is produced.[35]

The UN Convention on the Law of the Sea as well as various bilateral and multilateral agreements attempt to address parts of the fisheries problem, but the world community has yet to agree on the general (deontological) principles or a (teleological) cost/benefit allocation scheme to effectively manage the growing threat to global fishing stocks. These two decision-making approaches can work together or operate separately, sometimes leading in different directions. Environmental preservationist principles likely led to Lesotho's $2million effort to save the Maloti minnow.[36] Fishing quotas on cod involve more economic and political cost/benefit calculations that attempt to preserve the cod's utility for human consumption. Other fishing policies, such as "dolphin-safe tuna" rules backed by the United States and Europe, arose from animal rights campaigners who drew on public sentiment more strongly attached to images of "Flipper" than to other varieties of fish.[37] As the global

Exhibit 9.3   Calculating the Costs of Bottled Water

Global thirst for bottled water attacked

by ANDREW WARD

For growing numbers of consumers around the world, bottled water is a convenient, healthy and fashionable way to remain hydrated.

To critics, however, the product is a shameful extravagance, creating unnecessary waste, straining scarce water resources and using vast quantities of energy to produce and transport.

That latter view is reinforced by a new US study questioning the world's rising thirst for bottled water. The Washington-based Earth Policy Institute says global consumption of bottled water has grown by 57 per cent over the past five years, despite the fact the product is often no healthier than tap water and costs up to 10,000 times more.

Emily Arnold, the author of the report, complains that the $100bn (£57bn, €84bn) spent each year on bottled water is nearly seven times the sum invested in providing safe drinking water in developing countries.

The report highlights increasing scrutiny of bottled water producers such as Nestlé, Danone, Coca-Cola and PepsiCo by environmental and human rights activists, especially in places where water is scarce. Much of Ms Arnold's ire is focused on the energy wastage and pollution involved in producing and distributing a product that can, in many parts of the world, be obtained much more efficiently through a tap.

She says that 40 per cent of bottled water comes from a municipal source rather than a natural spring, including leading US brands such as Coke's Dasani and PepsiCo's Aquafina. "Often the only difference (from tap water) is added minerals," says the report.

In the US more than 1.5m barrels of crude oil are used annually to make plastic bottles for water, enough to fuel 100,000 cars for a year. Nearly 90 per cent of bottles are disposed of after one use and take 1,000 years to biodegrade. Of those that are recycled, nearly 40 per cent are exported to China, adding to the drain on resources.

Further fossil fuels are used to distribute the product, with nearly a quarter of bottled water crossing at least one national border to reach consumers, according to Ms Arnold. That contrasts sharply, she argues, with the energy-efficient distribution of tap water.

Bottled water has become one of the strongest sources of growth for beverage companies as consumers in much of the world shift away from sugary soft drinks to healthier alternatives.

The US is the world's largest consumer of bottled water and Italians drink the most per person. But the fastest growth is coming in developing countries, with consumption tripling in India and more than doubling in China over the past five years, according to the report.

Ms Arnold alleges that a Coca-Cola water bottling plant in India has caused water shortages in 50 surrounding villages. Coke says an independent investigation found it was not to blame.

Stephen Kay, a spokesman for the International Bottled Water Association, a trade group, dismisses the report as "narrowly subjective" and says producers are responding to consumer demand.

"Consumers are choosing water not in lieu of tap water but as an alternative to other beverages," he says. "We're an on-the-go society demanding convenient packaging and consistent quality and that's what bottled water provides."

Source: © *Financial Times*, 13 February 2006, p. 3. Reprinted with permission.

---

community addresses issues of water resource management, the ecosystem's interdependent links will require careful attention in setting priorities and determining public policies.

The United Nations' Millennium Development Goals cite water as one of four priority issues under ensuring environmental stability, seeking to cut in half the number of people without access to safe drinking water and sanitation. Nearly half the world's population faces a scarcity of water and almost one billion people go without access to improved drinking water.[38] Exhibit 9.3 illustrates how a simple consumer product such as bottled water can relate to this concern and, through interdependent environmental effects, also link to issues of energy consumption and waste disposal.

Bottled water consumption grew by over 50 percent from 2000 to 2005, with the fastest growth coming in developing countries, particularly India and China. The article cites a study's finding that many bottled water products, including some leading brands, obtain their water from public municipal sources, sometimes only adding minerals. The report claims that bottled water "is often no healthier than tap water and costs up to 10,000 times more." The $100 billion spent annually on bottled water represents seven times the expenditure on providing safe drinking water to people in developing countries.

Company representatives cite the growth of bottled water consumption as simply a response to consumer choice. In that respect, the issue might be discussed in Chapter 7's examination of marketing techniques. However, Exhibit 9.3 elaborates on several interconnected environmental impacts. The crude oil used to produce plastic bottles for water in the United States alone requires enough crude oil to power 100,000 cars for a year. Product distribution claims additional energy resources, with almost one-quarter of bottled water crossing at least one national border. Once the water is consumed, nearly all plastic bottles are discarded, with many requiring 1,000 years to biodegrade while other enter the international trade for recycled materials, claiming more transportation-related energy.

From one perspective, providing bottled water to populations without access to safe drinking water could address an urgent global need. Unfortunately, the people most in need lack the disposable income to purchase the product, while wealthy consumers generally already have access to safe municipal tap water. Distributive justice asks whether the marketplace can most efficiently and effectively address a basic human need for safe drinking water. On a more complex level, how should the public goods aspect of environmental impacts from energy consumption and persistent wastage be calculated and managed? Does the price of bottled water cover such impacts? How would you distribute responsibility along a subsidiarity chain that includes corporations, consumers and governments? Should a bottled water company produce and market its product anywhere, in any way, which is legally permissible?

HUMAN MODIFICATIONS OF NATURE THROUGH BIOGENETICS

The evidence of human ability to alter nature and the physical environment can appear visually with oil-polluted rivers and clear-cut forests, or disappear as invisible gas emissions, depleted fishing stock or landscapes drowned in dam reservoirs. On an initially smaller but equally important scale, the microscopic manipulation of plant and animal genes poses yet another contemporary ethical dilemma where globalization magnifies an action's potential benefits and costs. Much debate centers on safety concerns about whether genetically modified (GM) crops could directly or indirectly endanger consumers or upset critical ecological balances in nature. Equally important issues relate to distributive justice questions regarding who will bear the main risks, who will reap the major rewards, and who decides what experiments will be conducted, when and where.

Exhibit 9.4 presents this debate in the form of two dueling reports that reviewed available data but reached contrasting conclusions about the acceptance, effectiveness, and environmental impact of genetically engineered crops. The use of agricultural biotechnology may hold the promise to reduce harmful pesticide use, increase crop yields and supply more food to hungry people around the world. Or, these new techniques could increase pesticide use, threaten crop yields, decimate small farms and give MNEs concentrated power over global seed supplies. The tendency in such debates is to seek to determine which facts are "right" and endorse that argument's view. Unfortunately, facts are often not objectively right or wrong, requiring interpretation and future projection to establish their importance and validity. These more subjective steps can be influenced by the broader value construct adopted by the people making the judgments.

For example, a major obstacle to the expansion of GM crops has been resistance in the European Union to both planting and consuming genetically modified products. The chairman of Nestlé, reportedly the world's biggest food company, cited EU pressure as a reason why most African countries reject GM crops. EU officials disputed charges of pressure but acknowledged that African food exports destined for Europe need to meet market demands. An EU Commission survey found only 21 percent of Europeans willing to eat GM foods.[39] EU governments must have been slower to approve use of GM seeds and certify the safety of GM foods, creating trade tensions particularly with the United States where some leading business interests are based.

Much of the EU opposition to GM foods draws on a "precautionary principle" that favors avoiding new technologies until their theoretical risks are fully evaluated and understood. By contrast, the US government argues that short-term studies provide sufficient reassurance against potential harm and that the benefits of GM products should be endorsed and enjoyed.[40] How should the cost/benefit trade-off be assessed, and who should decide on the acceptable outcome? Should resolving an immediate food crisis take precedence over fears that genetic experimentation could go astray, leading to the production of "Frankenfoods" or upsetting natural plant and animal ecosystems?

Some scientists view potential gains from GM foods as too distant a solution when immediate improvements could more certainly come from investments in better fertilizer and crop management, or improving storage and transport to reduce food spoilage. Even where biotechnology holds promise to increase food supply, private MNEs often decide what crops to investigate, with most initial research occurring in the United States on crops such as corn and soy beans. Only limited research takes place on traditional staple crops such as cassava, bananas, sorghum, cowpeas and sweet potatoes in Africa or other regions with the greatest hunger problem.[41]

In May 2004 the FAO released a report on *The State of Food and Agriculture*,

Exhibit 9.4 Debates Over Genetically Modified Crops

2 Reports At Odds On Biotech Crops

Dispute Is Over Use of Pesticides

by RICK WEISS

Take your pick:

The widening adoption of genetically engineered crops by farmers around the world is reducing global pesticide use, increasing agricultural yields and bringing unprecedented prosperity and food security to millions of the world's poorest citizens.

Or, it is fueling greater use of pesticides, putting crop yields at risk, driving small farmers out of business and decreasing global food security by giving a single company control over much of the world's seed supply.

Dueling reports released yesterday—one by a consortium largely funded by the biotech industry and the other by a pair of environmental and consumer groups—came to those diametrically different conclusions.

The assessments highlight the controversy that still envelops agricultural biotechnology 12 years after the first gene-altered crops debuted commercially.

Both sides agree that genetically modified crops are gaining ground. More than 280 million acres of them were planted in 23 countries last year, a 12 percent growth in acreage and an increase of two countries compared with 2006.

Most are endowed with a bacterial gene that protects plants against a leading weed killer, Monsanto's Roundup, allowing farmers to spray that herbicide without worrying that it will kill their crops along with the weeds. Most of the others have a gene that helps plants make their own insecticide, and a growing percentage have more than one engineered trait.

But the implications of those statistics are open to interpretation.

To the International Service for the Acquisition of Agri-Biotech Applications, which gets its funding from foundations and the biotech industry, the numbers represent a virtual tidal wave of acceptance.

"Once farmers have got used to this technology, they recognize the significant benefits," said Clive James, chairman of ISAAA's board of directors and author of the new "Global Status of Commercialized Biotech/GM Crops: 2007." In a teleconference call, James said more than 90 percent of farmers in China and India who planted engineered varieties in 2006 did so again last year—evidence, he said, of their enthusiasm.

"Already those farmers who began adopting biotech crops a few years ago are beginning to see socioeconomic advantages compared to their peers," including better access to health care and higher school enrollment for their children, James said. Biotech crops will be essential, he added, if the world is to achieve the U.N. Millennium Development Goal of cutting poverty and hunger in half by 2015.

Not so fast, said Bill Freese, a science policy analyst with the Center for Food Safety, a District-based consumer organization that, with the environmental group Friends of the Earth, produced its own report, "Who Benefits from GM Crops?: The Rise in Pesticide Use."

Countries worldwide are largely shunning biotech crops, Freese said in an interview, with virtually all the increased acreage in a handful of countries such as Argentina and Brazil that are growing "Roundup-ready" soybeans on huge corporate farms—not for poor people but for export to rich countries and as animal feed.

Meanwhile, Freese said, studies such as a recent one in the journal Nature Biotechnology have found that insecticide-exuding Bt cotton is increasingly failing to control insects, so farmers "end up having to buy pesticides anyway, after paying roughly threefold more for the bt cotton seeds."

Each camp accused the other of using data selectively.

James said that farmers reaped $7 billion in benefits from biotech crops in 2006. He said that because of those crops, 289,000 fewer metric

230 • Ethics for International Business

tons of the active ingredient in pesticides were applied to fields between 1996 and 2006, resulting in a 15 percent reduction in negative environmental effects. Huge amounts of fuel were saved by not having to spray those pesticides, shrinking carbon dioxide emissions by 2.6 billion pounds in 2006, equivalent to taking half a million cars off the road, he said.

The Friends of the Earth report says that the growing use of Roundup-resistant crops has brought a 15 percent increase in the use of that herbicide on soybeans, cotton and corn from 1994 to 2005, with a 28 percent jump in 2006 alone.

Meanwhile, the resistance gene has spread to several weed species, making them immune to the herbicide. And some biotech genes have contaminated conventional crops, forcing major recalls and losses in the hundreds of millions of dollars, Freese and others noted.

"Significantly, biotechnology companies have not commercially introduced a single GM crop with increased yield, enhanced nutrition, drought tolerance or salt tolerance," the report finds.

Hope Shand of the ETC Group, a civil society organization based in Montreal, said that as the number of biotech acres has swelled, the seed industry has shrunk.

"In 2006, Monsanto's biotech seeds and traits accounted for 88 percent of the total world area devoted to genetically modified crops," she said. "This is a staggering level of corporate control over the world's seed supply."

Source: From *The Washington Post*, 14 February 2008, p. A4 © 2008 *The Washington Post*. All rights reserved. Used by permission and protected by the Copyright Laws of the United States. The printing, copying, redistribution, or retransmission of the Material without express written permission is prohibited.

commenting extensively for the first time on biotechnology. The report cited the potential for new research, including genetic engineering, to alleviate global hunger but noted that few current initiatives address the crops or animals likely to benefit subsistence farmers. Private companies invest ten times as much ($3 billion annually) on improving agriculture in developed countries compared to government expenditures for research on crops in developing countries. The FAO urged greater public funding of biotechnology research to improve subsistence crops in regions with serious hunger problems.[42]

Private control of discoveries through intellectual property rights (IPRs) can raise ethical issues regarding general use of genetic engineering on both plants and animals (including potential human applications). The Mexican yellow bean provides a simple illustration of how patents can affect food ownership and financial gain, even without sophisticated GM applications. For centuries Mexican farmers cultivated and bred these beans for local consumption and in the last half-century also exported them to the United States. A US citizen reportedly self-pollinated some beans obtained in Mexico and acquired a patent on them, because the bean's local breeding had not been well documented in Mexico. Ownership then allowed legal action against Mexican yellow bean exporters for patent infringement, a result one commentator labels "biopiracy."[43]

A contrasting example arose from announcements in 2000 that Monsanto would make research from its genetic mapping of rice available to the public and waive patent rights in developing countries for its so-called "golden rice." Reportedly the "first bioengineered plant altered specifically for humanitarian reasons," higher levels of betacarotene in "golden rice" can help overcome vitamin A deficiencies.[44] An

One kilogram of the hybrid cherry tomato seeds in this petrie dish sold to European growers for $350,000, over sixteen times the price of gold. The sweet-tasting yellow variety was developed by Hazera Genetics, an Israeli firm that uses advanced bio-technology R&D to breed non-GM hybrid varieties favored in Europe. Photo by David Silverman/ Getty Images.

estimated 1 million children die each year from vitamin A deficiencies while another 300,000 are left blind. For biotechnology advocates, this case illustrates how the industry can act teleologically to help meet pressing human need. Biotechnology critics may discount the example, inferring suspect deontological motives aimed at enhancing the industry's public image and acceptance. Who should make decisions regarding biotechnology research and applications, and do motives matter, or only results (for whom)?

A civil society opponent of biotech agriculture in Exhibit 9.4 expressed concern about Monsanto's control over the vast majority of seeds used for GM crops. This issue also emerged when a few large MNEs sought patents on a new generation of "climate ready" genes designed to help crops survive drought, flooding, saltwater, heat, and ultraviolet radiation. Three firms, BASF, Syngenta and Monsanto, reportedly filed patent applications to control almost two-thirds of these types of genes. Such patent applications can cover a gene's use on a broad range of different plants. Companies argue that GM crops are necessary to address crucial world hunger problems and patent protection is required to permit investments in genetic techniques to meet climate change challenges. Other experts worry that consolidated corporate control over plant genes could prove damaging in a food crisis and that public research efforts may be undermined, particularly for non-biotech plant breeding aimed at helping subsistence farmers.[45]

A core issue relates to the concept of ownership of nature, or alterations of nature, that arise from a Humanistic ethic. While a Naturalistic ethic would emphasize humankind's responsibilities to act as a trustee of nature for the welfare of all, the Humanistic ethic sanctions the ownership of private property. Moving well beyond traditional methods of plant breeding, genetic engineering now includes patented "improvements" to nature, even in the form of creating new "life." After Harvard University received a patent in 1988 on a genetically engineered mouse used for research, similar animal patents were issued in the United States and, somewhat more slowly, in Europe.[46]

Decisions on regulatory controls shape much of the public debate on biotechnology issues. Evolving European rules now permit some GM crop cultivation and marketing, shifting the focus from prevention to agricultural controls and consumer choice. Labels must inform EU consumers if products contain even 1 percent of GM food ingredients, based on records from a tracking system back to farm fields.[47] The UN Cartegena Protocol on biosafety, designed to inform importing countries about possible biotechnology risks, also incorporated new GM food information requirements in 2004.[48] Concerns over regulatory controls still apply to research and field applications for GM plants and, even more so, animals. Reports released in 2004 by the US National Research Council and the Pew Initiative on Food and Biotechnology highlight the need for much improved controls, particularly when research involves mobile animal subjects (such as honey bees and mosquitoes).[49] Essentially, biotechnology capabilities can outpace control techniques and official regulatory decision making.

Biotechnology debates also encompass genetic engineering of human stem cells and cloning. For example, European institutions have struggled to decide how to interpret and apply a European convention clause prohibiting patents for inventions "contrary to public order or morality," with some member states resisting a 1998 European Commission directive to restrict patents on processes for cloning and other human genetic modifications.[50] In 2005, the US Patent and Trademark Office denied a patent for a technique to combine human embryo cells with those of a monkey or ape, creating a blend called a chimera. The application was reportedly rejected because the creation could be much more human than not, a decision that paradoxically pleased the applicant who never intended to create such a creature but wanted a legal precedent to keep others from profiting from such inventions. Nevertheless, questions remain about what percentage might be allowed. A Patent Office official stated: "I don't think anyone knows in terms of crude percentages how to differentiate between humans and nonhumans."[51] Denial of patent protection would not itself preclude research or experiments, but patent regulations provide a society's practical standard for directing the role for-profit business enterprises will play in such research. What ethical principles should guide the formulation of a global societal standard for biogenetic modifications of nature, including the human species?

DECISIONS TO ALTER OR ADJUST TO THE NATURAL ENVIRONMENT

Nature encompasses the elements of land, air, water and biological life that comprise the earth's physical environment. The rapidly accelerating growth in human ability to affect environmental change has outdistanced humankind's understanding of nature's complex interdependences, leading to the emergence of new environmental problems that pose difficult ethical choices. Decisions based on cost/benefit outcome calculations must confront myriad factual unknowns, generational time projections and globe-spanning distributional effects, all of which present enormous challenges for quantification and judgment. The alternative search for decision-making principles encounters various attempts to formulate public and private sector guidelines, generally aimed at specific sets of newly identified problems. These incipient efforts to devise global standards also pose basic value choices, often seeking a balance between the polar extremes of altering nature or simply adjusting to the existing natural environment.

Although many concerns surfaced much earlier, the 1992 Earth Summit in Rio de Janeiro helped shape the search for middle-ground principles between a Humanistic and Naturalistic ethic. The human drive for economic growth had placed increased stress on world resources, threatening critical aspects of the natural environment. The Earth Summit sought agreement on goals for sustainable development, an approach that would channel the human use of natural resources within limits that protect the long-term viability of the global environment. The earlier 1987 Montreal Protocol and the subsequent 1997 Kyoto Protocol reflect efforts to apply balanced, sustainable-development principles to the respective battles against depletion of the ozone layer and global warming.

The World Summit on Sustainable Development, held in Johannesburg, South Africa, in 2002, aimed to evaluate progress achieved since the 1992 Earth Summit and to identify quantifiable targets and concrete steps needed to fight world poverty while protecting the environment. The implementation plan forged at the Johannesburg Summit incorporated measures for managing the earth's natural resource base, including specific categories covering water, oceans and fisheries, the atmosphere, biodiversity, and forests. Success will be measured by achievement targets scheduled as far out as 2015. To encourage progress, this summit promoted partnerships between governments, business and civil society groups. Conference preparations identified over 220 such partnerships, with 60 more announced during the meetings. Over 8,000 civil society representatives attended the summit and participated in numerous parallel events that coincided with official activities.[52]

The principle of sustainable development offers a conceptual middle ground that attempts to balance and merge the sometimes competing priorities of a Humanist and Naturalistic ethic. The challenge involves applying such a principle in practice to particular sets of issues or cases. Partnership projects among concerned stakeholders attempt to meet this challenge collaboratively, recognizing the legitimacy of competing or even conflicting viewpoints while seeking a "best choice" solution that can gain broad assent among government, business and civil society groups. This approach engages private sector actors in shaping global norms where insufficient consensus currently exists to support more binding governmental actions.

Private sector collaboration on developing environmental standards predates the Johannesburg Summit. For example, since 1989 the Coalition for Environmentally Responsible Economics (CERES) has promoted 10 principles addressing corporate responsibility for the environment. The coalition includes a variety of environmental organizations, investment firms, pension funds and public interest groups, with well over 60 firms having endorsed the principles. The CERES project developed the Global Reporting Initiative (GRI) that evolved into a broader effort to monitor corporate social and financial as well as environmental performance.[53] A different approach emerged from the International Organization for Standardization with the ISO 14000 series that sets environmental management standards appropriate for corporate systems. However, these standards focus on evaluating the management system used by an enterprise rather than on the actual environmental performance or impact of corporate activities.[54] Other standards originate with business groups, such as the 16 environmental principles adopted by the International Chamber of Commerce in 1991 as the Business Charter for Sustainable Development.[55]

Proliferating international activity over the past couple of decades points to emerging answers on several of the "W" questions relating to nature and the physical environment. Increasing recognition of the interdependent effects of natural ecosystems answers "where" questions by seeking normative standards with global application, realizing that many environmental problems cannot be confined or effectively addressed within the artificial political borders drawn by national governments. The invocation of sustainable development goals responds to "when" questions by attempting to balance the satisfaction of current human needs with the generational interests of nature's longer-term requirements. Although the sustainable development principle appears deontological, its attempt to balance current needs and future requirements can lead to a more teleological approach when the principle is put into practice. The selection of a "best choice" balance for exploiting ocean fisheries or restraining greenhouse gas emissions, for instance, can involve many of the cost/benefit calculation and projection problems associated with outcomes-based decision making.

These considerations place a premium on determining who should decide standards to measure and implement globally sustainable development. The movement toward growing partnerships among governments, business and civil society indicates both the limited reach of existing international law and the increasing potency of environmental problems. However, actual influence within all three partnership groups tends to reflect the disproportionate influence of developed countries. Richer governments and private MNEs can devote greater financial and personnel resources to negotiations on environmental standards than governments and enterprises based in developing countries or transitional economies. Although civil society groups often speak on behalf of broad public interests or requirements of the natural environment, many of these groups lack broad membership or effective influence from the majority of countries containing the majority of the world's population.

Because who will decide what particular standards constitute sustainable development guidelines, the representative composition of partnership groups becomes a critical determining factor for ethical analysis. How will global costs and benefits be distributed in programs where "balanced" principles attempt to address immediate human needs while safeguarding nature's long-term requirements? Is effective participation broad and representative enough to reflect the global scope and impact of interdependent environmental issues? Are unorganized or even non-human interests adequately represented? Who should determine the "what" of global common morality standards that will shape humankind's interaction with nature and the physical environment?

NOTES

1. H. Rolston, "Just Environmental Business," in T. Regan (ed.), *Just Business*, New York: Random House, 1984, pp. 324–59.
2. L. Westra, "The Problem of Sustainability: Traditional African or Islamic Land Ethics or Western Technological Approaches?" in Hoffman, M., Kamm, J., Frederick, R. and Petry, (eds), *Emerging Global Business Ethics*, Westport, CT.: Quorum Books, 1994, pp. 242–54.
3. R. De George, "Safety, Risk, and Environmental Protection," in T. Beauchamp and N. Bowie, *Ethical Theory and Business*, 6th edn, Upper Saddle River, NJ: Prentice Hall, 2001, pp. 210–17.
4. Information in this description is drawn primarily from A. Salpukas, "Ecuadorean Indians Suing Texaco," *The New York Times*, 4 November 1993, p. D4.
5. J. Stoner, "Oil Operation Did Not Harm Ecuador," *Chicago Tribune*, 30 August 1996, p. 26.
6. J. Brooke, "New Effort Would Test Possible Coexistence of Oil and Rain Forest," *The New York Times*, 26 February 1991, p. 4. A comparable issue arose later when Ecuador's national legislature passed a law in 1999, holding oil companies retroactively responsible for cleaning up past oil pollution. At the time of Texaco's operations there, Ecuador had no environmental protection law applying specifically to the oil industry. See S. Wilson, "Showdown in the Ecuadorian Jungle," *The Washington Post*, 23 October 2003, p. A18.
7. Wilson, "Showdown."
8. M. Yeomans, "Fools' Gold: In Ecuador's Rain Forest, The Case Against Texaco is Clear-cut," *The Village Voice*, 4 February 1997, p. 46.
9. J. Valdivieso, "Judge Quits Suit Against Chevron; Wrongdoing Investigated," *The Washington Post*, 5 September 2009, p. A16.
10. S. Romero and C. Krauss, "A Well of Resentment," *The New York Times*, 15 May 2009, p. B1.
11. "Suriname's Example," editorial, *The New York Times*, 21 June 1998, p. 14.
12. Drawn from G. Lee, "Proposal to Log Suriname's Rain Forest Splits the Needy Nation," Washington Post, 13 May 1995, p. A1.
13. L. Luxner, "Green Reserves for Suriname," *Americas*, vol. 51, no. 1, January–February 1999, p. 4.
14. J. McCarry, "Suriname," *National Geographic*, vol. 197, no. 6, June 2000, p. 43.
15. "Tropical Forests: Not Out of the Woods," *The Economist*, 15 March 2003, pp. 73–4.
16. Carbon credit trading also forms the basis of an experimental project to offer Brazilian ranchers money to preserve forests and engage in sustainable agricultural practices rather than clearing land to graze more cattle. See M. Reel, "Applying Capitalism to Protect Dwindling Brazilian Forestland," *The Washington Post*, 25 April 2008, p. A10.
17. L. Moore, "Reducing Emissions Paramount," *The Gazette*, 10 June 2008, p. B1.
18. World Bank, Press Release No. 2009/029/SDN; "World Bank Forest Carbon Partnership Facility meeting in Panama," UN Climate Change Conference available online at http://www.unfccc.int (accessed 16 June 2009).
19. A. Gore, *An Inconvenient Truth*, DVD. Directed by Davis Guggenheim. Los Angeles, CA: Paramount Home Entertainment, 2006.
20. D. Cogan, *Corporate Policies to Address Global Climate Change*, 2002 Background Report H2, Washington, DC: Investor Responsibility Research Center (IRRC), 4 March 2002, p. 2.
21. G. Gugliotta, "Warming May Threaten 37 Percent of Species by 2050," *The Washington Post*, 8 January 2004, p. 1.

22. Cogan, "Corporate Policies," pp. 10–13.
23. W. Drozdiak, "US Firms Become 'Green' Advocates," *The Washington Post*, 24 November 2000, p. E1.
24. J. Ball, "New Market Shows Industry Moving on Global Warming," *The Wall Street Journal*, 16 January 2003, p. 1.
25. Ibid.
26. United Nations Environment Programme (UNEP), "$440 Million Agreed for Phasing Out Developing Country CFCs," UNEP press release, 3 December 1999, mimeo.
27. M. Weisskopf, "Third World Demand for CFCs Raises Worries," *The Washington Post*, 14 March 1989, p. A18.
28. UNEP.
29. Issues of cost/benefit distribution appeared to shift toward a case of economic bargaining in late 2002. With US opposition to the Kyoto Treaty, final ratification required Russia's approval. However, Russia perceived an insufficient market for the "credits" it would realize under Kyoto rules and therefore sought improved financial or other concessions from treaty supporters. This negotiating approach reportedly achieved some success in May, 2004 when the European Union and Russia reached a favorable trade agreement that also advanced Russia's goal of joining the WTO. Formal Russian approval came later in the year, setting the stage for the Kyoto Treaty to come into force. See J. Ball, "Russia Will Ratify Kyoto, for a Price," *The Washington Post*, 12 December 2003, p. A6; P. Baker, "Russia Backs Kyoto to Get on Path to Join WTO," *The Washington Post*, 22 May 2004, p. A15; and P. Finn, "Russian Cabinet Backs Kyoto Pact," *The Washington Post*, October 2004, p. A22.
30. M. Grunwald, "Saved, or Ruined, by 'White Gold'," *The Washington Post*, 27 November 2002, p. A1.
31. For example, Laos pursued several projects where World Bank financing criteria were key to constructing the largest dam while several smaller ones could be undertaken with less stringent assistance from a neighboring country. See "Damned if You Do," *The Economist*, 29 November 2003, p. 38.
32. M. Boorstein, "Embrey Dam Explosion to Free the Rappahannock," *The Washington Post*, 22 February 2004, p. C1; F. Montaigne, "A River Dammed," *National Geographic*, vol. 199, no. 4, April 2001, pp. 2–30.
33. D. Pauly, V. Christensen, S. Guenette, T. Pitcher, R. Sumaila, C. Walters, R. Watson and D. Zeller, "Towards Sustainability in World Fisheries," *Nature*, 8 August 2002, pp. 689–95.
34. For a discussion of the problems that confronted Chilean fisheries, see J. Kline, *Foreign Investment Strategies in Restructuring Economies*, Westport, CT: Quorum Books, 1992, pp. 114–18.
35. Pauly et al., "Towards Sustainability," Another problem for aquaculture solutions emerged with the higher toxin levels found in farm-raised as opposed to wild salmon. See E. Planin, "Toxins Cited in Farmed Salmon," *The Washington Post*, 9 January 2004, p. 1.
36. Grunwald, "Saved, or Ruined."
37. "Tangled nets," *The Economist*, 4 October 2003, pp. 36–8.
38. UN Millennium Report, 2008.
39. R. Minder, "Nestlé Urges EU to Soften GM Line," *Financial Times*, 23 June 2008, p. 6.
40. J. Gillis, "Calculating the Risks," *The Washington Post*, 30 November 2003, p. A26.
41. Ibid. The choice of plant research projects suggests a parallel comparison with pharmaceutical research. Just as developed-country crops attracted early GM food research, WHO studies warn that genetic research on medicines, driven by market mechanisms, will focus on diseases most prevalent in developed countries and largely ignore tropical diseases common in many developing countries. See S. Okie, "Genetic Gains Unlikely to Help World's Poor, Report Predicts," *The Washington Post*, 1 May 2002, p. A3.
42. J. Gillis, "UN Touts Biotech to Boost Global Food Supply," *The Washington Post*, 18 May 2004, p. A2.
43. J. Van Fleet, "Protecting Knowledge," *Human Rights Dialogue*, Carnegie Council on Ethics and International Affairs, series 2, no. 9, spring 2003, pp. 18–19.
44. J. Degges, "Bioengineering," Social Issues Service, 2003 Background Report J1, Washington, DC: Investor Responsibility Research Center, 10 February 2003.
45. R. Weiss, "Firms Seek Patents on 'Climate Ready' Altered Crops," *The Washington Post*, 13 May 2008, p. A4.
46. C. Cookson, "Science and Ethics Clash Over Life Forms," *Financial Times*, 2 September 2003, p. 11.
47. S. Miller, "EU's New Rules Will Shake Up Market for Bioengineered Food," *The Wall Street Journal*, 16 April 2004, p. 1.
48. J. Burton, "International Conference Deals Blow to US on Labeling of Gene Modified Food," *Financial Times*, 28–29 February 2004, p. 5

49. J. Gillis, "Biotech Limits Found Lacking," *The Washington Post*, 21 January 2004, p. E1; J. Gillis, "Making Way for Designer Insects," *The Washington Post*, 22 January 2004, p. 1.
50. Cookson, "Science and Ethics Clash."
51. R. Weiss, "U.S. Denies Patent for a Too-Human Hybrid," *The Washington Post*, 13 February 2005, A3.
52. United Nations, "Johannesburg Summit 2002: Key Outcomes of the Summit," New York: United Nations, mimeo.
53. D. Cogan, "The Ceres Principles and Environmental Management Practices," Social Issues Service, 2002 Background Report H, Washington, DC: Investor Responsibility Research Center, 15 March 2002.
54. P. Utting, *Business Responsibility for Sustainable Development*, Occasional Paper 2, Geneva: UN Research Institute for Social Development, January 2000.
55. International Chamber of Commerce (ICC), "The Business Charter for Sustainable Development," ICC Publication No. 210/356A, Paris: ICC, 1991.

10

BUSINESS GUIDANCE AND CONTROL MECHANISMS

INTRODUCTION

The evolution of modern MNEs created a mismatch between traditional systems for regulating business based on national law and the globe-spanning reach of MNE operations. The MNE form of organization simply outdistances most national government controls, while international institutions lack the political authority and enforcement capability to pick up where national mechanisms stop at territorial borders. This disparity alarms actors in both the public and the private sectors who perceive growing MNE influence on national economic, social and even political processes. The ensuing search for effective business guidance and control mechanisms covers an array of alternatives, ranging from voluntary through coercive to mandatory. The challenge is to select and activate the best mechanisms to influence MNE actions in ways that maximize benefits and minimize potential harm to the many societies MNEs serve.

Concern that national regulations fall short of controlling MNE activity initially gained prominence in the 1970s.[1] Recent globalization trends exacerbated these worries, particularly after the Soviet Union's collapse discredited communist and many socialist economic policies, leaving the field open to dominance by US-style capitalism. A seeming consensus emerged centered on liberalization and privatization policies that open developing countries and transitional economies to international market forces. Privatization and deregulation reduce or remove many national government controls over business, while lower barriers to international trade and investment expose domestic economies to MNE penetration. In essence, private MNEs gained more legal rights and greater freedom of action within national economies, sparking calls for MNEs to accept explicit corresponding responsibilities toward meeting societal interests.

Some critics of globalization favor a re-energized national government role to control corporate actions while others advocate the development of international law to regulate MNE operations. However, many national governments face resource constraints that preclude effective supervision of complex and wide-ranging MNE activities. Potential international regulation of MNEs suffers from inadequate political consensus among nation states on both priority goals and necessary enforcement authority. Failing satisfactory progress through these legal channels, alternative paths emerged, championed by civil society groups with the acquiescence or support of governments. These approaches use moral suasion and market pressures to encourage or coerce changes in MNE behavior.

Voluntary "soft law" guidelines promote broad standards of conduct often endorsed by governments as measures of good corporate citizenship, but these measures lack the mandatory sanction of enforceable "hard law" requirements. Many MNEs adopt individual codes of conduct, subscribe to industry guidelines and develop partnerships with relevant societal groups. Such voluntary business self-regulation may respond to external pressures or arise from internal reassessments of company responsibilities, although the broadest change appears to develop in industries that have come under significant external criticism. Civil society groups use media campaigns as well as investment and procurement instruments to organize market pressures against targeted MNEs to induce change in corporate practices. Investment funds, shareholders' actions and product boycotts constitute some of the ways used to influence MNE policies through private market mechanisms.

Prior chapters discussed various business guidance and control mechanisms, primarily in the context of examining case scenarios. This chapter surveys these devices in a more systematic manner for two reasons. First, understanding the background and evolving use of such measures can provide insights to the dynamic interaction among business, governments and civil society groups. More broadly, sound ethical decision making should be followed by an equally sound choice of effective measures to alter behavior in the desired direction. Evaluating past events and determining standards for appropriate conduct ought to be coupled with a capacity to influence future actions. After determining *who* should do *what, when* and *where*, the next logical question becomes *how* one could make it happen.

NATIONAL AND INTERNATIONAL LAW

Governments hold ultimate power over the corporate entities operating in their jurisdiction, so standards set by national law embody mandatory norms that such companies violate only at their peril. In practice, however, governments may lack the administrative resources, expertise or political will to fully and effectively enforce legal mandates. More uniquely, even strong national governments face a difficult challenge when attempting to regulate part of an MNE organization where important corporate assets and capabilities reside outside the country. Although birthed by charters based in national laws, corporate entities linked through an MNE network can plan, coordinate and execute transactions using a global rather than a national strategy and vision. The constraints of nation-state sovereignty generally confine a government's actions within its own territorial borders, even when the activities of an MNE's foreign affiliates could significantly affect the nation's welfare.

The popular MNE image portrays a corporate entity able to evade national law by escaping into the unregulated space of some ethereal international arena. In reality virtually all MNE activity occurs within the legal jurisdiction of some nation state. Inadequate controls result when national governments fail to pass or enforce effective national laws and to coordinate those legal standards through international agreements. Differences among national legal regimes enable MNEs to exploit the disparities in ways unavailable to purely domestic enterprises, fostering frustration that the MNEs are escaping national law. For strong national governments with international political and economic clout, one possible response lies in the extraterritorial application of their national law.

Extraterritorial extension of a nation's laws generally creates diplomatic controversy because the law's application reaches into another nation's jurisdiction, creating potential legal overlap with resulting conflicts between sovereign political authorities. The United States attempts to extend its laws extraterritorially more than any other nation, employing this mechanism in areas such as antitrust, taxation, export controls and anti-bribery legislation. Such actions mark a national policy decision that US companies should follow these normative standards anywhere they operate, underlined by a willingness to risk political discord with other countries to enforce the mandates. Some other nations also adopt extraterritorial legal standards, but few countries possess comparable international leverage to pursue their enforcement, and even US attempts frequently fail when faced with a strong opposing government.[2]

Despite implementation difficulties, precedents exist for examining the extraterritorial extension of national law as a control mechanism for MNE behavior. Passage of the US Foreign Corrupt Practices Act (FCPA) constitutes the most obvious example previewed in earlier chapters. Political, economic and moral arguments persuaded the US Congress to develop a definitional standard, backed by criminal penalties, to prevent US companies from bribing foreign government officials in any country, whatever the local law and practice.[3] The United States has also included human rights goals among the foreign policy objectives for which export controls may be imposed on US companies, including the operations of their foreign affiliates.[4]

Developments on several other case scenarios also illustrate how national law may apply to MNE actions in other countries. Chapter 4 examined criticism of Unocal's business involvement in Burma where a military government engages in widespread violations of human rights. Using a controversial interpretation of the US Alien Tort Claims Act (ATCA), lawyers for villagers in Burma brought suit in a US court against Unocal for alleged human rights violations associated with abuse of workers forced to help build the natural gas pipeline. Enacted in 1789, the ATCA lay essentially dormant until a 1980 ruling upheld the right of foreigners to pursue tort claims in US courts for violations of US treaties and the evolving "law of nations." Over two dozen suits had been filed alleging various human rights violations abroad, but the Unocal case was the first to reach a trial stage. A ruling by the US Supreme Court in June, 2004 upheld ATCA's possible use in such cases but warned against interference with US foreign policy. Unocal's subsequent out-of-court settlement, reportedly for $30 million, precluded a trial that might have set binding precedent for this type of case.

Among the cases discussed in previous chapters that were brought against MNEs under the ATCA are Chevron's alleged complicity with Nigerian military action against protestors (the jury found Chevron not legally responsible); Shell's alleged involvement in Ken Saro-Wiwa's trial and execution (settled out of court); Yahoo!'s alleged assistance in the identification and imprisonment of a Chinese dissident (settled out of court); and ChevronTexaco's alleged environmental damage in Ecuador (trial still underway). Other cases have involved allegations against ExxonMobil, Coca-Cola, Occidental Petroleum, Drummond, and Del Monte Foods.[5] Over 50 MNEs faced a $400billion lawsuit under ACTA, charged with knowingly helping and benefiting from the apartheid regime's repression of blacks in South Africa. (The contemporary black-led government in South Africa opposed the lawsuit as a threat to further investment in the country.)[6] Occasionally similar legal actions occur in other countries, as with the cases brought in France against Total for its operations in Burma and in Britain against the Cape corporation for asbestos injuries in South Africa (both settled out of court).

The attempted resort to US courts often arises when local legal remedies are impossible (as in Burma under a military regime accused of the violations) or inadequate (where court backlogs, minimal penalties, futile enforcement or potential corruption compromise the legal system). Essentially this tactic seeks to use one nation's legal powers, and often different standards, to impose judgment and penalties on MNEs for actions allegedly taken by foreign affiliates legally incorporated in other sovereign countries. Although Ecuador might object less than Burma to the type of action taken in US courts, both situations basically reflect unilateral US law applications to MNE actions occurring in another country's legal jurisdiction. As such, these examples suggest an unusually fluid area for utilizing national law to address essentially international normative issues.

International law offers little effective regulation of business because no international body exists with the political authority and enforcement capability to charter and regulate MNEs at the global level. Fundamental differences persist among nations regarding the proper role, goals and methods of private business activities, as well as the appropriate distribution of commercial benefits and costs. Such differences impede progress toward the broad consensus needed to formulate detailed international legal standards that could be applied direct to corporations. Where international law does emerge, the accords generally require signatory governments to adopt and enforce the standards through the mechanism of national law.

The difficulty for governments to reach binding agreements regulating international business led to the development of "soft law" alternatives that seek to guide corporate conduct. As discussed in Chapter 2, the OECD Guidelines for Multinational Enterprises represented the first significant attempt by governments to endorse multilateral standards for good business behavior and to urge their adoption by MNEs. The sponsoring OECD governments emphasized the voluntary nature of the guidelines and resisted attempts to use the standards to judge individual corporate actions. However, cases brought before national "contact points" for clarification can serve to highlight complaints against particular MNEs, thereby increasing pressures for a change in corporate behavior.[7]

This "soft law" approach permits governments to act, reaching agreement on broad normative statements regarding corporate conduct, without resolving policy differences that preclude the more detailed legal definitions necessary for binding regulations. The burden of interpreting and applying general guidelines essentially shifts on to MNEs, leaving other private or public actors free to offer their own critique regarding how well a corporation complies with the broad standards. Subsequent intergovernmental agreements adopted this promotion of general business conduct guidelines covering such areas as competition standards, social policy and marketing practices.[8] UN Secretary General Kofi Annan proposed a similar approach in a speech to the World Economic Forum on 31 January 1999, challenging business leaders to support a Global Compact based on principles drawn from UN documents on human rights, labor and the environment. Formally launched in July 2000, this initiative seeks corporate reporting on implementation practices and encourages dialogue among various groups supporting the Global Compact's principles.[9]

BUSINESS CODES AND MONITORING MECHANISMS

Although some individual corporate codes of conduct predate governmental moves to "soft law" mechanisms, the vast majority of individual company codes and industry-wide standards emerged after the mid 1970s. In the United States many corporate codes stemmed from responses to foreign bribery scandals while other enterprises reacted to more broadly based calls for greater MNE social responsibility. MNE codes of conduct can help establish or clarify internal policies and procedures, promote a common company identity among an increasingly diverse international workforce and communicate corporate standards to interested external stakeholders. Voluntary codes can help encourage appropriate MNE conduct while also collectively reducing pressures for mandatory government action.[10]

In developing a code of conduct, corporate leadership generally relied on internal managers who began with core issues where legal standards already existed, such as on accounting practices, antitrust rules and conflicts of interest. Provisions relating to employees focused on worker obligations to the enterprise but sometimes addressed reciprocal company responsibilities as well. Sections dealing with other stakeholder groups, such as customers, competitors or communities, often employed broad language that lacked clear relevance to actual business operations. Individual corporate codes seldom addressed specific international issues, relying on generalities about promoting economic growth while obeying local laws and ignoring potential conflicts among differing national standards.[11]

Although companies often looked at other MNE codes when drafting or revising their own documents, great diversity still exists among these mechanisms in terms of their approach, content and implementation. Some codes bear little connection to operational decision making and represent little more than public relations pieces aimed at external constituencies to deflect criticism or portray a positive corporate image. Other companies adopt more detailed policies and operational guidelines but restrict these documents to internal use, leaving them unavailable to outside stakeholders. A more balanced approach seeks to develop a code of conduct that speaks to both internal and external audiences, providing sufficiently detailed links to actual operations that employees can use the guidelines for practical decision making while sharing substantive corporate standards with external stakeholders.[12]

In addition to establishing individual corporate codes, MNEs can join a growing plethora of cooperative arrangements that promulgate and promote business conduct standards.[13] Established business organizations sponsor some initiatives, such as the sector-specific marketing code developed by the International Federation of Pharmaceutical Manufacturers' Associations (IFPMA).[14] Other actions arise from cooperative approaches that span various types of enterprises and address general corporate social responsibility issues, for example the Caux Round Table or the Prince of Wales Business Leaders' Forum (PWBLF).[15] Social Accountability International (SAI) offers broadly applicable standards (SA8000) to verify management system compliance with basic labor conditions in the workplace.[16] Still other efforts center on specific product-related issues, such as the Rugmark Foundation's code for carpets or the Federation Internationale de Football Association (FIFA) standards for soccer balls that address child labor and other "sweatshop" labor conditions.[17]

Exhibit 10.1 describes the growth of such codes in the food sector, an industry with difficult supply chain challenges that reach from supermarkets to developing country farmers. The article reviews initiatives in several countries and the manner in which the industry's global MNEs are responding. Compliance is less burdensome if most purchasers collaborate on a common code of social and environmental responsibilities for their suppliers. As related by a Kraft Foods executive: "We had a horrible vision of a small farmer with seven codes tacked on to a palm tree." The broad range of the food industry can require some differentiation on how standards for safety, labor conditions and sustainable development are applied. Individual company commitments also vary in areas such as providing assistance for supplier education and training. Because adherence to industry codes can involve additional costs for complying companies, "free rider" issues arise for firms that do not follow the code but benefit from the industry's enhanced public standing. Product certification programs mentioned in the article and described later in this chapter are a partial response to this problem as well as to basic credibility issues regarding monitoring and assessing code implementation.

Whether individual or collective, business codes of conduct face scrutiny by civil society groups that question if the voluntary codes make any real difference. Responding to such skepticism, many MNEs issue reports outlining and illustrating their compliance, particularly on environmental performance but increasingly on other social responsibility issues as well. The UN Global Compact project specifically encourages MNEs to report on their operations and this approach may be enhanced by incorporating the Global Reporting Initiative into the Global Compact's procedures. Although reporting can broaden public knowledge of MNE activities, skeptics often discount such self-descriptions, urging independent monitoring procedures to ensure the accuracy of code implementation reports.[18]

Debates over monitoring procedures underline questions about the credibility of

Exhibit 10.1   Developing Codes for Food Companies

Pulling together puts progress at the top of the food chain's menu

A variety of approaches is bearing fruit in a high-profile industry's ability to show that it is behaving ethically, says **Sarah Murray**

For companies in the food industry wanting to manage their supply chains responsibly, the challenges might at times seem insurmountable.

Those sourcing coffee or cocoa, for example, are not necessarily dealing with workers in a factory, but often with thousands of smallholder farmers and commodities that may be traded dozens of times along the supply chain.

For those supplying supermarkets, the demand for fresh produce year-round means companies are constantly shifting their production bases.

Consumer demands create other challenges for the industry. "If it's raining in the UK, people don't want barbecued foods—but if there is a heatwave, they do," says Julia Hawkins of the Ethical Trading Initiative (ETI), a government-backed alliance of companies, non-governmental organisations and trade unions. "That puts pressure on suppliers to make last-minutes changes to orders. Reducing lead times and other buying practices make it harder for suppliers to implement international labour standards."

A further pressure is that of prices, with large supermarkets driving prices downwards, forcing suppliers to push their workers to work longer hours or to hire migrant or temporary workers who are more vulnerable when it comes to employment standards.

The challenges are not restricted to developing countries. In the UK, an ETI working group has been addressing the exploitative working practices of some temporary labour providers, also known as gangmasters. The ETI group—which includes supermarket chains, government departments, temporary labour providers and organisations such as the National Farmers' Union—successfully lobbied the UK government, which set up a Gangmasters Licensing Authority.

"What we've learned is how the power of collaboration works," says Ms Hawkins. She argues

that while the narrow audit-based approach is important, "it's generally not the answer. Companies have to have a joined-up approach and that's what we're trying to do with temporary labour in the UK—and because of the weight of the group together, we could lobby government to introduce a law."

Others in the food industry are beginning to recognise the power of collaboration. The Ethical Tea Partnership, an association of tea packers that includes Sara Lee/Douwe Egberts, Tetley GB, Brook Bond Tea and Finlay Beverages, is working to monitor and improve working conditions in the tea industry.

In South Africa, the Wine Industry Ethical Trading Association—a group of winery owners, trade unions, government and buyers with members that include Tesco, Co-op, Marks and Spencer and Asda—inspects conditions in the Western Cape wine industry, seeking improvements in, for example, housing for temporary workers, and health and safety.

In the coffee industry, producers, buyers, trade unions and NGOs have been developing a Common Code for the Coffee Community, or the 4Cs, as it is also known.

Annemieke Wijn, senior director of the commodity sustainability programmes at Kraft Foods, one of the participating companies, says that when it comes to dealing with smallholder farmers, having a jointly agreed on set of standards is essential. "We had a horrible vision of a small farmer with seven codes tacked on to a palm tree," she says. "So having a common code as opposed to one for each company is very important."

Nevertheless, Ms Hawkins argues that individual company efforts still have an important role to play, particularly when it comes to training workers and suppliers. "Some individual companies are putting workers to the front of the stage," she says. "They've been treated as passive recipients in the past, but we need to get more proactive education of suppliers and training for workers on their rights."

One company taking such an approach is M&S, which has a number of initiatives designed to spread good practice throughout its supply chain. The company has, for example, produced a DVD on workers' rights for suppliers and it provides workbooks in 11 languages on ethical trade for suppliers. It also runs one-day workshops around the world for suppliers and has devised and accredited a three-day social auditing course.

"The starting point is making sure the people that directly supply you are fully aware of your standards and requirements," says Louise Nicholls, foods ethical trading manager at M&S. "Then, armed with the knowledge and the tools, they are able to spread these messages and standards down to their own suppliers and other suppliers."

Yet another approach that is gaining momentum in the food industry is product certification. Leading the certification movement is the Rainforest Alliance, a conservation group based in New York, which has developed a system of auditing and certification that is overhauling the way companies operate. Using a system that tracks more than 200 different criteria it assesses whether companies are adhering to environmental and social standards.

The Rainforest Alliance works with companies such as Kraft Foods, Procter & Gamble and Chiquita, the US banana giant once criticised for poor environmental and labour practices. Kraft, which started working with the group in 2003, is now blending Rainforest Alliance certified products into its mainstream coffees and has started to sell some 100 per cent certified coffees in the UK, Scandinavia and France.

For a company such as Kraft, the advantage of working with the Rainforest Alliance is its local knowledge and experience, says Ms Wijn. "There are certifiers that do the certification and there are technical training people who help farmers get up to the right level," she says. "So they know their stuff, particularly on the ground."

Source: *Financial Times*, 28 November 2005, p. 3. Reprinted with permission.

---

voluntary business codes. Most issues relate to the agency examining corporate performance and how compliance is tested. The use of accounting firms to audit code implementation raised concerns that business relationships could color the reporting. Some civil society groups favor participation in code monitoring to assure its transparency and fairness. Other organizations see voluntary codes of conduct as fundamentally flawed, at best representing "stop-gap" measures on the way to the enactment of mandatory standards imposed by law.[19]

Differences of opinion and approach occur among civil society groups, sometimes resulting in direct competition and conflicting positions. For example, the Workers' Rights Consortium (WRC) challenges whether the Fair Labor Association (FLA) possesses sufficient independence from its sponsoring MNE members to provide credible compliance reporting, despite the involvement of several outside groups. Designed for greater distance from monitored corporations and incorporating more local representatives from monitoring locations, the WRC presents itself as an alternative to FLA operations, essentially competing for sponsorships.[20] As some civil society groups opt for closer participation or even partnerships with MNEs that adopt acceptable voluntary codes, other organizations retain a more confrontational style. Such differences should not be surprising, given the continuing growth of non-governmental organizations from around 10,000 in 1980 to well over 27,000 by 2007.[21]

The proliferation and expanding diversity among civil society groups can pose dilemmas for MNEs that seek to engage in dialogue or cooperative activities with external stakeholders. Enterprises could seek to exploit these differences by aligning with a relatively compatible group to help deflect criticism coming from other, more combative organizations. However, even with the best of intentions, MNEs face difficulty knowing how to select potential partners from among the variety of civil society groups whose self-defined mandates often overlap in terms of core issues and/ or geographic focus. A related problem arises from questions regarding whether such groups represent the views and interests of the people most affected by particular issues. The membership, leadership and resources of most civil society groups are heavily concentrated in the advanced industrialized countries, while many MNE issues impact disproportionately on populations in developing countries and economies in transition. Expanding collaboration among civil society groups internationally may help address this problem, but MNEs still lack clear public standards on how to evaluate and select the most legitimate and representative civil society groups as partners for cooperative actions.[22]

INVESTMENT, DIVESTMENT AND SHAREHOLDER ACTIVISM

Capital markets that supply equity funding for corporate growth also provide mechanisms for controlling and guiding MNE behavior. Publicly traded corporations are managed by executives hired to operate the firm on behalf of its shareholders, who "own" the corporation. While the managing executives hold a fiduciary responsibility to provide a return on their shareholders' investment, operating within the terms of governing legal requirements, shareholders possess the right, responsibility and power to define the nature of their expected return as well as operational guidelines for how the company conducts its business. Traditionally, most shareholders are primarily, if not exclusively, concerned about obtaining maximum financial return on their investment and only large, institutional shareholders possess the knowledge, resources and relative leverage to actively influence corporate behavior. However, spurred particularly by protests in the 1970s against business involvement with South Africa's apartheid policies, three contrasting approaches emerged whereby even smaller investors could exercise their ownership responsibilities regarding corporate conduct.

Investment and divestment represent mirror-image actions that shareholders can use to reward or punish companies for their behavior. Although "buy" or "sell" decisions generally respond to expected financial returns, investors may also purchase or dispose of stock in companies based on other criteria, including a firm's conduct on social responsibility issues. During the fight against apartheid, numerous shareholders divested stock in companies that continued to do business in or with South Africa, or refused to conduct their operations under the Sullivan Principles, as discussed in Chapter 4. Similar shareholder actions occur on other issues, motivated by a desire to bring pressure on a company to change its policies, penalize a firm for refusing to change policies, or simply to sever personal "ownership" ties to an enterprise that engages in unethical behavior. The first two motivations focus on teleological effects or outcomes whereas the third motivation reflects a deontological concern with role responsibilities or the shareholder's complicit connection to wrong behavior.

Comparable goals guide investor decisions to avoid purchasing stock in companies whose products or operations raise ethical concerns. This approach led to the development of socially responsible investment (SRI) funds based on exclusionary rules. These funds promise not to invest in enterprises with objectionable products or behavior, essentially "punishing" those firms while simultaneously assuring fund investors that their money will not help support such activities. Initially SRI funds excluded firms associated with certain products, such as tobacco, alcohol or armaments. Later efforts focused on particular aspects of corporate performance, with "green" funds excluding firms with poor environmental records and social funds assessing corporate practices such as hiring and promoting minorities.[23]

A more recent approach to SRI funds seeks to encourage and reward good behavior more than punish offending corporations. In July 2001 the FTSE (owned by the *Financial Times* and London Stock Exchange) established indices for corporate social responsibility called the FTSE4Good. Although companies dealing with tobacco, arms and nuclear power were excluded, selection for these indices depended on positive assessments of corporate performance on core criteria involving the environment, human rights and relations with stakeholders. Using an advisory committee of social responsibility experts to assess over 1,600 listed companies, the FTSE4Good selected fifty qualifying firms with the highest market capitalization for British and for European indices, with another 100 similarly chosen companies comprising American and world indices to provide an incentive for improvement, firms with some questionable performance record but a commitment to change could gain selection.[24] During its initial five years, the index progressively broadened and strengthened its social responsibility criteria, removing over 150 firms that failed to meet new requirements while adding three times as many new companies.[25]

SRI funds that use FTSE4Good indices to help determine their equity portfolios add a proactive reward dimension, supporting improved corporate performance to the traditional fund emphasis on reactive punishment for misdeeds. Of course, investment funds still reflect some financial limitations. Selection by the FTSE4 Good favors the most highly capitalized qualifying firms rather than strictly the best social performers, pragmatically balancing financial return objectives with social responsibility concerns. Much hesitation about using SRI funds to influence corporate behavior stems from investor fears of lower financial returns compared to funds investing in any corporations with profitable outlooks, unencumbered by non-financial performance criteria. In other words, individual investors often weigh how much lower a financial return they might accept in order to direct their shareholdings away from objectionable firms while encouraging socially responsible behavior.

Comparisons between SRI fund returns and general market performance tend to yield mixed results, depending both on time periods covered and methodology employed. SRI proponents argue that socially responsible operations often enhance corporate profitability over the longer term through such effects as cost savings

Exhibit 10.2   Shareholders with a Mission

Ethical crusaders resolve to redeem the corporate sinners

The influence of religious groups on business behaviour is growing, says
Elizabeth Wine

Of the many activist groups pressing US companies to change their ways, only Sister Patricia Wolf's Interfaith Center on Corporate Responsibility can really claim to be on the side of the angels.

As the season of annual meetings approaches, the group of 275 religious institutions headed by the nun is in the vanguard of institutional investors using shareholder resolutions to spotlight issues such as human and worker rights and global warming.

"Many people in the SRI [socially responsible investment] community understand that reputation is as important as the financial outcome," said Sister Pat. "If they haven't learned it from Enron, or Andersen, they haven't learned anything."

Religious communities such as the Sisters of Charity of St Vincent de Paul of Halifax, Nova Scotia, or faith-based charities such as Mennonite Mutual Aid, find themselves lined up alongside trade unions and Greenpeace in the battle for the corporate conscience.

But the group can claim financial as well as moral clout: ICCR's members collectively control $110 billion, almost all in pensions and endowments, some of which come from charitable donations.

ICCR was born thirty years ago as the US religious community looked for ways to fight apartheid by pressing corporations to divest from South Africa. Member organisations used existing investments as the lever to press for change.

Since then the group has campaigned for social issues, from human and worker rights to global warming, often taking the side of developing nations, where many religious organisations' members work. For that reason, international debt forgiveness for the world's poorest countries is a cherished goal.

This year, ICCR members sponsored 144 shareholder resolutions on social and environmental issues at ninety-nine companies.

Sister Pat said the group often achieves successes "through a back door" by creating opportunities to talk with a company.

For example, ExxonMobil, which recently admitted global warming is a problem after insisting for years it was an unproven theory, is being targeted for further improvement.

ICCR and other activists filed a shareholder resolution this year asking it to produce a report by next September outlining how it will promote renewable energy sources.

Richard Koppes, former general counsel of Calpers, the largest US public pension fund, and shareholder activist, was once a non-believer when it came to using shareholder meetings to raise broader issues.

But ICCR converted him. "There was the notion that these things did not belong on the proxy but I moderated that over the years as the importance of corporations in our global economy developed."

Other fans say ICCR's influence comes not from its shareholdings but from a reputation for thorough research and arguments.

Sister Pat cites Disney as one reforming corporate sinner that bowed to ICCR's argument. When ICCR started talking with the media company five years ago it did not have a corporate code of conduct outlining standards for the group and its vendors, such as the right of workers to form unions.

Now, after several years of discussions, Disney has overcome its reluctance and introduced a code on workers' rights. It recently invited ICCR representatives to a plant in the Dominican Republic to meet workers.

"It was quite an open meeting," said Sister Pat. She said Disney, while not yet a model of corporate governance, was making good progress.

But she sees the quest for more enlightened policies as a long-term project. "We've had corporations look at us and say, 'It's a four, five, six, seven-year issue'," said Sister Pat.

Perhaps ICCR can afford to be patient: like the poor, recalcitrant companies will always be with us.

Source: © *Financial Times*, 30–31 March 2002, p. 1. Reprinted with permission.

from energy conservation and improved productivity with lower turnover among contented workers. Whatever the potential difference in financial returns, an increasing number of investment firms utilize social responsibility criteria and offer SRI fund options to their investors. The Social Investment Forum estimates that in 2007, SRI investments in the United States amounted to over $2.7 trillion, or nearly one of every eight dollars managed by investment firms. In 2000 the UK government adopted new rules requiring pension funds to disclose whether they considered environmental, social or other ethical factors in their investment decisions.[26]

Beyond the criteria used for investment and divestment decisions, shareholders can attempt to influence corporate operations through activist strategies. As "owners" of an enterprise, investors can employ voting shares to offer and support resolutions that would alter corporate policies. Applying this mechanism to international issues also essentially grew out of the debate over apartheid in South Africa, although some earlier actions arose from opposition to companies involved in producing certain goods related to the Vietnam War, such as napalm or cluster bombs. One early promoter of shareholder activism was the Interfaith Center on Corporate Responsibility (ICCR), founded in 1971 by religious institutions drawn from the Protestant, Roman Catholic and Jewish faiths. The Center conducts research on issues to advise its institutional members on how to invest or vote their share holdings. Exhibit 10.2 describes the approach and some of the activities of this organization.

As suggested in this exhibit, shareholder activism as a mechanism to influence corporate behavior does not depend on direct control over a significant proportion of a company's stock. With management often holding enough proxy voting rights to defeat unwanted proposals, shareholder resolutions on MNE social responsibility issues seldom reach even double digits in percentage of votes cast. However, many enterprises seek to minimize or avoid the controversy that can surround public debate over shareholder resolutions, particularly when the issues involve assertions by religious organizations regarding unethical corporate actions. Wider coordination among civil society groups and other institutional investors can provide even greater incentive to settle policy disagreements in a mutually satisfactory way. By encouraging such dialogue, activist shareholders can sometimes exercise significantly greater impact on corporate operations than might be expected by assessing only their equity stake in an enterprise. Shareholding provides an investor with a potential avenue for inside access to corporate management. This mechanism focuses more on proactively influencing specific corporate operational decisions than on reactively assessing and penalizing business results.

CONSUMER BOYCOTTS AND CERTIFICATION SCHEMES

Consumer markets also offer opportunities to punish and/or reward corporate behavior. Product boycotts and product certification schemes represent contrasting mechanisms used by civil society groups, occasionally with governmental involvement or support, to influence MNE activities. Organized consumer boycotts usually target individual companies, either because the specific firm's actions are deemed particularly offensive or the company plays a prominent and influential role within an industry whose common practices generate opposition. Boycott mechanisms do not work equally well in all situations. Boycotts enjoy greatest success when directed against recognizable consumer goods whose market position relies on brand-name image and reputation, and where substitute products of satisfactory quality and price are readily available. In addition, the issue motivating the boycott must be conveyed in an easily understandable fashion that will evoke broad sympathy in the general consuming public. By contrast, companies that engage in minimal advertising and produce intermediate products for sale to other businesses are less vulnerable to a consumer boycott mechanism.

The use of consumer boycotts to protest MNE actions developed from the same general time period and set of issues that produced the capital market mechanisms discussed above. Anti-apartheid campaigns included product boycotts, such as the adoption by many US state and city governments of selective procurement regulations that restricted purchases from companies maintaining investments in South Africa. The loss of large sales contracts to state and municipal agencies may have provided more measurable effective leverage against MNEs than stock divestment actions by activist pension funds. Another high-profile campaign urged a boycott of Nestlé's numerous consumer products to protest the corporation's methods of promoting its infant formula in developing countries, as discussed in Chapter 7.

Similar to shareholder activism, the potential effects of consumer boycotts often surpass the actual financial loss in terms of immediate sales. In order to reach the broad consuming public, boycott organizers generally seek maximum publicity and may organize demonstrations, marches or even engage in acts of civil disobedience to draw media attention to their cause. The short-term demand on management response time and potential for longer-term damage to a company's reputation can add significantly to overall boycott costs.[27] Opponents often assert that boycott campaigns unfairly single out one or a small number of companies to protest actions undertaken by many enterprises, including MNEs in countries where comparable consumer actions seldom occur. Sometimes boycott targets show only minimal or distant causal connections to wrong actions. Similar to secondary rather than primary boycotts, the targeted firm or product may simply be used as a means to exert leverage on a different offending actor.[28]

For example, in 1990 a civil society group called Neighbor to Neighbor helped organize a boycott action against Folger's coffee, sold by Procter & Gamble. In this case, the boycott campaign stemmed from opposition to human rights violations by right-wing death squads in El Salvador, allegedly connected with that country's government. Although less than 2 percent of the beans in Folger's coffee reportedly came from El Salvador, those purchases represented an important share of the country's coffee exports, which in turn provided significant revenue to the government. To help publicize their cause, the boycotting groups sponsored a dramatic television advertisement attacking Folger's and showing blood running from an overturned coffee cup. The advertisement was characterized by a P&G spokesperson as "inaccurate, grossly misleading and offensive."[29] The company responded with its own type of boycott action, suspending advertising on some television stations that aired the anti-Folger's commercial. US government officials offered clear statements supporting

P&G's coffee bean purchases, calling the actions "in the best interest of the peace process and the people of El Salvador."[30] The case illustrates how boycotts, even when motivated by laudable objectives, may become ethically problematic as causal and capability connections grow more distant between a targeted product or company and the offending actor and actions.

Another case of a successful boycott describes a campaign organized by the Rainforest Action Network (RAN) against Scott Paper, aimed at stopping Scott's plans to use a rain forest concession on the Indonesian island of Irian Jaya to develop a eucalyptus plantation and sawmill to supply pulp for its various paper products. An observer reports that, despite corporate efforts to work with local representatives to limit the project's environmental and social impact, "RAN convinced environmental groups from all over the world to boycott Scott products if the company did not withdraw from Irian Jaya. The campaign focused on a single thing: Scott's name, the company's most valuable, and most vulnerable, asset." The company announced its withdrawal from the project just before the boycott began, prompting RAN to take out newspaper advertisements "declaring victory" and "hailing the power of consumer boycotts."[31] Without necessarily disputing the impact of the boycott mechanism, some critics subsequently questioned the substance of the victory as a state-owned forestry company replaced Scott in the project and, not subject to similar consumer pressures, reportedly engaged in broad deforestation actions.[32] This case points up the challenge of projecting a boycott's effects, which may depend on when outcomes are measured and whether or not potential impacts on other boycott actions are considered.

Product certification schemes also depend on consumer choice to provide leverage for influencing corporate behavior. Contrasted with boycott mechanisms, certification schemes focus less on penalizing bad corporate conduct to induce change and more on rewarding good corporate operations by giving their products a market advantage over uncertified competitors. To be credible, groups using this mechanism must demonstrate that consumers are sufficiently aware and concerned about an issue to affect their purchasing decisions. In addition, consumers need enough knowledge and understanding about the certification process to recognize and favor certified products. These requirements place a premium on media coverage and the development of alliances and support networks among sympathetic civil society groups, particularly in major consumer market economies.

No clear consensus exists regarding either the breadth or the depth of probable consumer response to product certification schemes. Certainly participation will vary depending on the nature of the issue, the location of the consumer market and the effectiveness of a particular campaign. Other important variables include the cost, quality and convenience differential in choosing certified over uncertified products. Some polling data suggests that a core of committed individuals will act on certification criteria while a larger portion of the general public is open to considering corporate actions and reputation in their purchasing decisions. For example, a Mori survey in Great Britain defined 15 percent of the population as corporate responsibility activists, reporting that ethical considerations led 17 percent of adults to boycott a product and 14 percent to purchase a company's product during 2003. The survey also reported that 38 percent of the public stated corporate social responsibility was very important in making their purchases. The head of Mori's CSR research speculated that more individuals from this broader group might follow through with concrete actions if provided with more effective information.[33]

The proliferation of product certification schemes touches many of the issues discussed in earlier chapters. Exports of soccer balls and rugs from South Asia feature certification processes to assure the goods were not produced using child labor. "Green" labels tout the environment-friendly record of many products, from recycled paper or plastic products to energy-saving devices to "dolphin-safe" tuna. Remarkable variety exists in the types of issues addressed and certification measures employed. The constellation of certifying and supporting organizations can also mix public agencies, business organizations and civil society groups.

Fair Trade initiatives represent a particular application of product certification schemes, usually but not exclusively applied to products based on agricultural commodities. The basic concept seeks to establish a dependable, long-term relationship with commodity growers in developing countries, offering them a higher price for their products by eliminating middlemen traders. Many schemes also provide an additional premium to growers for using environmentally friendly methods and/or for community social development projects. The general approach reportedly stems from efforts begun in 1986 by the Max Havelaar Foundation in the Netherlands to respond to desires for development projects that emphasize trade rather than aid. Starting with coffee and expanding to honey, bananas, tea and orange juice, the Foundation supported Fair Trade products sold primarily in Europe. During the 1990s, 14 other Fair Trade organizations were established, reaching over $200million in sales by the end of the decade, still largely concentrated in European markets. Some approaches expect consumers to pay a somewhat higher price for certified Fair Trade products while other efforts try to remain price-competitive, using cost savings in the distribution chain to redistribute profits toward developing country growers.[34]

An important extension of the Fair Trade mechanism to the US market occurred in 2000 when Starbucks announced the introduction of a blend of Fair Trade coffee certified by the non-profit TransFair organization that encourages farmer cooperatives in developing countries to sell direct to coffee roasters or retailers. The breakthrough with Starbucks came after some of its coffee houses were vandalized during anti-globalization protests at a World Trade Organization meeting hosted in the company's hometown of Seattle, Washington. This initiative complemented Starbucks' broader social responsibility programs and helped expand Fair Trade coverage in the United States beyond craft shops and a few grocery stores. Subsequent discussions between Starbucks and Oxfam also led to cooperation on a project to aid coffee growers in poverty-stricken areas of Ethiopia.[35]

As discussed in Exhibit 10.1, the Rainforest Alliance promotes another certification scheme covering several products and has forged agreements with major coffee MNEs that broadens the Fair Trade mechanism beyond the market for specialty coffees, which represents only about 2 percent of supply. Kraft Foods, purchaser of nearly 10 percent of the world's coffee, agreed to blend beans certified by the Rainforest Alliance into the company's major brands, paying farmers up to a 20 percent premium for their production, With existing production of certifiable coffee insufficient to go much beyond early commitments, the company agreed to help break through this bottleneck by training specialists to assist more farmers to meet the certification standards. Procter & Gamble also began to sell a special order brand of certified coffee while other companies employed the certification system for their products.[36]

SELECTING THE BEST MEANS TO AN END

Extraordinary growth in the scope and importance of global MNE operations focused attention on the unique characteristics and potential impact of these firms on national societies. Appearing to operate above or beyond national legal powers, these enterprises assumed an unusual role as new private actors in an international relations arena that had been the nearly exclusive domain of public sector authorities. Partly in response to MNE activity, and utilizing many of the same advances in communications and transport technologies that underpin MNE operations, civil society groups proliferated in a parallel fashion, expanding and coordinating their international reach. The intersection and interaction of these three types of actors stimulated experimentation and the development of new business guidance and control mechanisms to influence MNE policies and actions.

Pioneered over the past quarter-century, many of these mechanisms remain in a state of evolution, adjusting approaches and techniques in response to both experience and changing conditions. Mandatory international regulation of MNEs remains limited by the scope of international political consensus on standards and enforcement, while conflicts of national sovereignty restrain the practical extension of extraterritorial laws. "Soft law" standards provide a way for governments to encourage good international corporate citizenship but depend on responsible MNE interpretation, application and compliance. Voluntary company and industry codes of conduct represent a burgeoning MNE response to increased public attention to business conduct. However, the extremely broad array of these instruments, coupled with external skepticism regarding implementation, monitoring and reporting processes, leaves many groups unconvinced that MNE self-regulation constitutes a fully satisfactory option.

The rise of civil society groups sparked a surge in new instruments that use market mechanisms to influence MNE behavior. Campaigns to sell or buy stock based on a particular MNE's activities on international ethical issues grew into institutional SRI funds organized to promote normative goals through capital markets. Activist minority shareholders used their status as "owners" of a corporation to aggressively support change, employing both legal and public relations channels to promote dialogue with management and a modification of MNE policies. Civil society groups also organized boycotts, selective procurement policies and product certification schemes to utilize the marketplace power of consumer choice to influence MNE decisions.

This evolving array of guidance and control mechanisms provides both challenge and opportunity to public and private sector actors that seek to influence MNE behavior. The principal task involves selecting the most available, appropriate and effective mechanism to attain the desired end of improved business conduct. Dangers can arise that MNEs may receive unfair treatment if dealt with only as an instrumental means to generally desirable ends, especially when actual developments can turn out quite differently than anticipated outcomes. A tendency may also emerge to focus quickly on the easiest actor to influence rather than fully assessing where principal responsibility for action should reside. With growing success in fashioning instruments to influence MNE behavior, civil society groups may turn first in this direction rather than devoting resources to pursuing a more difficult (but perhaps ultimately more appropriate and effective) path of inducing action by governmental authorities.

It is worth remembering that a decision to focus on altering MNE behavior should come at a follow-up action stage, after ethical analysis of an issue has identified a best choice normative standard and goal as well as assessed the relative responsibilities of all relevant actors. For critical need issues, MNEs may become the most aware, knowledgeable, proximate and capable actor, especially when governments or other more responsible bodies fail to act. Absent sufficient international consensus to support governmental actions, civil society groups have turned increasingly to MNEs as the next best actor on a global subsidiarity chain to improve critical need situations on the world stage. This choice can be ethically justified, but such a decision merits careful evaluation and communication of the ethical reasoning for such a judgment.

NOTES

1. R. Vernon, *Sovereignty at Bay*, New York: Basic Books, 1971; F. Bergsten, T. Horst and T. Moran, *American Multinationals and American Interests*, Washington, DC: Brookings Institution, 1978, pp. 329–33.
2. G. Shambaugh, *States, Firms, and Power*, Albany, NY: State University of New York Press, 1999; G. Hufbauer and J. Schott, *Economic Sanctions in Support of Foreign Policy Goals*, Washington, DC: Institute for International Economics, October 1983; G. Hufbauer, J. Schott and K. Elliott, *Economic Sanctions Reconsidered*, 2 vols, Washington, DC: Institute for International Economics, December, 1990.
3. J. Kline, *International Codes and Multinational Business*, Westport, CT: Quorum Books, 1985, pp. 32–4.
4. T. Gladwin and I. Walter, *Multinationals Under Fire*, New York: Wiley, 1980, pp. 186–92, 244–6; Hufbauer et al., *Economic Sanctions Reconsidered*.
5. P. Magnusson, "A Milestone for Human Rights," *Business Week*, 24 January 2005, p. 63; A. Gomez, "Foreign Workers to Sue U.S. Companies Under Old Law," *USA Today*, 2 April 2007, p. 2.
6. D. Glovin, "Court's Apartheid Ruling Could Cost U.S. Businesses," *The International Herald Tribune*, 25 October 2007, p. 16.
7. Kline, *International Codes*, pp. 45–8, 76–80.
8. UN Conference on Trade and Development (UNCTAD), *The Social Responsibility of Transnational Corporations*, Geneva: United Nations, 1999, pp. 11–12, 42–5; and Kline, *International Codes*, chapters 3–4.
9. For information on the Global Compact, see the project's website, online, available http://www.unglobalcompact.org (accessed 15 June 2009).
10. Kline, *International Codes*.
11. Ibid., chapters 6–7.
12. Ibid. Also see K. Gordon and M. Miyake, *Deciphering Codes of Corporate Conduct: A Review of their Contents*, Working Papers on International Investment, no. 99/2, Paris: Organization for Economic Cooperation and Development (OECD), March 2000.

13. Investor Responsibility Research Center (IRRC), "Comparative Codes of Conduct and Their Auditing and Follow-up Procedures," Washington, DC: IRRC, 1999, mimeo; Gordon and Miyake, "Deciphering Codes"; R. Jamal, "USCIB Compendium of Corporate Responsibility Initiatives," New York: US Council for International Business, 2002, mimeo; Interfaith Center on Corporate Responsibility (ICCR), "Principles for Global Corporate Responsibility," *The Corporate Examiner*, vol. 26 (6–8), 29 May 1998.

14. International Federation of Pharmaceutical Manufacturers' Associations (IFPMA), *IFPMA Code of Pharmaceutical Market Practices*, fifth printing, Geneva: IFPMA, 1984.

15. Caux Roundtable, "The Caux Round Table Principles for Business," online, available at their website http://www.cauxroundtable.org/; Prince of Wales Business Leaders' Forum (PWBLF) and Amnesty International (AI), *Human Rights: Is It Any of Your Business?* London: PWBLF and AI, April 2000; see also the website at http://www.pwblf.org.

16. Social Accountability International, "Overview of SA8000," online, available at their website http://sa-intl.org.

17. T. Moran, *Beyond Sweatshops*, Washington, DC: Brookings Institution, 2002, pp. 91–2.

18. A. Maitland, "Truants, Nerds and Supersonics," *Financial Times*, 18 November 2002, p. 9; H. Williamson, "Making a Commitment to Corporate Citizenship," *Financial Times*, 12 February 2003, p. 9; M. Turner, "UN Group to Measure Companies' Social Virtues," *Financial Times*, 3 March 2004, p. 6.

19. J. Finer, "Monitoring Corporate Citizens," *The Washington Post*, 5 June 2003, p. E4; D. Brown, "US Urged to Monitor Global Labor Policies," *The Washington Post*, 12 January 2004, p. A15.

20. Moran, *Beyond Sweatshops*, p.93.

21. Union of International Associations (UIA), *Yearbook of International Organizations*, ed. 45, vol. 5, Munchen, Germany: UIA, 2008, pp. 34–7.

22. UNCTAD, *The Social Responsibility*, pp. 47–8.

23. E. Wine, "Getting to Grip with Some Ethical Issues," *Financial Times*, 11 July 2001, p. 28.

24. Ibid.; " 'Best Behaviour'," *The Economist*, 14 July 2001, p. 71; "FTSE4Good: Global Investment, Global Improvement, The FTSE4Good Index Series," online, available http//:www.ftse4good.com (accessed June 15 2009).

25. FTSE4Good, "Adding Value to Your Investment: FTSE4Good—5 Year Review, available online at http://www.ftse.com/Indices/FTSE4Good_Index_Series/F4G_Download_Page.jsp (accessed 15 June 2009).

26. "Ethical investment: Warm and Fuzzy," *The Economist*, 14 July 2001, p. 71; A. Maitland, "Profits from the Righteous Path," *Financial Times*, 3 April 2003, p. 9; Social Investment Forum, 2007 Report on Socially Responsible Investing Trends in the United States.

27. G. Solomon, "Applying Tactical Consumer Boycotts," *Financial Times*, 3 September 1996, p. A13.

28. M. Kinsley, "Rules for Consumer Boycotts," *The Washington Post*, 22 November 1990, p. A31.

29. P. Farhi, "Procter & Gamble Pulls TV Ads," *The Washington Post*, 12 May 1990, p. A9.

30. G. Stern, "P&G, Pressured by Boycott, to Market Coffee Blend Without Salvadoran Beans," *The Wall Street Journal*, 15 November 1991, p. B5. See also G. Stern, "P&G Backpedals on Plan to Cut Use of Salvadoran Coffee," *The Wall Street Journal*, 18 November 1991, p. B4.

31. A. Stern, "How They Won the Battle and Lost the Rain Forest," *The Washington Post*, 1 June 2003, p. B2.

32. Ibid.

33. A. Maitland, "The Influential Core of 'Socially Responsible' Consumers," *Financial Times*, 4 December 2003, p. 11.

34. R. Cowe, "Poor Farmers Taste Success," *Financial Times*, 5 March 2002, p. 11. Retail prices charged on "fair trade" products can provoke controversy when retailers are seen reaping excessive profit margins that do not aid the commodity producers. See S. Stocklow and E. White, "At Some Retailers, 'Fair Trade' Carries a Very High Cost," *The Wall Street Journal*, 8 June 2004, p. A1.

35. S. Schafer, "Activists Score Preemptive Win on Coffee Sales," *The Washington Post*, 10 April 2000, p. B4; E. Alden, "US Offered Coffee with Conscience," *Financial Times*, 4 October 2000, p. 9; and A. Maitland, "Starbucks Tastes Oxfam's Brew," *Financial Times*, 14 October 2004, p. 9. For a discussion of broader US applications of Fair Trade, see K. McLaughlin, "Is Your Grocery List Politically Correct?" *The Wall Street Journal*, 17 February 2004, p. D1.

36. S. Silver, "Kraft Blends Ethics with Coffee Beans," *Financial Times*, 7 October 2003, p. 10.

11

DECIDING ETHICAL DILEMMAS

INTRODUCTION

Contemporary policymakers confront decisions involving unprecedented levels of complexity, shaped and reshaped by globalization's kaleidoscope of interwoven political and socioeconomic factors. Once nearly the exclusive domain of governments, international relations now involves a proliferating array of organized private sector decision makers, including both business enterprises and a growing constellation of civil society groups. Interdependent international linkages, many forged through MNE commercial networks, transmit the impact of these actors' decisions into the daily lives of diverse populations around the world whose interests, or even existence, may be largely absent from the deliberations.

Does globalization portend the evolution of a global society where shared basic values link the welfare of people throughout a diverse world community? Or will the forces of globalization simply serve competitive interests defined by national boundaries or corporate objectives and asserted by political and economic strength? The script for this play, already under way on the world stage, is still being written. Normative standards and decision-making tools could help guide difficult choices in line with broad human interests, if a sufficient foundation exists in common global values and key actors incorporate reasoned ethical analysis into their decision frameworks.

The twenty-first century holds both promise and mounting challenge. Greater awareness of interdependent relationships and growing knowledge about the causes and consequences of interconnected actions provide the potential for more informed and responsible decision making. Heightened concern about globalization has focused attention on the need to develop international standards to evaluate actions and guide policy decisions. National governments, private business and civil society groups will all play a role in this task. The key challenge, however, rests at the personal level. A truly global society connects individuals, not just organizations, in a

257

community built around common concerns and interdependent interests. The impetus for more deliberately reasoned ethical analysis and decision making must come from a greater willingness among individuals in all organizations, including business enterprises, to utilize normative terminology and concepts when confronting the ethical dilemmas that arise in a global political economy.

EVOLVING GLOBAL CONCERN

Much of the popular reaction to globalization focuses on stories of disruptive personal or societal change under pressure from external forces that appear unaccountable to the people most affected. Yet the complex developments driving globalization can also bridge divisions and promote empathy in ways that permit the emergence of a global society. Revolutions in transport, communication and information technologies provide ways to surmount barriers of physical distance and individual ignorance that have sustained separations among the world's population. Unprecedented numbers of people now visit faraway countries with a speed and ease unimaginable a half-century earlier. Countless more people who choose not to travel or cannot afford the still significant expense have the world brought to them daily through ubiquitous television screens with round-the-clock news broadcasts and programmed visions of life in very different countries and cultures. Expanding millions can access extraordinary volumes of information and establish instantaneous direct links with individuals in distant locations through the wonders of the World Wide Web.

Considered in terms of ethical implications, these changes alter core factors that help determine the level of ethical responsibility borne by various actors in a world community. Communications media and the organized efforts of activist groups increase individual and societal awareness of critical need conditions among people living far outside a local community or nation. Remaining oblivious to situations of desperate foreign suffering now almost requires a conscious act of avoidance or a deliberate dulling of the emotional senses to escape the constant barrage of visual and verbal reports. Knowledge constitutes less of a constraint on responsible action as information becomes broadly dispersed or at least easily accessible through proliferating technical and organizational outlets. Proximity acquires a larger meaning as globalization tightens the interdependent links between regions still separated by substantial physical distance. Similarly, concepts of causality gain an extended reach as influence and control flow over far-flung networks of economic and corporate connections. Capabilities also grow, particularly those exercised by MNEs whose pursuit of commercial benefit propel many of the globalization changes.

Contemporary events offer evidence of an evolving global concern that corresponds to these changing notions of ethical responsibilities. Violations of international human rights standards draw increased attention to the interaction between government policies and MNE operations. As examined in Chapter 4, violations of political and civil human rights provoke concern and responses from individuals and organizations far removed from the national site of harmful actions. Subsequent chapters survey economic, social and cultural human rights that also claim new priority on public policy agendas. Labor and environmental issues achieve the broadest recognition, with environmental concerns reflecting the most easily understood example of how interdependent actions can impact the world community's shared interests.

International business plays a prominent and perhaps indispensable role in the dispersion of globalization forces. MNEs represent particularly significant conduits whose interconnected operations link diverse countries and cultures around the world. With increased size and scope, MNEs can exceed some national governments in their capacity to mobilize resources and exert effective influence on certain types of issues and outcomes. Growing MNE capabilities prompt calls for a parallel increase in MNE responsibility for societal welfare. In the "sweatshop" debate, applying subsidiarity concepts to the business supply chain illustrates the relatively recent tendency to assert ethical corporate responsibilities based more on potential capability for action than on considerations of proximity or causality. Past chapters offer numerous examples where MNEs faced ethical dilemmas posed by perceived harms or social needs that connect only distantly to the MNE's own direct operations.

EVOLVING GLOBAL STANDARDS

When confronted by international ethical dilemmas, where should MNEs turn for guidance in making "best choice" decisions when reasoned normative arguments can support action in several different directions? The complexities of this challenge emerge from the multiple case scenarios presented throughout the book. National legal requirements set a minimum floor of mandated action, but issues posed by illegitimate regimes or international "gaps" between national laws still raise troublesome questions. Intergovernmental organizations struggle to devise broader standards but usually lack the agreed consensus or political power necessary to establish binding law. MNEs may set their own normative standards in the absence of legal directives or follow maximal value principles above legal requirements. Civil society groups, often skeptical of MNE self-regulation, generally advocate strengthening national and international law while still promoting MNE adherence to voluntary codes of conduct.

These simultaneous developments yield a patchwork of progress toward evolving global standards. The various chapters identify a variety of approaches and instruments used to forge international cooperation. Practical actions appear most advanced with intergovernmental agreements in areas such as trade involving pesticides or other hazardous products where a type of common morality standard emerges. Recognized perils to human health lead governments to accept a responsibility to participate in cooperative arrangements to reduce potential dangers, even when the threat falls mainly on citizens of other countries and control measures can involve economic costs. Damage to the natural environment often poses a less direct and immediate danger than hazardous products, but the commonly shared risks and wider impact of environmental degradation are generating similar movement toward meaningful international standards and cooperative actions.

Patchy progress also describes the development of international marketing standards. Although the most advanced guidelines come from national regulations, a surprising degree of international consensus sets limits on the types of marketing techniques that should be used to promote particular products. The landmark WHO code on infant formula identifies specific marketing practices adjudged by the international community to essentially breach common morality standards. The code's application relies on national government action and/or voluntary corporate compliance, but the WHO instrument achieves a remarkable degree of specificity for a global marketing standard. The Framework Convention on Tobacco Control follows a similar if somewhat less detailed path, while new studies examine whether alcohol consumption and growing obesity rates raise comparable marketing issues. The WHO periodically reviews practices in the pharmaceutical sector, where coordinated industry action already promotes voluntary international marketing standards. Despite issues of cultural relativism, clearer delineations also emerge between internationally acceptable and unacceptable practices involving bribery and racial or ethnic marketing, with governments regulating the former and public consumer response driving action on the latter.

More broadly, the relationship and impact of international business on distinctive world cultures presents one of the most contentious globalization issues. Cultural diversity offers unique values that can be lost to the homogenizing trends introduced by internationally integrated MNE production processes and product promotions. Nevertheless, some change is inevitable and certain local practices may not deserve protection if they violate important minimum global norms. The debate over international human rights embodies the struggle to define and apply a common morality standard for individual rights that should be respected in all countries and cultures, regardless of historical or current local practices. Despite the UN Universal Declaration of Human Rights, important differences remain regarding how to interpret and apply these standards, particularly where conflicts develop between enumerated rights. International business may be caught in the middle when anti-discrimination standards clash with traditional customs or religious practice or in situations where general economic development becomes linked to the economic or political repression of minorities.

Traditionally, standards for MNE operations derive from host country regulations, even though the practical effect of such governance often varies with the legitimacy and efficacy of particular regimes. Concerns over the adequacy of national measures fuel movement towards evolving global standards on issues such as labor relations and workplace safety, presenting a potential challenge to both national sovereignty and competitive economic development strategies. Despite ILO conventions on a few core international labor standards, effective implementation falls far short of the agreed norms. In response, civil society groups advocate broad action through international trade agreements while simultaneously urging targeted industry groups and specific MNEs to adopt voluntary labor standards for application throughout their global business supply chain.

Perhaps unsurprisingly, global standards appear most problematic on issues of MNE involvement in political affairs. These situations can pose the greatest threat to principles of national sovereignty, interjecting foreign private actors into matters of local public policy. The same globalization forces that propel MNE influence generate attention and concern among civil society groups regarding individual human rights conditions in many countries around the world. Reacting primarily case by case, these groups may either condemn MNE involvement or press companies to confront or openly defy governments deemed unrepresentative of their citizen's best interests. Global standards have not yet evolved far enough to provide much normative guidance for MNEs on how to manage their involvement or impact on political issues, purposeful or unintentional.

ROLE RESPONSIBILITIES AND APPROACHES

The evolution in global concern and standards relating to international business signal accompanying changes in the role responsibilities and approaches used by governments, MNEs and civil society groups. Governments carry the predominant responsibility for organizing and enforcing norms governing conduct in the international system. The public, representative function of governments inherently dictates this essential task. Difficulties arise from the limitations of a nation-state system that is bounded by territorial political jurisdictions and restrained by national sovereignty principles and goals. National governments define their priority objective as protecting and projecting the interests of a specific population classified as national citizens. This defined function constrains the role of national governments in developing a truly global society. Although international relations relies on deontological, rule-based agreements, national governments also avoid many commitments that would curb unilateral discretion to pursue self-interest gains in teleological case-by-case situations.

The conundrum for governments, particularly nation states with significant unilateral powers, arises from the entangling ties established by globalization's interdependent bonds. Although these ties extend the potential reach of national influence, the enhanced powers are not fully subject to national government control nor are strong states immune from "blow-back" impacts channeled through interconnected global networks. The reach, resources and potential influence of MNEs provide them with options for decisions and actions not under the sovereign control or direction of single national governments. MNEs gain a vested interest in promoting global approaches that enhance free international flows of people, products and, of course, profits. Globalization also speeds the rise of civil society groups as increasingly organized and influential actors in international affairs. Particularly on human rights and environmental issues, many of these groups pursue agendas that reflect more the interests of a globally defined society than nation-state objectives.

Business enterprises generally resist accepting new social role responsibilities to accompany their expanding presence and influence on the international stage. Preferring to concentrate on the central function of achieving global market success, most MNEs formally defer to governments as the deontologically assigned actor responsible for setting the rules to assure societal welfare. However, glaring disparities among countries in the efficacy and representative character of national governments can thrust MNEs into uncomfortable positions where they appear as the next most proximate, capable actor in a global subsidiarity chain of responsibility. The development of clear international responsibility standards may help guide MNE conduct, but a lack of political consensus precludes such standards and, despite stated desires to have clear rules of the game, most MNEs prefer to avoid specific social responsibility commitments that detract from core business requirements. As a result, MNEs often adopt a teleological approach, responding in an *ad hoc*, case-by-case fashion when confronted with international ethical dilemmas.

Much of the impetus for MNE action derives from the growing ability of civil society groups to organize concerted pressure on target companies. Civil society encompasses a wide variety of groups, most pursuing rather narrowly focused objectives rather than broad societal welfare. These groups seek clearly prioritized deontological goals while employing a teleological approach to implementation that weighs the expected outcomes of alternative tactics and actions. Given their orientation toward single-issue advocacy, potential (and probably inevitable) clashes between these groups have remained remarkably muted. The inherent nature of ethical dilemmas portends more coming conflicts over priorities and trade-offs among worthy goals, such as current tensions between environmental preservation and economic development.

Lacking agreed global standards that embody their priorities, civil society groups devise methods to persuade influential actors to endorse and follow supportive guidelines. Governments constitute the obvious preferred choice due to their power to enforce required actions. However, marshaling the time, energy and resources necessary to change governmental policies often exceeds the capacity or patience of special interest advocates. Private companies, subject to marketplace pressures as well as government regulations, increasingly offer more promising and susceptible targets. For international issues, MNEs present a particularly attractive option as their continued growth expands corporate capabilities for action.

Civil society activism on international issues and their turn to MNEs for responsive actions transforms the historical dynamic of international relations by multiplying the number and type of involved actors. Combined with national governments and intergovernmental organizations, this expanding constellation of players can create or redefine role responsibilities in ways that augment possible approaches to meeting global needs. Indicative of this new creative potential are joint partnership programs linking governments, MNEs and NGOs, such as the agreement on how to develop Chad's oil resources or certify Cambodia's effort to eliminate "sweatshops."

Heightened awareness, expanded knowledge, enhanced capabilities and new perceptions of proximity nourish the search for fresh approaches to meeting international needs. Expectations regarding proper normative decisions and outcomes no longer stop at national borders as globalization increasingly weaves countries, cultures and individuals into a more interconnected world community. The effort to define agreed normative standards for actors within this evolving community will determine whether the bonds of common values will support the development of a truly global society.

PERSONAL DECISION MAKING

This book examines the decisions and behavior of organizational actors on the global stage whose conduct shapes the nature of the world community. However, the text also focuses on the development of a personal decision-making framework. Whether individuals hold positions in governments, MNEs or NGOs, the role of personal decision values is crucial to the process of organizational decision making. Achieving rational "best choice" outcomes in ethical dilemmas requires the active participation of individuals willing and able to inject clear normative analysis into the deliberations.

Decisions reflect value choices but organizational discussions often revolve around implicit assumptions about goals embedded so deeply in the institution's ethos that potential value trade-offs, conflicts or related impacts may go unrecognized. The new challenges presented by globalization's complexities require a more open perspective that can use normative standards and procedures to illuminate value choices. In order to stimulate and guide such discussion, individuals must first cultivate their own decision-making skills, developing their abilities to communicate clearly both the process and rationale of ethical decision making.

The book suggests using five "W" questions to organize and focus ethical analysis as a possible aid to individual decision making. No claim is made for unique advantages inherent in this particular formulation. Most individuals will develop a personal approach and style that best fits their own mental process and set of values. However, an organized, self-aware approach to decision making offers important assistance when confronting difficult ethical dilemmas. Asking and answering who should do what, where, when and why offers one possible way to organize this challenge. The main point, however, is that ethics can involve relatively simple ways to improve practical decision making.

The elaboration of ethical theory provides essential insights to understanding core values that give meaning to human activity. For most individuals, however, the intellectual complexity of theoretical systems can make ethics appear abstract and disconnected from everyday life. Applied ethical analysis provides a necessary bridge between the distant demands of formal theory and the immediate need to make "best choice" decisions under conditions of insufficient time and information. Without relatively simple guides for normative analysis, many people will dismiss a serious discussion of normative choices as too slow, complicated or confusing to use in practical decision making.

Individuals entering careers in international business face especially difficult tasks as MNEs operate at the forefront of globalization forces. Spanning many countries and cultures, these enterprises will play an important role in shaping the impact of global change and how distinctive populations react to the transformations. Which value choices will guide MNE operations and how will those decisions affect the development of a global society? The answers will arise largely from the way individuals perform their roles as business executives, or as government and civil society representatives. Both organizations and individuals possess options in their actions. Incorporating ethical analysis into personal and organizational decision making can help assure that outcomes reflect conscious "best choice" judgments, even in the demanding environment of a global political economy.

FURTHER READING

Barnet, R. and Cavanagh, J., *Global Dreams*, New York: Simon & Schuster, 1994.

Barnet, R. and Muller, R., *Global Reach*, New York: Simon & Schuster, 1974.

Beauchamp, T., *Case Studies in Business, Society and Ethics*, 5th edn, Upper Saddle River, NJ: Pearson Prentice Hall, 2009.

——, Bowie, N. and Arnold, D. (eds), *Ethical Theory and Business*, 8th edn, Upper Saddle River, NJ: Pearson Prentice Hall, 2009.

Bergsten, F., Horst, T. and Moran, T., *American Multinationals and American Interests*, Washington, DC: Brookings Institution, 1978.

Boatright, J., *Ethics and the Conduct of Business*, 6th edn, Upper Saddle River, NJ: Pearson Prentice Hall, 2009.

Buchholz, R. and Rosenthal, S., *Business Ethics*, Upper Saddle River, NJ: Prentice Hall, 1998.

Carroll, S. and Gannon, M., *Ethical Dimensions of International Management*, Thousand Oaks, CA: Sage, 1997.

Cavanagh, G., *American Business Values: A Global Perspective*, 5th edn, Upper Saddle River, NJ: Pearson, 2006.

Coicaud, J.-M. and Warner, D. (eds), *Ethics and International Affairs*, New York: United Nations University Press, 2001.

Crane, A. and Matten, D., *Business Ethics: Managing Corporate Citizenship and Sustainability in an Age of Globalization*, Oxford: Oxford University Press, 2007.

Davies, P., *Current Issues in Business Ethics*, New York: Routledge, 1997.

De George, R., *Business Ethics*, 6th edn, Upper Saddle River, NJ: Pearson Prentice Hall, 2006.

——, *Competing with Integrity in International Business*, Oxford: Oxford University Press, 1993.

DesJardins, J. and McCall, J., *Contemporary Issues in Business Ethics*, 5th edn, Belmont, CA: Thomson Wadsworth, 2005.

Dienhart, J., *Business, Institutions, and Ethics*, New York: Oxford University Press, 2000.

Donaldson, T., *The Ethics of International Business*, New York: Oxford University Press, 1989.

—— and Dunfee, T. (eds), *Ethics in Business and Economics*, Brookfield, VT: Ashgate Dartmouth, 1997.

——, *Ties that Bind: A Social Contracts Approach to Business Ethics*, Boston, MA: Harvard Business School Press, 1999.

Donaldson, T., and P. Werhane, *Ethical Issues in Business*, 8th edn, Upper Saddle River, NJ: Pearson Prentice Hall, 2008.

Enderle, G. (ed.), *International Business Ethics: Challenges and Approaches*, Notre Dame, IN: University of Notre Dame Press, 1999.

Fisher, C., *Business Ethics and Values*, 3rd edn, New York: Prentice Hall/Financial Times Press, 2009.

Freeman, R., *Strategic Management*, Boston, MA: Pitman, 1984.

—— (ed.), *Business Ethics: The State of the Art*, Oxford: Oxford University Press, 1991.

Friedman, M., *Capitalism and Freedom*, 3rd edn, Chicago: University of Chicago Press, 1963.

Fritzsche, D., *Business Ethics: A Global Managerial Perspective*, New York: McGraw-Hill, 1997.

Gladwin, T. and Walter, I., *Multinationals Under Fire*, New York: Wiley, 1980.

Goodpaster, K. and Nash, L., *Policies and Persons: A Casebook in Business Ethics*, 3rd edn, New York: McGraw-Hill Dushkin, 1998.

Hennelly, A. and Langan, J., *Human Rights in the Americas*, Washington, DC: Georgetown University Press, 1982.

Hoffman, M., Frederick, R. and Schwartz, M. (eds), *Business Ethics*, New York: McGraw-Hill, 2001.

Hoffman, M., Lange, A. and Fedo, D. (eds), *Ethics and the Multinational Enterprise*, New York: University Press of America, 1986.

—— , Kamm, J., Frederick, R. and Petry, E. (eds), *Emerging Global Business Ethics*, Westport, CT: Quorum Books, 1994.

Hufbauer, G. and Mitrokostas, N., *Awakening Monster: The Alien Tort Statute of 1789*, Washington, DC: Institute for International Economics, 2003.

Hufbauer, G., Schott, J., and Elliott, K., *Economic Sanctions Reconsidered*, 2 vols, Washington, DC: Institute for International Economics, 1990.

Iannone, P. (ed.), *Contemporary Moral Controversies in Business*, Oxford: Oxford University Press, 1989.

Jennings, M., *Business Ethics: Case Studies and Selected Readings*, 6th edn, Mason, OH: South-Western Cengage Learning, 1999.

Kline, J., *International Codes and Multinational Business*, Westport, CT: Quorum Books, 1985.

—— , *Foreign Investment Strategies in Restructuring Economies*, Westport, CT: Quorum Books, 1992.

Malachowski, A. (ed.), *Business Ethics: Critical Perspectives on Business and Management*, London: Routledge, 2001.

Minus, P. (ed.), *The Ethics of Business in a Global Economy*, Boston, MA: Kluwer, 1993.

Moran, T., *Beyond Sweatshops*, Washington, DC: Brookings Institution, 2002.

Newfarmer, R. (ed.), *Profits, Progress and Poverty*, Notre Dame, IN: University of Notre Dame Press, 1985.

Paine, L., *Cases in Leadership, Ethics, and Organizational Integrity*, Chicago: Irwin, 1997.

Powers, C., *People/Profits: The Ethics of Investment*, New York: Council on Religion and International Affairs, 1972.

Regan, T. (ed.), *Just Business: New Introductory Essays in Business Ethics*, New York: Random House, 1984.

—— and Singer, P. (eds), *Animal Rights and Human Obligations*, 2nd edn, Englewood Cliffs, NJ: Prentice Hall, 1989.

Roussouw, D., *Business Ethics in Africa*, 2nd edn, Oxford: Oxford University Press, 2002.

Rubin, S. and Hufbauer, G. (eds), *Emerging Standards of International Trade and Investment: Multinational Codes of Conduct*, Totowa, NJ: Rowman & Allanheld, 1984.

Sethi, S., *Setting Global Standards: Guidelines for Creating Codes of Conduct in Multinational Corporations*, Hoboken, NJ: Wiley, 2003.

Sethi, S. and Falbe, C. (eds), *Business and Society*, Lexington, MA: Lexington Books, 1987.

Sethi, S. and Steidlmeier, P., *Up Against the Corporate Wall*, 6th edn, Upper Saddle River, NJ: Prentice Hall, 1997.

Sethi, S. and Williams, O., *Economic Imperatives and Ethical Values in Global Business: The South African Experience and International Codes Today*, Boston, MA: Kluwer, 2000.

Sethi, S., Steidlmeier, P. and Falbe, C., *Scaling the Corporate Wall*, 2nd edn, Upper Saddle River, NJ: Prentice Hall, 1997.

Shambaugh, G., *States, Firms, and Power*, Albany, NY: State University of New York Press, 1999.

Shaw, W., *Business Ethics*, 6th edn, Belmont, CA: Wadsworth, 2008.

Shue, H., *Basic Rights: Subsistence, Affluence, and US Foreign Policy*, Princeton, NJ: Princeton University Press, 1980.

Smith, A., *The Wealth of Nations*, New York: Modern Library, 1937.

Soule, E., *Morality and Markets: The Ethics of Government Regulation*, Lanham, MD: Rowman & Littlefield, 2003.

Steckmest, F., *Corporate Performance: The Key to Public Trust*, New York: McGraw-Hill, 1982.

Sullivan, R. (ed.), *Business and Human Rights*, Sheffield: Greenleaf, 2003.

Tavis, L., *Power and Responsibility: Multinational Managers and Developing Country Concerns*, Notre Dame, IN: University of Notre Dame Press, 1997.

—— and Williams, O., *The Pharmaceutical Corporate Presence in Developing Countries*, Notre Dame, IN: University of Notre Dame Press, 1993.

Velasquez, M., *Business Ethics: Concepts and Cases*, 6th edn, Upper Saddle River, NJ: Pearson Prentice Hall, 2006.

Varley, P. (ed.), *The Sweatshop Quandary*, Washington, DC: Investor Responsibility Research Center (IRRC), 1998.

Weir, D. and Schapiro, M., *Circle of Poison: Pesticides and People in a Hungry World*, San Francisco, CA: Food First/Institute for Food and Development Policy, 1981.

Weiss, J., *Business Ethics: A Managerial, Stakeholder Approach*, Belmont, CA: Wadsworth, 1994.

Williams, O. (ed.), *Global Codes of Conduct: An Idea whose Time has Come*, Notre Dame, IN: University of Notre Dame Press, 2000.

INDEX

269